Shotguns & Shotgunning

LAYNE SIMPSON

Published by

700 East State Street • Iola, WI 54990-0001
715-445-2214 • 888-457-2873
www.krause.com

Please call for our free catalog. Our toll-free number to place an order or obtain a free catalog
is 800-258-0929 or please use our regular business telephone 715-445-2214 .

Library of Congress Catalog Number: 2003108893
ISBN: 0-87349-567-5

Manufactured in China

Table of Contents

This book is gratefully dedicated to readers who have bought my books and magazine articles through the years, and in doing so made it possible for me to spend much of my time doing things and writing about places I once could only dream about. To Jim Bequette, who has done a lot for me through the years. To Art, Bob, Brad, Dick, Dwight, Ed, Eddie, Gina, Jackie, Jay, Linda, Mary, Mike, Murph, Ron, Roxie, Ryan, Steve, Tom and others, who have shared with me many wonderful days in the field. To bird dogs called Iceman and Sierra and Fritz and Ruark. To beagles like Sue and Peaches and Kate who never failed to smile and wag their tails each time I spoke their names. To my father for taking me hunting at an early age. And to Phyllis, the love of my life who makes it all worthwhile.

Layne Simpson
Simpsonville, South Carolina

Introduction

I was born in the sleepy little South Carolina village of Liberty at a time when doctors still made house calls. We had two family practitioners at the time, and while Dr. Swords later became our family doctor and removed my tonsils, it was Dr. Kitchens who delivered me at home on a rainy night in April. I grew up in the best of times, but there were a few exceptions. During wintertime in those days, parents made children wear around their necks a small cloth bag filled with a foul-smelling witch's brew called asafetida. It was supposed to ward off germs and other evil stuff. In looking back, I am sure it worked mainly because its terrible odor kept anyone who might have a contractible disease a safe distance away from those of us who were forced to wear it.

It was a time of innocence we Americans will never again know and exactly as captured and depicted in Jean Shepherd's *A Christmas Story*. My father was an avid hunter, and when I was 12 we moved to a small farm located between Liberty and Six Mile, where he bred, raised, trained and sold beagles. We called them rabbit dogs, which is exactly what they were. It was a wonderful time to be young, and it was a wonderful place for a youngster who loved to hunt to be a part of. Cottontail rabbits and bobwhite quail were everywhere. The patch of giant hickory and oak trees behind Furman Mauldin's house was full of gray squirrels, and regardless of how hard I tried, I was never able to catch all the suckers, catfish and horney-heads from Golden Creek.

Christmas was a big thing back then, but it was much different than it is today. It had yet to become so heavily commercialized, and most people still remembered the real reason it was celebrated. Kids weren't so spoiled in those days, or at least this held true for my chums and me. In addition to clothing and some fruit, Santa usually brought me no more than one of the "luxury items" I had lusted for earlier in the year. On a really good year I might get two. One Christmas, I received a hand warmer that leaked cigarette lighter fluid in my pocket and blistered my leg each time I used it. That same year, I also received a cowboy suit. It was equipped with twin cap pistols and painted on each leg of its chaps was my hero, Roy Rogers, and his horse, Trigger. Another year I was the proud recipient of a spring-powered, double-barrel shotgun. It was designed to shoot little cork bottle stoppers, but I found it to be far more effective at fending off dry-gulching badmen, marauding redskins and neighborhood dogs when it was loaded with green acorns from the water oak tree in our front yard. Like Ralphie, I received my first BB gun, a Daisy Red Ryder, at the age of 10. Just as it is in the movie, Mom was always warning me about "shooting an eye out with that thing."

Gerald Holden, an older kid who lived next door, received his first shotgun on the same Christmas that I got my Roy Rogers cowboy suit. It was a .410 single-shot, but for the life of me I cannot remember what company made it. At the time, a patch of woods not far from my house was full of squirrels, so on Christmas morning, Gerald and I decided to bump off a few of the little critters with his new gun. When we arrived in the woods, we found squirrels running and jumping all around, but even after using up about half the shells in his pocket, the old boy still had not bagged one. Even worse, the selfish scoundrel absolutely refused to allow me to shoot the gun. Just as we came to the edge of the woods on our way back home, I suddenly stopped, pointed into a canopy of brown leaves above our heads, and whispered, "squirrel." "Where?" Gerald whispered back anxiously. "In that big hickory nut tree," I replied. "I can't see it," came back Gerald. "Gimmie the gun and I'll kill it," said I. Not one to allow an easy meal to escape, old Gerald handed me the shotgun. Shouldering the little .410, I pointed it at the top of the hickory nut tree, pulled its trigger and we both watched as the biggest, fattest squirrel we had ever seen came cartwheeling to earth with a loud thud. To this day, the old boy thinks I really saw a squirrel in the top of that hickory nut tree, when the truth of the matter is, I wanted to shoot his gun so badly, I only pretended to see one. I shot the .410 at nothing but a patch of dead leaves still clinging to an upper limb of the tree, and it just so happened that what had to be the unluckiest squirrel in all the world was in the wrong place at the right time just when I needed it most.

How I came to own my first real shotgun is one of my favorite childhood stories. We did not have gun shops back then, but each small town had at least one hardware or farm supply store that sold guns. Our town had two: Bruce Smith's Feed & Seed and Wallace Cantrell's Hardware. Dad knew how much I enjoyed visiting both, so I was greatly puzzled one day when he asked me to remain in the car while he did a bit of shopping in Cantrell's. After awhile he returned with a long parcel and placed it on the back seat of our 1941 Chevy. "What do you have in the package?" I asked. "A new shade for the living room window," replied Dad. Several weeks later that same package appeared under our Christmas tree with my name on it and the window shade had somehow been magically transformed into a new Iver Johnson .410-bore shotgun. A smaller package wrapped in green paper and covered with tinfoil icicles and fiberglass angel's hair turned out to be two boxes of Remington 3-inch shells loaded with 3/4 ounce of No. 7-1/2 shot.

In those days, Dad hunted everything with a 16-gauge L.C. Smith double. One of my older cousins owned a .410-bore L.C. Smith, and how I lusted for that gun! Dad's favorite hunting buddies were Lewis Gilstrap, Calvin Smith and Jim Galloway. Almost every grownup I knew shot a double. Lewis and Calvin were double-gun men, but Jim shot the shiniest Browning A5 in all the land. I really liked Jim Galloway. Each and every time I was allowed to hunt with him and Dad, he never failed to give me $2.50, which just happened to be the going price of a box of .410 shells.

The first gas-operated shotgun I ever saw just happened to be the first one introduced. It also came awfully close to ending my life. Built by High Standard and sold by Sears under the J.C. Higgins name, the one I will never forget was owned by a kid of about my age who lived just up the road from our place. By the time he and I got around to hunting rabbits together a few times, I had graduated to Dad's

L.C. Smith. One day, as we sat resting on the edge of an old wooden bridge with our feet dangling toward the creek running along beneath it, my hunting companion shifted the loaded shotgun resting in his lap and allowed its muzzle to point directly at my leg. Just as I pushed the muzzle away from me, the gun fired. After narrowly missing me, the shot charge buried itself in the creek bank within inches of one of Dad's prize beagles. Never again did I hunt rabbits with the owner of the J.C. Higgins shotgun.

Even though I hunted with my father's double-barrel shotguns a lot at an early age, a double was not the first type of shotgun I bought with my own money. The first one I purchased during the early 1960s was a Browning A5 in 12 gauge. It had a 26-inch barrel, and it was choked Improved Cylinder. I bought it because Jimmy Davis let me shoot his and I really liked it. The A5 was a very nice gun, and I shot it fairly well, but it did not take me long to decide it was heavier than an upland gun needed to be. Along about the same time, I also discovered that the 12 gauge was more shotshell than I actually needed for most of my shotgunning.

The next shotgun I owned was the first 20-gauge Winchester Model 101 to arrive at Pepper's Hardware in Easley, South Carolina, in 1966. I still own it. The Model 101 weighs 6-1/2 pounds, fits me perfectly and not a single one of its parts has broken or worn out in thousands of rounds fired. I have owned it longer than any other shotgun, and to this day I shoot it as well as any shotgun I have ever brought to my shoulder. I have also hunted in more countries with that gun than with any other. I used it on everything, too. Back when lead shot could still be used on waterfowl, the little 20-gauge Winchester was the gun I always reached for when shooting ducks at close range. When Phyllis and I lived in Nashville, Tennessee, Roger Bowman, Lester Smith, Tom Seckman and I along with other friends would make short trips to Stuttgart, Arkansas, where we shot ducks over decoys in flooded timber. The Model 101 proved to be perfect for that. Its 26-inch barrels are supposed to be choked Improved Cylinder and Modified, but with .008 and .014 inch of constriction, they are closer to Improved Skeet and Light Modified for the 20 gauge. I have probably killed more quail with fewer shots with it than with any other gun I have ever owned.

Today I own far more shotguns than I actually need, but I cannot think of a single one I would want to live without. Giving up all but one in each gauge would call for some extremely tough decisions, but I suppose I could do it if I had to. So which guns would survive the weeding-out process? Beginning with the smallest, I am torn between a 1930s vintage Iver Johnson Skeet-er in .410 and a Winchester Model 42 skeet gun of the same caliber built during the 1950s. A double man at heart, I would have to go with the Skeet-er in the end.

More of my shotguns are in 28 gauge than in anything else. A Winchester Model 12 pump in that gauge is my favorite ptarmigan gun, and I have taken all six species of quail with a Weatherby Athena over-under with three sets of barrels in .410, 28 and 20 gauge. Another of my favorites for quail is a 28-gauge Parker reproduction. I enjoy shooting doves with a 28-gauge Remington Model 1100, and a Krieghoff 32 with 28-gauge tubes is my favorite skeet gun. Then there is a very nice little deluxe grade Franchi 48AL. But if I had to choose one above all the rest, it would be a little 5-1/2-pound double built by the Spanish firm of Aguirre y Aranzabal or AyA, as it is commonly called. With that gun, I have taken quail, mourning doves, Hungarian partridge, sharptail grouse, prairie chickens, pheasants, chukar partridge and ruffed grouse. Not only do I shoot it quite well, it and a 20-gauge Westley Richards are the two most handsome shotguns I own.

The 20-gauge Westley Richards I mentioned weighs 5-1/2 pounds, same as the AyA. I have also used that gun on a variety of game birds ranging from South Carolina quail to West Virginia ruffed grouse to Huns in Montana. There is absolutely nothing special about the little double, and I am sure Westley Richards made hundreds just like it, but it fits like it was made just for me, which is probably why I shoot it so well.

Through the years, I have carried many different guns in the field, and not a single one has performed any better in my hands than a 16-gauge L.C. Smith. But then, I have been shooting it for a very long time. Built in 1949, Elsie was bought by my father, Bailey Simpson, during that same year. After using it for all of his

hunting for a couple of decades, Dad turned it over to me after he switched to a Browning Superposed Lightning in 20 gauge. If not for the L.C. Smith, I might not have learned to appreciate the 16-gauge shotshell as much as I do today.

I have never been a 12-gauge man at heart. I use the 12 for waterfowling with steel shot and when hunting turkey gobblers, but I prefer smaller gauges for most of the upland hunting I do. Of the few 12-gauge guns I do own, a Remington Model 3200, a Fox Sterlingworth and a Remington Model 11-87 are my favorites. Boiling those guns down to one is a tough task. The Model 3200 is my favorite trap gun, but since I had rather shoot feathered birds than those made of clay, I will have to go with the Fox. Built in 1924, it is a gun I really enjoy using in wide-open spaces, like the time I took it to the sandhills region of Nebraska for a go at wild-flushing pheasants and prairie chickens.

I still prefer the 10 gauge for hunting waterfowl with steel shot. This is not because I think it is capable of doing anything the 3-1/2 inch 12 gauge loaded with steel cannot do. It is because the Remington SP10 for which it is chambered is so much more comfortable to shoot than guns chambered for the super-long 12.

Over the years, I have hunted on five continents and would be hard-pressed to name a favorite game bird. If someone twisted my arm hard enough, I would probably have to say it is a tossup between Hungarian partridge, South American perdiz and bobwhite quail. Some of the most difficult shotgunning I have experienced was in Spain on driven red-legged partridge, but I find that type of shooting no more of a challenge than trying to connect with an early-season ruffed grouse in heavy timber. I have yet to meet a shotgun sport or game that I did not like, but upland hunting is my favorite cup of tea. Give me a good gun and a good dog in the company of an old hunting pal on a bright but cold day in the field, and I am a very happy man.

Photos in this book are by the author unless noted otherwise.

CHAPTER 1

Evolution of the Shotshell in America

By the end of the 19th century the British had already perfected the side-by-side double as represented by this 20-gauge gun built by Westley Richards.

As the 19th century drew to a close, all successful shotgun designs had been developed. The British had perfected the double, the Germans had introduced the bolt-action and in America the single-shot and the slide-action were moving along full steam ahead. Only the autoloader had not gone into production, and John Browning filled that slot when filing patents on his new Automatic-5 in 1900.

It is commonly believed that more major developments took place in rifle and handgun cartridges than in shotshells during the 20th century, but this is not true.

In addition to adopting the noncorrosive primer, manufacturers of metallic ammunition increased velocities, improved accuracy and developed better bullets as the 20th century rolled on. While all those things are important, shotshell makers were equally busy.

Once choke boring and fluid steel barrels came into common use during the 1800s, downrange shotgun performance progressed very little. Even today when the same shotshell loads are used in both, a scattergun such as the old Winchester 1897 will shoot patterns of about the same quality as those delivered by the latest models

John Browning filed patents on his Automatic-5 semiautomatic in 1900 and it went on to become one of the most popular shotguns ever built.

Introduced by Winchester in 1897, the slide-action Model 97 was the first truly successful repeating shotgun to become available to working America.

from Remington, Benelli, Franchi, Browning and others. Today's shotguns might kick less, they might look prettier and they may even be easier to repair, but their mechanical ability to take game or break clay targets is no better than those built 100 years ago. The giant steps forward in downrange performance enjoyed by today's shotgunners came not from any great improvements in the gun during the 20th century, but were due to tremendous improvements in its ammunition.

Crude forms of smokeless powders were loaded in shotshells a decade or so before they found common use in centerfire rifle cartridges, and while that represented one of the first giant steps forward in shotshell evolution, perfection was not achieved until well into the 1900s. The new 20th century nitro powders burned cleaner, but just as important, the more uniform chamber pressures they generated made the autoloading shotgun a workable invention, something that had not taken place during the black powder era.

By the 1920s, the development of new progressive-burning propellants made increases in velocity possible, but they also improved pattern quality by shortening the shot string in its flight. Further advances in powders after World War II brought on the introduction of "baby magnum" performance from shotshells of standard length. Whereas 1-1/4 ounces had once been the heaviest practical shot charge in the 2-3/4-inch 12-gauge shell, improvements in powder made the now-common 1-1/2 ounce load possible. Other gauges were affected as well; short-magnum shot charge weight became 1-1/4 ounces for the 16-gauge and 1-1/8 ounces for the 20. Federal boosted the shot charge of the 28-gauge shell first to 7/8 ounce and then on to a full ounce but eventually dropped both in favor of the standard 3/4-ounce load. As I write this, Winchester is the only company to offer a one-ounce loading of that shotshell.

Federal was first to make turkey hunters shout with joy by increasing the shot charge of the three-inch 12-gauge shell to a full two ounces. That same company was also first to load the 3-inch 20-gauge shell with 1-5/16 ounces of shot.

The early years of the 20th century saw English shotgun makers pretty much standardize on shotshell lengths of 2 and 2-1/2 inches, but not so in America. Prior to the early 1930s, the 20- and 28-gauge shells were 2-1/2 inches in length, the 16-gauge shell was a nominal 2-9/16 inches long, and while 2-3/4 inches was becoming popular for the 12-gauge, 2-5/8 inch shells weren't exactly uncommon either. As for the 10-gauge, it was available in 2-5/8, 2-9/16, 2-7/8 and 3-1/2 inches. Eventually, 2-3/4 inches became standard for the 12, 16, 20 and 28, the .410 was standardized at 2-1/2 inches and the big 10 settled on 3-1/2 inches as its standard length. As the 20th century rolled on, improvements in powders made it possible to increase shot charge weight even more without increasing chamber pressures, and as a result the hull lengths of several gauges were increased to accommodate the change. Three-inch versions of the 12, 20 and .410 were developed, and the 2-1/2 inch 28-gauge was replaced by a 2-3/4 inch hull. The latest in 12-gauge shotshell developments is the 3-1/2 incher, which comes close to duplicating 10-gauge performance in lighter shotguns, albeit at higher chamber pressures.

Standardization of shotshell lengths and improvements in smokeless powders were by no means the only great 20th century achievements in shotshell evolution. Thanks to the development of the nonmercuric primer by Remington around 1930, severe rusting in shotgun bores which in the past often took place overnight became virtually a thing of the past. A 1931 advertisement told hunters all about the advantages of

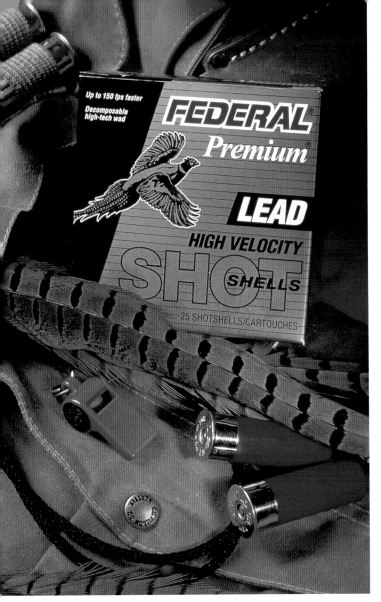

The 20th century brought with it many new and important developments in shotshells, including the plastic hull and the 2-3/4 inch baby magnum. (Photo courtesy of Federal Cartridge)

After the use of nontoxic shot in America's marshlands became law during the late 20th century, several companies quickly responded to the demand.

using Remington shotshells with the new Kleanbore primer. Extremely hard lead shot with a high antimony content was a 20th century innovation, as was lead shot plated with copper and nickel.

A lot of odd shotshell sizes made their last trips to the marshes and uplands during the 20th century with the 10, 12, 16, 20, 28 and .410 being the sole survivors. Among those not making the cut were the 4, 8, 11, 14, 15, 24 and 32 gauges, some offered as late as the 1930s. Some of those are still loaded in Europe, but they are as dead as yesterday's news in America.

The introduction of the plastic hull during the 1960s ranks right up there in importance with the development of the noncorrosive primer. I still miss the wonderful aroma that wafted from one of the old paper hulls just after it was fired on a cold winter's morn, but the use of paper in shotshell manufacturing had many

shortcomings. Wet or even mildly humid conditions could cause a shell to swell up and refuse to enter the chamber of a shotgun. Its tendency to become scuffed during its journey inside the pocket of a hunting coat caused many a pump gun or autoloader to grind to a halt just as the second bird from a covey took to wing. Not only was the new plastic shell weatherproof, its slick exterior surface allowed it to travel smoothly through the feed mechanism of a firearm, and this virtually eliminated ammunition-induced malfunctions in pumps and autoloaders.

As a bonus to handloaders, plastic hulls such as the Remington STS, Federal Gold Medal and Winchester AA can last for a dozen or more firings, while most paper hulls were good for no more than a couple of trigger squeezes. If any fault can be found in the plastic shotshell hull, it is the fact that if left in the field by a careless hunter, it remains on the scene as an ugly eyesore practically forever, whereas all but the metal head of a paper hull will eventually disappear back to the earth from which it came. Federal continues to offer a shotshell with a paper hull, but it is available only in the Gold Medal target load lineup. I know skeet and trap shooters who swear it churns up less recoil than the same load in a plastic hull, but my shoulder is too insensitive to detect any difference. Fiocchi and Bismuth Cartridge also offer paper-hulled shells, and the latter contains biodegradable wads.

Almost as important as the development of the plastic shotshell was the introduction of the plastic wad, which came along at about the same time. The cardboard wad column used in paper shells was inefficient due to its inability to completely seal off the bore of a shotgun barrel during firing, and this required heavy powder charges to be used in order to compensate for propellant gas that escaped around it. Not so with the new plastic wad, since its flexibility and the concave

Shotshell lengths became standardized during the 20th century and the fine, little 28 gauge ended up at 2-3/4 inches.

shape of its base serve to seal off the bore to the point where powder charges can be reduced considerably with no loss in velocity. A reduction in the amount of powder loaded in a shotshell reduced recoil, and this explains in part why many shotgunners believe today's shotguns shoot softer than those of yesteryear.

Benefits of the plastic wad do not stop with recoil reduction. The wall of its protective shotcup prevents soft lead shot from making direct contact with the bore during firing, and the resultant reduction in pellet deformity improves shot-pattern quality. In addition, whereas the rear layers of lead pellets in a shot charge suffered setback deformation during firing with the old fiber filler wad, the collapsible midsection of a plastic wad serves as a shock absorber and in doing so reduces the severity of pellet deformation. The petals of a plastic wad also act as an airbrake, and this prevents blown patterns that were common with the old card wad system. As if all that were not enough to produce pattern quality seldom seen by shotgunners prior to the 1960s, shotshell manufacturers reduced pellet damage even more by developing buffered loads with tiny pellets of a soft material filling the spaces between each lead pellet. The introduction of the one-piece plastic wad column also made handloading a bit more foolproof, and this can be important to the beginner who decides to start loading his own shotshells.

But the plastic shotshell wad still falls short of perfection, since like the plastic hull, it remains on the scene practically forever when left behind in the field. The English have already taken the easy way out by banning the use of plastic wads in its hunting fields, and unless my crystal ball is wrong (and it seldom is), American shotshell manufacturers who have long been more innovative and creative than the Brits will eventu-

ally develop a biodegradable wad with all the qualities of one made of plastic. Federal has developed what the company describes as a decomposable plastic wad for use in some of its steel shot loads, and I hope it is a sign of more to come.

The last really important 20th century step forward in shotshells was the development of various forms of nontoxic shot. While most of us managed to adapt to the different flight characteristics of steel shot for waterfowl hunting, it does have one really big shortcoming. Unlike lead shot, which can be used in any shotgun of serviceable condition, steel is suitable only for modern guns with barrels specifically designed for its use. If steel shot is fired in a gun designed for use only with lead shot, the extremely hard pellets can and likely will plow nasty grooves down that shiny smooth bore, not to mention the fact that it can also iron out any choke constriction in the barrel. For this reason the mandatory application of steel shot in America's marshlands virtually eliminated the use of thousands upon thousands of shotguns built before it came into use. The problem was solved with the introduction of ammo loaded with shot that performs exactly like lead, but is nontoxic to any duck or goose that might ingest it while feeding. Examples are the bismuth from Bismuth Cartridge and Tungsten-Matrix from Kent.

Just as important as the development of a nontoxic shot capable of equaling the performance of lead is the introduction of a material capable of outperforming lead. Remington calls it Hevi-Shot, but I simply refer to it as one of the top half-dozen developments in shotshells of the 20th century.

The 20th century was a busy time for shotshell manufacturers, and one can only guess what will take place during the next 100 years.

CHAPTER 2

Over-Under Versus Side-By-Side

Hunters will always debate the merits of over-under and side-by-side shotguns. I find that if a double fits me and I am having a good day I shoot it quite well regardless of how its barrels are oriented.

I have been shooting double-barrel shotguns for a very long time. The first gun I owned during my youth was an Iver Johnson single shot, but my father owned several doubles, and I eventually was allowed to use them as well. Dad's first shotgun was a 16-gauge L.C. Smith, but he eventually had others, including a Browning Superposed Lightning in 20-

gauge. The Browning was the first double with a single trigger I had ever shot. In those days, I thought nothing of hunting with an over-under with a single trigger one day and then switching to a side-by-side double with two triggers the next. I am glad I did because it is something I can still do today without ever giving it a second thought.

Of the over-under shotguns introduced by Remington since the company's first one in 1932, the Model 332 is the best yet for hunting because of its dynamic handling and light weight.

Since I started shooting both side-by-sides and over-unders at an early age, I really have no strong preference between the two. I do, however, recognize advantages and disadvantages in the two designs. Nothing feels better in my hands than a top-quality side-by-side double, but when all things are equal, I shoot the over-under just as well in the field. When I shoot skeet and use today's popular high-gun start position, I usually break more clay targets with a nine-pound Krieghoff 32 over-under than with a lightweight side-by-side, but it is due more to differences in heft than the way barrels are oriented. If I were to use a side-by-side double with the weight of the K32, I would probably shoot skeet just as well with it. From the old low-gun start position, which is actually better practice for hunters, I break a few more targets with a lightweight side-by-side like my 28-gauge Parker than with the heavy Krieghoff because it is quicker handling. But then, I break no more targets with the Parker than with an over-under weighing about the same.

I have seen it written on more than one occasion that the over-under is more durable than the side-by-side, but few of today's hunters will ever put enough rounds through either to know for sure. A fantasy comes to mind anytime I read such a statement. I chain the author to a tree, hand him my Fox Sterlingworth along with thousands of rounds of heavy duck loads and promise to turn him loose only when the gun is worn out. After many years of shooting heavy loads, a serious trap shooter

might wear out a good side-by-side, but the number of hunters who will do so are few and far between. Over on the other side of the argument, I hear the side-by-side has an edge because the gape of its barrels is shorter than for the stackbarrel gun. I'll admit, not having to swing the side-by's barrels down quite so far in order to load its chambers can be handy in the cramped quarters of a duck blind but everywhere else I see it as no great advantage.

There is also the matter of recoil. Critics of the side-by-side are fond of saying the over-under kicks less because the axis of its lower barrel is positioned closer to the centerline of the stock. What they conveniently fail to mention is when the top barrel of an over-under is fired, it seems to kick more than the side-by-side. And while I am picking nits, positioning the barrels of a gun horizontally is supposed to cause it to torque to the side when it is fired. This might be true in both theory and fact, but you can't prove it by me, and I have fired many thousands of rounds in side-by-side guns. If it were true, I would miss more often with the second barrel of a side-by-side than with the second barrel of an over-under, but when shooting quail or simultaneous doubles in sporting clays, I hit or miss just as often with one type of gun as with the other.

Ben Amonette of Alliant Powder and I once shot sporting clays at the prestigious old Homestead gun club in Hot Springs, Virginia. The 28-gauge gun I used on

An over-under with three sets of barrels like this Weatherby Athena in 20, 28 and .410 is capable of handling a lot of hunting territory.

clay targets was what I had brought along for hunting ruffed grouse, a 5-1/2-pound double built by AyA of Eibar, Spain. It is choked .006 inch (Improved Skeet) and .018 inch (Improved Modified). One of the stations we shot was especially challenging because it presented sharp left and right crossers as a true pair in a heavily wooded area. The trapper who pulled targets for us said he had never seen professional shooters break that particular pair of birds so quickly in registered tournaments held by the gun club. I say this not to boast of my prowess with a shotgun, but to drive home the fact that the side-by-side double can be as fast for two accurate shots as any other type of shotgun.

Some say the over-under with its so-called single sighting plane offers a better "sight picture" than the wide muzzles of the side-by-side. This may be a factor worthy of discussion for someone who has been using a single-barrel gun for years and first tries the side-by-side, but even then I am convinced it is more mental than physical. I am also convinced it is easily overcome by anyone who really wants to learn to use that type of gun. I personally consider this a rather silly argument because in wingshooting the shotgun should be pointed rather

than aimed. If the shooter is concentrating on the target as should be done, he will not notice the number of barrels he is looking over as he pulls the trigger.

One thing is certain: The side-by-side has fewer firing-pin problems than the over-under. This is because of the fact that the lower firing pin on a stack-barrel gun is usually positioned at a much sharper angle than the upper firing pin. This is why anytime an over-under develops misfire problems, it almost always takes place in its lower barrel. The sharply angled firing pin also has a tendency to peen its orifice in the standing breech out of round, and that can cause it to hang up when the gun is broken down for reloading. Those who have put many thousands of rounds through a Remington Model 3200 are familiar with this problem.

I could go on and on with my comparison of the two types of doubles and might eventually get around to choosing a side, but any points I make would be rather moot considering the excellence of both designs. If the owner of a shotgun is happy with his choice, it fits him reasonably well and he is convinced he can hit with it, he likely will, regardless of whether its barrels are stacked one atop the other or they lie side by side.

Doubles have the edge over pumps and autoloaders in some ways, but there are times when neither is a clear winner. When overall length is the same, the barrels of a double will be longer because its receiver is shorter. This is easy to see when comparing a couple of 20-gauge guns I own, a Westley Richards double and a Remington Model 1100 skeet gun. The double has 28-inch barrels, whereas the Remington has a 23-1/2-inch barrel and yet overall length of those two guns is almost exactly the same. I am quick to add that since both put muzzle blast the same distance from my ears, that characteristic alone does not make the double a better gun than the autoloader. The big difference is in the way the two guns feel, and while the Model 1100 feels better to me than most other autoloaders, it is not in the same league as the Westley Richards. On the other hand, you can buy a truckload of Model 1100s for the price of one Westley Richards, and even I will have to admit it most definitely does not handle that much better.

I would like to be able to say all doubles handle and feel better than pumps and autos, and while this is true in some cases, it not always is. Some pumps and autos have the balance and feel of a railroad tie, but then the same applies to some doubles. Any double-gun manufacturer that manages to improve on the dynamics of the Winchester Model 12 pump and Remington 1100 autoloader in 20 and 28-gauges should be congratulated for a job well done. The British and Spanish have done it time and again through the years, but few American companies have. In my opinion (and just about everybody has one), some of the best-handling doubles ever built in America are those in 16 and 20-gauges built up through 1928 by the old A.H. Fox Gun Company. I also am quite fond of the L.C Smith Lightweight in .410 and 20-gauge. Another classic is a neat little skeet gun from Iver Johnson called the Skeet-er. It is especially nice in .410, 16, 20 and 28. Small-gauge Parker, Ithaca and Lefever guns are also nice, and to keep over-under fans happy, I will include the Browning Superposed Lightning and Winchester 101 in those same three bore sizes in my list of old favorites.

The double-barrel shotgun has a number of advantages over pumps and autoloaders. For one, it offers a hunter the option of carrying one gun with two different choke constrictions. The versatility of a double can be greatly expanded by the use of subgauge tubes, something that cannot be done with the pump and autoloader. That idea has long been popular with skeet shooters and seems to be catching on a bit among hunters as well. I had Briley custom-fit to a couple of pairs of lightweight tubes in 28-gauge and .410 to the barrels of a 20-gauge Browning Superposed Lightning, and I use

My favorite side-by-side double is a No. 1 grade AyA in 28-gauge with which I took this sharptail grouse in Montana.

that gun even more now than I did before the job was done. A pair of tubes adds 10 ounces, but the gun was quite light to begin with and since much of the added heft is out front, handling is actually improved in a dove field. A double with two or more sets of barrels is also nice as it too allows its owner to shoot more than one gauge in the same gun. I have spent a great deal of time afield with a Weatherby Athena over-under with three sets of barrels in 20, 28 and .410 and with that one gun I can handle about 90 percent of my shotgunning.

American manufacturers are big players when it comes to turning out pumps and autos, but by and large they have never led the race in manufacturing sleek, smooth-handling doubles. Now don't take what you have just read in the wrong vein. Some the strongest and most durable doubles ever built were produced right here in the good old US of A. One example is the Fox side-by-side. Another is the Remington Model 3200 over-under. I own both, use them a lot and consider them great guns for what they once sold for and what they still sell for on the used gun market. And when it comes right down to how well I do in the field, I shoot just as well with some of the American-built over-under and side-by-side doubles I own as I do with any other gun built anywhere else

This Holland & Holland over-under looked and handled like a million bucks when I shot it in Uruguay but it cost its owner only a bit less than thirty thousand dollars.

doubles with 26-inch barrels, and it mostly comes from those who spend most of their time shooting clay targets or pass-shooting ducks. We could argue barrel lengths until we are blue in the face, but it would not change the fact that if I am having a good day and the gun fits, I shoot it fairly well. If a gun does not fit me, I do not shoot it well regardless of the length of its barrels. I am convinced the same applies to most hunters.

I prefer the looks of two triggers on a side-by-side double. I also like the instant choice of options they offer. If a bird flushes from underfoot I have the open-choked barrel with a light load ready for immediate action. If a bird gets up long before my dog can pin it down, I have the option of pulling the rear trigger and reaching out farther with a tighter choke and maybe even a heavier load with larger shot in the left barrel. A friend of mine says he can accomplish the same thing with the barrel selector of a single-trigger gun but I find most designs to be much slower than two triggers. Pushing the button to select the other barrel just gives me something extra to think about as I shoulder the gun, and anytime I start doing too much thinking when I am shooting, I start doing a lot of missing. There is one exception to what I have just written. The safety and barrel selector on the Remington Model 3200 is as fast and as fumble-free as having a gun with two triggers.

The biggest thing double triggers have going for them is they are simple in design and quite durable. This cannot be said of all single triggers. Some American- and foreign-built doubles of yesteryear with single triggers, even those of high quality, had plenty of problems. This is why the Miller Single Trigger Company of Millersburg, Pa. (now owned by Doug Turnbull Restorations) stayed in business for most of the 20th century. My 28-gauge Parker doubled more often than not until I had the Miller brothers install one of their triggers. Back in the 1930s, Iver Johnson charged $17.50 extra for a Miller trigger on its Skeet-er skeet gun, but the installation alone now costs about as much as a good over-under shotgun.

in the world. But the fact remains, when it comes to building a lightweight double that points like your finger, handles like a fistful of feathers and springs to shoulder as if it has a mind of its own, few compare to side-by-side game guns built by the British and copied faithfully by the Spanish. If anything of American make comes close, it is the new Ithaca gun being built by Ithaca Classic Doubles of Victor, New York.

Double-barrel shotguns I own have barrels ranging in length from 26 to 30 inches. When the mourning dove shooting is hot, I like the feel of a 28-gauge Weatherby Athena over-under and my 20-gauge Westley Richards side-by-side, both with 28-inch barrels. For hunting waterfowl, I like a Fox Sterlingworth and a Remington Model 3200. Both have 30-inch barrels. If ever I decide to keep score, I will probably discover that I am a bit better at pass-shooting with those guns because once I get their long barrels off and running, I am not as likely to get lazy and stop my swing too soon with them as I am when shooting guns with shorter barrels.

When shooting at targets that travel away from the gun at various angles, I don't shoot longer tubes any better or worse than I do when using doubles wearing barrels as short at 26 inches. In fact, some of the best quail shooting I have ever done was with a Remington Model 1100 Special Field with a straight grip and a 21-inch barrel. I own several guns with barrels measuring in the neighborhood of 26 inches and would not want them to be any longer. It has become fashionable among the younger generation these days to criticize

While the British have always held an edge in building trim, lightweight side-by-side doubles, an American-built gun like this 1930s vintage .410-bore Parker I once used to bag a few quail is close enough to perfection to suit me.

Just as some like blondes, others prefer brunettes or redheads, and so it goes with shotguns. In my eyes, the most handsome shotgun ever built is a sleek side-by-side double in 20-gauge or smaller with two triggers and a straight grip. When done up right, nothing else comes close to matching its grace and beauty. As for the over-under, I think the straight grip looks a bit out of place there and the curved grip gives that type of gun a better appearance. Like I said, almost everyone has at least one opinion. There are those who believe the straight grip is better on a gun with two triggers since it allows the hand to more easily slide from one trigger to the other. This is probably more true than not for shooters with short fingers. Those of us with longer pinkies are usually able to move our finger from trigger to trigger while the hand remains relatively stationary on the stock, and for us one style of grip works about as well as the other.

I like the straight grip on a dual-trigger gun because it allows me to position my rather large hand a bit farther back on the stock while some pistol grips are curved too tightly for comfortable use with two triggers. The stock on my Fox Sterlingworth is a good example. When shooting the right barrel (front trigger) first and then shooting the left, everything goes as planned, but its tightly curved grip positions my hand so far forward it feels a bit cramped when a wild-flushing pheasant requires my finger to seek out the aft trigger first.

When everything is thrown into the pot and allowed to simmer awhile, the half pistol grip as popularized in America by the old Browning Auto-5 and Browning Superposed may be the best style for use on either a single-trigger gun or a gun with double triggers. It is open enough to allow a larger hand to be positioned comfortably to the rear and yet closed enough to just about equal the more secure feeling some shooters prefer in a full pistol grip. This style of grip is being kept alive in the U.S. today by the Weatherby Athena over-under and several other guns imported into the United States by Sigarms and others. The stock of the Remington Model 332 does not quite have a half pistol grip, but it is close.

One reason the British have had such a long love affair with the double is because it is their invention. (Well, if we really must split hairs, the double is a French invention, but the British perfected it.) The Brits often gather in large groups and chat about the driven birds they are about to shoot or they have already shot, and this is another reason why they prefer doubles. When several dozen hunters are standing around with their doubles broken down it is easy to tell at a glance that all guns are safe. The safety aspect also makes the double an excellent choice for a youngster, although you will hear no argument from me if you think a single-loaded pump gun or autoloader carried with its chamber empty is any less safe under the close supervision of a responsible grownup. Trap and skeet shooters like doubles for the same reason British field gunners do – when unloaded and open, they are visibly safe.

CHAPTER 3
The All-American Pump Gun

Designed by John Browning, the Stevens Model 520 was one of the earliest successful slide-action shotguns.

Most shotgunners in other countries would not have a pump gun if it were wrapped in $100 bills and came with a lifetime supply of ammunition. In stark contrast, American hunters have for many years bought more shotguns with the trombone action than any other type. Back in 1988 the pump represented 58 percent of all shotgun sales in the United States for that year, while the autoloader trailed behind it by 31 percent. The over-under accounted for seven percent of sales, while single-shots and side-by-sides chalked up only four percent. I am sure those percentages read a bit differently today, especially for the over-under, but my guess is the

pump is either still number one or it is close behind the autoloader in second place. Either way, plenty of pump guns are still sold in the United States each year, and why this is true is easy to explain.

Everything considered, the slide action might be the closest we will ever come to the ideal shotgun. For starters, it is the most affordable repeating shotgun available. There was a time when the typical knock-about bolt-action scattergun was even less expensive, but it no longer counts, considering the small number now available and what they sell for. As for the slide action, you can buy two Remington Model 870 Express

More Remington Model 870s have been built than any other make or model of pump gun. This one in 16-gauge worked fine on Florida quail.

shotguns and then spend close to $100 on shotshells for what you will pay for a Remington Model 11-87 autoloader. Want pretty, too? The fancier Wingmaster version of the Model 870 costs only about two-thirds as much as the Model 11-87 Premier. The story reads about the same with other brands. The Benelli M1 Field semiauto sells for 2-1/2 times the price of the Benelli Nova pump gun. The Browning Gold Hunter will cost you 60 percent more than the Browning BPS.

Then we have the matter of weight. The 12-gauge Model 870 Wingmaster is rated at 7-1/4 pounds, the smaller-framed 20-gauge version weighs 6-1/2

pounds and the 28-gauge tips the scale at an even six pounds. Remington's Model 11-87 autoloader in 12-gauge weighs 7-3/4 pounds, while the 20-gauge version weighs 6-3/4 pounds. The 28-gauge Model 1100 usually pegs the scale at around 6-1/2 pounds. Any way you look at it and regardless of the gauge, the pump gun weighs anywhere from one quarter to one half pound less than the typical autoloader. That's not much if you mostly hunt a covey or two of quail out behind the barn, but it can be a lot in Montana sharptail country with many long miles between where you are and where you were during breakfast. Moving on to other compar-

The Winchester Model 42 skeet gun in .410 is fun to have in the field on early-season dove shoots.

isons, the Browning BPS at 7-1/2 pounds is a quarter pound lighter than the Browning Gold Hunter. The Ithaca Model 37 is one of the lightest 12-gauge shotguns available. It is rated at seven pounds, although several I have handled felt even lighter. Of course, there are exceptions to everything. The Benelli Nova pump gun looks light but feels quite heavy at eight pounds. Pump guns made by Mossberg usually weigh 7-1/2 to 7-3/4 pounds. Still, if weight matters and if you must have the lightest repeating shotgun available, you will eventually end up leaving the gun shop with a slide action in your hand. One exception in all of this is the Franchi AL48 autoloader in 20 and 28-gauge; at just over 5-1/2 pounds, it weighs less than any pump gun I have ever shot.

The handling and feel of some pump guns are as good as you will get in a repeating shotgun. Most who have hunted with the Winchester Model 12 in either 20, 16 or 28 gauge would agree. Having shot that gun rather extensively through the years, I never cease

to be amazed at how the old Winchester company managed to offer so much gun at so small a price. The 28-gauge Model 12 I am now shooting feels like it was made just for me even though it was mass-produced along with hundreds of others just like it. Same goes for my .410-bore Winchester Model 42 skeet gun, which is basically a scaled-down version of the Model 12. In a very close second place (if not in a three-way tie for first place) is the Remington Model 870 Wingmaster in 20 and 28 gauge. I have hunted quail a bit with a 28-gauge Model 870, and it seems to get lighter as the day gets longer. I would like to be able to add the 16-gauge Model 870 to this short list of dynamic-handling guns, but cannot since it is built on the larger 12-gauge receiver. The receiver of the Ithaca Model 37 in 16 gauge is properly sized for that gauge and it is an excellent gun, but some pump-gunners don't care for its bottom ejection of fired cases.

Reliability, durability and longevity are other things you often hear pump-gun fans discuss. When both are new, the reliability race between pumps and autoloaders will usually end in a draw. This assumes properly maintained guns of equal quality and good, clean ammunition. Forget to clean both types of guns a time or two after heavy use, and the slide action will still come out shooting while the semiauto might not. As for durability, there is no doubt in my mind that the pump gun will survive more years of extremely hard use. I have seen Winchester Model 97s and Model 12s and Remington Model 870s owned by waterfowl guides that worked without a hitch after spending countless seasons partially submerged in water in the bottom of a boat. Those guns had been beat-up, battered, dropped, stepped-on and occasionally used as boat paddles to the

Rudy Etchen, the best pump-gunner I ever shot with, worked for many years as a consultant to Remington. Here he shows me the then-new Remington Model 300 over-under.

point where very little finish remained on either wood or metal, and yet they performed to perfection when called on. No autoloading shotgun would tolerate such abuse. I won't say a good pump gun will last longer than a good autoloader, but I will say it will shoot longer without suffering parts breakage. And when a pump does stop working, its simple design and few moving parts are likely make the repair cost much easier on the family budget.

Those who are shopping for a first shotgun for a youngster should look long and hard at a pump gun in 20 or 28 gauge. Its light weight makes it an excellent choice, but the safety factor is even more important, something I had never thought about until I hunted quail with Tom Shepherd of Hodgdon Powder. Tom described to me how his father kicked off his shotgunning career with a slide-action shotgun. When hunting rabbits and quail, he was allowed to carry the gun with a round in its chamber, but he had to keep the slide all the way back in its unlocked position. With nothing more than an occasional glance his father could see that the gun was being carried in an entirely safe mode. Tom said he quickly progressed to the point where smoothly closing the action became such an integral part of bringing the gun to his shoulder for a shot, he never even thought about it. It sure makes a lot of sense to me.

The slide-action shotgun was not supposed to be with us for as long as it has. During the last decade of the 19th century, severe fluctuations in chamber pressures generated by black powder prevented manufacturers from finding success in the development of autoloading shotguns. Since the semiautomatic had to

wait until smokeless powder was perfected, some other means had to be developed for increasing the firepower of shotguns. The British designed breechloaders with as many as four barrels, but in addition to being rather expensive and quite a nightmare to regulate properly, they were a bit hefty. What was needed was a shotgun offering more firepower than the double at a cost the average working man could afford. Slide-action shotguns proved to be the first commercially successful answer, although those who manufactured them were convinced the design would not last very far beyond the introduction of the first autoloading shotgun that worked reliably. How wrong they were.

Most historians credit British designer Alexander Bain as first to patent a slide-action shotgun, but it took the quest for greater firepower at an affordable price to get it into the duck and goose blinds across America. Two of the first slide-action shotguns to be introduced in the United States were the Spencer and the Burgess, the latter manufactured by the Burgess Gun Company of Buffalo, New York. Both entered the marketplace around 1890. The Burgess utilized a sliding pistol grip to operate its action, whereas the Spencer had a sliding forearm much like pump guns of today.

None of the earlier designs proved to be anywhere near as successful in a competitive market as Winchester's first pump gun, the Model 1893.

This Browning reproduction of the Winchester Model 12 in 28 gauge is as effective on live birds and clay targets as the real thing and it is far less expensive.

Designed by John Browning, it was introduced in 1893 and along with it came several design improvements. One was a trigger disconnect that prevented the hammer from traveling forward unless the breechblock was all the way forward in its fully locked position. After manufacturing just over 34,000 Model 93s, Winchester replaced it with a smokeless powder version of the same shotgun in 1897.

With slightly more than one a million eventually built, the Winchester Model 1897 went on to become one of the most successful repeating shotguns ever designed. It was cheaper than a good double, more durable than a cheap double and its magazine capacity allowed it to be loaded on Sunday and shot all week. None of this went unnoticed during an era when the number of Americans who hunted to eat still far outnumbered those who hunted solely for the love of sport. Even today the old Model 97 can hold its on in the field when pitted against about any shotgun of modern design. Most seen today are in 12 gauge, although quite a few 16s were built as well. Some of the early ones also had Damascus barrels, but that extra cost option was dropped in 1914. A number of model variations and grades were available, including Trap, Riot, Brush, Pigeon, Tournament and Trench, the latter purchased by the thousands by the U.S. Army during World War I.

Had Winchester decided to scale down the Model 97 action and chamber it for the 20-gauge shell, the gun might have been with us later than 1957, the year it was dropped from production. I did not get around to owning one until more than 100 years after it was introduced. Mine has a 30-inch barrel, and while its barrel is marked Full, it actually is choked closer to Modified. One day I decided to shoot a few rounds of trap with the old Model 97, and the other fellows in my squad seemed quite surprised when I ended up with a 96x100 with a gun I had not previously shot a single time. Of course, they were nowhere near as surprised as me.

The Model 97 was and is a great shotgun, but it had an exposed hammer sprouting from the rear of its blocky receiver during an age when the trend in shotgun design was leaning heavily in the direction of hammers concealed within streamlined receivers. This prompted Winchester to introduce a totally new shotgun in 1912. Called the Model 12, it was designed by Thomas C. Johnson and first produced in 20 gauge with a 25-inch nickel steel barrel. The 12- and 16-gauge chamberings were added in 1914 and the 28-gauge came along in 1934. The Model 12 was often described by Winchester as the "Perfect Repeater," and few who have owned one would disagree.

As I mentioned earlier, few shotguns of any type handle and feel as nicely as Winchester's sleek Model 12 pump gun. Several model variations were produced, and as standard-production guns go, the Skeet Gun in 28 gauge usually brings the most money from hunters and collectors alike. One of the best buys in Model 12s as I write this is the Heavy Duck Gun with a 30-inch barrel in 12 gauge with a 3-inch chamber. Regular Model 12 production stopped in 1963 with 1,969,307 guns built. The grand old gun was reintroduced in 1972 in 12-gauge only, but with a price of $350 for the field grade, it was no match in a highly competitive market against the Remington Model 870 and its $134.95 price tag. The Model 12 was dropped a final time in 1980. Counting those guns along with limited edition guns such as the 800 built for Ducks Unlimited in 1975, just over 2,000,000 were built.

Incidentally, a lot of people do not realize that Winchester built a solid-frame version of the Model 12. Called the Model 25, it sold for $80.25 in 1953 at a time when the Model 12 field grade with plain barrel went for $93.85. The major difference between the two is the Model 25 cannot be taken down like the Model 12. It was not as nicely finished as the Model 12 either. The Model 25 was introduced in 1949 and even though Winchester built almost 90,000 units, it was discontinued only a short time later in 1954. Perhaps the company was beginning to see the handwriting on the wall since the Model 12 was discontinued less than 10 years later.

I enjoy shooting the Model 97 and few experiences rank higher on my priority list than being in the field with the Model 12, but neither is my favorite Winchester pump gun. That title belongs to a six-pound package of precision-machined steel, American walnut and greased lightning called the Winchester Model 42. Not only is it my favorite Winchester repeating shotgun, it is one of my favorite shotguns of all brands and types. Anyone who can pick up a Model 42 without falling head over heels in love with it either doesn't know how a woodcock gun is supposed to feel or, as an old farmer I once knew used to say, "he just ain't no shotgunner." The Model 42 and its equally new 3-inch version of the .410 shotshell were introduced in 1933 at a time when skeet shooting was really beginning to catch on in America. Before the year ended, it was dominating the .410 event and many skeeters shot it in the 28-gauge class as well. Soon thereafter, the littlest of pump guns was discovered by hunters.

A scaled-down version of the Model 12, the Model 42 is the only repeating shotgun I am aware of that was designed solely and exclusively for the .410

shotshell. It was designed by William Roemer, who went to work at Winchester as a draftsman in 1909 and ended up as chief designer for the entire company. Any Model 42 is nice, but my favorite and the one I own is called the Skeet Gun. Several features on my 1953-vintage gun make collectors foam at the mouth and reach for their checkbooks, but that doesn't prevent me from hunting with it at every opportunity. In addition to a ventilated rib, mine has a Cutts Compensator attached to the muzzle of its 26-inch barrel. The Cutts was an extra-cost option first offered on Model 42 skeet guns by Winchester in 1954 and it was never very popular. Incidentally, if a Model 42 originally left the factory with a compensator installed, it will have no choke stamping on its barrel. The previous owner of my gun returned it to the factory for installation of its Cutts, which explains why its barrel is marked "Skeet." Somewhere around 160,000 Model 42s were built, which is not many when you consider how many of today's shotgunners would love to own one. If the Winchester Model 12 really is the "Perfect Repeater," then the Winchester Model 42 has to be "The Shotgunner's Sweetheart."

Even though a number of excellent pump guns have worn the Winchester name, that company has never had a monopoly on the design. One of the first truly successful shotguns of that type was introduced by Stevens around 1904. Designed by John Browning, the Stevens Model 520 had a sliding safety on its tang and a humpbacked receiver. Steve Comus, who still shoots one, kindly allowed me to bag a duck or two with his while we were hunting in Old Mexico in 2000 with Mike Larsen of Federal. We were using Federal ammo loaded with Tungsten-Polymer shot. In 1927 Stevens replaced the Model 520 with the Model 620, a takedown gun with a more streamlined receiver. It looked like it might have been spooked from the bushes by the Winchester Model 12.

The 1960s and 1970s saw the introduction of more new pump guns than at any other time in history. To name but a few in no special order, there were the Harrington & Richardson M442, J.C. Higgins Model 20 (sold by Sears-Roebuck), Hi-Standard Flite King, Hawthorne Viking, Noble Model 60, Marlin M120 (another Model 12 look-alike), Savage Model 30, Smith & Wesson Model 916, Weatherby Patrician, Western Field M550. During the 1960s, a few foreign manufacturers also hopped aboard the slide-action bandwagon with the Silver Pigeon from Beretta and the La Salle from the French firm of ManuFrance Gun Works good examples.

If we go by sales numbers alone, Remington

Able to keep on ticking after most autoloaders have succumbed to the licking makes the pump gun an excellent choice for hunting where the nearest gunsmith is hundreds of miles away.

has the most successful slide-action shotgun every built by a margin so wide, there really is no second-place finisher. The Model 870 was introduced in 1950 and by 1996 seven million had been built. Remington has averaged building close to 1,000 Model 870s each day for the past dozen years, which means that production has surely exceeded eight million by now. Think about it: Winchester built Model 97s for 60 years and Model 12s for 50 years for a total production time of 110 years and ended up with around three million guns. That's less than half of the number of Model 870s Remington built in 52 years.

When it comes to introducing a hammerless pump gun with a streamlined receiver, Remington actually beat Winchester to the punch. It all started around 1906 when an inventor by the name of John D. Pedersen of Denver, Colorado, who had been issued patents for a number of firearms, entered into a business agreement with Remington that lasted for more than 20 years. Remington introduced Pedersen's streamlined slide-action shotgun in 1908, four years before Winchester introduced its Model 12. Simply described by Remington as the "Repeating Shotgun" during its first years of production, it eventually became known as the Model 10. Available only in 12 gauge, the Model 10 featured a takedown-style receiver and the bottom ejection of fired cases, the latter feature seen on today's Ithaca Model 37 and Browning BPS. The same basic gun was later refined a bit more and reintroduced as the Model 29 in 1929, but production came to a halt in 1933.

Remington introduced its Model 31 pump gun in 1931, and except for an interruption of production during World War II, it lasted until 1949, shortly before the Model 870 was introduced. Its smoothness prompted Remington to advertise the Model 31 as the gun with the ball bearing action, and anyone who has shot one would have a difficult time disputing the claim. The Model 31 was designed by Crawford W. Loomis and it was Remington's first side-ejection pump gun. A number of variations were offered, including field grade with a plain or ribbed barrel as well as guns built for trap and skeet shooting. Vic Reinders, who was one of the top trap shooters of his time, used a Model 31 to win a lion's share of tournaments, including the doubles event at the Grand Nationals with a 99x100. While never as popular in skeet shooting circles as the Winchester Model 12, Model 31s wearing Cutts Compensators still managed to break their share of clay targets from stations one through eight. Less than 38,000 Model 31s were built, so if you ever bump into a six-pound 20-gauge Model 31L with an aluminum receiver and in excellent condition, buy it quickly.

I seldom see a shooter today who can operate a pump gun the way it should be driven. I have been shooting pumps off an on all my life, and I don't mind admitting I probably will never completely master the design. This is due to the fact that I shoot other types of guns more often, and if you want to be good with a pump gun, you must shoot nothing else. As the old saying goes, if you can hear a shooter operate a pump gun, he is no pump gun man, and you can surely hear me operate mine.

During my lifetime, I have personally met two genuine pump gun maestros. One was exhibition shooter Herb Parsons, who worked for Winchester for many years. I once watched as Parsons threw seven clay targets into the air with his right hand and then used a Winchester Model 12 to break all of them before they hit the ground. Although I have never met him, I understand that exhibition shooter Tom Knapp who works for Benelli exceeded Parsons' long-standing record by throwing eight clay targets into the air by hand and breaking all before they hit the ground with a Nova pump gun.

The best pumper I have ever actually shot with was the late Rudy Etchen. Like Parsons, Rudy was poetry in motion except he used a Remington Model 870. I once stood next door to him on the trap field of the Ilion Gun Club in New York. We were shooting doubles with Model 870 trap guns. Regardless of how hard I concentrated, I could hardly see Rudy's hand move as he operated the action. He was quicker than quick, faster than fast. As he explained to me, the secret to driving a pump gun at top speed is to make operating its action a continuation of the previous shot rather than preparation for the next shot. Remington sent one of the first Model 870s built to Rudy, and shortly thereafter he used it to break 100 straight targets while shooting doubles at the 1950 Grand American. I believe that made him the first person to shoot a perfect score at trap doubles with a pump gun. Thirty-two years later, while recovering from a stay in the hospital, Rudy used that same old Model 870 to win the doubles event at the Shreveport Gun Club in Louisiana with another perfect score. He never did much trick shooting, but breaking 104 straight targets while standing on one foot and extending his shotgun out in front with one arm as if he were shooting a handgun most certainly qualifies for that category. Not long before his death in 2001, Rudy told me how many rounds he had fired in his 1950 vintage Model 870 and while I have forgotten the exact number, I do recall that it was in the hundreds of thousands.

CHAPTER 4
The Soft-Shooting Autoloader

Its ability to handle heavy loads while softening perceived recoil is one of the reasons why the autoloader has become quite popular among pheasant hunters.

The autoloading shotgun was invented during the final years of the 19th century. In those days, shotshell manufacturers were undergoing the transition from black to smokeless powders, and ammunition containing both types of propellants was still in common use. Chamber pressure curves generated by the two powders varied considerably, and this made it virtually impossible for designers of semiautomatic shotguns to come up with a mechanism capable of handling all types of ammunition interchangeably. But progress did not grind slowly for very long.

One of the first giant steps forward in repeating-shotgun evolution took place in 1900, when John Browning patented his recoil-operated Automatic-5. By changing the location of a sliding friction ring in relation to the recoil spring (both located on the outside of the magazine tube), the owner of an Auto-5 could switch back and forth between low-recoil field loads and heavy-recoil duck loads. The autoloading shotgun was about to be off and running.

John Browning first presented his new design to Winchester, but he was turned down. He then decided to call on Marcellus Hartley, president of Remington, but Hartley died before a meeting could take place. Undaunted, Browning traveled to Belgium where he struck a deal with Fabrique Nationale. A shrewd businessman, Browning sold to FN the rights to manufacture his new shotgun for much of the world market, but retained the U.S. manufacturing rights, which he later sold to Remington. FN started producing Auto-5 shotguns around 1903, and Remington started producing the same gun as the Model 11 in 1905. By the time Model 11 production ceased in 1948, more than 850,000 units had been produced. Add to this the almost 3 million Auto-5s made up until its discontinuance in 1998, and it becomes easy to see why John Browning's old humpback was the repeating shotgun by which all others were judged by hunters and shooters during the first half of the 20th century.

But as great as the Auto-5 design proved to be, changing positions of the friction ring when switching between light and heavy loads required removal of the forearm, and some shooters found that to be a bit inconvenient in the field. Also, the standard Auto-5 handled 2-3/4 inch shells only. While a 3-inch magnum version was eventually introduced, it was not designed to function with light 2-3/4 inch target loads. On top of all that, some who tried the Auto-5 never quite grew accustomed to its recoiling barrel. Still, the design of Browning's A-5 was far superior to other autoloading shotgun designs such as the German-developed Walther with its toggle operation.

Urged on by the success of the Browning A-5 and the Remington Model 11, Winchester management decided to introduce their company's first autoloader in 1911. Like the A-5, the Winchester Model 1911 was recoil-operated and its receiver had a similar humpback shape. The receiver shape of the Model 1911 was actually reminiscent of Winchester's earlier Models 1905/1907/1910 family of autoloading centerfire rifles. This was due in large part to the fact that Thomas C. Johnson designed them as well as the new shotgun. Winchester discontinued production of its first autoloading shotgun in 1925 and did not come up with its replacement, the Model 40, until 15 years later. The new Model 40 also operated on the long-recoil princi-

Phyllis loves the 28-gauge Franchi 48AL. It points naturally and at 5-1/2 pounds it is easy to carry through a long day in the field. She finds the little gun quite comfortable to shoot, even with one-ounce loads.

ple, but its streamlined receiver profile was a sign of better things to come. The Model 40 was produced for only about a year, but the fact that close to 12,000 units were sold during that time seems to indicate the American sportsman was ready for an autoloading shotgun with a modern look.

In 1954 Winchester introduced its Model 50, a rather heavy autoloader that operates on the short-recoil principle. Quite unique as shotguns go, the barrel remains stationary during firing, but its chamber recoils to the rear by about 1/10 inch, thereby causing the bolt to travel rearward far enough to eject the fired hull and chamber a fresh round. Almost 200,000 Model 50s were produced before it was dropped from production in 1961.

The year 1959 brought what I consider to be greatest autoloading quail gun ever built by Winchester and one of the greatest ever built by anyone, anywhere in the world. Called the Model 59, it was produced from 1959 until 1965 and weighed a mere 6-1/2 pounds. An aluminum receiver along with a composite Win-Lite barrel built by wrapping 500 miles of glass fiber around a thin steel tube are what made the shotgun so light. Production guns were made only in 12 gauge, but a few were made in 20 and 14 gauge for experimental purposes only. The Model 59 was available with screw-in chokes, a system referred to by Winchester as the Versalite. Despite the fact that Winchester's glass-barrel shotgun is one of the most dynamic handling quail guns ever built, it never won any popularity contests and fewer than 85,000 were made.

In contrast to Winchester's limited success with autoloading shotguns during the early part of the 20th century, Remington entered the market in 1905 with a best seller, which, as mentioned earlier, was nothing less than an American-made version of the Browning

When production numbers of all the various models are added up, it becomes obvious that Remington has built more semiautomatic shotguns than any other firearms manufacturer. When teamed up with Remington ammunition loaded with Hevi-Shot, the 20-gauge Model 11-87 seen here is a fantastic waterfowl gun.

Auto-5. Originally described in Remington catalogs as the "Autoloading Gun," it became known as the Model 11 in 1911 and remained in production until 1948. Remington replaced its Model 11 with the Model 11-48 in 1948. Also called the Sportsman-48, it was, like the earlier gun, recoil-operated but the smooth and streamlined shape of its receiver would go on to become a familiar sight on other guns built not only by Remington but by many other companies during the remainder of the century. The trigger assembly of the Model 11-48 was easily removed for cleaning by the removal of two pins, a desirable feature that would appear on future Remington shotguns.

The major shotgun manufacturers received rather a rude awakening in 1956, when Sears-Roebuck introduced the world's first gas-operated shotgun under its highly successful J.C. Higgins brand name. Developed by High Standard Manufacturing, the gas system of the Model 60 was quite similar in concept to that of the earlier M1 Garand military rifle. A small hole drilled through the wall of the barrel allowed propellant gas to flow into a cylinder where it pushed against a piston. The piston was connected to the bolt. The new shotgun was capable of handling both light and heavy 12-gauge loads without the need for any kind of mechanical adjustment. Even though High Standard's application of the gas-operating principle fell a bit short of perfection in execution, the Model 60 proved quite successful. More important, it set the pace for autoloading shotguns that would soon follow.

Within months after J.C. Higgins woke up the shotgunning world with its Model 60, Remington intro-

Roger Bowman used a Browning Auto 5 to bag his limit of ducks in the flooded timber of Stuttgart, Arkansas, during the 1960s. That gun virtually owned the autoloading shotgun market during the first half of the 20th century.

duced its first gas-operated shotgun, the Sportsman-58. But like most autoloaders developed during that era, it had at least one shortcoming. Whereas the Sears-Roebuck gun was capable of handling all 2-3/4 inch loads interchangeably without mechanical adjustment, the magazine cap of Remington's new gas gun had to be twisted to its "H" position when heavy loads were used, and to its "L" setting when switching to light loads. While shooters found this far more convenient than removing the forearm and relocating a friction ring as was required of the old Browning A-5, the Model 58 still fell a bit short of the latest in gas-gun design.

Remington's next step toward perfection in autoloaders came in 1959 with the introduction of the Model 878. Also called the Automaster, it was basically the same as the earlier Model 58 except it would handle

all 2-2/4 inch loads without requiring the twisting of a knob or any other mechanical adjustment. But Remington design engineers had better things in mind, and the Model 878 remained in production for only four years.

In 1963 Wayne Leek and his team of engineers at Remington stepped forward with what would eventually become the best-selling autoloading shotgun built anywhere in the world. In addition to quickly becoming a favorite of millions of hunters, the Model 1100 would go on to dominate both trap and skeet competition like no other shotgun gun had ever done. The Model 1100 eventually became the autoloading shotgun by which all others were judged, and any other manufacturer who had enough clout to get away with it would eventually copy its receiver shape. As good as the Model 1100 was, still is and always will be, total versatility had yet

Shotguns made by the Italian firm of Beretta have a reputation for reliability and durability.

to be reached because it would not handle 2-3/4 inch and 3-inch ammo interchangeably.

A year after Remington introduced its Model 1100, Winchester came forward with its first gas-powered shotgun. Simply described, the Model 1400 was an economy-quality, knockabout firearm designed to cut production cost rather than rule the shotgun market. Many have been sold but few are cherished.

The classiest autoloading shotgun ever produced by Winchester was the gas-operated Super-X Model 1. It was introduced in 1974. Unlike other autoloaders with their mix of machined and stamped metal parts, just about everything about the Super-X was precision-machined steel. Unfortunately, all that steel made the gun heavier than its competition, and while the additional heft is what made many trap and skeet shooters stand in line to buy the gun, the average hunter wanted something easier to tote over hill and dale. And anytime hunters ignore a new shotgun, it is not long for this world.

Another great event in 20th century autoloader history was the mid-1970s introduction of the gas-operated Ithaca Mag 10. A number of single- and double-barrel shotguns had previously been chambered for the 10-gauge shotshell, but the Mag-10 was a first in autoloaders. Several years after all Ithaca shotguns disappeared from the scene, Remington bought the design rights to the Mag-10, spent a good-sized fortune on improving its durability and introduced it as the SP-10. Introduction of the 3-1/2 inch version of the 12-gauge shell along with lighter guns chambered for it have not exactly helped the popularity of

the SP-10 but I will always consider it to be the all-time greatest waterfowl gun every built for use with steel shot.

During the late 1970s, the shotgunning world was turned on its ear once more when the first gas-operated 12-gauge shotgun capable of handling 2-3/4 inch and 3-inch shells interchangeably came on the scene. Initially called the Super 12 and later renamed Model 1000, it was introduced not by Remington, Winchester or Browning as one might logically have expected in those days, but by Smith & Wesson, the manufacturer of handguns. A spring-loaded relief valve in the gas chamber of the new gun remained closed when light target loads were used, but automatically opened to vent excess pressure when heavy magnum loads were fired. Never before had such versatility been available in a semiautomatic shotgun. Offered in both 12 and 20 gauge, the Model 1000 stayed around for only a few years, but it did prove once and for all the feasibility of building a gas-powered gun capable of handling the full range of shotshell loads.

Introduction of the new S&W shotgun saw other companies scurrying back to the drawing board and by the mid to late 1980s the Remington 11-87, Browning A-500G, Browning A-500R and Beretta Model 303 were in full production. Like the S&W gun, all were capable of handling the full range of 2-3/4 inch and 3-inch loads. With the exception of a few internal improvements along with a new gas relief valve design, the Remington 11-87 is nothing less than a more durable version of the time-proven Remington 1100. The two guns even look the same on the outside. The Beretta 303 was also gas operated, as was the Browning A-500G, but when designing the A-500R, Browning engineers chose to go with a short-recoil system quite similar to that originated by the Italian firm of Benelli.

Another step forward in autoloader evolution took place at the tail end of the 20th century, when 12-gauge shotguns capable of handling everything from 2-3/4 inch quail loads to 3-1/2 inch goose loads appeared. I believe Benelli beat everyone to the punch on this one, but it was not long until every other major manufacturer was riding on the same bandwagon. One of the first to scramble aboard was the USRAC/Winchester Super X2, which looks a bit like the old Winchester Super X on the outside but is a mixture of that gun and the Browning Gold on the inside. Shortly thereafter, Browning (which is owned by the same European company as USRAC) introduced a 3-1/2 inch version of its Gold shotgun. Remington eventually caught up with the pack by chambering its Model 11-87 for the 3-1/2 inch shell.

Many other new autoloaders made their initial appearances during the 20th century and to name all the many model variations would take up more space than I have. To name but a few in no particular order; Beretta AL391 Urika, Mossberg 9200, Weatherby Centurion, Benelli Super 90, Hi-Standard Supermatic, Browning B-2000, Ithaca 51, Franchi 48AL, Browning B-80, and one I'd like to see brought back, the Browning Double-Automatic. The best-selling autoloaders during the tail end of the 20th century were the Remington Model 11-87, Weatherby SAS, Benelli M1 Field, Beretta AL391, Franchi Model 912 and the Browning Gold. Excellent guns all, they are still going strong.

The semiautomatic has a lot of things going for it, but it also has a few things against it as well. Of all the various types of shotguns, it is the one most likely to be put out of action by neglect from its owner. When maintained properly and fed good ammunition, I find the autoloader to be about as reliable as any other type of shotgun, but it will not tolerate a lot of neglect and abuse. I have seen pump guns dropped in the water, stepped on with muddy boots, sat on by wet dogs and hauled for an entire season beneath piles of ducks in the bottom of a boat, and they never failed to feed or fire when called on by their owners. Mistreat an autoloader in the same manner and you will probably find yourself hunting with a single-shot, if it will fire at all. But treated right, the autogun will seldom let you down.

Two of the most impressive exhibitions of reliability and durability I have ever witnessed starred two different autoloaders. One was a Beretta AL391 in 20 gauge. While shooting a clay target game called the flurry at The Willows near Tunica, Mississippi, three of us took turns shooting the same gun virtually nonstop. The barrel became so hot we eventually had to stop and let the gun cool off after enough heat had flowed through the receiver to make the trigger too hot to touch. The little Beretta never missed a single beat. Then there was the time I shot ducks in Uruguay for a week with a 12-gauge Remington Model 11-87. Anyone who has experienced high-volume duck shooting in South America knows what a pounding guns are subjected to there. I cleaned the bore and the outside of the magazine tube of the 11-87 every other day and experienced not one malfunction during the entire trip.

Modern autoloaders are easy to keep clean, so there is no good excuse for not doing it. This holds especially true for guns that allow removal of the trigger group by pushing out a couple of pins. With the trigger removed, dirt, gunk and powder residue can be blasted from inside the receiver with a good quick-drying degreaser such as Gun Scrubber from Birchwood Casey. Then, use a cotton Q-tip to apply an extremely thin film of Rem Oil to moving parts. Dirty chambers cause more malfunctions in autoloaders than anything else. A brass brush of the proper size attached to a cleaning rod and dipped in Brownells Shotgun Wad Solvent along with a bit of elbow grease takes care of that. Use the same brush and solvent to scrub powder fouling and plastic wad from the bore, apply a thin coat of Shooter's Choice Rust Prevent and your gun is ready to work flawlessly during its next hunt.

The autoloader can be rather expensive. The latest price list I have shows the Remington Model 11-87 Premier to cost about a third more than the Remington Model 870 Wingmaster pump gun. The Browning Gold Hunter is about 45 percent more expensive than the Browning BPS. More pricey autoloaders such as the Benelli Legacy and Beretta AL390 Xtrema cost about as much as the least expensive over-under shotguns from Weatherby and Beretta. This is something few of us ever thought we would see.

Then we have the matter of weight. Autoloaders are usually heavier than pump guns, although the Italian-built Franchi 48AL is an exception. Back to the positive side, its ability to prolong the recoil impulse during firing makes the selfloader more comfortable to shoot than any other type of shotgun. Many shooters believe this one positive characteristic far outweighs all the negatives I have mentioned. I fully agree. I am often asked what shotgun is best for a youngster or lady who desires to hunt game such as quail and doves but is sensitive to recoil. My answer has long been the

Most shooters can handle the 12-gauge when light one-ounce loads are teamed up with the soft recoil of a gas-operated autoloader.

My friend Nick Sisley who hunts ruffed grouse every single day of the Pennsylvania season each year had on several occasions mentioned how much he liked the Franchi autoloader. I had never shot one until I was invited to hunt birds at Pintail Point, a classy hunting preserve on the eastern shore of Maryland. That place is located not far from the city of Accokeek, where the home office of Franchi USA is located. So I asked Jason Evans of Franchi to send a couple of deluxe grade guns to the lodge where I would be staying. Jason must have spent several hours going through every gun in the warehouse, because the contrasting figure in the European walnut stocks and forearms of the pair of guns he sent was absolutely breathtaking.

I hunted with the 28-gauge gun and shot it so well on chukar and Hungarian partridge, I decided it had found a new home. I did not get around to hunting with the 20-gauge gun at Pintail Point, but its stock was so handsome, I took it home as well. My plan was to wring out both guns at the pattern board and then shoot some skeet and sporting clays with them. I would keep the gun I shot best and return the other. As it turned out, both guns shot dead on my hold point at the 25-yard pattern board and both delivered beautiful patterns with every load I tried in them. On top of that, I shot them equally well. It was as if someone was trying to tell me they were made just for me. I needed two more guns like higher taxes, but those two performed so nicely in my hands, I could not bear the thought of anyone else owning them. On a postal scale, the 28-gauge gun weighs exactly 5 pounds, 12 ounces while the 20-gauge gun is 2 ounces lighter. I can carry either for days on end without ever growing tired.

The British who have long looked down their noses at repeating shotguns have even gone so far as to declare them as unsporting. To me, this has always seemed quite hypocritical, since the fashionable thing among Brits who can afford to do so is to own a pair of matching double-barrel shotguns and to retain the ser-

same – the Remington Model 1100 or the Franchi 48AL in 28 gauge. The autoloader also tames extremely heavy loads that are virtually intolerable in other guns. The 3-1/2 inch 12-gauge shell is a good example.

I am sure many hunters buy autoloaders because of their ability to send lots of lead downrange fast, but I have not found that to be an advantage. If having a third shot on tap gives the hunter who uses the selfloader an edge over his pal who shoots a double, you cannot prove it by me. A friend and I hunt quail a lot together, and our proficiency with the shotgun is about the same. When he hunts with an autoloader and I hunt with a double, we almost always average about the same number of shells per bird taken. When we switch guns and he hunts with a double while I hunt with an autoloader, the score still reads about the same.

I can shoot just about any over-under or side-by-side double I pick up fairly well. Why this does not hold true for autoloaders is a question I cannot answer. I shoot some quite well, but with others I have a difficult time hitting the side of a barn. The 20-gauge Benelli Legacy is among those I shoot as well as any double. The same goes for a couple of 12-gauge Remington guns, a Model 11-87 and a Model 1100. A pair of guns I shoot even better than those three were made by the Italian firm of Franchi and called the Model 48AL. One is in 28 gauge and the other is in 20 gauge. How I came about those two gems might be of interest.

If a hunter could own only one shotgun for all of his shooting, a 12-gauge autoloader would not be a mistake.

vices of a peasant known as a "loader" during a driven bird shoot. When shooting pen-raised birds driven to the "guns" by other peasants, the shooter empties one double and then quickly hands it to his loader in exchange for a loaded gun. This goes on until the birds stop flying. An experienced shotgunner armed with a pair of doubles and assisted by a top-notch loader can keep the air filled with more lead than someone who shoots a pump or autoloader and who has to load his own gun. I fail to see that hunting with a repeating shotgun is any less sporting than two grown men with their pair of doubles ganging up on one bird.

Possibly the worst that can be said of the "automatic" is it may not always be welcomed with open arms in some social circles, even in America. Some years ago I got to know a fellow who managed a quail plantation in the state of Georgia. The farm had been in continuous operation since the early 1900s. The drive leading to the grand old antebellum mansion was lined with ancient oak trees, each dripping with Spanish moss. I expected to see Rhett and Scarlett walk out onto

the veranda at any moment. Several of the quail hunters sat arrow-straight atop fine saddle horses. Others rode in rubber-tired shooting wagons pulled by matched pairs of mules. Some wore tweed coats and ties and high-top leather boots. Most carried high-grade doubles built by Parker, Ithaca, L.C. Smith, Fox, Westley Richards and others. I think I even saw a Purdey or two. As far as I could tell, the 20 and 28 gauges were most popular, although plenty of 16s and a few .410s were there as well. How my friend managed to finagle an invitation for me to hunt quail with such nobility, I never asked. Even the bird dogs were uppity. Some pointed and others retrieved, but not a single one broke tradition by doing both. My friend had warned me that the Elhew pointers, Llewellin setters and French Britannys were trained to search out any dolt carrying a repeating shotgun and show their disgust by hosing down his pants legs just in case they might catch fire. Whether it was true or not, I cannot say, since I played it safe by showing up with a 16-gauge double – a side-by-side double at that!

CHAPTER 5

Single-Shots and Bolt-Actions

Imported by Stoeger, the Hammerless Hunter I used to take this chukar is one of the best buys available in a single-barrel shotgun. It is one of very few economy-grade, single-barrel field guns to wear a ventilated rib on its barrel.

When I was growing up in the 1950s, the double-barrel shotgun was what everybody wanted and what most who could afford it had, but in farmhouses all over the South the single barrel probably outnumbered it by at least ten to one. Most of the farmers I knew hunted with single-barrels. We also lived on a small farm, but my father's "city" job enabled him to buy an L.C. Smith double. Iver Johnson and Harrington & Richardson made the most popular single-shots, but it was not unusual to bump into a rabbit hunter toting a Savage, a Stevens, a J.C. Higgins or a Winchester. Regardless of who made them, all cost about the same in those days. At a time when the Winchester Model 21 double sold for $355 and the least expensive Model 12 pump gun cost $93.85, anyone with an extra $23.55 in his pocket could buy a

The Winchester Model 37 Steelbilt was once quite popular mainly because of its low price. This one cost Phyllis' father, Barney Link, less than $30 during the 1950s.

Winchester Model 37 single-shooter. The Savage Model 220 with an optional 36-inch barrel was the most expensive at $25.25. By today's standards, shells were also rather inexpensive. Remington and Winchester field loads ranged in price from $2.30 for the 20 gauge loaded with 7/8 ounce of shot, to $4.05 for 12-gauge 3-inch magnums loaded with 1-5/8 ounces of shot.

Most of the single-barrel shotguns built by major American manufacturers were good buys for the money, but some of those imported from abroad were real dogs. A friend of mine owned one made by some unknown Spanish company, and its locking mechanism would come unlatched and allow its barrel to break down about every time he fired it. Some shotguns of this type have extremely rough and heavy triggers and the strong springs of their hammers make them difficult to cock with a cold hand. I received my first shotgun, a single-barrel, at the age of 12, and I had to use both thumbs when cocking its hammer. Anytime I cocked the gun but did not fire it, I would trip the top lever and break down its barrel before attempting to lower its hammer. This is something youngsters of today who use this type of shotgun should be taught to do.

Because of the simplicity of its design, a good single-barrel gun is reliable and some are also quite durable. Some I have seen in use in the field should have been retired long ago, but they were still bringing home the bacon for their owners. The only gun owned by an ancient old black man who worked part-time for my father when I was a youngster fit that description. We kids called him Uncle Ned, and I distinctly remember that the extremely long barrel of his rusty old 12-gauge Stevens made the gun taller than I was at the time. Even though his shotgun was held together by an assortment of hay-baling wire, black tape, nails, screws and probably an occasional prayer, it was death and destruction on any rabbit foolish enough to allow Uncle Ned within range of its full-choked charge of No. 4s.

The age of the single-shot game gun has come and gone, but quite a few are still built each year by New England Firearms, a company owned by Marlin. One of the more interesting single-shots I have examined lately is the Hammerless Hunter from Stoeger. Imported from Brazil, it comes with screw-in chokes and as its name implies, it has no external hammer. Neither does it have any type of top lever; a pull to the rear on its trigger guard unlocks the barrel and allows it to hinge down for loading. The Stoeger Hunter also has a ventilated rib, something not seen on an inexpensive field gun since Winchester stopped producing its Model 20 in 1924. I shot a round of wobble trap with a Hammerless Hunter and don't recall missing a single target. I later shot a few liberated chukar and Hungarian partridges with it, and I hit a lot more often than I missed. Like the Pardner from New England arms, the single-barrel gun from Stoeger sells for less than $125 as I write this in early 2003.

My bear guide used a 12-gauge New England single-barrel gun to harvest this ptarmigan dinner in Alaska.

Despite the fact that the single-shot takes a back seat in firepower to the double, pump and autoloader, it has a few advantages. For one, it is still the least expensive shotgun available. It is also lighter than any repeater. I just weighed a 12-gauge Winchester Model 37 Steelbilt that once belonged to Phyllis' father and it went exactly 6-1/4 pounds on my postal scale. Most guns of this type sold by New England and Stoeger weigh around six pounds. Low price, lightness of weight and the fact that the single-shot can be taken down into a compact package are the primary reasons why it continues to enjoy popularity as a wilderness gun. Seldom will you enter a remote cabin in Alaska without seeing one resting behind the door.

My first shotgun was a .410-caliber Iver Johnson, but once I graduated to doubles and repeaters, I did not hunt with a single-shot for many years. The opportunity to bring back old memories came during a hunt in Alaska. After bagging my bear, I had several days remaining in my hunt and it just so happened that my guide had brought along his old single-barrel gun in 12 gauge. At some point through the years, the fellow had painted its stock and forearm white, probably his way of having a camouflaged gun for use in snow country. He had also spray-painted its barrel with Rust-oleum. I used up my remaining time on the tundra hunting ptarmigan and ducks with that beat-up old gun and I could not have had more fun had the name "Purdey" been marked on its action.

Since that trip to Alaska, I have made it a point to hunt with a single-shooter at least once each year. It is my way of remembering how times once were. Believe it or not, I seldom fail to bring home just as many doves and quail when hunting with a single-shot as I do when hunting with a shotgun that shoots two or three times between reloads. Having only one round on tap forces you to pause just long enough to make that first shot count. This along with the fact that the single-shot can be safer than a repeater in the hands of an inexperienced shooter is why I will always remain convinced it is the best choice for a youngster's first gun. It is the type of firearm my father started me on, and I am convinced I am better hunter and a better shot in the field because of it.

I used to hunt big game a lot with single-shot rifles like the Ruger No. 1 and the Browning B78. I still enjoy hunting with a couple of muzzleloading rifles, a .45 caliber Knight Disc Extreme and a .50 caliber Remington Model 700ML. So it stands to reason that if I were to buy a single-shot shotgun tomorrow, it would probably be a slug gun with a fully rifled barrel. Because a scope can be mounted directly to its barrel, the old single-shooter has the potential of delivering excellent accuracy. A friend of mine who owns a Tracker II slug gun made by New England says it will drive tacks at 100 long paces with saboted slugs. The Encore slug gun from Thompson/Center also has a reputation for excellent accuracy.

Single-shot shotguns have long been popular among trap shooters, but they are not the inexpensive knockabout guns rabbit hunters once carried in the field. Companies like L.C. Smith and Ithaca made them, and they were never cheap. In 1959, when the Browning Superposed cost $260, Ithaca's single-barrel trap gun was priced at $450 for the standard grade and $2,500 for the highest grade. L.C. Smith built the same style of gun from 1917 until 1950, and when compared grade for grade with the company's double-barrel guns, it was always more expensive. Single-barrel trap guns continue to be made, and they are still a bit pricey. The Remington 90-T I shoot is no longer in production, but when it was one like mine with adjustable comb, adjustable butt, ported barrel and fancy wood, it sold for close to $4,000. The same type of gun built by Perazzi, Krieghoff and Ljutic is even more expensive. One of the fellows I shoot trap with paid almost $7,000 for his stainless steel Ljutic Mono Gun. Another shelled out $8,000 for his Krieghoff unsingle. The Browning BT-99 has long been one of the best buys in trap guns, because it costs about half as much as the BT-100 from the same company.

Most serious trap shooters own both double-barrel and single-barrel guns. They use the over-under when shooting the doubles game where two targets are thrown simultaneously. They then switch to the single-barrel when shooting long-yardage targets at handicap distances. Some also use the single-barrel when shooting 16-yard singles, but about as many use their over-unders there. Shooting trap from the longer handicap yardages requires breaking targets as far away as 60 yards, and since an extremely long barrel puts enough weight out front to make a gun swing more smoothly than one with a short barrel, the guns of most shooters wear barrels measuring 32 or 34 inches long. Some are quite heavy. My Remington 90-T has a 34-inch barrel and it weighs 10-1/4 pounds.

The two types of single-barrel trap guns are called top-single and unsingle, the latter short for under-single. The barrel of the top-single is positioned at the top of the receiver, same as on your grandfather's old single-barrel rabbit gun. Think of the unsingle as an over-under shotgun with its top barrel replaced by an extremely tall ventilated rib, and you get the picture. Since the barrel of the un-single sits lower in the receiver, muzzle jump is reduced a bit and some shooters are convinced this dampens perceived recoil. I have shot trap with a Krieghoff unsingle and I have also shot a Remington Model 3200 equipped with an unsingle barrel made by Stan Baker. Both were slightly more comfortable to shoot with heavy trap loads than my Remington 90-T, but I did not find the difference to be as great as some trappers claim.

The most single-barrel trap guns I have ever seen in one heap were at the 100th anniversary of the Grand American trap championships held in Vandalia, Ohio, in August 1999. One of the ammunition companies sponsored a squad of firearms writers that year, and three of us brought along single-barrel guns. I shot my Remington 90-T, Steve Comus was shooting his old Ithaca, and I believe Bill Miller's gun was made by Beretta. During the week-long event, more than 7,000 shooters stood on 100 trap fields and shot at more than five million targets. If all the single-barrel trap guns shot during that week were sold at auction, the money would probably pay off the national debt!

The Bolt-Action Shotgun

There was a time when the bolt action was the least expensive repeating shotgun available. When

The author (second from left) along with Bill Miller (extreme left) and Steve Comus (extreme right) hold the single-barrel trap guns they shot at the 100th anniversary of the Grand American.

Remington's Model 870 pump gun sold for just under $78 and a really cheap knockabout such as the Stevens Model 77 was priced at only $59, most bolt actions sold for a few cents less than $30. In 1956, the Marlin Model 55, the J.C. Higgins Model 10 (which was also made by Marlin) and the Stevens Model 58 had the same price tag of $29.50. The difference in cost between the bolt action and the pump gun may not sound like much today, but it was a lot at a time when the average factory worker made less than a hundred bucks per week. Leaders in the manufacture of bolt-action shotguns during the 1950s were Harrington & Richardson, Marlin, Mossberg and Stevens. Some of those companies offered guns with adjustable chokes.

Some bolt guns were built only in 12 gauge, but others were also made in .410, 16 and 20. When I was a youngster on the farm, a neighbor owned one in 28 gauge, but I do not remember what company made it. In today's market, small-gauge guns often cost more than those in 12 gauge, but it was often just the opposite back then. One of the Mossberg guns sold for $28.95 in .410, $29.95 in 20 gauge, $31.95 in 16 gauge and $32.95 in 12 gauge. One of the longest-lived bolt actions was the Marlin Model 55 Goose Gun. If the ducks and geese were flying low enough, you could save ammunition by reaching into the sky with its 36-inch barrel and whacking dinner over the head. Marlin later built the Model 512 slug gun around that same action, and it was a good one.

Even in its heyday, the bolt-action shotgun was not very popular in my neck of the woods, but someone somewhere must have liked them because I used to see lots of them on the used gun market. One of the few people I knew as a youngster who hunted with one was a fellow of questionable repute who lived on the other side of Golden Creek from our place. He and his wife stayed in a dilapidated old shack, and they practically lived off the land. I recall visiting them one evening, just as they sat down at the dinner table to devour a meal of "possum,"

With its fully rifled barrel, the Marlin Model 512 bolt-action slug gun is accurate enough for shooting deer and black bear as far away as they should be shot with any saboted slug load. One of the groups I fired at 100 yards, has five shots inside two inches.

stewed turnips, crackling cornbread and buttermilk. Butch and Mary considered opossum to be a real delicacy, but only if the animal was kept penned up for a month and "cleaned out" on a diet of raw sweet potatoes before it was slaughtered. Butch had the mangiest bunch of mixed-breed hounds I had ever seen, but anytime he took them and his old 16-gauge Marlin bolt gun to the field, the local cottontail rabbit population was in big trouble

A reader once scolded me for not mentioning the bolt-action in an article I wrote on turkey guns. I intentionally did so because when I wrote the piece, only a couple of manufacturers offered that type of shotgun, and they had rifled barrels for use with slug loads. Neither offered a bolt-action turkey gun. At any rate, the fellow who wrote the letter went on to mention how much faster the bolt-action shotgun is on the second shot than a single-shot gun. This might be true for the average shotgunner, but a man who is accustomed to shooting a single-shot equipped with an ejector is about as fast as a good bolt-gun man. I recall just such a shooting contest between a couple of my boyhood chums, Forrest Kelly and his brother Kenneth.

Forrest owned a 20-gauge J. C. Higgins single-barrel, and "Hambone" (as we called him) owned a Mossberg bolt gun in 16 gauge. Hambone enjoyed kidding his brother about his slowpoke rabbit gun, and I just happened to be present when the two decided to prove who was quickest by shooting it out. After placing a row of tin cans about 15 yards away, both started with guns loaded and, upon my signal, they shouldered them, blasted a tin can, reloaded and fired at another. Even now I can see the desperate look on his brother's face as Forrest rolled his second tomato can a split second before Hambone managed to get off his second shot. They dueled six more times, and even though Hambone did manage to win twice, he never again kidded his brother about that old single-shot. What was Forrest's secret? His gun had been shot a lot so it was as loose as a goose. Immediately after firing the first round, he tripped the top lever with the thumb of his trigger hand and allowed gravity to open the barrel and eject the fired shell. As the smoking hull rocketed into the sky, he threw in a second

Shooting a single-barrel gun on a dove field is good practice because you either make every shot count or you go home empty handed.

shell he had been holding between the fingers of his left hand, closed the gun, thumbed back its hammer and blasted the second can. He was so smooth, he could do it all while his brother was operating the bolt of his gun. Forrest had plenty of practice, and although I had seen him do it several times when we were hunting quail, I did not realize just how fast he was until I watched him outgun his brother.

The bolt-action shotgun is an excellent choice for hunting game that requires careful aiming, as one would do with a rifle. An example is ground-sluicing a turkey as has become both customary and acceptable among many hunters. Another is the hunting of big game with slug loads. I have two bolt-action slug guns, neither of which is still in production. Both have fully rifled barrels. One is an A-Bolt Stalker made by Browning. It was introduced around 1996 and stayed in production for no more than three or four years. Capable of consistently shooting three slugs inside two inches at 100 yards with Remington and Federal saboted ammo, it is the most accurate slug gun I have ever worked with. Some guns I have shot would occasionally put three shots inside two inches, but the Browning is the only one I have tried that will do it group after group on a consistent basis. I also own a Model 512 Slugmaster once made by Marlin, and while it is not quite as accurate as the Browning, it is accurate enough for shooting a deer or black bear as far away as it should be shot with any slug load. I don't hunt deer with a shotgun very often, but when I do it is usually with one of those guns.

As far as I know, a bolt-action shotgun that handles the way a gun should handle for wingshooting does not exist, and this is the main reason why it is not more popular today. Most hunters want a shotgun they can use when hunting quail, rabbits, deer, turkey and everything else and the double barrel, the pump and the autoloader are much better for all-around use. I suppose a hunter could get by on everything with a bolt gun if he had to, but few of today's hunters have to make that choice.

CHAPTER 6
Understanding and Choosing the Right Choke

The barrels of the 20-gauge Winchester Model 23 double used by ace sharptail grouse and Hungarian partridge hunter Ryan Busse are choked Improved Cylinder and Modified. After years of carrying the same gun on the plains of Montana he has found no reason to change its chokes.

Choke is a word other shooters in my squad often use to describe what is about to happen to me as I step up to station eight during the last round of a registered skeet tournament and attempt to break my 100th straight bird. That same word is just as commonly used to describe a slight amount of bore constriction at the muzzle of a shotgun barrel. No one has proved beyond doubt exactly how choke in a shotgun barrel works, but since we know without doubt that it does, I won't use up a lot of space in speculation. Neither will we ever know for sure who uncovered the fact that the range of a shotgun could be increased by slightly reducing or "choking" its bore to a smaller diameter at the muzzle, but in the United States, Illinois duck hunter Fred Kimble is usually given credit for coming up with the idea during the mid-1800s. Before the invention of choke, the maximum effective range of most shotguns was not much over 20 yards. Introduction of the choke

extended the range on out to 70 yards or so when shotshells capable of that level of performance were eventually developed.

The degree of choke constriction in a barrel is usually expressed in either thousandths of an inch or in "points." The actual amount of choke in a barrel is determined by subtracting the inside diameter of the choked area from the diameter of the main bore, both measured with special gauges available from Brownells and other suppliers of gunsmith tools. If, for example, the bore of a 12-gauge barrel measures .729 inch and its choke measures .694 inch, it has .035 inch or 35 points of constriction, which is rated as Full choke for that gauge. The bores of 12-gauge guns built by various manufacturers can vary considerably in diameter, but regardless of what the bore actually measures, the barrel is choked Full if its choke diameter is .035 inch smaller than the bore. Here are two examples. The barrel of my Remington 90-T trap gun was overbored at the factory to .745 inch, which is .016 inch larger than is standard for the 12 gauge. The bore tapers down to .710 inch at the muzzle for .035 inch of constriction, or Full choke. The barrel of my Remington Model 11-87 field gun has a .727-inch bore. One of the screw-in chokes that came with it measures .692 inch at the muzzle for .035 inch of constriction, so it, too, is Full choke. Different bore diameters, but the amount of choke is the same in those two guns because their bores are constricted by the same amount.

I am glad to see Briley and a few others list the amount of constriction in their screw-in chokes, but some companies have adopted the irritating habit of listing only inside diameter. If a company tells me that a particular 12-gauge choke has, say, .010 inch of constriction, it means something and I immediately know it is Improved Cylinder. If, instead, a company tells me the inside diameter of a choke is .719 inch, I can determine its constriction, but only if I know the nominal bore diameter of the barrel it was made for. One maker of turkey chokes confuses the issue even further by not knowing the difference between inside diameter and constriction. That company advertises the inside diameter of a choke as its constriction by listing an Extra-Extra-Full choke made for Remington 12-gauge barrels as having a "constriction" of .675 inch. Why the fellow who wrote the specs for that company chose to do that, I really can't say, but I can say there is no such thing as a choke with .675 inch of constriction. The tightest chokes available usually have no more than .070 inch of construction, and very few are anywhere close to being that tight. What that company really means is its XX-Full choke has an inside diameter of .675 inch. When used in a Remington barrel with a bore measuring .729 inch, its actual constriction is .054 inch.

It is not uncommon to see an old-timer check the barrel of a 12-gauge shotgun by attempting to push a dime into its muzzle. As many shotgunners still believe, if a dime will not enter the bore, the barrel has a Full choke. If the dime will enter the bore, the barrel is choked looser than Full. A few of the younger generation of writers enjoy ridiculing that method of checking the choke in a gun at every opportunity, but they only show their ignorance when doing so because there is some truth in it. It works on older guns, since the bores of most of them seldom exceed a diameter of .730 inch. In the old days Full choke meant .040 inch of constriction, and a full-choked barrel with a bore diameter of .730 inch measures .690 inch at the muzzle. Since a dime in good condition is .705 inch in diameter, it is easy to see why it will not enter a barrel choked Full. On the other hand, because the muzzles of barrels choked Modified and looser are larger than .705 inch, the dime will pass through. That method works just

The 20-gauge Browning Superposed Lightning used by my father, Bailey Simpson, to hunt quail during the 1960s was choked Skeet and Improved Cylinder. Open chokes along with his ability to shoot quickly made him a deadly shot at close quarters. Pointing bobwhites is Cricket, Dad's favorite English setter.

as well with .035 inch of choke (which is considered Full today) so long as bore diameter is not oversized. It does not work on drastically overbored barrels. My Remington 90-T trap gun has a .745-inch bore, and it measures .710 inch at the muzzle for Full choke by today's standards, so a dime will pass through it with room to spare.

A chart at the end of this chapter shows the amount of constriction assigned to various degrees of choke by Briley Manufacturing. In addition to being the largest manufacturer of aftermarket screw-in chokes in the country, Briley also makes chokes for Remington, Weatherby and several other manufacturers of shotguns. As illustrated in the chart, choke constrictions are the same for the 10, 12 and 16 gauges. The 20 and 28 gauges are also the same, but the .410 differs from those two. This is done in order to keep constriction percentages close to the same. If we squeeze down a 12-gauge .729-inch bore by .035 inch, we have a barrel choked Full. In doing so, we have reduced bore diameter by 4.8 percent. If we reduce the .550-inch bore of a 28-gauge barrel by .035 inch (6.3 percent), we are completely off the chart, since only .027 inch of constriction is considered extra full constriction for that gauge. If the 28-gauge bore is reduced by 4.8 percent, same as we did with the 12 gauge, the barrel will have .026 inch of constriction, which is closer to Full choke for that gauge.

The ability to quickly and conveniently change the amount of choke in the barrel of a shotgun is something we now take for granted, but it is one of the most

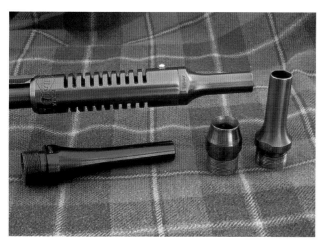

Changing chokes on the Cutts Compensator of this Winchester Model 42 is as easy as screwing out one tube and screwing in another. The shortest tube shown is an experimental Spreader choke while the longest is choked Full.

important shotgun developments in history. The idea is also much older than many of today's shooters realize. Around 1870, an American shotgun designer by the name of Sylvester Roper developed a short tube with threads inside that allowed it to be attached to the muzzle of a shotgun barrel. The old Roper choke was much shorter than modern screw-in chokes and it attached to the outside of a barrel rather than inside, but both types work on the same principle.

Another device that enabled a shotgunner to change the amount of choke in his barrel at will was the Cutts Compensator. Developed by U.S. Marine Corps veteran Colonel Richard M. Cutts, the compensator alone was first used successfully by the U.S. military on the Thompson submachine gun. The Army also used the same device, but with interchangeable choke tubes on the Winchester Model 97 shotgun. Lyman bought the manufacturing rights to the Cutts in 1929 and went on to sell many thousands to shotgunners. The device attaches permanently to the outside of the barrel and consists of a set of interchangeable choke tubes that screw into the muzzle of a ventilated cage. The vents reduce muzzle jump and perceived recoil by directing propellant gas to the side. There was a time when about every skeet gun of every gauge in America wore a Cutts Compensator, but it never became as popular among hunters because its gas vents direct muzzle blast back toward the shooter. If bird dogs could rise up from their graves and talk, those who hunted with hunters using Cutts-equipped guns in the old days would tell you how unpleasant the muzzle blast can be. My Winchester Model 42 was popular among skeet shooters back when the Cutts was in style, so it wears one out on the end of its barrel. I enjoy hunting quail with the little gun, but I always wear ear protection when shooting it and I am

careful to never shoot at flushing birds if the dog that pointed them is standing in line with the gas vents of its compensator.

There was a time when adjustable choke devices were also quite popular. Several different designs were tried, but the most successful utilized a collet fitted to the inside of a rotating sleeve. Twisting the sleeve in one direction decreased the interior diameter of the collet for an increase in choke constriction, while turning it in the opposite direction reduced the amount of choke. Lyman, Weaver and other companies once offered adjustable chokes, but my guess is the Poly-Choke outsold them all. The old mail-order firm of Herter's offered the same type of device in two versions, one with a ventilated cage like that on the Cutts Compensator, and another without the vents. The collet-type adjustable choke is much handier than the screw-in chokes of today because a twist of the wrist instantly changes it from one constriction to another. Over on the negative side, screw-in chokes do not change the outside appearance of a barrel, while some consider the Poly-Choke and other such instruments to be rather ugly. I am sure my old-fashioned opinion is in the minority today, but I think the Cutts Compensator on my little Winchester Model 42 makes it look quite racy.

Probably the most interesting adjustable choke ever developed was called the Adjustomatic. Designed for installation on pumps and autoloaders, it automatically adjusted to its next tighter choke setting with each firing of the gun. If the rig was set on Improved Cylinder, the first shot would switch it to Modified and the second shot would cause it to squeeze on down to Full. It probably worked OK when a hunter kept shooting and missing at the same bird or rabbit traveling away from the gun, but very little more than feathers would have been be left of a bird hit by the third shot in a close covey rise.

Screw-in chokes like we use today have been around for quite a long time in one form or another, but they didn't begin to win the hearts of American hunters and shooters until sometime after Winchester introduced the Versalite system in its Model 59 fiberglass-barreled autoloader in 1959. The story reads quite differently today, and it is just about impossible to buy a new gun without screw-in chokes. The idea has become accepted by the multitudes to the point where interchangeable chokes are considered as much a necessary part of a shotgun as its stock and trigger. It is doubtful if a gun would sell very well without them today.

Interchangeable chokes are quite popular simply because they offer the owner of a shotgun the ability to transform it into an entire hunting and shooting battery, one capable of handling wingshooting, deer hunting, waterfowling and clay target sports such as trap, skeet and sporting clays. The switch-choke option is now standard-issue on most pump guns, autoloaders, single barrels and doubles, in all the popular gauges plus the .410 bore. Most chokes are made of stainless steel with either a natural or black oxide finish. There are chokes designed to be used with lead shot and others intended for use with shot made of harder materials such as steel and Hevi-Shot.

One of the great things about screw-in chokes is they give us the option of conveniently and inexpensively trying different choke constrictions with different loads. If you hunt quail or ruffed grouse in country where extremely close shots require the biggest possible pattern at 15 to 20 yards, and that box of shells you recently bought is delivering overly tight patterns for those conditions, just screw out the Improved Cylinder choke and screw in a Skeet, Cylinder or perhaps even a Spreader choke. At the opposite extreme, if the box of ammo you have is not delivering a dense enough pattern at 40 yards to saturate the head and neck of a turkey gobbler, simply replace the Full choke with Extra Full. But be careful when using extremely tight chokes, because once the optimum amount of choke is reached for a particular load, a further increase in constriction can actually decrease the effective range of a load by disrupting pattern uniformity. This holds especially true when shooting lead shot.

Choosing chokes for specific hunting applications is quite important. For upland shooting where most game birds are taken inside 30 yards, Cylinder bore, Skeet and Improved Cylinder are our most useful chokes. When teamed up with the right load, those three deliver adequate pattern density for shots out to 25 long paces, and yet pattern size is large enough to make hitting birds that flush just off the muzzle of your shotgun possible. If I had to do all of my wingshooting with one choke, it would be Improved Cylinder. For shooting at extremely close range, as is sometimes done on woodcock and ruffed grouse, some hunters choose Cylinder bore or Spreader choke. The spreader was once popular among skeet shooters who shot guns wearing the old Cutts Compensator, and Briley still offers the same idea in screw-in style for most guns. I have not tried the Briley Spreader choke, but the one on my Winchester Model 42 throws a pattern no larger in diameter than Cylinder bore.

For all-around use, Modified choke is less useful than Improved Cylinder, but there are times when it and even Improved Modified are better choices. One sporting clays shooter I know has a couple dozen different screw-in chokes in his shooting bag and uses a battery-powered wrench to switch them from station to station. He sometimes changes chokes several times at the same station! The hunter can get by with a lot less. If I could have only four chokes, three of them would be Skeet, Improved

These chokes extend beyond the muzzles of the barrels for easy removal and installation with the fingers alone.

Cylinder and Modified. Those would cover all of my upland hunting and most of the waterfowl hunting I do. The fourth would be Full unless I used the gun for hunting turkeys, in which case it would be Extra Full.

When hunting quail with a side-by-side or over-under in brushy or wooded areas where shots are extremely close, I prefer Cylinder bore or Skeet in both barrels or Cylinder bore in one barrel and skeet in the other. If I move into relatively open country with that same gun, but the birds are still holding tight to the point of a good dog, I will install Light Modified in the second barrel. Improved Cylinder and Light Modified is also an excellent combination for close- to medium-range shooting of ducks and geese over decoys. For hunting plains-dwelling birds such as pheasants, Hungarian partridge and chukar, the combination of Improved Cylinder and Modified covers everything from close-flushing birds to those that flush wild. I also like that combination when shooting doubles in the game of trap. I have used double-barrel shotguns choked Improved Cylinder and Improved Modified when hunting sharptail grouse and prairie chickens. As a rule, and depending on the load used, Improved Modified will extend the effective range of a shotgun by 5 yards or so farther than Modified with some loads, yet it is a bit easier to hit with than Full choke.

About the only times I ever use more choke than Improved Modified are while hunting turkeys, when pass-shooting waterfowl and when shooting trap from handicap yardages. There will be exceptions, but as a rule, once .040 to .045 inch of choke is reached with lead shot, an additional increase in constriction fails to yield any increase in pattern tightness. Too much choke can actually cause pattern quality to become worse, probably because of increased deformation among the rather soft pellets. Tighter chokes can be used with extremely hard shot such

By using Hevi-Shot, Eddie Stevenson of Remington and I were able to take ducks at long range in Uruguay with open chokes in our guns. Eddie used a Model 11-87 autoloader choked Improved Cylinder while the barrels of the Model 332 over-under I used were choked Improved Cylinder and Modified.

as steel and Hevi-Shot, so long as pellet size it not too large. Even then, there are limits. Hevi-Shot in sizes ranging from No. 4 to No. 7-1/2 produces its tightest and densest patterns when used with .055 inch of choke, and any increase in constriction beyond that offers practically no improvement. Which is just as well, since Hevi-Shot often produces pattern percentages in the 95 to 100 percent range at 40 yards with .055 inch of choke.

One of the most useful chokes, and yet one of the most neglected, is no choke at all, or Cylinder bore as it is commonly called. Many shotgunners and quite a few shotgun manufacturers consider it good only for use with slug loads, but it is just the ticket for close-range shooting on birds such as ruffed grouse and woodcock. Some guns deliver patterns with low-density centers with Cylinder bore, but a gun that will shoot uniform patterns with it is to be cherished. My two Franchi 48AL autoloaders in 28 and 20 gauge will do just that with any load I feed them, and with shot sizes ranging from No. 7-1/2 to No. 9. Any bird that manages to escape their patterns out to 25 yards has pilot error and not shotgun performance to thank.

Always keep in mind that just because your gun delivers Modified (or whatever) performance with one load doesn't necessarily mean it will do the same with other loads. Also keep in mind that just because the barrel of a gun or its screw-in choke was marked "Modified" or "Improved Cylinder" at the factory does not mean it will deliver Modified or Improved Cylinder choke performance with all loads. Different loads from various manufacturers or even different loads from the same manufacturer can vary in a number of ways and those variations can

result in performance differences even when choke constriction remains the same. Even though the load you tested delivered Modified performance in your particular gun, another load might deliver Improved Cylinder performance while the next might perform as if your gun is choked even tighter. The same rule also applies to different guns. If you test two seemingly identical shotguns with exactly the same amount of choke constriction in their barrels, one might deliver Improved Cylinder choke performance with Remington's high-velocity load of No. 4s, while the other gun might deliver Modified performance with the same load. Whether fixed or the screw-in type, actual diameters of chokes can also vary, even when they are marked the same. This is clearly illustrated in the chart containing various shotgun barrels I have measured. The only way you will know for certain how a particular gun, load and choke combination is performing is to spend some time at the pattern board.

It is also important to remember that identification markings given to chokes by their manufacturers are not always correct. The Improved Cylinder choke of a 28-gauge over-under I once hunted with had no constriction so it should have been marked Cylinder Bore. Another of its chokes was marked Skeet but rather than having the proper .005 inch of constriction, its inside diameter was actually .006 inch larger than the bore of the barrel for no choke at all. Whereas its Modified choke should have had around .015 inch of constriction, it had only .003 inch, which is about right for Light Skeet for the 28 gauge. One of the deadliest quail guns I own is a Franchi 48AL in 28 gauge. One of its chokes is marked Improved Cylinder, but because it has .013 inch of constriction, it actually is closer to Light Modified. Another choke for that same gun is marked Skeet, and while its .007 inch of constriction puts it close enough to that classification for government work, American clay target shooters would call it Improved Skeet. I also have a Franchi 48AL in 20 gauge and its three chokes are close to dead on the money. Like I said before, the only way you will know for sure is to actually measure bore and choke diameters or spend some time at the pattern board with your gun.

Extended Chokes

Some chokes fit flush with the muzzle of the barrel. Others extend an inch or so beyond the muzzle and have a knurled surface for easy gripping with slippery hands. I like the extended choke on a modern pump or autoloader for several reasons. It makes the jobs of switching from one constriction to another and checking for looseness easy. It also protects the muzzle of the barrel from possible damage in the field. Putting the constriction in an extended choke rather then back in the barrel also reduces the possibility of bulging the muzzle of the barrel with steel shot.

Browning once made a sporting clays version of the Citori with what had to be the mother of all screw-in chokes; when installed, they extended the length of 28-inch barrels to 32 inches. The extra length did not increase velocity enough to notice, but it did change the handling of the gun by making it a bit more muzzle heavy. It also pushed muzzle blast a bit farther away from the ears of the shooter. Small gas ports in yet another style of extended choke are put there to reduce muzzle jump during firing, and while that design is very effective when used on centerfire rifles, it is less so on shotguns due to the considerably lower muzzle pressure generated by shotshells. Some say the gas ports also improve pattern quality by retarding the plastic wad as it exits the muzzle, but I have my doubts.

The Intentionally Eccentric Choke

Anyone who has done a bit of pattern testing knows it is not exactly uncommon to see a shotgun place the center of its shot pattern either above, below or off to the side of where its barrel is pointed. This is usually caused by misalignment of the screw-in choke and the bore or by a warped barrel. Only a tiny amount can cause the gun to shoot away from your hold point by a considerable degree. The old-fashioned way of curing this ailment is for a gunsmith to gently place the muzzle of the barrel in a padded vise, carefully place both feet against the side of the bench, close his eyes tightly, grit his teeth in determination, and bend the devil out of it in what he figures is the desired direction. This might still work OK for a single-barrel gun, but only if it does not wear a ventilated rib and then only if it needs no more than a slight tweak. It is not a solution for doubles of either over-under or side-by-side orientation. The modern way to correct this problem is to install eccentric screw-in chokes. The bore of this type of choke is intentionally misaligned with the bore of the barrel just enough to shift pattern center point of impact in the desired direction and by the desired amount. The Excentrix (as Briley calls it) can be machined to change the impact in any direction and anywhere from an inch to a foot at 40 yards. My 28-gauge Model 12 shot far off my hold point when I bought it, and a set of Excentrix chokes fixed it perfectly.

Accessories

You and your screw-in chokes will live happily every after if you own a wrench for removing and installing them and a storage box designed to protect their threads from damage. The wrenches furnished by manufacturers with their guns are all most shooters need, but if you are an impulsive choke-switcher you won't be very

Most shots presented in the American version of sporting clays are easily handled by Skeet or Improved Cylinder chokes. Those two along with Modified have the entire game covered.

happy until a speed wrench is in your possession. At the risk of repeating myself to the point where I begin to sound like a company stockholder, I'll also add that Briley makes just such an item as well as a pocket-size plastic box with individual compartments for stowing up to five chokes.

Don't Choke On Maintenance

If a screw-in choke is allowed to loosen up in the barrel, its threads and those in the barrel can suffer great damage during firing, so check its tightness every 25 rounds or so (with the gun unloaded, of course). There are other things to watch out for as well. If rust is allowed to form in its threads the choke can be impossible to remove. To prevent this from happening, remove the choke after each hunt, thoroughly clean its threads and the threads inside the barrel with an old toothbrush dipped in bore cleaning solvent, and then apply a thin coat of lubricant to the threads before screwing the choke back in. You can buy the special lube from Birchwood-Casey, Briley and Brownells. Various lubes formulated to prevent breech plug seizure in muzzleloading rifles also work quite well.

When modern ammunition is used, the bore of a choke can become coated with plastic residue left behind by wads and sabots. Scrubbing the bore with a brass brush and a solvent formulated to dissolve plastic takes care of that. A product called Shotgun and Choke Tube Cleaner from Shooter's Choice works rather nicely, as does Shotgun Wad Solvent from Brownells. Never fire a gun with its choke removed as doing so can damage the threads in the barrel. And one last really important safety note: Make doubly sure any gun is unloaded with its action open and then check it two more times before messing around with its muzzle.

BRILEY MANUFACTURING CHOKE CONSTRICTIONS (Inches)

	10/12/16 GAUGE	20/28 GAUGE	.410 BORE
Light Skeet	.003	.003	.003
Skeet	.005	.005	.005
Improved Skeet	.007	.007	.007
Improved Cylinder	.010	.009	.008
Light Modified	.015	.012	.010
Modified	.020	.015	.012
Improved Modified	.025	.018	.014
Light Full	.030	.021	.016
Full	.035	.024	.018
Extra Full	.040	.027	.020

APPROXIMATE EFFECTIVE PATTERN DIAMETERS (Inches)

	10 YDS	20 YDS	30 YDS	40 YDS
Spreader	23	37	51	66
Cylinder Bore (no choke)	20	32	44	57
Improved Cylinder	15	26	38	51
Modified	12	20	32	46
Full	9	16	26	40

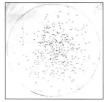 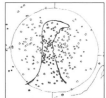

ACTUAL BORE DIAMETERS AND CHOKE CONSTRICTIONS (Inches)

GUN - CHOKE*	BORE	MUZZLE	CONSTRICTION
.410			
Briley subgauge tube Light Skeet	.405	.402	.003
I-Johnson Skeet-er, left barrel Skeet	.398	.392	.006
I-Johnson Skeet-er, right barrel Skeet	.398	.392	.006
Weatherby Athena Improved Cylinder	.406	.401	.005
Weatherby Athena Modified	.406	.397	.009
Weatherby Orion Improved Cylinder	.406	.400	.006
Weatherby Orion Modified	.406	.390	.016
28 GAUGE			
AyA No. 1 Improved Cylinder	.547	.541	.006
AyA No. 1 Modified	.547	.534	.015
Franchi 48AL Cylinder	.555	.555	.000
Franchi 48AL Skeet	.555	.548	.007
Franchi 48AL Improved Cylinder	.555	.542	.013
Remington Model 1100 Skeet**	.548	.532	.006
Remington Model 1100 Improved Cylinder**	.548	.540	.008
Remington Model 1100 Light Mod**	.548	.533	.015

GUN - CHOKE*	BORE	MUZZLE	CONSTRICTION
28 GAUGE			
Remington Model 1100 Modified**	.548	.529	.018
Remington Model 1100 Full**	.548	.520	.028
Browning Superposed Skeet*	.535	.530	.005
Browning Superposed Light Modified**	.535	.524	.011
Browning Superposed Modified**	.535	.520	.015
Browning Superposed Full**	.535	.510	.025
Krieghoff Model 32 Skeet	.549	.542	.007
Parker (RB) Quail-1	.552	.550	.002
Parker (LB) Quail-2	.552	.545	.007
Winchester Model 12 Skeet**	.553	.549	.004
Winchester Model 12 Improved Cylinder**	.553	.544	.009
Winchester Model 12 Modified**	.553	.540	.013
Winchester Model 12 Full**	.553	.533	.020
20 GAUGE			
Franchi 48AL Cylinder	.627	.627	.000
Franchi 48AL Improved Cylinder	.627	.617	.010

GUN - CHOKE*	BORE	MUZZLE	CONSTRICTION	GUN - CHOKE*	BORE	MUZZLE	CONSTRICTION
20 GAUGE				**12 GAUGE**			
Franchi 48AL Modified	.627	.611	.016	Remington M1100 Slug Unmarked	.728	.720	.008
Krieghoff Model 32 Skeet	.614	.607	.007	Remington Model 11-87 Skeet	.728	.724	.004
Remington Model 1100 Skeet	.623	.618	.003	Remington Model 11-87 Improved Cylinder	.728	.716	.012
Remington Model 1100 Improved Cylinder	.614	.605	.009	Remington Model 11-87 Modified	.728	.705	.020
Remington Model 11-87 Improved Cylinder	.611	.602	.009	Remington Model 11-87 Full	.728	.690	.038
Remington Model 11-87 Modified	.611	.585	.026	Remington Model 11-87 XF Turkey	.728	.688	.040
Remington Model 11-87 Full	.611	.577	.034	Remington Model 11-87 SF Hevi-Shot	.728	.673	.055
Winchester 101 Improved Cylinder	.615	.607	.008	Remington Model 11-87 SF Turkey	.728	.663	.065
Winchester 101 Modified	.615	.601	.014	Remington M3200 Field Modified	.730	.710	.020
Weatherby Athena Improved Cylinder	.618	.613	.005	Remington M3200 Field Full	.730	.690	.040
Weatherby Athena Modified	.618	.603	.015	Remington M3200 Trap Full	.735	.695	.040
Weatherby Athena Full	.618	.584	.034	Remington M3200 Trap Full	.735	.695	.040
Westley Richards Skeet	.620	.615	.005	Remington M332 Field Improved Cylinder	.730	.721	.009
Westley Richards Modified	.620	.605	.015	Remington M332 Field Modified	.730	.710	.029
16 GAUGE				Ruger Red Lab (BB) Skeet	.726	.724	.002
L.C. Smith, right barrel Improved Cylinder	.655	.645	.010	Ruger Red Lab (TB) Improved Cylinder	.724	.718	.006
L.C. Smith, left barrel Modified	.655	.630	.025	SKB M685 Trap Full	.725	.690	.035
12 GAUGE				SKB M685 Trap Improved Modified	.725	.700	.025
Browning Citori, right barrel Light Modified	.715	.700	.015	Win. M37 Steelbilt Full	.731	.695	.036
Browning Citori (BB) Modified	.712	.695	.017	Winchester M1897 Full	.726	.697	.029
Brown Citori Top-Sing (TB) Improved Modified	.715	.690	.025				
Fox Sterlingworth, right barrel Modified	.728	.718	.020				
Fox Sterlingworth, left barrel Full	.725	.684	.041				
Kimber Improved Cylinder	.725	.715	.010				
Kimber Modified	.725	.710	.015				
Rem 870 Spec Field Improved Cylinder	.725	.715	.010				
Remington Model 870 Improved Cylinder	.724	.713	.011				

Choke constrictions measured by author

*As marked by manufacturer **Briley screw-in chokes
NOTE: The industry-standard bore diameters among American manufacturers are: .775 inch (10 gauge), .729 inch (12 gauge), .670 inch (16 gauge), .615 inch (20 gauge), .550 inch (28 gauge) and .410 inch for the .410 bore.

CHAPTER 7

Sizing Up Shot

Game birds of different sizes require the use of shot of various sizes. I prefer No. 7-1/2s when hunting California quail although some hunters prefer No. 6 shot for late-season hunting.

In about every way we can think of, lead is the perfect material for making shotgun pellets. Due to a plentiful supply, it is quite inexpensive when compared to other materials being used to make shot. It is also quite soft. This is good from a manufacturer's point of view, because its softness makes lead easy to form into about any desirable shape. That same characteristic allows it to travel through the barrel of a shotgun at high speed without damaging its bore. In addition to all of those positive things, lead is extremely dense and even the smallest sizes shed momentum rather slowly as they travel through the air. All things considered, the only material that would be better for making shot is gold, and it takes no genius to figure out why it is not used for that pur-

pose. The downside to lead is its toxicity, which becomes a potentially lethal problem once it enters the digestive system of bottom-feeding waterfoul.

Shot is formed by melting lead and then pouring it into a huge steel pan with its bottom full of tiny holes. The size of the holes roughly determines the size of the finished shot. Vibrating the pan causes the molten lead to flow through the holes in tiny droplets, and as they freefall through the air, the surface tension of the lead causes each droplet to take on a spherical shape. A pool of water serves to cushion the landing and to cause the shot to go completely solid. The pellets then go through an inspection process where misshapen pellets are culled out. Since the pellets vary a bit in size at this point, they

Hevi-Shot as loaded by Remington in waterfowl, turkey and upland loads is the benchmark by which the downrange performance of materials used to make all other types of shot, including lead, are now measured. (Photo courtesy of Remington)

are separated by mechanical screening. Each pellet is then coated with graphite powder to improve the fluidity of the shot. This causes it to flow smoothly through the measure of a shotshell loading machine. The manufacturing process for lead shot is less than precise, and even after the pellets are graded to size, their diameters will almost always vary somewhat within a particular size designation. Even the highest grades of shot will usually vary by about half a size, or around .005 inch. The bag of No. 8 shot you buy for handloading will likely contain a mixture of No. 8 and No. 7-1/2 pellets, or it might be a mixture of No. 8s and No. 8-1/2s. The same applies to the shot loaded into shotshells by various manufacturers.

Magnum and chilled are the two types of lead shot commonly seen today. Magnum-grade shot costs more to manufacture, because it contains a higher percentage of an expensive metal called antimony. The exact amount of this additive varies slightly among the various manufacturers, but top-grade magnum shot in sizes No. 7-1/2 and No. 8 as loaded by Remington, Winchester and Federal in loads used for trap shooting contains six percent. It is the hardest lead shot available. Shot in sizes No. 8 and No. 9 made for skeet shooting is not quite as hard, since targets are broken closer to the muzzle of the gun in that game than in trap. Chilled shot is the softest available, and it usually contains around two percent antimony.

Adding antimony to shot makes it harder, and the more antimony added up to a point, the harder it becomes. The harder the shot is, the better it is able to resist setback deformation during firing, not the mention the damage that can occur as it slams first into the forcing cone of the barrel and then squeezes through its choked section. As the shot charge exits the muzzle, the undamaged pellets tend to hold a straight course toward the target, while air resistance on irregular surfaces of the deformed pellets cause them to stray from the main pattern more quickly and in a more erratic fashion. All else being equal, nice round pellets shoot straighter and therefore deliver more uniform patterns of higher density than severely deformed pellets. This is why extremely hard shot made of iron (but called steel shot by duck hunters) often delivers such beautiful patterns. This is also why extremely hard lead shot produces shorter shot strings during flight than soft lead shot. Magnum-grade lead shot in sizes larger than No. 6 seldom has a very high antimony content, because the larger the pellet, the less its flight is affected by minor deformation.

One of the reasons why premium-grade shotshells sold by Federal, Remington and other companies cost more than economy-grade field loads is because they contain shot with a relatively high antimony content while inexpensive field loads made by those same companies are often loaded with chilled shot. It is not

Before reaching this Texas gobbler, the charge of No. 6 Hevi-Shot I fired from a Remington Model 11-87 had to penetrate the pads of several prickly pear cactus. It was the most amazing demonstration of penetration either my guide or I had ever seen.

Steel shot works fine out to about 30 yards as long as the correct size is chosen. I prefer to use BB when hunting Canada geese although BBB in the 10 gauge or 3-1/2 inch 12 gauge might be an even better choice.

uncommon to see hunters make the mistake of buying mart-special shells when they should be spending a few more dollars on the premium-grade stuff. But I've seen it happen the other way, too; some hunters spend more money than they really need to by buying the best premium-grade ammo available when economy-grade ammo would deliver the performance they need. It never hurts anything but the old wallet to use the very best regardless of the type of hunting one decides to do, but if shots in the field seldom exceed 25 yards, economy-grade field loads teamed up with the right choke constriction will deliver all the performance a shotgunner needs. Someone who hunts ruffed grouse or quail in thickets where 20 yards is considered long-range shooting should find nothing about standard loads to complain about. On the other hand, for late-season hunting when shots at quail, pheasants, sharptail grouse, chukar and other birds are often beyond 25 yards, premium ammo is worth every cent of its cost difference because it almost always delivers patterns of higher density at longer range. Turkey hunters who carry tight-choked guns and aim for the head and neck of a gobbler should

also use the best ammunition available.

I know hunters who are under the impression that plated shot is far superior to unplated shot, but this is not always true. If the shot hiding beneath that shiny copper or nickel skin was soft to begin with, it is actually inferior to unplated, high-antimony shot because it is softer. I have never been able to prove it, but plating shot just might cause the pellets to flow more smoothly through the forcing cone and choke of a barrel and in doing so help to prevent pellet deformation. Plating also makes the shot look pretty, but many long hours spent pattern-testing have convinced me that the amount it contributes to improving the downrange performance of magnum-grade shot is insignificant compared to the contribution made by its high antimony content. I am also convinced that nestling the shot in a bed of buffer material, as is often seen in premium-grade ammunition, contributes more to pattern quality than plated shot. Still, the use of plated shot in high-performance loads doesn't hurt anything, and it is often an indicator of the very best ammunition a company can possibly make.

I have no idea who came up with the numerical

system we use to indicate the various shot sizes, but it tells us very little about the actual diameter of a pellet. If anything, it can be downright confusing to new shooters because the larger the number the smaller the shot. For example, No. 9 shot is much smaller than No. 6 shot. The catalogs of most shotshell manufacturers contain approximate diameters for shot of various sizes, but if you don't have one on hand, you can arrive at the nominal diameter of American shot in thousandths of an inch by subtracting its number from a constant of .17. As an example, subtracting 6 from .17 gives us .11 inch, which is the diameter of No. 6 shot. The diameter of No. 4 shot is .08 inch, while the diameter of a No. 9 pellet is .08 inch. This method works for all shot smaller than BB. Regardless of what material shot is made of, it is supposed to conform to standard diameters used within the industry. For this reason, No. 4 pellets made of lead, steel, Tungsten-Polymer, Tungsten-Matrix or whatever should measure about the same.

Some shotshells imported into the United States today are loaded in England, so it might be helpful to add that actual diameters of shot made in the two countries differs a bit for all sizes except No. 9. As you can see in the chart at the end of this chapter, when the same numbers are compared, shot made in America is actually one size larger than shot made in Great Britain. For example, American No. 4 shot is the same diameter as what the English label as No. 2. This can be rather confusing because the shot in some ammunition loaded "over there" is identified on the box with the American numbering system because its importer special-ordered it that way. So, the only way to know for sure how actual pellet diameter of foreign-manufactured shotshells actually compares to our standards is to cut open a shell and measure several pellets with a micrometer. As a rule, the best grade of English shot is softer than the best grade of shot made in America simply because it does not contain as much antimony.

The exact number of pellets in an ounce of shot will vary slightly from batch to batch due to slight variations in density, but charts published by the various manufacturers are close enough for government work. I have included a chart for lead shot put together by Federal and a steel shot chart from Remington, but those published by other companies usually agree quite closely with them. I have also included a chart of recommended shot sizes, and while it might not totally agree with the opinions of others, it has worked for me through the years. If I had to weed out some of the options, I would go with No. 9 for skeet and some sporting clays presentations, No. 8-1/2 for woodcock, No. 8 for 16-yard trap, mourning doves, sporting clays and bobwhite quail, No. 7-1/2

for handicap trap, ruffed grouse and the other five species of quail, and No. 5 for pheasant, sage grouse, cottontail rabbits and head shots on turkey gobblers. If I had to boil it on down to only a couple of choices, I would hate to have to give up No. 8 shot, but I'd do it in order to end up with No. 7-1/2s and No. 5s. Given only those two, I would use No. 5 shot for the shooting I have already mentioned for it and use No. 7-1/2 on everything else. Those two shot sizes fall a bit short of being ideal for all aspects of shotgunning, one example being shooting skeet with 1/2 ounce of No. 7-1/2 shot in the .410, but a fellow could most certainly get by with them.

Nontoxic Shot

Back when only lead shot was loaded in shotshells, the biggest decision hunters had to make was what pellet size and shot charge weight to use on various game. When it was finally decided in 1987 that shot made of materials less toxic than lead had to be used on waterfowl, the picture began to grow a bit more complex. In addition to lead, ammo is now commonly loaded with shot made of iron (or steel as it is commonly called) as well as Tungsten-Matrix, Bismuth, Tungsten-Iron and Hevi-Shot. Those materials vary considerably in density with steel the lightest at 7.86 grams per cubic centimeter. Then we have Bismuth at 9.60 gms/cc, Tungsten-Iron at 10.30, Tungsten Matrix at 10.60, lead at 11.00 and Hevi-Shot, the real heavyweight, at 11.80 gms/cc. Steel was the first nontoxic shot to be adopted by U.S. ammunition manufacturers in 1987, and while its performance was nothing to brag about early on, it has been greatly improved. Either that, or we finally got around to learning how to use it.

When thinking about shot, it is important to remember that the lower the density of the material it is made of, the more rapidly it sheds velocity and therefore energy during flight. Steel is only about 70 percent as dense as lead, so pellets of the same size made of those two materials differ considerably in the amount of energy they deliver down range. As an example, if No. 4 pellets made of both materials exit the muzzle of a shotgun at 1350 feet per second (fps), the lead pellet will strike a 40-yard target with 4.4 foot-pounds (ft-lbs) of energy compared to only 2.4 ft-lbs for the steel pellet. In order to deliver the same amount of energy per pellet with steel as with lead, we must increase its diameter by two sizes. In this case, we would move up to No. 2 steel, which delivers 4.4 ft-lbs at 40 yards, same as for No. 4 lead. But even when using the two-sizes-larger rule, ammunition loaded with steel shot cannot possibly equal the performance of ammo loaded with lead shot at all ranges. This is because a shotshell of a given length can only hold so much shot, and it is incapable of holding as many of the larger steel pellets. Staying with those same two shot sizes in our comparison, a common loading of the 3-1/2 inch, 12-gauge shell for turkey hunting is 2-1/4 ounces of No. 4 lead shot for a total count of 303 pellets. The heaviest steel shot charge commonly seen in 3-1/2 inch waterfowl loads contains only 1-9/16 ounce of No. 2s for a total of 195 pellets, not because the ammo companies are too stingy to put in more shot, but because it is all a 12-gauge shell of that length will hold. So as you should be able to see, even though the steel shot load delivers the same amount of energy per pellet, it has a shorter effective range simply because it contains only about 65 percent as many pellets. Such a drastic reduction in pattern density results in an equally drastic reduction in effective range.

Magnum shot usually delivers better patterns than chilled shot because its higher antimony content makes it harder and therefore more resistant to deformation during its violent trip down the bore of a shotgun barrel.

All of this may sound like I am against the use of steel shot on waterfowl, but it is not true. When hunting with a modern shotgun capable of handling steel, and shots at ducks and geese don't greatly exceed 30 yards, I seldom use anything else simply because out to that distance it performs well enough so long as the correct pellet size is used. The performance advantage realized by the use of shot made of higher density materials really does not become apparent until ranges begin to exceed 30 yards or so. On top of that, steel is considerably less expensive than the other nontoxics. After trying various sizes of steel shot on waterfowl, I have come to the conclusion that No. 2 offers the best combination of pattern density and energy delivery for ducks, although No. 1 is not a bad choice. For geese, BBB might be the best all-around steel shot size, although I seem to always shoot better when using BB.

Bismuth followed steel by several years in the nontoxic shot parade, and while it too suffered a few problems early on, shot now being made of that material performs quite satisfactorily. I have used bismuth shot quite a bit on both waterfowl and upland game birds, mainly because its softness allows it to be fired in older shotguns without damaging their barrels, and I enjoy hunting with vintage guns. It has a higher density than steel, but since it is a bit lighter than lead, I usually choose one shot size larger than lead, with No. 5 being my favorite for ducks. For quite a long time, Bismuth was the only nontoxic shot offered in all the gauges as well as the .410. I have shot ducks over decoys with the 28-gauge load and found it to be quite effective out to about 25 yards.

Tungsten-Matrix shot was developed by Kent Cartridge, and it too is soft enough to be used in vintage guns. Because its density compares more closely to that of lead, I use one shot size smaller than for Bismuth, or the same as I used in the old days when shooting waterfowl with lead shot. In addition to the 2-3/4 inch, 3-inch and 3-1/2 inch 12 gauge, it is available in the 2-3/4 inch and 3 inch 20 gauge. While hunting with vintage guns, I have bagged more ducks and geese with Tungsten-Matrix than with any other nontoxic shot, and its performance is so close to that of lead, it is impossible to tell any difference between the two. Back when it was first introduced, I used it on ducks in South America, and since the country I was in still allowed the use of lead on waterfowl, it was an excellent opportunity to do a side-by-side performance comparison of the two types of shot. Believe me when I say that duck hunters of today can do anything with Tungsten-Matrix that duck hunters used to do with lead.

Tungsten-Iron from Federal has about the same density as Kent's Tungsten-Matrix, and for this reason it delivers more individual pellet energy than steel when pellets of the same size are compared. The extreme hardness of Tungsten-Iron requires Federal to use a plastic shotcup with extremely thick petals, and this reduces the amount of shot that can be loaded compared to Bismuth and Tungsten-Matrix. Even so, I still find it to be one of the best choices available for dropping Canada geese at ranges beyond the reach of steel. Tungsten-Iron should be used only in guns designed for use with steel shot.

Duck and goose hunters have long compared the various types of nontoxic shot to lead shot, just as I have been doing here, but what we must now do is compare all types of shot, including lead, to Hevi-Shot. I first tried this revolutionary new shot in 2002, the year Remington started loading it in the 20- and 12-gauge shells, and I had never seen anything like it. Not only is it capable of outperforming all other types of nontoxic shot, it reaches beyond the performance boundary of lead shot. Using choke constrictions ranging from .050 to .060 inch in 12-gauge guns, I have shot patterns at 40 yards that averaged darned close to 100 percent, something I have never been able to do with any other type of shot, including steel. The extreme hardness of Hevi-Shot is what enables it to deliver unheard of performance at the pattern board. Composed of a tungsten, nickel and iron mix, it is considerably harder than lead. It is also harder than steel, although it can be used in any shotgun designed to handle steel shot. Hevi-Shot, with its density of 12.0 gms/cc, is 54 percent heavier than the iron alloy used in making steel shot, and slightly heavier than lead.

While Hevi-Shot was developed with duck and goose hunting in mind, turkey hunters in their never-ending search for the tightest and most dense patterns possible have grown fond of it too. I have used it a lot on waterfowl, and while it has proven to be an outstanding performer there, I am just as impressed by what it does to a turkey gobbler at ranges I had previously considered impossible with a shotgun. When Hevi-Shot was first introduced, I took several gobblers with the 1-5/8 ounce of No. 6 load, and all were dead-in-their-tracks, one-shot kills. During the 2002 spring season in Kentucky, Harold Knight of Knight & Hale Game Calls laser-ranged the longest shot I made on a hunt with him and came up with 59 yards. Harold was amazed. So was I, but I was not surprised because only a couple days earlier I had pattern-tested the load at various distances in a Benelli Super Black Eagle, the gun with which I would

be hunting. The gun had .060 inch of choke constriction in its barrel and wore a Burris electronic sight with a three-minute dot. During my pattern-testing, I began to run short of ammo at 70 yards, where I was still putting no fewer than 17 pellets into the head/neck zone of a turkey target. Incredible performance to say the least.

For hunting waterfowl, Remington recommends dropping down three steps in shot size from what is usually recommended for steel shot. This means that if you use No. 2 steel on large ducks as I do, you can switch to No. 5 Hevi-Shot for the same energy delivery per pellet. When this is done pellet count is drastically increased. For example, when 1-1/2-ounce charges of both are compared, No. 2 steel contains approximately 185 pellets compared to over 300 pellets for No. 5 Hevi-Shot. This is a good plan for anyone who desires to do nothing more than match the individual pellet energy of steel with patterns of higher density, but I have bagged enough ducks with Hevi-Shot to become convinced that dropping back one size smaller than the lead we once used is a better idea. Rather than using No. 4 lead on ducks and No. 1 lead on geese as many of us did before the use of steel shot was mandated, we would now use No. 5 Hevi-Shot on ducks and No. 2 Hevi-Shot on geese.

I am absolutely convinced that because of its phenomenal performance on game birds, Hevi-Shot will rewrite many of the rules of wingshooting. I say this because I have done things with Hevi-Shot that simply cannot be explained. Like the time Nick Sisley and I shot ducks in Uruguay with 20-gauge Remington Model 11-87 shotguns. Using Remington's 3-inch shells loaded with 1-1/8 ounces of Hevi-Shot, we consistently killed ducks as far out as 50 and 60 yards. And we were not guessing about the range because the distances were accurately measured with a laser rangefinder. Now comes the part that I would not have believed had I not been there, done it and seen it for myself. We were using Improved Cylinder chokes and No. 6 Hevi-Shot.

AUTHOR'S RECOMMENDED SHOT SIZES FOR LEAD SHOT

| | Lead Shot Sizes | |
| | Close To | Longer |
	Medium Ranges	Ranges
Woodcock, snipe, rail & other small shore birds	9	8-1/2
Quail, doves (early season)	8	7-1/2
Quail, doves (late season)	7-1/2	7-1/2
Mountain quail	7-1/2	6
Grouse; ruffed, sharptail, spruce, ptarmigan	7-1/2	6
Pheasant,	6	5
Sage grouse	5	4
Cottontail rabbit, squirrel	5	4
Swamp rabbit	4	4
Turkey, for shots to head & neck only	6	5
Turkey, for shots to body	2*	BB*
Skeet	9	NA
Trap	8	7-1/2
Sporting Clays	9	7-1/2

*Only where larger sizes may legally be used on turkey.

NOTES: These same recommendations apply to nontoxic shot with densities similar to that of lead. Steel shot should be two sizes larger.

LAWRENCE BRAND LEAD SHOT (Antimonial Content)

SIZE	PERCENT ANTIMONY	PELLETS/OUNCE
CHILLED SHOT (GRAPHITE COATED)		
9	2	570
8	2	400
7-1/2	2	340
6	2	220
5	2	168
4	2	132
MAGNUM SHOT (Graphite coated)		
9	6	585
8-1/2	6	490
8	6	410
7-1/2	6	350
7	6	310
6	6	225

COPPER-PLATED SHOT (Wax coated)

7-1/2	6	359
6	6	226
5	2	172
4	2	135

DIAMETERS OF AMERICAN & ENGLISH SHOT
(In Thousandths Of An Inch)

SIZE	AMERICAN	ENGLISH
FF	.230	——
F	.220	——
TT	.210	——
T	.200	——
BBB	.190	——
BB	.180	——

SIZE	AMERICAN	ENGLISH
Air Rifle	.175	——
B	.170	——
1	.160	——
2	.150	.130
3	.140	——
4	.130	.125
5	.120	.110
6	.110	.100
7	.100	.095
7-1/2	.095	.090
8	.090	.085
8-1/2	.085	——
9	.080	.080
10	.070	——
11	.060	——
12	.050	——
Dust	.060	——

NOTE: Some of the sizes listed are no longer readily available

APPROXIMATE NUMBER OF PELLETS PER LOAD
(Lead Shot)

SHOT CHARGE (OZS)	9	8	7-1/2	6	5	4	3	2	1	BB
1/2	293	205	173	112	86	68	53	44	35	30
5/8	366	256	216	139	108	85	66	55	44	37
11/16	402	281	237	153	118	94	73	61	49	41
3/4	439	307	259	167	129	102	80	66	53	44
7/8	512	358	302	195	151	119	93	77	62	52
1	585	409	345	223	172	136	106	88	71	60
1-1/8	658	460	388	251	194	153	120	99	80	67
1-1/4	731	511	431	279	215	170	133	110	89	74
1-3/8	804	562	474	307	237	187	146	121	98	82
1-1/2	878	614	518	335	258	204	160	132	107	89
1-5/8	951	665	561	362	280	221	173	143	116	97
1-3/4	1024	716	604	390	301	238	186	154	125	104
1-7/8	1097	767	647	418	323	255	200	165	134	112
2	1170	818	690	446	344	272	213	176	143	119
2-1/8	1243	869	733	474	366	289	226	187	152	127
2-1/4	1316	894	756	492	378	307	240	196	161	134

NOTE: Pellet count for Tungsten-Matrix and bismuth is only slightly lower.

APPROXIMATE NUMBER OF PELLETS PER LOAD
(Steel Shot)

SHOT CHARGE (Ozs)	6	5	4	3	2	1	BB	BBB	T	TT
3/4	236	18	144	118	94	—	—	—	—	—
15/16	295	230	180	149	117	—	—	—	—	—
1	314	243	189	155	125	—	—	—	—	—
1-1/8	335	274	212	175	141	116	80	—	—	—
1/1-4	—	—	237	194	156	129	89	76	67	56
1-3/8	—	—	60	212	170	141	97	84	73	62
1-9/16	—	—	300	247	195	161	112	97	81	71
1-3/4	—	—	—	—	215	177	125	108	92	82

DENSITY OF VARIOUS SHOT PELLET MATERIALS
(Grams Per Cubic Centimeter)

Hevi-Shot	12.00
Lead	11.10
Tungsten Polymer	11.10
Tungsten Iron	10.04
Tungsten Matrix	10.05
Bismuth	9.89
Steel	7.86

ENERGY COMPARISON

TYPE SHOT	SHOT SIZE	MUZZLE VELOCITY (FPS)	RETAINED ENERGY PER PELLET (FT-LBS)	
			40 Yards	60 Yards
Lead	7-1/2	1330	1.4	0.9
Lead	6	1330	2.5	1.7
Lead	5	1330	3.6	2.5
Lead	4	1330	4.8	3.4
Lead	2	1330	8.0	5.8
Lead	2	1240	7.3	5.4
Hevi-Shot	7-1/2	1325	1.6	0.9
Hevi-Shot	6	1325	2.8	1.7
Hevi-Shot	5	1325	3.9	2.5
Hevi-Shot	4	1325	5.3	3.5
Hevi-Shot	2	1325	9.1	6.2
Steel	6	1365	1.3	0.2
Steel	4	1365	2.4	1.4
Steel	2	1275	4.1	2.4
Steel	2	1365	4.4	2.6
Steel	BB	1275	8.3	5.2
Steel	T	1300	12.5	8.0
Steel	TT	1300	15.0	9.9

CHAPTER 8

Guns and Loads for Quail

The topknot of the Gambel quail consists of two or three feathers. It has an apostrophe-like shape, same as the one worn just as proudly by the California species of quail. What a magnificent bird!

I am sure quite a few hunters have taken more than one species of quail in America, but those who have taken all six are fewer in number. This is because in the United States, the Mearns quail is found mainly in Arizona and New Mexico, and even in those states, there are not many of them. Some American hunters call it the harlequin quail, and in Old Mexico it is referred to as the Montezuma quail. Regardless of what you decide to call the cocky little game bird, to me the Mearns looks like a miniature guinea fowl. I once set

out to take the grand slam of quail and I pulled it off with a .410-bore Weatherby Athena shotgun. After taking the mountain and valley species in California, I then went after Mearns, scaled and Gambel in Arizona and finished up on bobwhite in both North and South Carolina.

My love for quail hunting goes back to the days when as a youngster I hunted bobwhite on small farms belonging to my father and several neighbors. In those days, I mostly used the only shotgun I owned, an Iver

Like all quail, the mountain species ranks among the most handsome of game birds. I bagged this one while hunting in the Sierra Nevada mountains of California with Mike Schwiebert and Bob and Mary Koble.

Cactus-proof running shoes are the ideal footwear when hunting scaled quail in the Arizona desert. If not for the efforts of Brian "Murph" Murray and his magnificent dogs, Fritz and Hans, I would never have been successful in taking a fleet-footed bird that acts more like a pronghorn antelope than a quail.

Johnson chambered for the little .410 shotshell. Occasionally, I would head to the field with Dad's 16-gauge L.C. Smith double, but most of the time I used my own "Ivy" Johnson. Back then, I hunted quail because I enjoyed eating them, not to mention my love for guns and hunting in general. Today, I hunt the little buzz bombs for those same reasons, plus I enjoy the casual and relaxed pace of the sport. I also like nothing better than watching good dogs work; to me, a well-trained pointing dog is as important a part of quail hunting as a fine shotgun. Something else I really like about the sport is that it has given to me many opportunities through the years to be afield with friends who love quail hunting as much as me. Quail hunting has often been described as a gentleman's sport, and it is as good a name as any as far as I'm concerned because I know plenty of gentlemen who participate.

As United States game bird harvest figures go, the number of quail bagged annually by hunters is second only to the number of mourning doves taken. The population of this grand little bird is highly influenced each year by a number of things, with weather being near the top of the list, but it is not unusual for hunters to take upwards of 40 million in a good season. Roughly 80 percent of the quail taken each year are bobwhites, with the remaining 20 percent made up of the five western species, which include Gambel, Mearns, mountain, scaled and California, the latter just as commonly called valley quail.

Quail hunting is extremely popular for a number of reasons, not the least of which is its availability across the nation. In lumping together the bobwhite with its Western cousins, we find that quail hunting is available in all but a few states in the country. Last time I looked, there were no huntable populations in Maine, Vermont, Alaska, Wyoming and Montana, and the same might apply to a few others, but most of the remaining states including Hawaii have at least one species. In some of the states where wild-bird hunting ranges from slim to nonexistent, commercial shooting preserves offering liberated quail have become quite popular. Some states offer both planted and wild birds. In California and Oregon, I have hunted on commercial operations that offered liberated bobwhite and wild valley quail. In South Carolina, I have hunted both wild and released bobwhites on the same preserve.

Most states from the East Coast to the Midwest have only bobwhite quail, making it the most common, but two or more species thrive in a number of our Western states. In California, for example, you can hunt mountain and valley quail in areas ranging from the central portion on up to the Oregon border, and then head south to the other end of the state for a go at the Gambel. Move farther north into Oregon, and it is possible to hunt three species there as well: valley, mountain and bobwhite. Head southeast to Arizona, and you'll find Gambel, scaled and Mearns on the menu. Move next door to either Nevada or New Mexico, and you can try your luck at Gambel, scaled, Mearns and bobwhite.

I am often asked which of the six species available to hunters in the United States offers the most challenge to an accomplished shotgunner. Under the right circumstances, all can be difficult to intercept with a swarm of shot. At other times, all can be quite easy to hit. Hunting mountain quail can be the most physically demanding, due to the type of country it calls home. Gambel and scaled quail would really rather run than fly, so you'd best be in good shape and wear your track shoes when hunting them. I have never ground-sluiced a Gambel or a scaled quail, but I would never criticize some tired soul who decides to do so with revenge in his heart.

Mearns quail are sometimes the easiest to hit simply because they often hold so tight to a dog's point, they have to literally be kicked from the grass before they will fly. But the Mearns can become a rather challenging target once it is airborne. Valley quail also like to run, but in my experience, not as much as Gambel and scaled quail. Once a covey is broken up, the singles often hold as tight as the most gentlemanly of bobwhites. But I have also seen the same happen when hunting the Gambel and the scalie. In looking back, I'd say the scaled quail presents the toughest shooting I have experienced, but that may be because I have had more bad days than good when hunting that particular bird rather than it being more difficult to intercept with a swarm of lead pellets.

So which species would I rather hunt? I will have to say it is almost a tossup between mountain, bobwhite and Mearns. I love hunting mountain quail because I enjoy being in some of the magnificent alpine country they call home. Same goes for hunting the Mearns in Southwestern desert country. Still, I'll have to rank the mountain species a close second best to bobwhite and Mearns. Both have more of a tendency to hold tight to the point of a dog, allowing the hunter to get close enough for a shot before flushing. Mearns and bobwhite would rather fly than run. When they do explode into the air, their speed can make them rather

challenging to hit. Attempt to draw a bead on either as it flies through woods or tall brush and you will find it every bit as difficult to hit as a ruffed grouse. Not only do the Mearns and bobwhite fly faster than their four cousins, they are smaller targets. I should mention that I am referring to bobwhite quail that hatch naturally and grow up in the wild. Liberated bobs found on commercial hunting preserves are fun to shoot, and I hunt them quite a bit with .410 shotguns because of the long season, but the only thing many of them have in common with wild quail is they both wear feathers and they both taste the same after shedding them.

It might be of interest to note that hunters account for only a small percentage of the wild bobwhite quail taken each year, even in heavily hunted areas. A study that took place in the Packsaddle Wildlife Management Area of Oklahoma during the late 1990s showed that avian and mammalian predators accounted for 65 percent of the birds, while only 14 percent were taken by hunters. The mortality rate of young chicks was extremely high, with only 37 percent of those hatched surviving longer than six weeks. Video-monitoring research conducted in Georgia by Auburn University and the University of Georgia showed that of the quail that fell victim to predation, 44 percent were taken by snakes, 22 percent by raccoons, 20 percent by armadillos, 8 percent by fire ants and 4 percent by opossums. Other predators such as fox squirrels, chipmunks, skunks, coyotes, bobcats, barred owls and gray foxes accounted for only about 2 percent. There are those who are convinced the wild turkey comeback has had its toll on quail in the Southeast, and while this may be true, I doubt if all the predators combined have impacted the quail population as much as a severe loss of habitat, much of it caused by drastic changes in farming practices.

As much as I enjoy hunting the bobwhite, I'll have to admit some of my best hunts have been for his Western cousins. Like the time I hunted valley quail with Ed Weatherby, Brad Ruddell and Mike Schwiebert, all of Weatherby Rifles. After hunting for several days at High Desert Hunting club not far from Los Angeles, Mike and I drove north and joined up with Stacy Twissleman of Twissleman Outfitters and her Lab, Biscuit. A few days later, Brad and I concluded the adventure even farther north at Rock Springs Ranch. Never had I seen so many quail, and never had I seen coveys containing so many birds. Late one afternoon, Mike and I spotted a covey several hundred yards away as the birds ran along the opposite end of a vast meadow. They were on their way to water, and we figured the covey had to contain somewhere in the neighborhood of

Bagging this Mearns in the rolling hills of southern Arizona concluded my quest for the grand slam of quail in America. I took all six species with a .410-bore Weatherby Athena.

200 to 250 birds. We tried to get close enough for a shot, but the entire bunch vanished into thick brush before we could get there.

Just about every time we flushed a covey of valley quail on those hunts, the singles would land in wooded or brushy areas. When followed up and flushed again, they presented shots that reminded me of bob-white hunting back east. The valley quail is every bit as good as the ruffed grouse at putting a tree or bush between you and him just as you pull the trigger. I mostly used the 28-gauge and .410-caliber barrels of a Weatherby Athena three-barrel set, and both worked quite well. For the 28, I had a supply of Winchester Super-X ammo with an ounce of No. 7-1/2 shot, and in the .410 I used Federal's 3-inch load with 11/16 ounce of the same size shot. Both were quite effective.

Mike Schwiebert and I later met up with Bob and Mary Koble for a hunt for mountain quail in California's Sierra Nevadas. It was my first hunt for mountain quail but it was the 16th consecutive year Bob and Mary had hunted opening week of the season. Believe it when I say those two know mountain quail

hunting. Just sharing that beautiful country with such nice people made the trip from South Carolina worthwhile, and the fact that I had my limit before noon of the first day really iced the cake. I was shooting the same Weatherby three-barrel set I had used on valley quail, and after taking four birds with the .410, I switched to the 20-gauge barrel and took a couple more. After switching to the 28 gauge and taking another three birds, Mike Schwiebert suggested that I take my last bird of the day with a 12-gauge Weatherby SAS autoloader. I am glad I did because it is doubtful that anyone else had ever taken their first limit of mountain quail with four different gauges — all before lunch on opening day of the season. Mountain quail country can be extremely thick and quite rugged — and for those reasons, few people manage to bag their limit — but thanks to Bob, Mary, Mike and two wonderful Brittanies named Sierra and Kelly, I did it the first time out. The second day jolted me back to reality; I flushed only three birds and missed one of them.

Only a few weeks after hunting mountain quail with Bob and Mary Koble, I headed to Arizona, where I hooked up with Brad Ruddell, Roxie Kelso and our guide, Bryan "Murph" Murray. Two other important members of our group were a German shorthair named Fritz and a pudelpointer that went by the name of Hans. Wise old cactus-scarred veterans of desert hunting, they belonged to Murph.

We started out on Mearns, and I did okay by taking three of the first five birds I shot at with only five .410 shells. What a beautiful little bird, and what a great pleasure it was to hunt a species of quail few hunters have ever even seen. The next day, things got worse. Or I should say my shooting got worse. The scaled quail really had my number, and I would really rather not say how many shells I used up before bagging my first bird of the day. Day three started out much better. In only a few minutes, five Gambel quail were in the game pocket of my vest, and I had fired only eight shells. It went downhill from there; despite the fact that I had managed to regain both composure and confidence, I finished up the day with some of the poorest shooting I have ever suffered through. Brad Ruddell made things a lot worse by having one of his best days. But like he told me as I apologized for my poor showing, the worst quail-hunting day is far better than the best of days without quail.

A shotgun of any gauge can be used for hunting quail, but some are better suited for the purpose than others. I also believe gun size and weight should be in direct proportion to gauge. When it comes to choke constriction, I see too many hunters attempting to use too much of it. In areas where most shots are inside 25 yards, Cylinder Bore, Skeet and Improved Cylinder are the best choices, and a combination of either two is what I often choose in a double. I usually tighten things up a bit when Gambel and scaled quail are doing their usual wild-flushing thing, but even then I seldom go beyond Improved Cylinder and Modifed in a double or Light Modified in a pump or autoloader. When hunting mountain quail for the first time in California, I used a bit greater spread in choke constrictions. Most birds flushed inside 20 yards, but a few preferred to run apiece and then flush farther away. By the time I squeezed the trigger on one of those long-distance runners, it was often crossing the 30-yard stripe. In an attempt to cover as many bases as possible, I used a Skeet choke in the bottom of my Weatherby Athena and Improved Modified up top. The combination worked perfectly.

There was a time when the 12-gauge was simply too much shell for shooting quail inside 25 yards (where the majority are shot), but the introduction of factory ammo with light shot charges has changed all that. Among the really great quail loads I have tried is Winchester's AA Xtra-Lite with an ounce of shot at 1180 fps. Other excellent reduced-recoil quail medicines include the Federal Gold Medal Extra-Lite and Remington's Premier STS target load, both charged with an ounce of high-antimony shot. In addition to churning up less recoil than most field loads, they deliver extremely uniform patterns from most guns, and the extremely hard shot they are loaded with penetrates more deeply and breaks bone better than softer shot.

Under certain circumstances, heavier loads are preferred. I remember my first hunt for bobwhites in Old Mexico. One area we hunted had obviously been hit hard by hunters who were there before us, and the birds flushed so wild, I doubt if I killed a single one inside 30 yards. The small supply of 12-gauge shells loaded with 1-1/8 ounces of No. 7-1/2 shot I had on hand saved the day. I seldom use the 12 for hunting quail simply because the lighter weight and trimmer lines of guns scaled to size for the smaller gauges make them so much more pleasant to carry for miles on end. Still, if a fellow could own only one quail gun, he could do a lot worse than make it a 12 gauge.

Few hunters choose the 16 gauge today, which is rather sad since I can remember when it was second in popularity only to the 12 gauge. Even those of us who still occasionally sing the praises of Sweet 16 have to admit it is virtually dead. One has only to look at the availability of factory ammo to see how deep it lies in its grave. The biggest thing the 16 has against it as a quail cartridge is the lack of reduced-recoil factory ammo. The typical 3-1/4 dram factory load with 1-1/8 ounces of shot can be uncomfortable to shoot in a relatively lightweight double, not to mention the fact that it is more than actually needed for some hunting conditions. Best choices in quail medicine for shots out to 30 yards are the 2-1/2 dram loads available from Remington, Federal, Winchester and Kent, all loaded with an ounce of shot. I'd really like to see at least one of those companies introduce a new "Lite" loading of the old 16 with 7/8 ounce of shot at a muzzle velocity of 1100 fps or so. That, my friends, would transform thousands of the old doubles out there into superb close- to medium-range quail guns.

The 20 gauge is the classic quail cartridge of the Deep South. This is true for a number of reasons, not the least of which is its availability in guns that are trimmer and usually lighter than most in 12 gauge. In its various loadings, the 20 throws all the shot needed for all terrain and conditions. Most of the time, the various 7/8 ounce and one ounce loads will do. The quintessential quail gun is a light side-by-side double in 20 gauge, like my 5-1/2 pound Westley Richards. An over-under like my old Browning Superposed Lightning is just as good, even if those who prefer side-by-side doubles do think its barrels are stacked the wrong way. You don't have to shop for a double in order to own a great quail gun, but you do have to look a bit to find an autoloader that's actually scaled down in size for the 20-gauge shell. The Remington Models 1100, 11-87 and 870 are. So are the Beretta 391 and Franchi 48AL. Even though I had rather hunt quail with a good double, I'll have to admit that come sundown on most days, I will have averaged as few shells per bird with my Model 1100 LT-20 skeet gun or my Franchi 48AL as with any other gun I own.

While the 20-gauge shotshell has long been my favorite for hunting quail, the 28-gauge is gaining on it fast, and has just about pushed the 20 from the No. 1 spot in my heart. If I added up the number of birds I bag each year with the 28 to the number of clay targets I break on the skeet and sporting clays fields with the little cartridge, it already is my favorite. When the right load is squeezed through the right choke, it will do anything the 20 will do out to about 35 yards. Guns built to proper scale and weight for the 28 are trimmer and lighter than in 20 gauge. And if that's not enough to whet any bird hunter's appetite for a new gun, a box of 28-gauge shells weighs half a pound less and takes up less space in a hunting coat than the same number of 20-gauge shells.

A bit more gentlemanly than the scaled and Gambel quails, the California species is more likely to hold to the point of a dog and wait until the hunter is within shotgun range before flushing. These two taken by Ed Weatherby and me made the mistake of doing just that.

Remington offers two excellent 28-gauge quail loads, the Premier STS Target with 3/4 ounce of No. 8 shot at 1200 fps and an Express load with the same amount of No. 7-1/2 shot at a rather speedy 1295 fps. Federal offers equally good 3/4 ounce loads, one in its Gold Medal Target lineup with 3/4 ounce of No. 8-1/2 shot at 1200 fps, the other a member of the Premium Lead family with 3/4 ounce of No. 7-1/2 and 8 shot at 1295 fps. Kent and Estate target ammo loaded with 3/4 ounce of shot also perform quite nicely in the field. Winchester is the only company presently offering a one-ounce loading of the 28. A member of the Super-X family, it is available with Nos. 6, 7-1/2 and 8 shot at 1200 fps. That load offers 20-gauge performance from a smaller shell. The various 3/4 ounce loads work great on quail at ranges where most of them are shot, but when hunting birds that have a tendency to flush further away from the gun, Winchester's heavy loading of No 7-1/2 shot has no peer in the 28 gauge shell. Winchester occasionally offers its AA target shell with 3/4 ounce of No. 8 shot, and it too is excellent quail medicine.

When it comes to 28-gauge bird guns, I am shotgun poor. One among my favorites is a No. 1 grade side-by-side double made by the Spanish firm of AyA. Its 26-inch barrels are choked .006 and .018 inch. When carrying that gun, I am nicely equipped to take tight-holding birds that flush just off the toes of my boots as well as wild-flushing birds out to about 35 yards. A shotgun I enjoy using in heavily forested or thick, brushy country where most shots are inside 20 yards is a Winchester reproduction of the Parker double. It too has 26-inch barrels, but they are marked "Quail-1" and Quail-2" and have respective choke constrictions of .002 and .007 inch. According to Briley, those constrictions could also be called Light Skeet and Improved Skeet. Those chokes work great for close-range shooting, but patterns become too thin when shots exceed 25 yards. I just weighed those two guns on a postal scale and both went 5-1/2 pounds dead on the money. Either is a delight to carry over those many long miles in the field.

My picks in 28-gauge over-unders for hunting quail are a Weatherby Athena with 28-inch barrels and a 1960s-vintage Browning Superposed Lightning. Both guns are outfitted with Briley screw-in chokes. The Franchi Veloce is another great little 28-gauge over-under quail gun. The one I carried on a hunt in Maryland had 26-inch barrels and weighed only 5-1/2 pounds. As 28-gauge autoloaders go, I like the Remington Model 1100 and the Franchi 48AL, the latter weighing only 5-3/4 pounds. In pump guns, I am partial to the Winchester Model 12, although the Remington Model 870 is lighter.

Those who have never hunted with the .410 shotshell will be surprised to see me include it in a chapter on quail hunting. Those who have given it a fair chance in the field (and who are decent shots) would have been disappointed had I not included it. And too, since this book is in large part about personal choices and favorites, I have no other choice but to devote some space in this book to our smallest shotshell. I am quick to admit, though, the .410 is not for everyone. I choose it for the same reason most of us have at one time or another hunted deer with handguns, muzzleloading rifles and the bow and arrow — doing so adds a greater sense of accomplishment to the game. In addition, some .410-bore guns are extremely light, and the shells don't take up as much room in a pocket of my hunting vest as the larger gauges.

One of my favorite close-range bird guns is a side-by-side double called the Skeet-er. It was built by Iver Johnson during the 1940s for the game of skeet, so both of its 26-inch barrels are choked rather loosely at .006 inch. This is in the neighborhood of Improved Skeet on the Briley chart. Another favorite is a 1960s-vintage 20-gauge Browning Superposed Lightning fitted with Briley subgauge tubes in .410 and 28 gauge. I enjoy hunting with both of those guns, but the one I shoot best is a Weatherby Athena with 26-inch barrels choked .006 and .009 inch. It is the gun I used to take the grand slam of quail, and it also has barrels in 28 and

Doug Kennemore and I took these bobwhites while hunting at Brays Island Plantation in coastal South Carolina.

20 gauge. I first used the Athena on valley quail in California, and I shot so well with the .410 barrels, I never got around to removing its other two barrels from the leather case until the last afternoon of the hunt. Regardless of whether a bird got up at 10 yards or 30 yards from the muzzle of that .410-bore Weatherby, it was as good as dead.

When hunting quail with a .410 double in thick country where most shots are inside 20 yards, I like Skeet in the first barrel and Improved Cylinder in the second barrel. A combination I prefer when ranges and conditions call for a bit more choke is Improved Cylinder and Light Modified, which are usually around .009 and .012 inch for the .410 bore. When hunting with a Winchester Model 42 pump gun or a Remington 11-48 autoloader, I use Cylinder Bore and Improved Cylinder more than any other chokes, but I sometimes switch to Modified for longer shots or when using shot larger than No. 8.

For shots beyond 15 yards, the 3-inch .410 shell outperforms the half-inch shell by leaps and bounds. This is becausethe longer shell allows the use of larger shot without sacrificing pellet count. For example, a 1/2-ounce charge of No. 8 shot in the 2-1/2-inch shell contains approximately 205 pellets compared to 240 No. 7-1/2 pellets in the 11/16-ounce charge of the 3-inch shell. The Weatherby Athena I mentioned earlier shoots beautiful patterns with No. 7-1/2 shot, and I actually prefer that size when hunting valley and mountain quail because they seem harder to kill than bobwhites. I seldom use less choke than Improved Cylinder when hunting with that shot size. Federal offers No. 7-1/2 and No. 8 in the 3-inch shell, while only the latter size shot is available from other companies such as Remington, Winchester and Estate. Regardless of the shot size I might choose, I seldom ever use anything tighter than Modified when hunting quail with .410-bore guns.

Have you been quail hunting lately? If not, the time has come for you to dust off that old bird gun, throw a few shells into your hunting coat and give yourself a gentleman's treat. Even better, take a kid along and introduce him or her to one of our finest shooting sports. My father did just that many years ago, and I wish I had thanked him for it more often than I did.

CHAPTER 9
Outgunning the Ring-Necked Pheasant

Because of its size, its brilliant colors and the loud cackle it often makes when flushed, the cock pheasant is a master at causing the shotgunner to shoot where it was rather than where it is about to be.

Long of tail and brilliantly colored, the ring-necked pheasant is a wingshooter's delight. Even though it prefers to escape from its enemies by running along the ground, the magnificent bird can sometimes be made to flush into the air, where it protests the intrusion on its privacy with loud cackles and strong wing beats, both guaranteed to cause any shotgunners' heart to skip a beat. The ringneck is suffering terribly from predation and habitat decimation caused by modern farming practices, but not as badly as the bobwhite quail. Despite it all, one of our most beautiful game birds continues to thrive in huntable numbers in about half the states in the U.S.

The ring-necked pheasant is often described as an Old World species. Romans transported the bird from Asia Minor to Europe, but it did not immigrate to North American shores until much later. Avid wingshooters both, George Washington and Thomas Jefferson brought black-necked pheasants from England during the late 1700s and stocked them in Virginia and New Jersey, but the birds failed to adapt to their new home. The Chinese ancestors to our ringnecked pheasant arrived on these shores in 1881, when Judge Owen N. Denny, who was the U.S. Consulate

General stationed in Shanghai at the time, shipped around half a dozen birds to his brother's farm in the Willamette Valley of Oregon. A dozen years later, Oregon declared its first hunting season for pheasants. Descendents of those birds were eventually transplanted in corn-growing areas located north of an irregular line running from Los Angeles to Baltimore. The state of Pennsylvania released around 2,000 pheasants in 1915, and by 1930 hunters there were taking more than a quarter million per year. The pheasant population in the United States peaked during the late 1940s and on into the 1950s, when it was not unusual for hunters to check in more than 15 million birds in a single year. During the 1946 season, more than one million were harvested in California alone.

Wild pheasants are now found in 39 states, as far east as Pennsylvania and as far west as Oregon, Washington and California, but the Midwest is where it is seen in its greatest numbers. With around two million birds harvested annually, South Dakota tops them all, while Iowa usually runs a close second with upwards of 1-1/2 million taken in a good season. Other top producers include North Dakota, Illinois, Kansas and Nebraska. While states like Ohio, Michigan, Idaho, Minnesota, Montana, Indiana, Missouri, Oklahoma and Utah do not ring up such great numbers each year, all have open seasons on pheasant. Dozens of commercial hunting preserves of various sizes offer liberated birds in most states, and this greatly increases the number taken. Of the 300,000 or so bagged each year in California, about a third of them come from private preserves. So how many ringnecks do hunters now take in the United States each year? The numbers will fluctuate from year to year but the latest estimate puts the number at about seven million. When we consider the average seasonal bag is said to be in the neighborhood of six birds per hunter, it is easy to see that this Chinese immigrant entices well over a million hunters to the field each year. The fact that other game birds such as sharptail grouse and prairie chickens often live in ringneck country is like icing on the cake. I absolutely love pheasant hunting, especially late in the season when plenty of snow is on the ground and the temperature is cold enough to freeze the hairs in your nose.

I grew up in South Carolina, a state where wild pheasant hunting has never existed. It was not until Phyllis and I made our first trip west that I got around to hunting them. Then and there, I became hopelessly addicted to chasing what many consider to be the king of game birds. Through the years I have shotgunned for ringnecks at every opportunity in a number of states from coast to coast. At the beginning of my pheasant

Mike Larsen of Federal Cartridge and faithful companion Emma after a successful morning in the field. (Photo courtesy of Mike Larsen)

hunting career, I used a 12-gauge Browning A-5 and made most of the common beginner's mistakes. One was using too much choke. Another was using more powerful loads than I actually needed. I also started out with too small a shot size. A mature cock pheasant is a tough cookie, one that pound for pound takes a lot more killing than any other North American game bird with the possible exception of the wild turkey and the Hungarian partridge. I really can't explain why but some birds seem to be far less tenacious of life than others. Another of my favorites, the chukar partridge, is a good example. While that bird is considerably larger than the scaled quail, it seems to give up the ghost with a hit that would allow a quail to escape wounded on foot. Like the scaled quail, a mature cock pheasant can soak up lots of lead without missing a single wing beat, but its larger body size makes it even more difficult to bring down. This holds especially true on a going-away target where the shot has to penetrate a lot of pheasant before reaching its vital area.

Liberated pheasants hunted on commercial preserves look the same as their country cousins that

Because of its extremely light weight of 5-1/2 pounds, the 20-gauge Franchi 48AL used by my hunting pal, Tom Latham, to bag this beautiful bird is ideal for covering lots of ground in pheasant country.

hatch out and grow up in the wilds, and they can be just as tough to kill. But the preserve pheasant that has not been released from its pen for very long usually holds better for a pointing dog, and in doing so allows the hunter to walk in closer before flushing. There are, however, exceptions to those and other rules. I have killed many wild pheasants inside 20 yards, but I have also taken a few beyond 30 yards. I have also bagged wild-flushing commercially raised birds that wouldn't allow me or my dog to approach closer than 35 or 40 yards. But if I had to guess, I'd say my average shot on wild birds is somewhere in the neighborhood of 20 to 30 long paces, while most of the preserve birds I kill bite the dust no farther away than 15 to 20 yards from the muzzle of my shotgun. The fact that preserve pheasants are usually shot closer to the muzzle of the gun allows a hunter to use one of the lighter loads in the 12 bore or leave it at home and hunt with a shotgun of smaller gauge.

While I am on the subject, some of the long-range shots at pheasant we read about are often the exception rather than the rule. When talking about distances, many hunters tend to think in terms of the longest shot they have ever made rather than the average of all their shots, and this applies to pheasant hunters as much as deer hunters. I too have experienced a few exceptionally long shots, but they certainly were not typical. Once while hunting ringnecks in the sandhills of Nebraska with Jim Casada, I killed a cock bird at so great a distance that our guide insisted on carefully pacing it off. The bird was flying from right to left, much like a low-house shot from station

five in skeet, and it was dead before it hit the ground. I was hunting with my 12-gauge Fox Sterlingworth and made the shot with its right barrel, which is choked Modified. I was also using a factory recipe Remington had just introduced. Called the Express High Velocity Extra Long Range load, it pushed 1-1/4 ounces of No. 4 shot along at 1400 fps. After the three of us paced off the distance from where I shot to where the bird hit the ground, we agreed on 72 yards. Later that very same day, I killed a prairie chicken at 66 yards with the same gun and load. I seldom attempt such long shots, but I knew the gun I was shooting was capable of getting the job done at extreme distances with a good load, and that gave me enough confidence to pull those off. The long shot I made on the pheasant does not change the fact that my average on wild birds is much closer.

There are those who will use no choke other than Full when hunting pheasants, but most of the time most hunters are better off with more open chokes. During the early season, Improved Cylinder is probably as close as we will ever get to ideal for pumps and autoloaders, and if a better combination than Improved Cylinder and Modified ever becomes available for double-barrel guns, I'll be the first to stand in line. Later in the season, when birds have been pushed around by hunters and have a tendency to flush farther from the gun (if they flush at all), Light Modified and Improved Modified is not a bad combination for a side-by-side or over-under. Modified teamed up with Full will also work at long range, although Improved Modified often throws better patterns than Full when a shot size larger than No. 6 is used.

My 12-gauge Fox Sterlingworth is choked 20 points in its right barrel and 41 points in its left (Modified and Extra Full). Both barrels pattern nicely with No. 4 shot. If there is such a thing as a lucky pheasant gun, that old Fox is mine. Even for late-season shooting, its left barrel is choked a bit tighter than it needs to be for some hunters. But I have learned to handle its tight chokes by shooting trap with it from the 27-yard line, where clay targets are usually broken at 45 to 50 yards from the gun. When no one else is shooting from one of the trap fields at our gun club, a friend and I often back off from the trap house even farther than that and see how many targets we can break out at 60 and 70 yards. It is darned good practice for long-range shotgunning in the field.

The most popular shot sizes among pheasant hunters are No. 6 and No. 7-1/2. The latter is OK for most preserve birds, and I have even used 8s with success there as well. However, if all the dope and data on

The over-under shotgun is popular among pheasant hunters but the autoloader exceeds it in popularity because of its ability to soften the recoil of heavy loads.

what it takes to consistently kill pheasants stone dead from all angles and at various distances were fed into a computer, the machine would likely make a terrible noise, belch a great cloud of smoke and choose No. 5 shot with No. 6 in a very close second place. Smaller shot sizes work OK at closer ranges, but they lack the ability to break wing bones and penetrate to the vitals of a bird at longer distances. Later in the season, when shots can be extremely long, I prefer No. 4 shot and it works great so long as enough choke is used to keep pattern density high. One of the two most effective long-range loads I have ever tried in my Fox is Remington's Premier high-velocity loading with 1-1/4 ounces of copper-plated No. 4s at 1400 fps. The other is Federal Premium ammo with 1-1/4 ounces of No. 5s at the same velocity. Those two loads work quite well for me because the barrels of my Fox are choked tightly enough to deliver killing patterns away out yonder with coarse shot.

Before leaving the subject of pellet size, I must mention that the use of nontoxic shot is now required in some areas of the country, regardless of the game being hunted, and this includes pheasants. Steel shot works

fine on ringnecks out to about 30 yards so long as pellet diameter is a couple sizes larger than lead. Those who prefer No. 6 lead shot would go with No. 4 steel, while fans of No. 4 lead shot would opt for No. 2 steel. When using nontoxic shot such as Tungsten-Iron, Tungsten-Matrix and bismuth, the same size shot as lead can be used since all have similar densities. I have used No. 5 bismuth and No. 4 Tungsten-Matrix in both the 16 and 12 gauges and both work as well on pheasant as No. 4 lead.

A friend of mine who eats, sleeps, lives and breathes pheasants, and who believes shotgun evolution began and ended with the introduction of the Model 870 pump gun, has switched to No. 7-1/2 Hevi-Shot loaded by Remington when hunting in areas where nontoxic shot is required. Since that material is more dense than shot made of other materials, he may not be all wrong. Still, I consider 6s a better choice. Hevi-Shot, Tungsten-Iron, Tungsten-Matrix and bismuth are noticeably superior to steel, and while they are also more expensive, most hunters are not likely to spend a fortune on shells with today's daily game bag limits on pheasant being what they are. Actually, anyone who

The 12 gauge is more popular but a good 20-gauge gun will handle pheasants as far out as they should be shot at by most hunters.

12 Gauge

More pheasants are bagged each year with the 12-gauge shotshell than with all the other gauges combined, and it is easy to see why. While many who choose the 12 do so because of its heavier payload compared to the smaller gauges, there are those who also recognize its tremendous flexibility. Regardless of whether you need a relatively light load for preserve hunting or a heavy load for long-range gunning, the 12 gauge has all the bases covered.

I prefer the smaller gauges for preserve hunting because I enjoy being in the field with trim, quick-

desires to use an older gun built prior to the steel shot days in an area where nontoxic shot must be used on upland game has no choice but to use bismuth, Tungsten-Matrix or other approved material. Now let's take a a brief look at shotshells of various gauges and how they fit into the pheasant hunting scheme of things.

handling guns. On those rare occasions when I do use the 12 there, a light 7/8 ounce or one ounce load that duplicates 28-gauge or 20-gauge field load performance is what I am likely to choose. On the other hand, when hunting long-flushing wild birds, I reach for premium-grade shells with heavier payloads. An excellent combination for a double-barrel gun is 1-1/8 ounces of 5s or 6s in the first barrel and 1-1/4 ounces of 4s in the other barrel for any second shot that might be needed. The single best all-around load for pumps and autoloaders might just be 1-1/4 ounces of 5s exiting the muzzle at 1300 to 1400 fps.

Some of the deadliest 12-gauge handloads I have ever used on pheasants are built around Hodgdon's LONGSHOT powder. A favorite recipe of mine, one I first used on a pheasant hunt in Kansas, consists of the Remington STS case, Winchester 209 primer, 32.0 grains of LONGSHOT, Remington's Figure-8 wad and 1-1/8 ounces of No. 5 or No. 6

magnum shot. Velocity in the 28-inch barrels of my Krieghoff 32 averages just over 1500 fps. Believe me when I say this combination really hammers them from the sky.

16 Gauge

One of the best wingshots I have hunted with is a farmer who lives in a Midwestern state. As far as I know, the only shotgun he has ever used on pheasants is a 16-gauge Lefever with the chokes of its 30-inch barrels opened up to about Improved Cylinder and Improved Modified. A handloader, his favorite ringneck medicine pushes 1-1/8 ounces of No. 6 nickel-plated shot along at just over 1200 fps. Incredibly, long shots I've seen my friend make with his old double have convinced me Sweet Sixteen will do about anything the 12 gauge is capable of doing in the field.

While each new hunting season sees fewer and fewer choices in 16-gauge factory loads, Federal has long offered one of the best for use on late-season pheasants. A member of the Premium family, the 16-gauge loading has 1-1/4 ounces of copper-plated shot nestled in a buffer material. Available with No. 4 and No. 6 shot, muzzle velocity is 1260 fps. I have used this load on pheasants and found it to be quite effective. I have also checked it out at the pattern board, and when fired from a L.C. Smith double with Modified choke, it produced excellent pheasant-killing patterns out to an honest 45 yards.

Because of limited choices in factory ammo, the 16 is an excellent candidate for handloading. Winchester no longer sells its AA16 wad for that purpose, but Remington's SP16 is still available and it is a good one for shot-charge weights ranging from one to 1-1/4 ounces. For 16-gauge load data, see Hodgdon's *Shotshell Data Manual* and the *Shotshell Handbook* from Lyman.

20 Gauge

I use the 20-gauge quite a bit on pheasant hunts, mainly because some of the guns are light enough to carry a long way. I also like the way they handle and feel. An over-under with 3-inch chambers is nice because it offers the option of more variety in loads than a 2-3/4 inch gun. Two of my favorites are 1960s-vintage guns, a Browning Superposed Lightning and a Winchester 101, although the Browning does not like 3-inch loads. A Weatherby Athena with 28-inch barrels is another double I have enjoyed hunting with. My pick in 20-gauge autoloaders is Remington's Model 11-87 with a 28-inch barrel.

As 20-gauge ammo goes, I prefer the premium-grade stuff with buffered shot. When birds are holding tight for the dog and flushing close to the toes of my boots, I like an ounce of 7-1/2s, but at other times I use heavier loads. A tough combination to beat when hunting with a double-barrel shotgun is the 2-3/4-inch shell loaded with an ounce of 7-1/2s in the first barrel, and a 3-inch shell with 1-1/4 ounces of 6s (or 5s if they can be found) for the second shot if needed. Three-inch turkey loads available from Remington and Winchester with 1-1/4 ounces of shot, and from Federal with 1-5/16 ounces of shot, are deadly long-range pheasant medicine when used in a gun that will produce acceptable patterns with them. Unfortunately, all 20-gauge guns will not deliver decent pattern uniformity with 1-1/4 ounces of No. 6 shot. Remington's other turkey load with 1-1/4 ounces of No. 6 Hevi-Shot is another matter entirely, and I have yet to find a gun that did not deliver excellent patterns with it. The chokes I use for late-season hunting with a double are Improved Cylinder (around .010 inch of constriction) in the first barrel and Improved Modified (.018 inch or so) in the other. Plain old Modified is my pick for a pump gun or autoloader. Combine the right load with the right choke, and the 20 gauge will do anything that needs to be done to a pheasant so long as range does not exceed 40 yards.

28 Gauge

The 28 gauge is overlooked by most pheasant hunters, but it has been with me on some of my best early-season hunts. One of my favorites for hunting on commercial preserves is a Parker in 28 gauge. While I actually prefer 28-inch barrels on a side-by-side pheasant gun, this one just happened to have 26-inch tubes when I bought it. Its barrels are choked Quail-1 (.002 inch of constriction) and Quail-2 (.007 inch), so it is by no means a long-range gun. It works just fine out to 25 yards, which is about 5 yards farther than I have killed most of my released birds from coast to coast.

It takes a bit more choke to make the 28 gauge entirely suitable for shooting wild pheasants at longer range. The little AyA double I often use is choked .006 and .018 inch for ratings of Improved Skeet and Improved Modified on the Briley scale. With Winchester's one-ounce loading of 7-1/2s in its right barrel, and the same load with No. 6 shot in its left barrel, I am ready for anything a pheasant can offer out to 35 yards. I have also found the Winchester load to work quite nicely in a Winchester Model 12 with Modified choke, a Franchi 48AL with Modified choke and a Weatherby Athena choked IC and Modified.

Many hunters consider the 28 too small for use on pheasants, and this is true for some conditions, but for shots no more than 35 long paces out, it is capable of grassing birds with the best of them when the right choke and load are used. I and several other writers once hunted wild pheasants in South Dakota as a guest of Browning. They supplied us with plenty of Citori Feather XS shotguns in 12 and 20 gauges, but only one in 28 gauge. Each and ever day saw a couple of us racing to see who would end up with the six-pound gun in 28 gauge. Using Winchester Super-X ammo loaded with an ounce of No. 6 shot, we consistently killed birds stone dead out to 30 yards with that gun. The limit was three birds per day, and over a period of two days, I bagged a pheasant on six consecutive flushes with exactly seven shots. Using the same gun and load, Ron Spomer went six straight dead birds with only six shots.

Several fine 28-gauge pheasant loads are available. For preserve hunting, I have enjoyed excellent performance from the Winchester Super-X, Remington Express and Federal Premium loadings with 3/4 ounce of No. 7-1/2 shot. The Estate and Kent high-velocity loads are also quite good. When hunting wild birds with my AyA double, I use the Winchester 1 ounce load with No. 7-1/2 in the right barrel and No. 6 in the left. Seems like every time I mention the Winchester load in print, some snooty purist reminds me the 28 was designed to use a lighter shot charge. While that may very well be true, the 1 ounce load has consistently outperformed any 3/4 ounce field load in almost every gun I have tried it in. It does generate a bit more recoil than the 3/4 ounce load, although I never notice the difference in the field, even when shooting it in guns as light as 5-1/2 pounds. Considering how popular the 28 has become among hunters, I would not be surprised to see other companies join Winchester in loading a shot charge heavier than 3/4 ounce.

.410 Bore

I thought long and hard before including the .410 bore in a chapter on hunting a bird as big and tough as the pheasant, simply because in the wrong hands it can be a wounder of game, and no true sportsman wants any part of that. But since it along with the 28 gauge are growing in popularity among experienced hunters who go after ringnecks on commercial hunting preserves, I decided to include it but emphasize its limitations. And besides, it is about the only thing I use on preserves anymore, even when hunting pheasants.

The biggest thing the .410 has against it is its light shot charge when compared to the larger gauges. The heaviest shot charge available in factory ammunition weighs only 11/16 ounce, and while any handloader worth his salt can stuff 3/4 ounce of shot into the 3-inch shell, the .410 is still a 25-yard pheasant gun at best. It will kill birds deader than a lamp post farther away than that, but not on a consistent basis. Incidentally, when Winchester introduced its Model 42 pump gun along with the 3-inch version of the .410 in 1933, they loaded it with 3/4 ounce of shot. This is now the standard shot-charge weight of the 28 gauge, and while it contains a few pellets more than are in the more common 11/16 ounce loading of the .410, it still falls short of the bigger bores in payload. Regardless of how much choke the relatively light shot charge is squeezed through, pattern density becomes quite patchy beyond 25 yards when loaded with shot big enough to be used on pheasants.

Hunting pheasants with the .410 might be compared to catching 10-pound bass on a fly rod with a 2-pound leader. To do it right, you've got to absolutely refuse to push your equipment beyond its limitations. The secret to living happily ever after with the little .410 is to combine the heaviest loads available with the right chokes, and refrain from taking a shot at any pheasant once it passes the 25-yard line. Anyone who cannot live by those rules will do everyone (including the game) a big favor by leaving the .410 at home.

Notes on Pheasant Guns

The older I become, the closer I get to coming around full circle in my choice of firearms. One of the first shotguns I hunted with as a youngster was my father's 16-gauge side-by-side double. Passing decades saw me stray from that type of gun, but I am now right back where I started and actually prefer the double for much of the wingshooting I do. I like a double because it gives me an instant choice of two chokes. If a bird flushes close, I use the open choke. If a bird flushes some distance away, I use the tighter choke. I have done it for so many years I can select the left or right barrel without actually thinking about it. It is just like driving a car with a manual transmission. After you have driven it for some time, you are able to change its gears while your mind is on something else. I also prefer two triggers simply because the barrel selectors on most guns are much too slow to use. One exception is the one on the Remington Model 3200; most shooters find it to be as quick to use as two triggers.

I am sure more pheasants fall victim to hunters armed with autoloaders than with any other type of shotgun. This is easy to understand considering the ability of the gas-operated models to soak up part of the recoil from heavy loads. When it comes to that, I have not found anything better than the old Remington Model 1100 or its offspring, the Model 11-87. But

Remington is not the only game in town, as Beretta, Franchi, Browning, Benelli, Winchester and others offer autoloaders of excellent quality. I have shot Benelli guns a great deal and like them a lot.

As slide-actions go, I still see a few hunters toting Winchester Model 12s, but the Remington 870 is America's favorite pheasant gun. I seldom hunt with the pump gun, but when I do, I usually choose a 28-gauge Winchester Model 12 for early-season hunting and then switch to a 12-gauge Remington Model 870 Wingmaster later in the season. An old Winchester Model 42 skeet gun is one of my favorites for preserve hunting. Two other pump guns that presently enjoy some popularity among several pheasant hunters I know are the Browning BPS and the U.S. Repeating Arms Model 1300 Ranger. The Benelli Nova is also becoming quite popular. A number of older pump guns will work as well on pheasants today as they did back then. A friend of mine continues to hunt with a Remington Model 31 trap gun, and anytime he invites me to come along, I use my Winchester Model 97 just to keep him happy.

I have hunted and shot pheasants about every way they are normally hunted and shot. My favorite way is to share all the fun with a good dog. Actually, two dogs is the way to go on wild birds in some areas, a flusher for digging them out of the thick stuff and a good pointer for everything else. On a number of occasions I have shot pheasants put up in the air by driving and blocking, which is a tradition in the Midwest. If you want to try your hand at hitting birds at various ranges and from angles you never thought of, this is for you. Then we have pheasants that for one reason or another are shot as incomers as they fly over tall trees. Once you figure out how many school bus lengths to pull out front before squeezing the trigger, the bird is easy to kill because its wings, head, breast and other vital areas are exposed to a swarm of pellets that don't have to penetrate as much pheasant before getting to where he lives.

I am sure my Western friends will head my way with buckets of tar and sacks of feathers when they read this, but as much as I love to hunt the ringneck pheasant, I'll have to admit I don't find him as challenging to hit as some hunters claim. While a late-

A lightweight over-under such as this 12-gauge Browning Citori Lightning Feather at about seven pounds is a joy to carry on long treks afield.

season cock wrapped in heavy feathers can be difficult to kill, I find it far easier to hit than some of the other flushing game birds I have hunted, even when shots have to be taken at long range. Old John Ringneck is a big target, and he is usually shot in open country. He flies quite slowly until he manages to build up a full head of steam. Some hunters miss at close range because they become unnerved by the cackle of a flushing rooster and rush the shot. Other hunters concentrate on those long tail feathers and shoot at where a bird was rather than where it is about to be. Then we have hunters who find connecting with late-season birds all but impossible, simply because they never practice long-range shotgunning. Concentrating on the bird's head and taking more time for the first shot on a close flush will take care of the first problem. Shooting the game of trap is the best practice I know of for learning how to bump off pheasants at long range.

CHAPTER 10

Grouse I Have Known and Missed

Hunting ruffed grouse with old friends on an autumn day is one of life's greatest pleasures.

Ruffed Grouse, the Toughest Target

Don't you just hate ruffed grouse? Me too. Most game birds will occasionally allow a shotgunner to pull off a nice shot and in doing so look good in the presence of friends. Not so for Ol' Ruff. I am convinced he was put on this earth for no purpose other than to make me look like a blundering idiot who has never fired a shotgun. Like the time brothers Bud and John Louck and I were hunting on their Upper Peninsula Michigan farm when we spotted a grouse standing flat-footed on the side of the old abandoned logging road we were walking along. The bird calmly stared at us as if it knew it was about to be shot at by someone who hadn't

hit anything flying since President Truman left office. "Shoot that silly grouse," Bud half whispered as I dropped two shells into the chambers of my 28-gauge double. Stepping confidently forward to make the foolish bird fly, I could already see myself being congratulated for making one of those fabulously nice shots we tuck away in our memory and replay over and over in our dreams. I even found myself wishing the fellows standing behind me had a video camera rolling at full speed. As I approached to within about 20 yards, the grouse exploded into the air, not zig-zagging off into the thick stuff as the bird was supposed to do, but flying arrow-straight directly away from me down the exact center of the open trail. If you are a skeet shooter, you know what I mean when I say it was a station seven low-house shot. It was the easiest shot I have ever had on a ruffed grouse, and probably the easiest I will ever get in my entire life, and I missed with both barrels! What makes the experience really special is I did it in front of witnesses who until that very moment had been convinced I was a good shot. Served them right for believing everything I had told them.

Actually, I don't hate ruffed grouse, but I do hate being made a fool by them, and they have refined that to a razor-sharp edge. It's like an ancient old black man who farmed a few acres of bottom ground near the little Southern farm I grew up on once told me about a covey of wild quail that spent a lot of their time in a swamp on his small farm. "Ah just hates to be discombobulated, and nuthin kin discombobulate a soul like dem buhds what live in dat swamp over yanner." Like old Ned and his quail, I hate being discombobulated by ruffed grouse, but I'll have to admit I absolutely love hunting them. And it has very little to do with actually shooting birds since few hunters shoot very many, even in an entire season. Mike Larsen, who has hunted "pa'tridges" much more than I, once told me the following are good rules to keep in mind. For every three grouse you flush, you will see one. For every three grouse you see, you will get a shot at one. For every three grouse you shoot at, you will hit one. Whether or not Mike's birds-flushed-to-birds-bagged ratio holds true for all hunters in all places, I really cannot say, but I can say my average has been only a bit better than that. Actually, hunting ruffed grouse is not about putting a lot of meat on the table. It is about much more than that. It is sharing the woods with a good friend. It is watching a fine dog work. It is being lucky enough to be in country where grouse and woodcock live. When I hunted grouse on Michigan's Upper Peninsula for the first time, the woods were absolutely ablaze with color. It is a sight I will never forget.

As rule, ruffed grouse shooting is a close-range proposition. My friend Nick Sisley, who hunts every single day of the Pennsylvania season each year, once paced off every kill he made in an entire season and came up with an average of 25 yards. But that was from where he stood when he shot, to where he picked up the birds from the ground. Since their momentum surely carried them several yards beyond where they were hit in the air, the actual shooting range was probably a bit closer. William Harnden Foster also kept records on his shots, and came up with an average of 23 yards from where he stood to where he thought each bird was struck in the air. Such close-range shooting calls for a

This Winchester/Parker in 28 gauge does not have a lot of choke. That along with its 5-1/2 pound weight, its short 26-inch barrels and the fact that I sometimes shoot it quite well makes it the best ruffed grouse gun in my battery.

quick-handling gun with little or no choke in its barrel or barrels.

In *New England Grouse Shooting,* Foster broadly describes the ideal grouse gun as one that a certain hunter will find most pleasant to carry to the spot where a grouse is to be shot at. I will add to that by saying the perfect grouse gun is one that fits its owner well enough to allow him to intersect the flight of a grouse with a swarm of shot. It is also light enough to be carried in the ready position with one hand while the other hand stays busy parting brush. Some believe the ideal grouse gun is extremely short of barrel, but I believe that within reason, weight and balance are more important than overall length. To me, any gun that exceeds seven pounds in weight is heavier than I want to carry in grouse country, and the lighter the better to a certain point. Heavy guns have their place on the dove field and

I have taken more ptarmigan with a 28-gauge Browning/Winchester Model 12 pump gun than with any other shotgun. A deluxe grade, this one has a set of Briley screw-in chokes.

in the duck blind, but they are out of place in the grouse woods. Truth of the matter is, I have yet to try a shotgun that proved to be too light for ruffed grouse hunting.

I consider several of my shotguns ideal for hunting old ruff, and of those, only one exceeds six pounds in weight. It is a 16-gauge L.C. Smith double with 26-inch barrels and weighing 6-3/4 pounds. I occasionally force myself to carry the extra weight simply because I shoot that particular gun so well. Three of my favorites are in 28 gauge. The two doubles, a Winchester/Parker and a No. 1 grade AyA, have 26-inch barrels and weigh precisely 5-1/2 pounds each. The other is an autoloader, a Franchi 48AL with a 26-inch barrel and weighing 5-3/4 pounds. Two of my grouse guns are in 20 gauge. The double was made during the 1930s by the English firm of Westley Richards. It weighs 5-1/2 pounds. The other is a Franchi 48AL with a 26-inch barrel. It weighs 2 ounces less than my 28-gauge Franchi. Which am I most likely to hit a grouse with? I have had good days and bad days with all of them, and while this might seem hard to believe, I shoot all of them equally well on one of my better days. Grouse that allow me to get quite close before flushing are probably in greater danger from the

Winchester/Parker double and the two Franchi autoloaders because of their open chokes, but birds that get out apiece before I pull the trigger are as safe from one gun as from any of the others.

My favorite choke is no choke at all, or Cylinder Bore, as it is commonly called. Skeet is also good, but if you go any tighter, then Improved Cylinder, you are overchoked for the bird of the forest. I have never found it necessary to use heavy loads on ruffed grouse. The 28-gauge loaded with either 3/4 ounce or a full ounce of shot will get the job done. The same goes for the 20 gauge loaded with either 7/8 ounce or an ounce of shot. Target loads such as the Federal Gold Medal, Remington Premier STS and Winchester AA are excellent choices. I have taken more birds with No. 8 shot, but if someone told me No. 7-1/2 shot is the best all-around choice, I would not argue with them.

Long Live the Sharptail Grouse

The best part of hunting sharptail grouse is being where they like to be. I have flushed them in other places, but the state of Montana is where my heart is now and will be tomorrow. In much of the country I have hunted there, you can stand over here and see far beyond over there. They call it Big Sky country, and for good reason: On a clear day (and the days are almost always clear in Montana), the sky goes upward and onward forever. The country is too big for anyone who has not seen it to imagine. Think of a place where a day's walk from here probably won't take you all the way over there, and you get the picture. But eight to 10 miles of steady walking each day might put you within shotgun range of a few sharptail grouse. Take it from one who knows for certain: Anytime you are lucky enough for that to happen, you will immediately forget how many steps are between where you are at the moment and where you were when you ate breakfast.

The sharptail grouse has been a part of the Western scene for a very long time, and it has proven time and again capable of surviving its share of hardships. Market hunters once shipped thousands to the Eastern market, but despite heavy hunting pressure, along with drastic land-use changes over much of its territory, this fine game bird goes about its business as usual. The sharpie sometimes shares its territory with sage grouse and prairie chicken, and I have even flushed a few coveys of Hungarian partridge in sage grouse country. While populations of some birds continue to decline, the sharptail seems to hang on, often in great numbers in some areas. Experienced hunters often mistake a flushing sharpie for a prairie chicken, and even though the latter is a bit darker overall, I'll have to admit

A Kimber over-under skeet gun accounted for this brace of sharptail grouse.

I share that problem unless the two birds are quite close. Up close and in the hand, their differences are as plain as day to see; the dark markings on the chicken are bar-shaped, while the sharpie has dark spots. I am sure no small number escape the guns of hunters each year, because the sharptail is often mistaken for a hen pheasant. Tip-offs to remember are a "yuka-yuka" alarm call often made by a disturbed sharpie, white feathers on its underside and a rather short, light-colored tail.

Like most birds, sharptail grouse are found where habitat is favorable. The birds thrive in rolling prairie country covered with grass tall enough to serve as a hiding place but thin enough to allow easy walking. Sharptails seem especially fond of areas broken up by tree-lined streams and brushy windbreaks. They often inhabit abandoned farms and can even be seen gleaning in cultivated fields during their favorite morning and evening dining times. Find where they like to be along with a good supply of food, and you might just locate enough birds to make your day. During summer, the sharpie eats lots of grasshoppers if they are available. Come autumn and winter, they will eat just about anything not nailed to the ground, including cultivated grains such as soybean, milo, wheat, barley, sorghum and sunflower. Also high up on the menu are various naturally growing foods such as juneberry, buffaloberry, blueberry and bearberry. When snow makes those items difficult to find on the menu, the buds of cherry, willow, birch and aspen can get them through hard times.

If nothing else, the sharptail grouse is an unpredictable bird. I have hunted them during the early season when flocks consisted mostly of hens and their young birds, and they held tight to the point of a dog; a shotgun of small gauge got the job done with room to spare. September of 2001 comes to mind. On that hunt, I carried a No. 1 grade AyA side-by-side double in 28 gauge. That particular gun is choked Improved Cylinder and Modified and throws beautiful patterns when fed Remington Express ammo loaded with 3/4 Oz of No. 7-1/2 shot. It also likes Winchester Super X loaded with an ounce of 6s. My hunting buddy, Ryan Busse, used the only gun he has ever used on sharptail, a Winchester Model 23 side-by-side in 20 gauge. I do not recall either of us wishing for more gun during the entire hunt. But the shooting is not always so easy. During another year on a late-season hunt, I used a 1924-vintage Fox Sterlingworth in 12 gauge choked Modified and Full, and not once during that outing would I have swapped it for a small-gauge gun. I have enjoyed some of my best shooting on sharptails with an old field-grade L.C.

Grouse I Have Known and Missed **77**

Brown chocolate bars in its plumage identify this bird as a prairie chicken as opposed to the more spotted appearance of its cousin, the sharptail grouse. A shotgun like my 12-gauge Fox Sterlingworth with its Modified and Extra-Full chokes is an excellent choice for days when these birds have a tendency to flush wild.

prairie chicken is a bit larger than the sharptail, with a mature male tipping the scale at about 2-1/2 pounds. Its cousin, the lesser prairie chicken, runs more the size of the sharptail and will seldom exceed two pounds by more than an ounce or two. A third species called the Attwater is supposed to still exist along the Gulf coast of Texas, but it is on the endangered list. While more numerous than the lesser grouse, the range of the greater species is much smaller than that of the sharptail grouse. The sharpie calls about a dozen states in the United States and three Canadian provinces home, but once you leave the two Dakotas and Nebraska, you are just about out of really good prairie chicken country.

Another difference I see between the two birds is the prairie chicken has a tendency to flush farther away from the gun. Or at least this has been my experience. Later in the season when the juveniles have matured a bit, sharptails will quite often flush wild as well, but I have found chickens to have more of a tendency to do it on opening day of the season. I hunted prairie chickens for the first time in the sandhills of Nebraska. I was using a 12-gauge Fox Sterlingworth and Remington ammunition. I started out with 1-1/8 ounces of No. 7-1/2 shot, and it worked fine out to about 35 yards, but birds kept getting up even farther away. After knocking only a few feathers from a couple of birds, I switched to 1-1/4 ounces of No. 6 shot and could immediately see the difference. Before that hunt was over, I was shooting 1-1/4 ounces of 6s in the right barrel and 1-1/4 ounces of 5s in the left barrel. That combination in my Fox proved to be one of the best I have ever used on wild-flushing chickens.

All hunts I have been on have not required such massive doses of firepower. During other years, I have hunted them with great success with a 28-gauge Browning Citori and a Remington Model 11-87 in 20-gauge. Both proved to be quite effective, since most flushes were well inside 40 yards. Some of the most effective 20-gauge medicine I have used on chickens is the Remington Express High Velocity loading with an ounce of No. 7-1/2 copper-plated shot at 1300 fps. A combination worthy of a try on days when birds are flushing both close and wild is that load in the first barrel of a double and the Remington Premier 3-inch turkey load with 1-1/4 ounces of No. 6 shot in the second barrel. I have found that combo to work especially well in a Weatherby Athena and a Browning Superposed

Smith double in 16 gauge and standard field loads containing 1-1/8 ounces of shot.

Some say hunting pressure is what causes the sharpie to flush wild during the late season, and while I am sure this holds true for some areas, I have hunted them on private property where no one else had been before me, and they still flushed wild. More likely, as the birds mature, they grow a bit wiser and become more street smart from dodging winged and four-legged predators.

You need a good shotgun for hunting sharptail grouse in Montana, one light enough to be carried over hills and through dales, quick-handling enough to get on birds that flush close to the gun, and true enough in shot-charge placement to shoot precisely where you are looking when a bird flushes wild. With that, and a good dog, you have all you need for hunting sharptail grouse.

Prairie Chickens

Most of what can be said of the sharptail grouse can also be said of the prairie chicken. From a great distance, they even look a lot alike, but up close it is easy to see a few differences. The sharptail grouse has a spotted appearance, and the lightly colored feathers on its breast and belly have pointed brown tips. The plumage of the prairie chicken is probably best described as bars of brown chocolate on a light background. The greater

Ptarmigan country.

Lightning. I also enjoy hunting chickens with a 16-gauge L.C. Smith, and have found 1-1/8 ounce loads from Remington, Federal and Winchester adequate most of the time. The Federal Premium Lead load with 1-1/4 ounces of No. 6 shot is an excellent choice for long-range shooting, but it churns up a good bit of recoil in a light gun.

Ptarmigan

I have never traveled to Alaska for the specific purpose of hunting ptarmigan, but I have managed to hunt them during several big-game hunts there. It is not unusual to finish up early when hunting for moose, bear, caribou or other game, and while some hunters prefer to spend the final days of a hunt fishing or catching up on their reading, I prefer to be in the hills after ptarmigan. I shot my first ptarmigan many years ago during a brown bear hunt on the Alaska Peninsula with outfitter Keith Johnson. Each day, as my guide Tom Hundley and I returned from many long hours of glassing the countryside for a bruin big enough to shoot, we would be greeted by toad-like croaks from several dozen birds that had taken up residence around the little 8x8 foot plywood shack we rested in each night. Tired of a steady diet of Spam and beans, I asked Tom about the possibility of harvesting some fresh meat with the Remington 870 he

had standing in the corner of the shack. He said go ahead, but quickly added that while we needed the breasts from four birds for a good meal, he had only three shells. "No problem" I remarked confidently as I headed out the door. Long story short, with Tom watching over my shoulder, I bagged the first two birds we flushed with only one shell and then took one bird each with the remaining two. To this day, Hundley is convinced everything went exactly as I had planned. After filleting the breasts of those birds, Tom pan-fried them in butter, and even today my mouth waters at the thought of so fine a meal.

I've heard it said that as game birds go, ptarmigan are pushovers and no real challenge to an accomplished shotgunner. There are times when this can be more true than not. I have hunted in a few areas where a slingshot would have been plenty of firepower, but just a wee bit of hunting pressure changed that. Even in remote areas, they can get plenty of pressure from native hunters who obviously enjoy eating them as much as I do. During our early-morning hike from the drop-off point on Lake Iliamna to the tent camp, we saw hundreds of birds, and while we were not actually hunting them, every single one flushed long before we were within shotgun range. Ours was the third group to hunt out of that camp, and it

The spruce grouse is seldom as challenging to hit as other members of the grouse family, but if allowed to flush in thick woods it is not exactly a pushover either.

was quite obvious that those before us had pushed the birds around quite hard. If anything, ptarmigan can be quite unpredictable; I have also chased them in country where hunting pressure was absolutely nonexistent, and yet they were as wild as they could possibly be.

I mostly have hunted ptarmigan by the glass-and-stalk method, where you cover lots of country on foot while carefully looking over bits and pieces of the countryside with a good binocular. Once a flock of birds is located, it is best to choose a route that will get you within shotgun range without being spotted. In some areas, slightly rolling terrain or clumps of brush make for an easy stalk, but on a number of occasions, open country with no places to hide has forced me to crawl on hands and knees for the last 50 yards to prevent flushing the birds out of range. After the shooting is over and any dead birds are carefully marked down, the open country will often allow you to make a mental note of where the survivors landed. Doing so has enabled me to stalk within range for additional shooting, although two flushes is about all you are likely to get from the same flock before they become virtually impossible to approach.

As the weights of various grouse go, the ptarmigan is near the bottom of the pecking order. I have yet to actually hang a willow ptarmigan on a scale, but my guess is that it would average about the same as a ruffed grouse at about 1-1/4 pounds. That puts it only slightly heavier than the average spruce grouse, and also a bit heavier than the rock ptarmigan, which probably weighs about a pound. Regardless if which species is hunted, a cannon is not required to bring them down.

My favorite medicine for ptarmigan is the 28 gauge. My AyA double and my Model 12 pump gun absolutely love Winchester's one ounce Super-X load, as does a Remington 1100 I enjoy hunting with. For close-range shooting, the 3/4 ounce loads from Remington and Federal do about as well, but the heavier Winchester load has the edge beyond 25 yards. A great handload for ptarmigan consists of the Winchester AA hull, W209 primer, 13.0 grains of Universal Clays, WAA28 wad, and 3/4 ounce of No. 7-1/2 high-antimony magnum shot.

I also enjoy using the .410 on ptarmigan, mainly because the Winchester Model 42 I own is so easy to pack along and it gets the job done on tight-holding birds. The 3-inch shell loaded with 11/16 ounce of No. 7-1/2 shot by Remington, Winchester and Federal works great out to 25 yards or so, but even better are handloads with high-antimony shot. A load that patterns very nicely in my Model 42 consists of Remington's 3-inch plastic hull and 209P primer, the Winchester WAA41 wad and 16.5

grains of Hodgdon's H110 for a muzzle velocity of 1250 fps with 11/16 ounce of No. 7-1/2 Lawrence magnum shot. An even heavier load that works quite well in an Iver Johnson Skeet-er and Remington 11-48 I occasionally take afield is made up of the Federal plastic hull, Winchester 209 primer, 16.0 grains of H110 and the Winchester WAA41 wad with its shot petals trimmed back enough to make room for 3/4 ounce of 7-1/2s. With a muzzle velocity of 1200 fps, that particular load will hold its own with most 3/4 ounce loadings of the 28 gauge.

The 20-gauge guns I have used most in the Far North are a Winchester 101, a Browning Superposed Lightning and a Remington 1100. All take down into compact packages, and neither adds a lot of weight to my duffel. Any good 7/8 ounce load will usually do, but when the birds flush wild and the wind blows hard, the one-ouncer has an edge, and there are times when the 3-inch shell loaded with 1-1/4 ounces of No. 6 shot is none too much. For the very worst of conditions, even small-bore lovers like me will have to admit that a 12-gauge double with 1-1/4 ounces of No. 6s in the first barrel and 1-1/2 ounces of No. 4s in the second barrel is the right choice. I have used that recipe in a Fox Sterlingworth choked Modified and Full, and it worked to perfection, although Improved Cylinder and Modified is usually a more useful combination. The 12 gauge is an especially good bet in Alaska if waterfowling is also on the agenda, although nontoxic loadings of the smaller gauges work quite well when shooting over decoys.

Sage Grouse

Even in places where there are lots of sage grouse, there are not many sage grouse these days. There are other reasons for this, but the rapid disappearance of sagebrush under the plow is a big factor. With a three-foot wingspan and weighing six pounds and up, the sage is the largest grouse in America and second largest in the world. Only the capercaillie of Europe is larger.

The sage grouse is a most unusual bird. Legend has it that it eats no seeds from weeds or cultivated grain because it has no gizzard for grinding then up for digestion. The sage grouse does have a gizzard of sorts, but it does not have the ability to grind seeds into meal, and for this reason it lives mostly on various forms of vegetation. Dick Keenan, a Wyoming rancher I used to hunt elk, mule deer and antelope with, told me the bird lives on the buds and tips of sagebrush, and cultivated plants such as alfalfa, with a few bugs and grubs occasionally added to spice up the diet. The sage grouse prefers to stay reasonably close to a source of water, but if it has to, it can survive in extremely arid areas where its only moisture comes from the plants it eats. Some of the sage grouse hangouts I have seen seemed quite desolate and inhospitable, with grass too short from overgrazing by domestic cattle. On a number of occasions, the big birds have bordered on following the heath hen to extinction, but somehow it manages to hang on. During the early 1950s, over 46,000 birds were reported taken during six days of hunting in Wyoming and Nevada, but that was during a peak in population cycle the likes of which will probably never be seen again. These days, I doubt if one-fourth that many birds are taken each year.

Of the grouse I have hunted, the sage has to be the easiest to hit. It is big and it flies slowly when compared to most other flushing birds. But its size can make it difficult to kill with a hit around its fringes. I enjoy hunting sage grouse because I love to walk the country they call home, but I don't enjoy killing a great many of them. One or two during several days of hunting the more abundant sharptail grouse or Hungarian partridge is enough to make me return home a happy man. A friend of mine takes several sages each year with a 28-gauge Beretta over-under and No. 6 shot. Because of the size of the target, I believe No. 4 shot is a better choice, and No. 2 is none too big if shots are taken much beyond 30 yards. I love the 28 gauge, but I believe a gun in 20, 16 or 12 gauge loaded with 1-1/4 ounces of shot is a much better choice. Improved Cylinder and Modified in a double or Modified in a pump or autoloader are not bad choices, although I have seen times when Improved Cylinder in one barrel of a double and Improved Modified or Full in the other covered more bases. Late in the season, after the birds have been pushed around a lot by other hunters, they have a tendency to flush wild, and a 40-yard shot can be a close one. This is when a 12-gauge double choked Modified and Full, and a load containing anywhere from 1-1/2 to 2 ounces of No. 2 shot, is none too much medicine for our largest grouse.

I used to see quite a few sage grouse while hunting antelope in Wyoming during the 1960s and 1970s, but I never had any desire whatsoever to shoot one. In places, they were so thick, I found stalking an antelope all but impossible. When I changed my mind a few decades later and decided to shoot a few of the big birds, they were never again so cooperative. My first serious attempt took place in Montana. To make sure I was prepared for any and all shots that might be presented, I took along loads for my 16-gauge L.C. Smith containing 1-1/4 ounces of No. 4 shot for its right barrel and the same amount of No. 2 shot in its right barrel. As it turned out, sagebrush was scarce in the area I hunted, and sage grouse were even scarcer.

CHAPTER 11

To Shoot a Silver Bullet

Ronnie Gillis and his Boykin spaniel, Dixie, patiently await a flight of mourning doves in a South Carolina cornfield.

I absolutely love to shoot doves the way generation after generation of hunters have done in the Deep South. It is as much a September social gathering as it is a bird shoot. Some come to those gatherings to remind others of their proficiency with a shotgun. Others are there to show off their new Purdey, their new retriever, their new Chevy Suburban or perhaps even their new wife or husband. I suppose some are there for all the above reasons. But many show up on opening day not to see how many birds they can bring to bag (because they could care less), but to renew old acquaintances, to see how many shells they can shoot without hitting a bird, and to see how much barbeque or Beaufort stew can be eaten before they tip over like bowling pins. Very few genuine Southerners take dove

A 20-gauge autoloader like this Remington Model 11-87 is the ideal shotgun for most dove shooters.

shooting seriously, and to them just being there is as serious as anything should ever get. Call it an autumn tonic, call it a coming-out party after a long, hot summer, but never call it a dove hunt to anyone who was born and raised south of the Mason-Dixon line. In the South, doves are either shot or shot at; hunting them would require far too much effort.

Some states don't allow mourning doves to be shot. This is a real puzzler when you consider that of the 450 to 500 million birds estimated by the U.S. Fish and Wildlife Service to reside in the United States each year, only about 10 percent are taken by hunters. Another 20 percent manage to migrate to South America. Approximately 70 percent die from predation and other natural causes. According to the statistics, about 2.5 million shotgunners spend an average of four days in pursuit of doves each year. A camo-clad dove hunter will never make the front cover of the PETA Gazette or The Tree-Hugger Chronicle, but shotshell manufacturers love each and every one like a rich uncle.

We have long been told that the average dove hunter squeezes the trigger five times for each bird taken home. Based on personal experience along with what I have observed on many dove shoots through the years, I'd say five shells per bird is being a bit too kind to most dove shooters. I remember reading the results of surveys taken among those who shot over public fields prepared by the South Carolina Wildlife Department, and they went a long way toward backing up my opinion. The most recent report

I read revealed that 29 survey participants who shot in one of those fields bagged an average of 7.6 birds each. While doing so they fired 1,700 rounds of ammo for an average of 7.7 shells per bird. The 25 guns who watched and waited around another field fared a bit worse; they grassed 5.2 birds each with just over 1,300 rounds of ammunition for a per bird average of about 10 rounds. Throughout the state, the average was 8.5 bangs per dove. Something to keep in mind when reading such statistics is the fact that dove shooting in the South is more social event than serious hunt, and some shotgunners never touch their shotguns either before or after dove season. Those shooters, along with inexperienced wives and youngsters who join in on the fun, have a serious impact on the number of shells fired per bird.

So how many shotshells are fired at doves in the United States each year? Assuming that hunters actually do take 10 percent of 450 million birds, and assuming that eight shells are fired for each one bagged, we arrive at 360 million yanks on the trigger. That's more than 514 tons of shotshell powder going up in smoke in only a few days. If we also assume that dove hunters pay an average of five bucks for each 25-round box of shells, we're talking serious money to the tune of around 72 million dollars. A pal of mine who works for one of the ammunition companies believes the figure is closer to 100 million dollars each year, and he may very well be correct. Now you know why shotshell manufacturers are in love with dove hunters. Those figures are even more amazing when you consider

A favorite dove gun of veteran shotgunner Tom Latham is this extensively modified Beretta AL391 in 20 gauge. Its stock has been fitted with an adjustable comb and a pneumatic recoil absorber.

that I write this, a dozen states don't allow doves to be shot.

How does the degree of difficulty in a dove field compare with the various clay target sports? Although I have shot worse, I usually break over 90 percent of the targets I shoot at on the skeet field. On a really good day, I might hit two or three more, but according to an annual report published by the National Skeet Shooting Association for 2001, I had a 94 percent average with the 12 gauge, a 95 percent average with the 20 gauge, a 93 percent average with the 28 gauge and a 88 percent average with the 2-1/2 inch .410 during that year. In other words, for every 100 registered targets I shot at, I averaged breaking 94 with the 12-gauge, 95 with the 20 gauge, 93 with the 28 gauge and 88 with the .410. In my best tournament of the year, I shot the 28 gauge in all except the .410 event and had a 96 and two 98s along with a 91 with the .410-bore gun.

I usually average around 95 percent at 16-yard trap, and I often miss about 10 additional birds per 100 when shooting doubles in that game. As for sporting clays, one of the best rounds I have ever enjoyed took place at the

beautiful Willows facility near Tunica, Mississippi. Using a SIG Arms/Rizzini over-under, I shot 86 percent on the green course, which is exceptionally good for me. As a rule, I seldom do better than 75 percent at sporting clays, which is not as bad as it might sound since I never shoot more than a half-dozen rounds each year and I seldom use guns bigger than .410 and 28 gauge.

Most of the time, I am not a bad shot in the field. I can usually hold my own with most other hunters when shooting flushing birds such as quail, pheasants, Hungarian partridge, ruffed grouse, chukar, woodcock and sharptail grouse. Once while hunting perdiz behind a good pointing dog in Uruguay, I went 14 straight birds with a 20-gauge Winchester 101 before missing a single shot. Years later, on another hunt in the same country, I hunted ducks with a 20-gauge Remington Model 11-87 and Remington 3-inch ammo loaded with 1-1/8 ounces of No. 6 Hevi-Shot, and probably averaged no more than two shells per duck on my better days. But when it comes to hitting doves, I will have to admit my usual performance is nothing to brag about. Anytime I can bag a limit of 12 mourning doves with less than 50 shells, I have had a good day in the field.

There occasionally comes a time when everything clicks, and I suddenly become the dove shot I should be rather than the dove shot I am. One of the best shoots I have ever experienced took place down in Old Mexico with J.B. Hodgdon of Hodgdon Powder Co. We flew into Hermosillo and then drove west to Kino Bay, where we stayed in a beautiful villa on the shore of the Gulf of California. When we weren't stuffing ourselves with fresh seafood or ogling at scantily clad senoritas as they strolled along the beach, we were out shooting doves. The fields we hunted were only about a half-hour drive from where we stayed. I was shooting a Krieghoff Model 32 over-under fitted with Briley 20-gauge insert tubes choked Skeet and Improved Cylinder. The shells I used were loaded in Mexico with an ounce of No. 7-1/2 shot. During three days of morning and afternoon shoots, I took a crack at doves as they came, with practically no picking and choosing of shots, and I averaged 2.08 shells per bird. Most were mourning doves, although we did take a couple dozen whitewings, which I find much easier to hit. I was most definitely shooting over my head. Considering how I usually shoot doves, I would have been quite happy averaging twice as many trigger squeezes per bird.

Through the years I have seen a few top-notch dove shooters in action. J.B. Hodgdon is no slouch with a shotgun, and neither are Ronnie Gillis and Jackie Rogers. But when all is said and done, Jerry Tuten ranks among the top five shooters I have ever observed. Jerry is an avid trapshooter, and when not shooting doves with his

A good 28-gauge double will handle most shots on doves out to 35 yards.

Remington Model 3200 trap gun choked Modified and Full, he uses a Remington Model 870 with Modified choke. He also shoots handloads with 1-1/8 ounces of shot, No. 8 during the early season and No. 7-1/2 later on. Regardless of which gun he has in his hands, any dove that flies within 50 yards of his stand is likely to join its ancestors in that big sunflower field in the sky. One year, while shooting next door to Jerry on a small field near Woodruff, South Carolina, I watched him raise his gun and shoot at a dove as it flew behind him and across an open pasture. I had passed up the bird when it flew by my stand, and by the time it got to him it was even farther away. I could hardly believe my eyes when the dove tumbled from the sky at his shot. I just had to see for myself how long the shot was, so while he was walking out to retrieve the bird, I walked over to his stand with my laser rangefinder. From where I stood next to his shooting stool to where the dove hit the ground was 68 yards.

Doves fall victim to various and sundry hunting methods each year. In South Carolina, where I have done most of my shooting, it is customary for hunters to form a ring of guns around a field the birds are known to fly into for a bite to eat. The shoots I enjoy most take place in small fields among a few close friends. A really big dove shoot often involves dozens of shooters and hundreds of acres. If it is a good one, it will be organized with military precision as farm tractors pulling rubber-tired trailers deliver the hunters and their gear to pre-established stands in the field. This is quite nice, since a really serious gunner will have, in addition to his gun, ammo and a dozen or so screw-in chokes, shooting glasses with interchangeable lenses of various colors, electronic ear muffs, a binocular, a laser rangefinder, insect repellant, a folding stool (or chaise lounge), a jug of iced tea (pre-sweetened, please), a cooler loaded with boiled peanuts, bubble gum, Oreo cookies and other snacks, and a portable radio tuned to the Clemson or Carolina football game. If the sun is as intense as it can be during an early-season Southern dove shutzen-fest, a see-through beach umbrella would not be out of fashion. On a top-drawer dove shoot, a couple of youngsters piloting a golf cart will come by your stand every hour on the hour with jugs full of ice water.

After being shot at and missed a time or two, a dove switches to its evasive action mode with a level of aerobatic skill matched by no other game bird I have wasted ammunition on. I really get a kick out of watching a lonely little old dove as it twists, zigs, darts and zags its way through a gauntlet of shooters, each of whom empties his or her gun in vain. The untouched bird then calmly lights on a power line or in a tree as if oblivious to the fact that it has just been missed by enough rounds of ammo to keep the Remington, Federal and Winchester factories running full speed for an entire day.

Doves are taken each year with all the various shotshell sizes. Years ago, during my first dove shoot in Old Mexico, I was being pounded to a pulp by a recoil-operated autoloader loaned to me by someone who obviously was not one of my fans. Another hunter in our group

Skeet is excellent practice for dove shooting.

who somehow managed to sneak a supply of .410 shells into the country noticed my suffering and offered the loan of his Winchester Model 23 double. The pain immediately went away. Since the birds were flying close, I shot just as well with the .410 as I had been shooting with the 12 gauge. I probably shot better! Few things in life are more fun than having a .410 shotgun in my hands on a dove field, although a gun in 28 gauge can be rather enjoyable as well. Resting in the chamber of the first barrel of my 28-bore gun is a Winchester AA, Remington STS or Federal Gold Medal skeet load with 3/4 ounce of No. 8s, while its left barrel will be loaded with a bright red shell with a horse and rider on its outside and an ounce of 7-1/2s inside.

I enjoy shooting doves with the .410 and 28, but anytime feasting on barbequed dove breast after the shoot is over becomes more important than just having fun during the shoot, I unlimber more serious artillery. When they are flying beyond reach of the 28 gauge, I am likely to be shooting one of a pair of Remington 20-gauge autoloaders. One, a Remington Model 1100 LT-20 skeet gun with a 26-inch barrel, was one of my father's favorite quail guns. The other is a Model 11-87 with a 28-inch barrel. The Model 1100 still has its original Skeet choke; the 11-87 came from the factory with Rem Chokes. For serious dove shooting with the 11-87, I often use Modified choke. As for ammo, if 1-1/8 ounces of No. 8 shot handloaded in the 20-gauge shell doesn't reach out far enough, I usually switch to a bigger gun. I don't shoot doves with Hevi-Shot because of its cost, but I did it once just to see what would happen. Using the Remington 3-inch factory load with 1-1/8 ounces of No. 7-1/2 shot at 1300 feet per second, I killed birds deader and farther away than I ever had with lead shot. While shooting in Uruguay, I found the same

load to be extremely effective on pigeons out to a good 50 yards, and one those birds takes more killing than any five doves I have shot.

Sometimes I shoot doves with a Krieghoff 32 with 28-inch barrels. When outfitted with a pair of Briley 20-gauge insert tubes, it weighs exactly nine pounds, and I can shoot it all day long, day after day, with no stress, strain or pain. It is the gun you will usually find me shooting these days when doves literally darken the sky over fields of wheat down Uruguay, Argentina and Old Mexico way.

All great dove shooting does not involve cultivated fields or an army of camouflaged gunners. Some of the best I have ever enjoyed was in south Texas. One afternoon a friend and I backed up against a couple of mesquite trees and had a ball shooting birds with .410 skeet loads as they sailed in low overhead for a drink of water from a cattle tank. He was shooting a beautiful little Parker double, and I was shooting my Winchester Model 42 pump gun. The shooting was as fast and as furious as I have enjoyed in South America, and our limits came much too soon each day. Most of the doves we killed fell no more than 25 yards from where we stood.

I also occasionally shoot doves in areas where the best bet is to walk them up as they feed on seeds from various native plants or grain left behind by a farmer. Shots can be rather long, and it is one of the times when I stick with the 12-gauge shell when gunning for the bird of peace. One of my favorites for long-range dove gunning is an old Fox Sterlingworth with 30-inch barrels choked .020 and .041 inch, about Modified and Extra Full by today's standards. Another favorite for reaching away out yonder is a Remington Model 3200 with 30-inch barrels. At .020 and .040 inch, it is choked about the same as the Fox.

Lighter than either of those is my Model 1100 skeet gun with a 28-inch barrel and Briley screw-in chokes. I only recently started shooting a Remington Model 332, and it also works rather nicely. Regardless of which of the those guns I might choose, I usually use trap loads with 1-1/8 ounces of No. 7-1/2 shot. The Fox shoots its best patterns with Federal's Gold Medal recipe, and with their preferences for Remington's Premier Nitro 27 trap load, the Model 3200 and Model 332 are about as faithful to the home team as shotguns could possibly be. The Model 1100 shoots beautiful patterns with any good trap or skeet load.

Back several shotgunners into a corner, and you are likely to get different opinions on the proper shot size to use on doves. A dove is not difficult to bring down, and while a wounded quail may make plenty of tracks after it hits the ground, a dove prefers to stay put until picked up by a two- or four-legged retriever. A friend of mine uses nothing but open-choked guns and skeet loads with No. 9 shot. I have tried 9s and they worked fine out to 20 yards, but too many birds flew off with feathers missing when I hit them only a bit farther downrange. For shots as far away as 30 to 40 yards, I find No. 8 to be plenty effective. One of the softest-shooting 12-gauge loads I have used on doves is Remingson STS Low Recoil with 1-1/8 ounces of No. 8 shot at 1100 fps. It also patterns beautifully in most guns. Winchester's sporting clays load with 1-1/8 ounces of No. 8s at 1300 fps is also quite effective, but it punishes the shoulder more than the Remington load. While No. 8 shot will get the job done most of the time, the ideal medicine for bringing down high-flying silver bullets is the standard 12-gauge trap load with 1-1/8 ounces of No. 7-1/2s at about 1200 feet per second. Recoil is tolerable in a gas-powered shotgun, and if you can't put the brakes on a dove with such a load, chances of you bringing it down with anything smaller than a 105mm howitzer are none too good.

I know dove shooters who use Full-choked guns and drop birds from incredible heights, but I always average fewer shells per bird when using less choke. If the birds are flying within 30 yards from where I am standing, I prefer Skeet, but no less than 1-1/8 ounces No. 8 shot should be used in order to keep pattern density adequate. When shooting a double in 12, 16 or 20 gauge, I like Skeet in both barrels or Skeet in one barrel and Improved Cylinder in another. When shooting an ounce of 8s in the 20 and 28, I find Improved Cylinder best, while Light Modified is the way to go when using the 28 with 3/4 ounce of shot or the .410 with 11/16 ounce of shot.

A good double-barrel shotgun with two triggers is not a bad choice for dove shooting, because it offers the instant option of an open choke for close-range shooting

Opening day on a dove field with a good 28-gauge double, a generous supply of shells, plenty of iced tea and snacks.

and a slightly tighter choke for longer shots. But as much as I love the double, I will have to admit the gas-operated autoloader is probably a better choice. Most dove shooters burn up lots of ammo in a day, and its lighter recoil makes it easier on the shoulder. If I were starting all over tomorrow and would be buying a gun to be used for nothing but dove shooting, I would take a serious look at a soft-kicking 12-gauge gas-operated autoloader. I might even seriously consider the Remington Model 1100 trap gun. Excellent balance along with a 30-inch barrel makes it one of the best shotguns I have ever used for pass shooting. Once you get all that out-front weight rolling along, the momentum encourages proper follow-through. I have a 12-gauge Remington Model 11-87 with a 28-inch barrel, and I probably average fewer shells per dove with it than with any other gun I own.

I like the 20 gauge, and I absolutely love the 28 and .410, but from a practical point of view, the one-gun dove shooter is better off with the 12 due to its versatility. Loads containing 7/8 ounce of shot will do anything the 20 can do when it is loaded with the same number of pellets, and since 12-gauge guns are usually heavier than those in 20 gauge, they are more comfortable to shoot on a day when the number of shots fired are counted by the box rather than by individual rounds. Move on up to heavier 1-1/8 and 1-1/4 ounce shot charges, and the difference in recoil between 12- and 20-gauge guns becomes even more apparent. Lighter guns in the smaller gauges are great for hunting game birds that require walking for many miles each day. But since most dove shooters carry their shotguns no farther away than they are forced to park their pickup trucks, few ever notice the extra weight of a 12-gauge gun.

CHAPTER 12

Medicine for Those Other Game Birds

Count out six fence posts in front of me, look about six feet above it against the sky and you will see a perdiz that has just taken the shot charge from my 20-gauge Remington 11-87. Close by to my left, a Brittany named Lulu is just beginning her run to retrieve the bird. (Photo courtesy of Nick Sisley)

The small farm I grew up on was loaded with bobwhite quail, so it was only natural for me to become an avid wingshooter at a very early age. There was a time when the various species of quail were my favorite game birds, but that was before I got around to hunting wild Hungarian partridge with a good pointing dog. I now rank the Hun alongside quail on my preference list, but other birds I have hunted have been about as much fun. One is a rather funny-looking little

feathered South American buzz bomb called perdiz. Here, then, are a few of my field notes on other game birds I have known.

Perdiz in Uruguay

Thousands of shotgunners travel to South America each year for its excellent wingshooting. Some go for waterfowl. Others prefer to pound their shoulders to bloody pulps while shooting doves in such numbers as to blacken the sky. As for me, a perky little partridge called perdiz is my favorite South American game bird. About the size of an overweight bobwhite quail, perdiz colorado is one of 45 different species of tinamous, a family of birds found in Central and South America. Picture in your mind a bobwhite with a long neck and curved beak, and you have the perdiz. When flushed, its wing beat sounds about the same as a flushing quail. The perdiz holds to the point of a good dog like bobwhite were once known to do, and while it almost always flies straight and low, its speed can make it difficult to hit. This grand little game bird can be up and out of range long before a slow shooter can shoulder his gun. Perhaps the most amazing thing about the perdiz is its ability to hold tight and remain unseen in grass and weeds that seem too short to hide a starving grasshopper.

I have hunted perdiz in Uruguay on several occasions. One of my most enjoyable hunts took place during 2002. I was hunting about 60 miles south of Chuy, a sleepy little village divided almost exactly in half by Brazil on the north side of its main street and Uruguay on the south. Our group was headquartered at the beautiful Fortin de San Miguel, a picturesque hotel with stone walls over a foot thick. The grand old building is tied historically to the Fort of San Miguel, which was built during the 17th century.

We hunted ducks each morning, and then after lunch and a short siesta, we hunted perdiz in the afternoon. My hunting partner was Scott Hanes of Remington, and we both used Model 11-87 autoloaders in 20 gauge. The guns had 28-inch barrels and were choked Improved Cylinder. Our ammo was 2 3/4-inch Remington Express High Velocity loaded with an ounce of No. 7-1/2 copper-plated shot at 1300 fps. We were hunting with a guide named George who spoke four languages. His dog Lulu was absolutely the most wonderful Brittany I have shot over. As is often seen in bird dogs trained in South America, Lulu's point was more of a crouch, and anytime the scent trail became quite hot, she would drop to her belly and crawl forward with her eyes locked in the direction of the bird. In less than three hours we flushed 17 birds, and Scott and I missed only one each. The bird I missed flushed wild as we were crossing a pasture fence with unloaded guns. As far as I know, Scott never came up with a good excuse for the bird he missed.

I have no idea how sociable perdiz become while mating, but I find it rare to catch more than two or three fairly close together during hunting season. Even then, they are likely to be 40 to 50 long steps apart. More often, you'll find single birds only, but there's nothing wrong with that because in a highly populated area it is

This is one of the few perdiz I have taken with something other than 20-gauge guns, a 12-gauge Remington Model 332 in this case.

not unusual to see the dog go on point every few minutes. Some birds sit tight while others choose to slowly move away from a dog's point, but you seldom have to walk more than 50 to 75 yards before flushing the bird.

On my first trip to Uruguay, I used an old 20-gauge Winchester Model 101. I bought that gun during the 1960s. Except for the time I took a few perdiz with a 12-gauge Remington Model 332, I have used only 20-gauge shotguns simply because they just happened be what I had on hand at the time. I have hunted other birds enough with the 28 gauge to know it too would work quite well, as would the 16 gauge. Shells in 20, 28 and 16 gauges are loaded in Argentina and available in Uruguay, and while the ammo is not of the same quality as is loaded in the United States, a good shooter can get by with it. I would love to hunt perdiz with the 3-inch .410, but I have been told that when loaded south of the border, its performance leaves a bit to be desired.

In addition to being great fun to hunt, the perdiz has a breast almost as light in color as the bobwhite quail, and that makes it excellent table fare. If anything, the meat is even better than quail because it is not as dry. Some of the best I have tasted was prepared by outfitter Eduardo Gonzalez, who books hunts in Uruguay through the American firm of Trek. After wrapping the

The Spanish loader is holding red-legged partridges I took with a matched pair of doubles during an exciting and challenging driven shoot.

part of the country for a wingshooting treat any shotgunner would happily trade his spare Purdey for.

There are several things you should know before attempting to shoot red-legged partridge driven to the "Guns" by human beaters. First of all, they are in a great hurry to get from where they are to where they want to be. Just as important to take note of, they tend to fly quite high when pushed off a tall bluff and over the heads of the shooters standing far below. They often dart by at so great an altitude, they appear as mere flyspecks on a ceiling painted with clouds.

As the double-barrel shotguns were being issued to us before the shoot, John Zent and I were a bit puzzled by the absence of guns in 20 gauge. As we later watched several partridges escape over our heads unscathed by the swarms of shot we threw at them, we understood why. If memory serves me correctly, we were shooting shells loaded in Spain with about 1-1/8 ounces of No. 5 shot. Once I finally figured out how far to lead, I started killing birds.

After the morning drives were over, we retired to a canvas shelter set up in the field, and there we sat down to tables covered with fine linen and set with bone china, sterling silver and Waterford crystal. Then we went out and shot some more birds. And we repeated it all for several days. And what grand and glorious days those were.

Woodcock

With a long, pointy bill and eyes set toward the rear of its head, the woodcock is rather unusual to say the least. Some will say I am quite silly for saying this, but the woodcock seems to have more personality than most game birds. Look deeply into those big brown eyes and you may see what I mean.

I enjoy hunting woodcock, but I don't enjoy shooting a large bag of them these days because their numbers have dwindled at an alarming rate in recent years. One or two taken during a week of ruffed grouse hunting satisfies me. Through the years I have bagged a few woodcock in the Deep South, the majority taken incidentally to the bobwhite quail I was hunting at the time. The most woodcock flushes I have experienced packed into the shortest length of time took place much farther north on Michigan's Upper Peninsula. After we had hunted ruffed grouse all day, fate led us to an area that held more woodcock than I had ever seen before. Ron Reiber and I took a couple each and then stopped shooting because a brace is more than enough for any hunter to have.

I have not shot all that many woodcock during my lifetime, mainly because most of the bird hunting I

breasts in a strips of bacon and marinating them with soy sauce, he cooked them over charcoal. The experience was enough to make your taste buds explode!

Red-Legged Partridge, Driven

They still burn a lot of soft coal in Spain, and I was happy when our little car finally left behind the choking blanket of smog hanging over the city of Madrid. We were on our way to the Basque village of Eibar, where most of the double-barrel shotguns made in Spain are turned out by Aguirre y Aranzabal (AyA), Garbi, Grulla, Arrieta, Arrizabalaga and others. After spending a few days there, we were off to the southern

Going after chukar among the cliffs and rockslides of Idaho is the most physically demanding bird hunting I have done.

have done was not in prime woodcock country. During most of the times I have hunted them, I have been in the company of a good pointing dog, and that may be why I do not consider them as difficult to hit as some hunters have claimed them to be. Shooting too quickly is probably the most common mistake made by inexperienced hunters. A woodcock rises quite rapidly when flushed, but if you are too hasty on the trigger, you are likely to miss low before the pattern has time to open up. On the other hand, some hunters hesitate too long and allow the bird to disappear behind a screen of limbs and leaves before they get off a shot. I find the woodcock much easier to hit if I count to three before shouldering my gun and pulling the trigger.

Averaging about the same in weight as four or five 28-gauge shotshells, the woodcock is quite easy to kill with a light charge of small shot. Anytime I set out to hunt nothing but woodcock the shotgun I will be toting will be .410 caliber. My favorite woodcock gun is a six-pound skeet gun built during the 1930s by Iver Johnson and called the Skeet-er. It is choked .006 inch in both barrels. I also enjoy hunting with a 1950s-vintage Winchester Model 42 skeet gun. With the spreader choke screwed into its Cutts Compensator, it has no choke at all. When hunting woodcock with either gun, I mostly stick with 2-1/2 inch skeet loads with half an ounce of No. 8-1/2 or 9 shot, but I have used the 3-inch shell with 11/16 ounce of 8s or 9s, and it works quite well too.

There is certainly no law against choosing bigger firepower for woodcock. A light, quick-handling gun like my 28-gauge Parker is not a bad choice, and when charged with an ounce of No. 7-1/2 shot, it has a performance edge over the .410 in ruffed grouse country. For that matter, a good one ounce load in the 20, 16 or 12 will also get the job done, even though shooting a woodcock with a 12-gauge gun does seem a bit like swatting a housefly with a 20-pound sledge hammer.

Hunting this curious little bird called the woodcock is great fun, but holding a dead one in my hand as the warmth of life fades from its body never fails to make me sad all over. The woodcock always makes me think of wonderful days that have been and never again will be.

Chukar Partridge

Of all the upland shooting I have done, hunting for chukar partridge has been by far the most demanding physically. Nothing else has come even close. I find the

Due to their declining numbers I have no desire to shoot a lot of woodcock each year but to occasionally take a pair or three with my .410-bore Iver Johnson Skeet-er is a wonderful experience I simply cannot resist. I bagged this one on Michigan's upper peninsula.

ruffed grouse to be more difficult to hit, but the chukar is the most difficult to get to. I have hunted chukar when they held tight to the point of a dog and the .410 was plenty of gun, but I have also hunted them when the 12-gauge was none too much. I have never found this import from India to be all that difficult to hit, but the terrain it prefers to call home can make getting close enough for a shot no job for the faint of heart.

I once traveled to Idaho to hunt pheasants, and since I expected most of the hunting to take place over relatively flat farmland, I took boots designed for that type of walking. After hunting ringnecks for a few days, we decided to go after chukar on canyon walls steep enough to cause a mountain goat to wear a parachute. Blisters on my feet eventually caused me to throw in the towel, but not before I killed several birds. The combination I used on that hunt was a Weatherby Orion side-by-side double in .410 and the Federal 3-inch shell loaded with 11/16 ounce of No. 7-1/2 shot.

Another chukar hunt I will never forget took place in north-central Oregon at wonderful place called Highland Hills Ranch. The sheer cliffs and rock slides we had to traverse reminded me more of a hunt for mountain sheep than for a game bird. It was a tough place for dogs to be, and even tougher on the hunters and the guns we carried, but I surely loved being there. I used two guns on that hunt. One was a Weatherby SAS autoloader in 12 gauge. In it, I used a couple of

Remington Express loads, one with 1-1/8 ounces of No. 7-1/2 shot, the other with 1-1/4 ounces of 6s. When my hold was true, both worked quite well. The other gun I used was a 12-gauge double-barrel muzzleloader. I loaded it with 80.0 grains (bulk measured) of Hodgdon Triple-7 and 1-1/8 ounces of high-antimony No. 7-1/2 shot. I found it to be just as effective as the modern autoloader for the first two shots.

Some of the open country in which chukar are often found can mean shooting at 25 yards and beyond, so Modified choke is not a bad choice for an autoloader or pump gun. For double-barrel guns, I like Improved Cylinder and Modified, but when hunting in an area where birds tend to flush both close and wild, I have been known to switch to Improved Cylinder in one barrel and Improved Modified or Full in the other. Where shots will average more than 25 yards, the 28-gauge loaded with 3/4 ounce of shot is a good minimum to stick with. When hunting with a double of that gauge, I usually load its first barrel with 3/4 ounce of No. 7-1/2 shot and its second barrel with an ounce of No. 6s. The 28 gauge is nice, but a 20-gauge double loaded with an ounce of shot has an edge over it in chukar country. It is light enough to carry in steep country and versatile enough to handle most shots to be found there. Standard one-ounce loads will do most of the time, but for really serious hunting, I like high-velocity loads with an ounce of No. 7-1/2s at 1300 fps from Federal and Remington.

Once found only in the Western states, the chukar is now available on many commercial hunting preserves in the East. The little gray import offers a nice break from quail hunting, and it usually costs about a third as much as a pheasant. Anytime chukar are available, I always request that a few be added to a day's quail hunt. Hunting plantation chukar is great fun, but very few of the liberated birds I have shot through the years were as challenging to hit as those taken in the wild. Most of the preserve birds I have hunted were easily bagged with various .410-caliber shotguns and 11/16 ounce of No. 7-1/2 shot. My friend Tom Latham takes most of his with a .410-bore Beretta and 1/2 ounce skeet loads.

Hungarian Partridge

If someone twisted my arm long enough and hard enough, I might eventually confess that the Hungarian partridge is my favorite game bird. I simply cannot think of anything more fun to hunt. Visualize a bird about twice the size of a bobwhite quail, one just as good to eat, one capable of flying about as fast, is just as difficult to hit, is more difficult to kill and sometimes holds quite nicely to a pointing dog, and you have the

Sharptail grouse and Hungarian partridge taken on the same day with a 20-gauge Westley Richards.

Hungarian partridge. Flush as many coveys as I have through the years, and you will likely agree.

They say a son-in-law of Benjamin Franklin released a few Huns on his farm in New Jersey. If this is true, that may have made it the first successful importation of an exotic game bird to America. Many years later, in 1908, a group of sportsmen led by Fred Green released 800 Huns near Calgary, Alberta, and descendents of those birds eventually spread like wildfire throughout western Canada and south into the United States. Ray P. Holland, former editor of *Outdoor Life* magazine, once wrote about flushing 105 coveys of Huns in a single day while hunting in Saskatchewan. That was in 1934. Hunting is not as good today as it was back then, but during some years and in some areas of the country it can be good enough. Shortly before I wrote this chapter, a couple of friends and I flushed 22 coveys of wild Huns in a single day, and if you don't think that was exciting, you are reading the wrong book.

Wild Hungarian partridge are found in huntable numbers if you know where to look, with Idaho, Montana, North and South Dakota, Oregon, California, Washington and Nebraska good places to start. Liberated birds have also become quite popular among those who hunt on commercial preserves throughout the western and midwestern parts of the United States. Unfortunately, the Hun has never migrated to the southern half of our country. I have hunted wild Huns in several states. I have also hunted liberated birds on preserves in a number of places, including South Dakota and California. Since one flies about as well as the other, it is often difficult for me to tell which was raised in a pen and which grew up in the wild. Most liberated quail don't fly nearly as well as

Medicine for Those Other Game Birds

Ounce for ounce, the pigeon is the toughest and most bulletproof game bird I have hunted. This one succumbed to my Krieghoff 32 and the Remington Nitro 27 trap load with 1-1/8 ounces of No. 7-1/2 shot.

their cousins that grow up out in the country, but I do not find this to be true for the Hungarian partridge. When flushed, both the Hun and the bobwhite make plenty of noise, but the Hun makes more of a whistling sound as its wings thrash the air. Listen closely, and you might also hear a few chirps as the birds quickly put distance between you and your gun. The entire covey may fly in the same direction, or they might decide to split up and head in all directions. If you are not quick to stuff in more cartridges, a few stragglers may catch you with an unloaded gun after you emptied it on the early risers.

Most of the Huns I have taken required a bit of walking. I once kept pretty close tabs on how much country I covered during six days of hunting and came up with close to one mile for each bird in the bag. My best average was eight birds in just under five miles, and I took three of them from the same covey flush with a 16-gauge L.C. Smith double. I grassed two birds with my first two shots and then managed to load the right barrel just in time to take a straggler. I have never kept up with the number of shells I average per Hun, but when I am shooting well, it is probably no more than two. Sometimes I have averaged very close to one shell per bird. I would rather not talk about my bad days.

Some of the best-flying liberated birds I have hunted were near Paicines, California, on Rock Springs

Ranch. The magnificent English setter I hunted with went by the name of Iceman, and it was one of the very best dogs I have ever shot over. The Huns Steve McKelvain and I shot at Pintail Point on the eastern shore of Maryland also flew like wild birds, and that, along with an extremely windy day, made them quite sporting. I was shooting far over my head that day, and I am sure the 20-gauge Benelli Legacy I had in my hands had a lot to do with it. The typical preserve bird might have a tendency to hold a bit tighter to the point of a dog, but once it is off and flying, it is usually about as difficult to hit as its country cousin.

Most of us who have hunted birds for many years have on occasion taken two with one shot for a genuine double, but I know of only one person who has pulled off a double-double on Huns. It happened while my friends Allen Rumley and Ryan Busse were hunting together early in the 2002 season. I know it to be true because I was there. As a covey flushed, Allen took two birds with the first shot from his 12-gauge Remington Model 870 and then took two more with his second shot. Once, when I was very lucky, I chalked up a couple of doubles on bobwhite quail during the same season, but never have I ever managed to do it from the same covey rise and on the same day.

One of my favorite shotguns for going after

Huns with a good pointing dog is a No. 1 grade AyA in 28 gauge with two triggers. It has six points of choke in its right barrel and eighteen points in its left. I killed the very first bird I ever shot at with that gun, and it just happened to be a wild Hungarian partridge. I was hunting in Montana with Ryan Busse and immediately upon my arrival, I could tell he was a bit skeptical about my showing up with a shotgun I had never hunted with. Several days and just as many bag limits of Huns and sharptail grouse later, he seemed convinced that my 28 was capable of doing just about anything that could done with his 20-gauge Winchester Model 23. For that matter, the three other hunters in our group were shooting 12-gauge guns, and both Ryan and I managed to hold our own with our small-gauge doubles. I have also taken Huns with a Weatherby Athena in .410 and the 3-inch shell handloaded with 3/4 ounce of high-antimony No. 7-1/2 shot. It too worked rather nicely out to about 30 yards.

When found in more open country, the Hungarian partridge tends to flush far enough away to require the use of guns bigger than the .410 and 28. Some of the best shooting I have ever done took place in Montana. The gun I used was a field-grade L.C. Smith double that once belonged to my father. It weighs 6-3/4 pounds, and its 26-inch barrels are choked Improved Skeet and Improved Modified. I have also used a 20-gauge Westley Richards double. Its 28-inch barrels are choked Skeet and Light Modified on the Briley chart.

Ounce for ounce, the Hungarian partridge can pack as much lead as most other birds I have hunted. It can run like the wind with wounds that would put most other feathered creatures down for the final count. I remember a Hun I shot with my 16-gauge L.C. Smith. When I picked it up, it appeared to be totally lifeless. About half an hour later, I felt a strong flutter of wings against my back, and before I had time to react, the bird suddenly flew from the game pocket of my hunting vest. That was the first time I had to kill the same bird twice! At about a pound, a mature bird is twice as heavy as a bobwhite quail, and even though the chukar is a bit heavier, I do not find it to be as difficult to kill. Out to 20 yards or so No. 8 shot packs enough punch, but for all around use on Hungarian partridge, No. 7-1/2 is a better choice. One of the most effective combinations I have come up with when chasing Huns with my L.C. Smith is an ounce of No. 7-1/2 shot in its first barrel and 1-1/8 ounces of 6s stowed over on the left side. When hunting with a 28-gauge double, I load No. 7-1/2 shot in both barrels, 3/4 ounce in the first barrel and a full ounce held in reserve in the other barrel.

Pigeon

The wild pigeon of South America is the toughest game bird I have ever shot. Called paloma grande, or "big dove" by the Spanish-speaking guides, the birds I have engaged in battle were not, I was told, blue rock pigeons, but they appeared to be the same as the blue rocks I once shot in Old Mexico. Some also looked about the same as the birds you see whitewashing a statue in a city park, but they are much more difficult to kill.

I'll never forget my first south-of-the-border pigeon shoot. About a dozen of us were shooting 12-gauge autoloaders and ammo loaded in Argentina with 1-1/8 ounces of No. 6 shot. Time and again, we would pound a passing bird several times only to see it shake off solid hits with puffs of feathers and eventually disappear over the horizon. And we weren't shooting off tail feathers either. It just so happened that we were on that trip to field test Kent's new nontoxic waterfowl load on ducks and had a good supply on hand. After we switched to No. 5 Tungsten-Matrix shot, doves began to die stone-dead in midair.

The most effective medicine I have ever used on pigeon is Remington's Hevi-Shot. I was hunting in Uruguay with a Remington Model 11-87 in 20 gauge, and after killing ducks at a laser-ranged 50 and 60 yards with 1-1/8 ounces of No. 6 Hevi-Shot in the 3-inch shell, I decided to try it on pigeon. Never had I ever killed those birds as far away with any other gun, gauge or load. I watched as Nick Sisley, who was shooting the same gun and load consistently, dump them at ranges exceeding 50 yards.

The Game Birds of Africa

In my book *Rifles and Cartridges for Large Game*, I devote a chapter to selecting a battery of rifles and cartridges suitable for hunting in various parts of the world. I also mention the importance of either including a shotgun in a battery to be used in Africa, or making sure a shotgun will be at your disposal once you arrive there. I have taken about every big-game animal I ever want to take on the Dark Continent, including lion, leopard and Cape buffalo, but some of my most enjoyable hunting has been for sand grouse, guinea fowl, doves, francolin and other game birds.

During my first hunt in Rhodesia in the 1970s, I shot francolin and doves with an old Greener double. It belonged to Bob Swift, who was my professional hunter. Then and there I decided that any hunt in Africa should include a bit of wingshooting if it is available and if it does not interfere with hunting for big game. I have shot Africa with guns in 28 and .410, but the 12 gauge is a more sensible choice because the ammo is easier to find.

CHAPTER 13

Cottontails and Beagles Have More Fun

As South Carolinian Jackie Rogers will attest, beagles always have more fun than hunters on a cottontail rabbit hunt. His dogs are the small 13-inch variety.

I just tried to think of any type of hunting more fun to do than chasing cottontail rabbits with a pack of beagles, and I failed to come up with a single thing. Actually, anyone who has hunted cottontails knows the rabbits and the beagles have all the fun, and the hunters are merely along for the ride. I grew up on a small farm in South Carolina during the 1950s, when rabbit hunting was at one of its peaks in popularity. While still popular today, it is now a mere ghost of what it was back when about every briar patch and honeysuckle-choked gully in rural America was called home by at least one bunny, and every country kid older than 12 owned his own shotgun. Pesticides and modern farming usually get the blame for the decrease in cottontail population, but I am convinced the uncontrolled growth of predators is having just as big an impact. Back then, we shot every hawk on sight and still had plenty of them, but now they are off limits to the shotgunner. But there are other factors. Too many roads full of too many speeding cars have caused many hunters to hang up their guns after seeing their best dog run over as it attempted to cross one of them. Many places to hunt have also disappeared. Much of the favorite rabbit-hunting country of my youth is now covered with vinyl houses, each of which looks exactly the same. "No Trespassing," "Keep Out" and "Beware of Dog" signs are nailed on every tree and fence post by unfriendly people who have moved into the neighborhood from other states where the people they left behind were equally unfriendly.

A good 20-gauge double like this Fox Sterlingworth is an excellent choice for ending the career of a bunny as it is chased by a pack of beagles.

An avid rabbit hunter, my father always kept at least a half-dozen good beagles, most of which he raised from puppies and trained himself. The beagle may be the easiest breed in the world to train because from the day it is born until the day it dies, it knows it was put on this earth for the sole purpose of chasing rabbits. Dad usually started off a new crop of puppies by allowing them to chase an old domesticated rabbit we had owned for many years. With its gray coloration, it looked like a wild rabbit, and judging by how those little beagles would tear out after him at such an early age, he must have smelled like a rabbit is supposed to smell. Those harmless chases amounted to nothing more than fun and games to Old Buck. After allowing the puppies to follow his hot trail all around our back yard, he would eventually grow bored and end the chase by ducking into the wood pile out beside the barn.

Dad always gave his hunting dogs names like Kate, Belle, Susie, Blackie and Peaches. Every serious rabbit hunter had at least one good "jump" dog. Fearful of no briar patch, it worked slowly enough to sniff out a cottontail from places the other dogs had passed by. Once a rabbit was pushed from its resting place by the jump dog, the others would join in the chase. Dad would never tolerate a cold-trailing dog or one that would follow a trail made by a rabbit several hours before. He also considered any dog that could not be called in from the chase less than fully trained. And a dog that dared chase a fox, a raccoon, a deer or anything other than a rabbit was eventually sold or traded away.

Even though rabbit hunting will never again be what it once was, the fact that several million cottontails are still bagged each year is a good indication of its continued popularity. There are eight different species of the genus Sylvilagus, and they range in size from the six-pound swamp rabbit (or cane-cutter as we kids always called it) to the pygmy, which is the smallest at about a pound. The eastern cottontail, Sylvilagus floridanus, is the most common and the most abundant. It inhabits the southeastern part of the United States and weighs two to three pounds when fully grown. The western part of the country is inhabited by the mountain and desert cottontails, but they, along with the eastern bunny, all look alike to me. They also taste the same. Anyone who heads off into that final big covert in the sky before eating chicken-fried rabbit with cream gravy, steamed rice, homemade strawberry sauce and piping-hot scratch biscuits has not lived a full life.

Many rabbits are taken each year by hunters who kick them from brush piles while hunting alone, but rab-

This 12-gauge muzzleloader is one of my favorite rabbit guns. I load it with 80.0 grains (by volume) of Hodgdon's Triple-7 powder and 1-1/8 ounces of No. 6 shot.

bit hunting is not the real thing without beagles. Just listening to those long-eared, doe-eyed little pooches cry their hearts out during the chase is far more pleasurable than shooting any rabbit. Most serious rabbit hunters can easily recognize the voices of each of their dogs from a distance, even though a half-dozen others might be barking at the same time. "That choppy voice," my father would say, "is old Kate, and do you hear that fine squeal? It's Peaches for sure."

Regardless of how much a rabbit darts and dodges or how far it runs, a good pack of beagles will stay on its trail through thick and thin. Most of the time the bunny does not run all that far, and since it eventually leads its pack of yelping pursuers back to the original starting point in its home territory, the wise hunter finds a good stand, makes himself comfortable and waits. A cottontail rabbit may not be as exciting to look at as a whitetail buck or a bull elk, but few things in life are more fun than standing atop a stump or brush pile with an entire pack of barking beagles headed your way. Suddenly, there he is running across the snow at full speed. You swing your shotgun and pull the trigger — just as the target decides to change directions to avoid the swarm of shot you just threw at it. If your gun is a single-barrel, you are done until the next rabbit is jumped. If you have a second round on tap, you might just be able to get off another shot before that round ball of cotton is swal-

lowed up by a patch of honeysuckle, kudzu or blackberry vines.

One mistake I see made by those who have not done a lot of rabbit hunting is thinking the dogs stay right on the bunny's tail. Our fledgling rabbit slayer keeps his eyes glued on the position of the dogs rather than a good piece in front of them. The rabbit is often quite some distance ahead of the beagles, especially if they are the small 13-inch breed like those owned by my friend Jackie Rogers. I used a muzzleloading shotgun during my most recent hunt with Jackie, and the rabbit I bagged was several minutes in front of the dogs. I had missed a long shot on that same rabbit earlier, but I stood my ground and killed it as it ran along the same trail as before but in the opposite direction.

Hunting rabbits with beagles and bassets has long been popular in America. It is a sport enjoyed by more than farm boys wearing tattered overalls and toting single-barrel shotguns. Back in 1889, The National Beagle Club was formed in the state of Virginia to promote a new "foot-sport" called beagling. The club still exists and is headquartered at Oak Hill, once the home of President James Monroe. James W. Appleton, who was master of the Waldingfield Beagles of Ipswich, Massachusetts, headed up the organization from 1892 until his death in 1942. Each November, a few who own packs of registered beagles are invited to participate in

The 28 gauge works as well on rabbits as it does on quail.

field trials held there. They stay in rustic log cabins and dine in an old building that rests on the site of the first agricultural college in the United States.

Any good shotgun is a good rabbit gun. I enjoy hunting bunnies with a single-barrel because it is what I started with as a kid, but since I enjoy rabbit hunting more than rabbit shooting, any old shotgun will do. If I could have only one, it would be the little .410-bore Winchester Model 42 pump gun sitting in the rack as I write this. Hunting rabbits with a muzzleloading shotgun is also high up on my list of fun things to do. I am sure most of the cottontails taken across the country each year fall victim to 12-gauge shotguns. Team up a 12-gauge gun choked Improved Cylinder with an ounce of No. 7-1/2 shot, and you have all the firepower needed for shots out to about 25 yards. A 12-gauge double choked Improved Cylinder and Modified with an ounce of 7-1/2s in the open barrel and 1-1/4 ounces of 6s in the tight barrel is about as good as it gets in rabbit guns.

From a practical point of view, the 16 gauge is as good on rabbits as the 12 gauge. My father's favorite was a 16-gauge L.C. Smith double with 26-inch barrels choked Skeet and Improved Modified. He was an excellent shotgunner, and I watched him make many spectacular shots not only on rabbits, but on quail and dove as well. For bunnies, he preferred Remington ammo loaded with 1-1/8 ounces of No. 4 shot. He preferred that size shot because it killed a rabbit dead, and not as many pellets were found at the dinner table as when smaller shot was used. I now own his old L.C. Smith, and I try to take it rabbit hunting at least once each year. I load an ounce of No. 6 shot in its right barrel and Federal's 1-1/4 ounce loading of No. 4s in its left barrel.

Back when I was a youngster, the 20 gauge was nowhere near as popular as the 12 and 16 gauges, but quite a few hunters used it. I have carried several 20-gauge guns while hunting cottontails. For quick shooting in tight places, a Remington Model 1100 choked Skeet is tough to beat, but a bit more choke is better for all-around use. Equally effective and considerably lighter is my Franchi 48AL. Its best choke for rabbits has .010 inch of constriction, which puts it close to Improved Cylinder for the 20-gauge. My Winchester Model 101 is choked .008 and .014 inch (about Improved Skeet and Light Modified), and I seldom have a need for more gun. I also enjoy chasing bunnies with a Westley Richards double. Its 28-inch barrels are choked .004 and .014 inch. When hunting with a 20-gauge double, I usually load the first barrel with 7/8 ounce of No. 6s and in the second barrel I carry an ounce of the same size shot.

Cottontails and Beagles Have More Fun **99**

I took these cottontails in Missouri while hunting with Allen Corsine and his pack of beagles. The shotgun is a Browning Gold autoloader.

Only one of Dad's hunting pals used the 28 gauge, and he was always complaining about the difficulty of finding shells. This is no longer a problem since more hunters now use the 28 than ever before, and the owners of many stores that sell shotgun shells keep a good stock on their shelves. Inside 25 yards (which is about where most rabbits are shot), the 28 gauge loaded with an ounce of 6s will do about anything the 2-3/4 inch

20 is capable of doing. Modified is the best all-around choke for a rabbit gun, although Improved Cylinder and Skeet are better when hunting in heavy brush or thickly wooded country where most shots are inside 20 yards.

As a youngster, I never used anything but the .410 on rabbits, and it works as well today as it did back then if the right choke and load are used. The 3-inch shell loaded with 11/16 ounce of No. 7-1/2 shot combined with a Modified choke will take cottontails as far away as they are usually shot in honeysuckle thickets of the South. Modified choke is the best choice in a pump or autoloader, while Improved Cylinder and Modified is an excellent combination for a double. I have a variety of Briley screw-in chokes for my Browning Superposed, and Light Modified in the bottom barrel and Improved Modified up top do an excellent job. I have also taken a few bunnies with a .410-bore Weatherby Athena choked Improved Cylinder and Modified and it too works quite well.

Confessions of a Market Hunter

I made some of my spending money as a kid by trapping cottontails and selling them to one of the grocery stores in Liberty, a little town in South Carolina we lived close to. In looking back, I am sure it was not exactly legal, but folks were so busy trying to scratch out a living, they had no time to be concerned about so trivial a matter as a 12-year-old market hunter. Alfred Smith, who was a meat cutter by trade, owned the store. He paid me 50 cents for any rabbit I bumped off with a shotgun and 75 cents for one caught in one of my homemade traps. A "rabbit gum," as we called it in those days, was a long, narrow box made of weathered wood. You could build one with new wood, but everybody knew a rabbit was too smart to enter it until it had "seasoned" outdoors for a year or more. A section of hollow log worked even better, if one of the right size could be found. The box was closed at one end, and a sliding trap door at the other end was operated by the pull of gravity. When a rabbit entered and attempted to reach the lettuce or other bait at the far end, it would trip a trigger protruding down through the top of the box, causing the trap door to drop behind it like a guillotine. Made of a narrow piece of wood with a notch in one end, the trigger was connected to a wooden link supported by forked stick stuck into the roof of the box and with its opposite end attached to the top of the trap door. I built so many of them back in those days, I could still build one today with my eyes closed.

Alfred Smith was always kidding me about not bringing in enough rabbits to satisfy the demand from his customers. Then one day I fixed him good. Back in those days, members of the Simpson clan would gather in late December for our annual rabbit hunt. It was not unusual for a couple of dozen to participate, each with his own pack of beagles. Most of the time, no more than four of us would hunt together with each group on a different farm. On the hunt I am thinking about, our group consisted of me and my Iver Johnson .410, Dad and his 16-gauge L.C. Smith, Uncle Clifton with his 12-gauge Fox

Sterlingworth and cousin Coy (a spoiled brat who got everything he wanted) and his .410-bore L.C. Smith. How I used to lust after that shotgun!

As two dozen hunters stood before a very large pile of very dead bunnies at the end of the day, it was decided that I should have 54 of them. I do not recall why it was 54 and not 53 or 55, but that's how many I loaded into the trunk of Dad's 1949 Chevrolet coupe. To be caught within five miles of so many defunct bunnies would not be a pleasant thing to experience today, but like I said before, back then people had more important things to worry about. After spending most of the night skinning, gutting and washing 54 rabbits, I had their carcasses iced down in a couple of big tin tubs. Next day I was off to Smith's Groceries & Meats.

Boy, was old Alfred surprised. As I entered the door, I was greeted by his usual "How many rabbits did you bring today, Layne?" When I said 54, he almost fell over his chopping block. That was on Monday morning, and after a bit of serious negotiating Alfred proposed that he would take all of the rabbits but he would rather not have to pay for any not sold by the following Saturday. I agreed on the condition that for each rabbit he did sell, I would receive a 10-cent bonus. (In those days, one thin dime would buy an Orange Crush and four pieces of Double-Bubble gum or an entire Saturday of movies at Albertson's Theatre). At closing time six days later, Alfred had exactly three rabbits left, and he decided to eat those himself. Rich beyond my wildest dreams, I had enough money to buy the used 20-gauge Fox that had long gathered dust in the show window of Wallace Cantrell's hardware store. But dreams and reality did not always intertwine. Part of the money went into a savings account, and some of it bought new clothing for the upcoming school year. I spent what was left on .410 shotshells.

Incidentally, one of my favorite hobbies through the years has been to translate certain words and terms that are popular in the Deep South into plain English for the benefit of the rare Northerner who desires to become a bit more sophisticated. For example, "ros'n ear" translates to roasting ear and means an ear of fresh corn. "Oker" is okra, "arn" is iron, "mater" is tomato, "far aint" is fire ant and "tar" is one of the four round rubber things your car rolls on as it speeds down the road. A "hi-pared raffle" is a high-powered rifle. "Yonnagowimmie?" is a Southerner's way of asking you if you want to go with him. "Y'all come back" is something no true Southerner would ever say to a Yankee. Despite the fact that I can speak Southern with the best of them, I have yet to figure out why many of us who grew up in the rural South call a rabbit trap a rabbit gum.

CHAPTER 14

Big Game with the Shotgun

Mike Larsen took this very nice black bear on Vancouver Island with a 12-gauge shotgun and the Federal saboted slug load. (Photo courtesy of Mike Larsen)

There was a time long ago when a deer hunter who needed more reach from his shotgun than buckshot offered had no choice but to shoot round-ball loads offered by various shotshell manufacturers. Since the ball was solid lead, it had to be made a bit smaller than bore diameter to avoid damage to the choked section of the barrel. For this reason, accuracy even at ranges no farther away than 50 yards sometimes left a great deal to be desired.

In the United States, the first giant step in slug-load technology took place just prior to World War II, when Winchester first offered the rifled slug. Called the Foster-type slug after its designer, Karl Foster, it is hollow through much of its length, like the minie ball used in rifled muskets during the Civil War. During firing, rapidly expanding propellant gas causes the hollow base of the slug to expand outward for a tight fit with the bore of a shotgun, and that makes it much more accurate than the

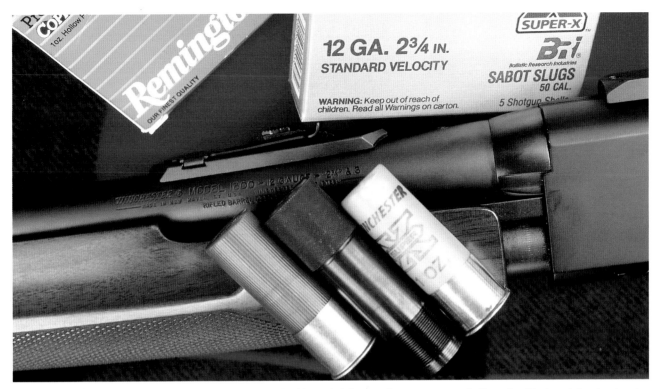

When the modern saboted slug load is fired in a rifled barrel, it is usually more accurate than the Foster-style slug load. Still, some deer hunters continue to believe the old Foster slug drops game more quickly due to its larger diameter.

undersized round ball once loaded by various manufacturers of ammunition. The thin skirt of the slug also enables it to squeeze through tight chokes without damaging the barrel. And since its center of gravity is located considerably forward of its center of mass, the slug is somewhat self-stabilizing in flight, same as is the case of a badminton cock as it flies through the air. This is why the rifled slug does not have to spin around its axis for in-flight stability.

When the right load is matched up with the right choke, accuracy of the Foster-style slug is plenty good for shooting deer-size game out to 100 yards or so. While living in the great state of Kentucky during the late 1960s, I decided to hunt deer in a couple of areas where only shotguns and slugs could be used. The Fort Knox military reservation was one. So I bought an Ithaca Model 37 pump gun called the Deerslayer. It had adjustable sights and a barrel said to be choked specifically for use with slug loads. Its rear sight was grooved for the installation of a long-eye-relief scope made by Redfield in those days. After buying the gun, I rounded up various brands and types of slug loads and headed to the range for a bit of accuracy testing.

A friend of mine had found the German-made Brenneke slug to be the most accurate in his Browning Auto-5 Buck Special, but it shot all over the paper when fired in my Ithaca pump gun. As it turned out, the Winchester slug was the most accurate of all and averaged five inches for five shots at 100 yards. I eventually figured the reason the slug was most accurate, and that was because it was slightly larger in diameter than slugs loaded by other companies. Years later, while working with a Remington Model 1100 with screw-in chokes, I found that gun to shoot best when I chose a choke constriction the same size as or a bit smaller than the diameter of a particular brand of slug. If memory serves me correctly, the Winchester slug shot most accurately with Improved Cylinder choke, the Remington slug shot best in Modified, and since the Federal slug was smallest of all, it was most accurate in a Full choke barrel. When the various brands of slugs were matched up with the correct choke, all delivered about the same level of accuracy at 100 yards. Anyone who decides to hunt with the Foster-type slug load today should keep those accuracy results in mind.

The introduction of the sabot-enclosed slug along with fully rifled shotgun barrels improved accuracy quite a bit, but since the maximum practical range for slug loads of all types is usually inside 150 yards, the saboted slug load is not something we really have to have. Incidentally, the word sabot (pronounced say-bow) is French for wooden shoe. The word sabotage comes from an age when irate factory workers threw their wooden shoes into the machinery as a form of protest. I have shot saboted loads that averaged less than two inches for five-shot groups at

A good slug gun wearing a scope is capable of shooting saboted slugs into groups measuring two inches and less at 100 yards.

100 yards, but I have also shot Foster-type loads that averaged four inches at the same distance. An improvement in accuracy never hurts anything, but considering the size of a deer's vital area, it is obvious that either type of slug will get the job done for anyone who spends enough time accuracy-testing various loads in his gun before the hunt.

The biggest advantage I have found in favor of the various saboted slug loads is this: Most shoot to about the same level of accuracy in a particular gun, while the accuracy of Foster-type loads from various shotshell manufacturers can vary considerably in the sizes of groups they shoot when fired in different guns. I have also found some saboted slug loads to be as accurate out to 50 yards when fired in a smoothbore barrel with a rifled screw-in choke as they are when fired from a fully rifled barrel. Most, however, are a bit more accurate in a fully rifled barrel when the range is extended to 100 yards. The saboted slug load is quite popular, but I remain convinced that when it comes down to which is more effective on deer and black bear, Karl Foster's big, fat slug has the edge simply because it punches a bigger hole through the target. The Buckhammer slug loaded by Remington may be the most effective of all, due to the large diameter of its flat nose.

Practically every shotgun manufacturer offers at least one slug gun, and some even peddle a slug gun on more than one type of action. A look at a few of the

things each type has to offer might make your decision a bit easier.

Whether or not you can be happy with a single-shot deer gun depends a great deal on how confident you are in your ability to place that first shot where it must go. Quite a few years ago, I decided it would be fun to do all of my big-game hunting during several consecutive seasons with nothing but single-shot centerfire rifles. Those were good years, and I ended up taking, among other things, elk, moose, mule deer, pronghorn antelope, whitetail deer, black bear and caribou with various single shots chambered for cartridges ranging in caliber from .243 Winchester to .45-70 Government. Not once during a single hunt did I find myself in need of greater firepower. While I have not gotten around to hunting big game with a single-shot slug gun, I would not hesitate to do so should the opportunity ever decide to knock on my door.

The single-shot has a lot of things going for it, but it also has a few strikes against it. Most important of all to hunters on tight budgets, it represents an economical way to get into deer hunting. As a rule, a single-shooter will cost less than half of what you would pay for a pump gun such as the Remington Model 870, and about one-fifth of the cost of a good autoloader like the Remington Model 11-87. Some single-shots are as light as 5-1/4 pounds, and that makes for easy toting up hills and over dales. A simple design means the gun is either fully loaded or fully unloaded with no in-between mode to confuse a young mind; this always has and always will make the single shot an excellent first gun for a youngster. This holds especially true when it is chambered for the mild-kicking 20-gauge shell. The single-shot can also be incredibly accurate. A T/C Encore with a rifled barrel in 12 gauge is one of the most accurate slug guns I have ever fired. Also high up on the things positive list, when done up right, the single-shot is not a bad-looking firearm.

As for the negatives, the single-shot is slower on follow-up shots than the repeaters, but this is neither here nor there if your aim is true and your hold is steady while squeezing the trigger. While lightness of weight is in its favor for walking, it works against it in actual shooting because light guns kick harder than heavy guns. This is why the 20-gauge chambering is not a bad idea in this type of slug gun.

The bolt-action slug gun sounds like a good idea, and it is. A Browning A-Bolt in my battery is so accurate, I am no longer surprised to see it shoot five of those big, fat saboted bullets into two-inch groups at 100 yards. I have worked with bolt-action rifles that were not as accurate. A Marlin 512P I once spent some time at the range with was not quite as precise in slug placement as the Browning, but it was plenty accurate just the same. Less important then punching out the X-ring, the bolt-action slugger simply looks like a gun you'd take on a deer or bear hunt, whereas slug guns built on other types of actions look more bird gun than deer gun. But, alas, the bolt-action shotgun is an idea America's deer and bear hunters may never entirely warm up to, and the fact that both Marlin and Browning discontinued production of their turn-bolt slug-shooters is most certainly proof of just that.

But all manufacturers of bolt-action slug guns have not given up on the American deer hunter. As I write this in June 2002, Savage still offers its 12-gauge 210F Master built around the famous Model 110 action. Chambered for the 3-inch shell, it has a 24-inch barrel with a rifling twist rate of 1:35 inches. The Savage gun weighs 7-1/2 pounds and holds two 12-gauge cartridges in its magazine. The Mossberg Model 695 Slugster is also still available. It has a 22-inch barrel, is available with a camo finish and comes with fiber optic sights.

If all the dope and data on the ideal slug gun were entered into a computer, the machine would probably spit out the old pump gun as best of the best. For starters, its lightness makes it a pleasure to carry. Pump guns offered by Remington, Browning, USRAC/Winchester, Fabarm, Ithaca and Mossberg weigh from 6-1/2 to 7-1/2 pounds. The Benelli Nova as another great slug gun, although it is heavier than the other pump guns. At prices lower than for

the autoloader and bolt action, the pump is second only to the single shot in affordability. Also right up there at the top in importance, the old corn shucker can hold its own in accuracy with the best of them. And for whatever it might be worth to some hunters, it is second only to the autoloader in firepower. A really good pump-gun man can make second place so close, it seems like a tie in speed between the two. Pump guns can also be totally reliable under terrible conditions, although a well-maintained autoloader fed good ammunition is no slouch in this department either.

I seldom hunt big game with a slide-action slug gun, but when I do I usually reach for an old Remington Model 870 Special Field. It has two barrels, one a smoothbore for shooting Foster-style loads, the other fully rifled for use with saboted slug loads. Sometimes it wears a Burris electronic sight called the SpeedDot. At other times, it wears a Burris 2-7x compact, not because I need so much magnification on a slug gun, but because the little scope weighs less than nine ounces.

More deer hunters carry autoloading slug guns than any other type, and it takes no more than a little common sense to understand why this is true. Since the autoloader is preferred by more American hunters than any other type of shotgun, it stands to reason that this is what they will buy when shopping for a deer gun. Equally important, a gas-operated autoloader tends to soften recoil, and this makes it the most comfortable type of shotgun to shoot with heavy loads. And believe me, some of the more powerful slug loads generate plenty of backward push. I once decided to compare the accuracy of various loads offered by the major ammunition manufacturers in four types of slug guns. I completed my ammunition tests, but long before the project was over, I began to wish I had not included the pump gun, the single shot and the bolt gun in the program. Whereas those three eventually became rather uncomfortable to shoot over a sandbag rest, I could have gone on forever with the Remington Model 11-87 and Browning Gold included in those tests. The Weatherby SAS with its Monte Carlo-style stock is one of the most comfortable slug guns I have ever shot. It is also one of the more accurate.

As a rule, the autoloader is not quite as accurate as the bolt-action, but when we consider the limited range of slug loads along with the size of the vital area of a deer, it stands to reason that accuracy is more than good enough. If the autoloader has anything going against it as deer medicine, it is the fact that some models are a bit heavy. Outfit an eight pound shotgun with a scope, a sling and a magazine full of shells, and its hunting weight will increase to well over nine pounds.

One of the most fun slug gun hunts I have ever

I bagged this Missouri buck at about 60 yards with the Winchester saboted slug and a Browning Gold shotgun. The deer dropped in its tracks but it did require a finishing shot.

been on took place in Missouri. It was actually the last in a series of hunts sponsored by Winchester, during which I started on the Flying B Ranch in Idaho and hunted my way east using the same Browning Gold autoloader and a variety of Winchester ammunition. With that combination, I hunted, among other things, pheasants, chukar, bobwhite quail, Hungarian partridge, mourning doves, waterfowl, cottontail rabbits (with beagles) and white-tailed deer. The deer I took during that huntathon is not the biggest I have ever taken, but it is the best I have taken with a slug gun.

I find it interesting that while quite a few European hunters hunt with various 12-gauge slug loads, many still do not use special slug guns. I recall a hunt I was on for driven boar, stag and bear in the beautiful Transylvania mountains of Romania, during which several German, French and Italian hunters used Benelli shotguns with no sights, and yet several managed to take game with them. Most of the shooting was inside 100 yards. Slug guns intended for the American market come with open sights, and while younger hunters who grew up with telescopic sights might find this hard to believe, they are precise enough for shooting deer out to as far as those animals are normally taken with that type of firearm. Open sights are by no means perfect, and other types of sights are better for shooting when ambient light conditions are not the best, but you can get by with them if you have to. I know this to be true because I did just that during my innocent youth. In fact, if your eyes are up to the task, the middle and front beads on a standard shotgun barrel can be aligned precisely enough for accurate shooting out to 100 yards or so.

Even better than open sights on a slug gun is the receiver-mounted aperture sight, something seldom seen these days on rifles owned by anyone who has yet to celebrate his 50th birthday. This type of sight adds almost no weight to the gun, leaves most of the receiver bare for a comfortable one-hand carry and it is easily installed by a gunsmith who knows how to drill and tap the receiver. The old Williams Gunsight Company still offers its excellent Foolproof and 5D sights for several shotguns, including the Browning A-Bolt and BPS, the Remington 1100, 870 and 11-87, the Browning A5 and the Mossberg 800 and 3000. The Lyman 66U will work on Remington pumps and autoloaders as well as other shotguns with receivers of similar shape. Brownells, by the way, is an excellent source for receiver sights.

So how good is the receiver sight? I once checked out the accuracy of a Marlin Model 336 in .30-30 by first shooting five-shot groups with its factory open sights. I then tried the same gun with a Williams Foolproof receiver sight, an electronic sight with red dot and a 4X scope. Regardless of the sighting system the rifle wore, my accuracy was about the same at 100 yards. That changed at longer distances. At 200 yards, five-shot groups fired with open sights measured twice as large as those fired with the other three types sights. The important point to remember here is my accuracy was as good out to 200 yards with the receiver sight as with the electronic sight and the 4X scope. Considering that the limited effective range of most slug guns, it stands to reason that an expensive sighting system is not an absolute necessity.

With that said, I will admit to one advantage offered by the telescopic sight — its ability to transmit light to the eye during early morning and late afternoon, when light conditions are at their worst and game movement is often at its best. Long before it is light enough and long after it is too dark to shoot with iron sights, a good scope will deliver enough light to the eye for the shot, and this can be important when the beginning of legal shooting light is only minutes behind you or the last rays of sunlight are disappearing from the woods in the afternoon. Not a lot of magnification is needed on a slug gun. I lean toward a variable-power scope with 1x or 1.5x at the lower end of its magnification range and no more than 3x to 5x at the top end. A fixed-power scope with anywhere from 2.5x to 5x on tap is also a good choice.

The electronic sight with a dot subtension of three to six inches at 100 yards works quite well on a slug gun. It is lighter than most scopes, does not add a lot of additional bulk to the gun, and it is precise enough for shots as far away as a slug gun should be used on game. On the negative side, some are not as weatherproof as a top-of-the-line scope. Four I have used in rainy weather with no problem whatsoever are the Aimpoint from Springfield Inc., the Bushnell HoloSight, the C-More from C-More Systems and the Burris SpeedDot.

Compared to most centerfire rifles, the slug gun is a short-range tool and should be sighted in accordingly. When using a Foster-style load, I prefer to zero the gun two inches high at 25 yards. That puts the slug approximately three inches above the line of sight at 50 yards, about two inches high at 75 yards and close to dead-on point of aim at 100 yards. Due to the rainbow trajectory of the Foster-style slug, I consider 115 to 120 yards to be its maximum effective range. When zeroing a gun with the faster saboted slug, I first zero the gun dead on at 25 yards and then check out trajectory at longer ranges. When one of the Federal loads with its 325-grain slug at a velocity of 1900 fps is zeroed to point of aim at 25 yards it is about an inch high at 50 and 75 yards, dead on at 100 and only a couple of inches low at 125 yards. The Remington Core-Lokt Ultra with its 385-grain bullet shoots about as flat as the Federal load, and it is the one my Browning A-Bolt prefers.

CHAPTER 15

Hunting with the .410

While hunting pheasant and Hungarian partridge in South Dakota as guests of Browning, another writer and I raced to the barn each morning in our attempts to be first to grab the only .410-bore Citori Ultra XS in the gun rack. On this day I won the race.

While other shotshells are identified by their gauge, the designation .410 comes from the caliber of its barrel, since nominal bore diameter is .410 inch. Technically speaking, our smallest shotshell is .410 caliber and not .410 gauge as is sometimes written and often heard spoken. If the .410 had been named in the same manner as the others, it would be 67 gauge. Original shell lengths were 2 and 2-1/2 inches, but others have been available. The last time I looked, the British firm of Gamebore still offered the 2-inch shell with 5/16 ounce of shot, the 2-1/2 inch shell with 3/8 ounce and a 2-7/8 incher with 9/16 ounce. American manufacturers at first loaded the 2-1/2 inch shell with 3/8 ounce of shot, but increased the charge to 1/2 ounce during the mid-1930s. Today, thou-

sands of rounds of the 1/2 ounce load are fired by American skeet shooters each year.

The 3-inch .410 shotshell is an American invention. Winchester engineers had a scaled-down version of the Model 12 slide-action shotgun called the Model 42 ready for introduction to the shooting world in 1932, but company president John M. Olin decided to delay its introduction until development of a stretched version of the 2-1/2 inch .410 was completed about a year later. Delivery of the first Model 42s took place in May 1933, and before the year was over the little pump gun was dominating the .410 and 28-gauge events in skeet shooting. Early on, Winchester also spent a lot of advertising money promoting the Model 42 shotgun and its equally new 3-

A perfect match of gun and game bird; my .410-caliber Iver Johnson Skeet-er and a woodcock taken with it.

inch chambering for hunting upland game such as quail, rabbits and pheasants.

In America today, the 3-inch shell is commonly loaded with 11/16 ounce of No. 4, 6, 7-1/2 and 8 shot. The 2-1/2 inch shell is available in various skeet and sporting clays loadings with 1/2 ounce of No. 8-1/2 and 9 shot. It is also available in field loadings with the same amount of No. 4, 6 and 7-1/2 shot. You can buy a slug load with a 1/5 ounce Foster-style slug at 1830 feet per second, and while I have seen it used to take game as large as deer, its use should be limited to targets no larger than a coyote and even then only at close range.

The .410 shotshell has long had a couple of strikes against it. For one, many of the shotguns chambered for it have been choked too tightly, and this can make hitting moving targets extremely difficult. Rather than criticizing the guns and suffering the wrath of the advertisers who manufacture them, politically correct authors often place the blame on the shotshell. That same breed of writer also has a tendency to be a bit lazy, so rather than actually giving the .410 a fair shake in the field or at the pattern board, he takes the easy way out by simply repeating what has been written by those who never actually went to the trouble of finding out what makes the little cartridge tick. Those of us who know how to make the .410 work and who accept its limitations continue to spend many pleasant days afield with the little shotshell.

At the age of 12, I received my first shotgun from my father. A .410 bore, it was made by Iver Johnson. Dad knew enough about shotguns to ream out its Full-choked barrel to Improved Cylinder. While he approved of the 2-1/2 inch shell for shooting clay targets thrown across our pasture with a hand trap, he insisted that I use the 3-inch shell for hunting. When introducing the 3-inch .410 in 1933, Winchester loaded it with 3/4 ounce of shot, same as was loaded in the 28 gauge. Remington and Federal later followed suit. As late as the 1970s, all three companies still offered that same charge weight of No. 4, 5, 6, 7-1/2 and 9 shot. In those days ammunition was priced they way it was supposed to be, and the smaller the gun you shot, the less money you needed for a box of shotshells. Three-inch .410 ammo sold for $3.50 per box of 25 while the 2-1/2 inch version was $2.95. This was at a time when a box of 20-gauge field loads cost $3.85, a box of 16s went for $4.05 and a box of 12s would set you back $4.40.

The 3/4 ounce loading of the 3-inch .410 remained standard until about the mid-1970s, when the adoption of the one-piece plastic wad with its integral shotcup necessitated a reduction in charge weight to 11/16 ounce. The new wad took up more space inside the case than the old fiber and felt wads. During the 1930s and for awhile following World War II, many shooters who desired to compete in all four events of skeet got by with three guns by using the 3-inch .410 with its 3/4 ounce shot charge in the 28-gauge event and

Contrary to what is often written by those who know very little about the subject, a shotgun in .410 with open chokes is an excellent first gun for a youngster.

then switching to the 2-1/2 inch shell loaded with 1/2 ounce of shot for the .410 event. In those days skeet ammunition of both lengths was loaded with No. 9 shot.

As a rule, shot string length increases as bore size decreases so long as shot charge weight remains the same. The .410 is a clear winner in this department. When both are loaded with 3/4 ounce of shot, the .410 produces a longer shot string during flight than the 28 gauge. Even so, I am not totally convinced differences in shot string lengths matter all that much in the field. There was a time when the longer shot column of the .410 allowed a greater number of pellets to suffer deformation by scrubbing against the wall of the bore as the charge traveled through the barrel, but the introduction of the one-piece plastic wad with a shotcup that encloses the shot virtually eliminated that problem. I have shot thousands of rounds of 28 and .410 shells in a variety of guns and chokes, and if the difference in pattern quality is enough to give the 28 a big edge over the 3-inch .410 in the field or at the pattern board, I have not been able to detect it so long as high-antimony shot and modern plastic shotcups are loaded in both. Load extremely soft lead pellets in the two, and the 28 gauge will sometimes show an edge in pattern quality, but even then it has no more than a five-yard advantage in effectiveness over the 3-inch .410 in the field.

There was a time when I was puzzled by the ability of various .410 guns to pattern so nicely when the 3-inch shell was handloaded with the same No. 7-1/2 shot I used in 12-gauge trap loads. Then it dawned

in me that it was due to the quality of shot I was using. The shot used in handloads by trap shooters and as loaded in target loads such as the Remington STS and Federal Gold Medal has a six percent antimony content, which is higher than in shot loaded by the factory in standard field loads. Trap shooters insist on the harder shot for long-range shooting at 50 yards and beyond, where pattern quality can mean the difference between 100 straight breaks and lost targets. As I explain in the chapter on lead shot, the higher the antimony content of shot up to a certain point, the less damage it suffers during its violent trip through a shotgun barrel, and it is not at all unusual to see pattern quality improve as pellet deformation is decreased. Using extremely hard shot in the 3-inch .410 is the key to top performance.

Some say giving a .410 to a youngster as a first gun is a mistake, but it did not prove so for me. During my youth I averaged about the same number of shells per quail, dove or cottontail rabbit with my .410 shotgun as did my father and his hunting cronies who used guns of larger gauges. I find the same to be true today so long as shots are rather close. Given the right load, choke and shot size, I will kill just as many game birds out to 30 yards with the .410 as with any other shotgun, including the 12 gauge. Beyond that distance, patterns delivered by its relatively light shot charge begin to lose adequate density for consistent multiple-pellet strikes. All of what you have just read holds true for the 3-inch shell, but the 2-1/2 incher is another story entirely. The shorter shell is adequate only when the game bird is small and within range of its half-ounce charge of extremely small shot. If the target or range requires the use of shot larger than No. 8-1/2, it is best left at home. The 2-1/2 inch shell simply cannot hold enough of the larger pellets.

With the Scatter choke screwed into the Cutts Compensator of my Winchester Model 42 skeet gun, it shoots beautiful patterns out to about 20 yards with various 2-1/2 inch skeet and sporting clays ammo loaded with 1/2 ounce of No. 8-1/2 and 9 shot. I have used those loads in the Model 42 and in an Iver Johnson Skeet-er for knocking woodcock from the air at close range in thickly wooded terrain. Under those conditions, I doubt if I would shoot any better with any other gun or shotshell. Ron Reiber and I once hunted woodcock on Michigan's upper peninsula at that time of year when the forests were ablaze with color. Also along on that trip were Ken Berger and our gracious hosts Bud and John Loucks. Due to the thick foliage, shooting was close and quick or not at all and, even though Ron is a far better shotgunner than I ever will be, I managed to match him shot for shot and bird for bird. He was shooting a lightweight 28-gauge Beretta, and I was shooting my .410-bore Iver Johnson Skeet-er. Considering how quickly we had to shoot, I am sure neither of us would have fared as well with heavier guns.

I have also used the 2-1/2 inch shell quite a bit for shooting liberated quail when they hold tight to a dog's point and flush close to the gun. Once while hunting bobwhites with Mike Baker on his Sunshine Hunting Preserve, he and my hunting buddy Tom Latham watched as I dropped three consecutive birds from the same covey flush with three shots from my Winchester Model 42. The quail at Sunshine fly better than on most of the other preserves I have hunted, so I was definitely pumping and shooting beyond my natural ability when chalking up that triple. Only a couple of days before I wrote this, Art Wheaton, Jay Bunting, John Trull and I hunted liberated quail at a preserve in North Carolina. On the first day we used .410-bore shotguns and the Remington STS 2-1/2 inch sporting clays load with 1/2 ounce of No. 8-1/2 shot. On the second day, we switched to 28-gauge guns and the Remington STS load with 3/4 ounce of No. 8 shot. Most of the shots were inside 25 yards, and if the 28 gauge was any more effective than the .410 for that type of shooting, you could not have proven it by us.

Under the right conditions and in the hands of someone who can shoot, the 2-1/2 inch shell can work on larger birds as well. Tom Latham and I have been known to shoot a chukar partridge or two at a South Carolina preserve called Riverbend. I remember one January day when it was snowing so hard we could hardly see a bird more than a couple of dozen steps away. Of the 25 chukar we flushed that day, Tom and I killed 24, all with 2-1/2 inch loads. The bird we did not get flushed wild and disappeared behind a curtain of falling snowflakes before either of us could get off a shot. If memory serves, Tom was using his Beretta skeet gun and Federal Gold Medal ammo loaded with 1/2 ounce of No. 9 shot. I was using my Iver Johnson Skeet-er and Remington's STS sporting clays load with the same amount of No. 8-1/2s. Most of the birds we shot that day were dead before they hit the ground. I have seen Tom drop pheasants out to 25 yards with the 2-1/2 inch shell, but he is a very good shot.

I have also taken wild chukar with the .410,

I used a Weatherby over-under in .410 and the three-inch shell to bag my first California quail.

but I used the three-inch shell. I'll never forget hunting those birds in Idaho with Mike Swiebert of Weatherby. We were there to wring out prototypes of the new Athena and Orion side-by-side doubles his company would soon introduce. Aware of my fondness for the .410, Mike made sure I had a shotgun chambered for it during our hunt. After bumping off our limits of pheasant in the lowlands, we hunted chukar on canyon walls steep enough to make a mountain goat dizzy. Despite a great deal of slipping and sliding in boots designed for flat-country walking, I managed to bag a few birds. My best shot of the day came when another hunter flushed a chukar from 40 yards above me and it decided to fly directly over my head. The swarm of 7-1/2s caught the incoming bird much like a high-house shot in skeet from station eight. Its momentum caused it to travel stone dead through the air for another 100 yards or so before hitting the ground farther down the steep mountainside.

I have used various .410 shotguns on many other hunts. Another in the unforgettable category took place at Rock Springs Ranch, which is located near Paicines, California. Brad Ruddell and I hunted pheasants, bobwhite quail and Hungarian partridge, he with a Weatherby Athena in 28 gauge. I was using an Athena three-barrel set in 20, 28 and .410, but I never got around to removing the 20- and 28-gauge barrels from their leather case. Brad and I both shot quite well, and I recall few birds missed by either of us. I especially enjoyed shooting those California Huns as they flew just as well as the same birds I have shot in the wilds of Montana and other places. On that particular hunt, I

Out to 25 yards the three-inch .410 works as well on pheasant as any other shotshell but at longer ranges it is badly outclassed by the larger gauges.

used 3-inch ammo exclusively, Remington Express loaded with 11/16 ounce of No. 7-1/2 shot and Federal Classic loaded with the same amount of No. 8s. Using that same gun, I later bagged the other five species of quail in the United States for my first grand slam on those birds.

I also look forward to an annual outing in which Art Wheaton and Jay Bunting of Remington and I get together to hunt quail. The rules are simple: We have as much fun as the law allows, and only .410 shotguns can be used. We held the first one in 1999 at Little River Plantation in Mt. Carmel, South Carolina. John Edens was our guide. Art hunted with his beautiful little Parker, and I used my Winchester Model 42 skeet gun. Jay did not own a .410 back then, so he used my Iver Johnson Skeet-er. We did not kill every bobwhite we flushed, but we bagged our share and we laughed so often and so hard even the misses were fun. Our most recent annual outing was held at a quaint little place called the Tobacco Stick in North Carolina. On the first day we shot .410s, Art with his Parker, Jay with his Model 870 and me with the Skeet-er. We were really in the groove, and I am sure we averaged fewer than two shells per bird. I even managed to pull off a couple of doubles with my Skeet-er. On the second day we fudged a bit by hunting with 28-gauge guns, not because we needed more firepower than the .410 has to offer, but because we could not resist hunting with some other favorite guns we had brought along. Jay

and Art used their Parkers and I hunted with my AyA until noon. After lunch, I switched to a recent acquisition, a deluxe-grade Franchi 48AL in 28 gauge. What a wonderful time we had.

When hunting wild birds such as chukar, quail and Hungarian partridge or for bagging pheasants on commercial preserves, I prefer the 3-inch .410 over the 2-1/2 inch version. Its greater capacity allows the use of enough shot in the bigger sizes to be effective on larger birds at greater distances. The 1/2 ounce charge of the 2-1/2 inch shell contains approximately 295 No. 9 pellets, 205 No. 8s, 173 No. 7-1/2s and 112 No. 6s. With its 11/16 ounce charge, the 3-inch shell contains 402 No. 9s, 280 No. 8s, 240 No. 7-1/2s and 153 No. 6s. Increase Shot charge weight to 3/4 ounce by handloading the 3-inch shell, and those pellet counts move up to 440, 305, 259 and 167. Because of the relatively low pellet count with larger shot, I have about decided that if the bird I will be hunting is too large or the range will be too long for No. 6 shot, moving on up to a larger gauge is not a bad idea. I am just about convinced that No. 7 -1/2 is the best shot size for all-around hunting with the 3-inch shell.

When hunting pheasants during the early season in areas where shots seldom exceed 25 yards, I almost always use a handload with 3/4 ounce of No. 7-1/2 shot. The Federal 3-inch plastic case has a bit more capacity than the Remington and Winchester hulls, and that makes it the best choice for the slightly heavier shot charge. Even when the Federal hull is used, the shotcup petals of the WAA41 wad have to be shortened a bit with scissors to make room for the additional 1/16 ounce of shot. When both are loaded with relatively soft shot, 3-inch factory ammo will do about anything my handload is capable of, but when the handload contains No. 7-1/2, high-antimony shot, it has as much as a 10-yard advantage in pattern density and uniformity with most guns I have tried it in. I have a lot of confidence in the ability of that load to grass birds at surprisingly long distances. The two guns I most often use it in are a Iver Johnson Skeeter with .006 inch of choke constriction in both of its barrels, and a Weatherby Athena with .006 inch in its bottom barrel and .009 inch up top.

One of the events I look forward to each year is an annual .410-only quail hunt with Jay Bunting (center) and Art Wheaton (right). On this hunt I used my Iver Johnson Skeet-er, Jay used an experimental gun and Art used his Parker.

Today, more shotguns in 28 gauge are sold in the United States each year, but the .410 leads it in shotshell sales simply because far more guns of that bore size have been built through the decades. As American-built .410-bore repeaters go, more Remington Model 1100s and Model 870s are sold each year simply because they rank among the more affordable. The Weatherby over-under in .410 is also quite nice, although like many doubles of the same caliber, it is built on the 20-gauge frame. The Weatherby side-by-side double in .410 is built on the smaller 28-gauge frame. In the used gun market, top-quality .410 doubles by L.C. Smith, Parker, Iver Johnson, Ithaca and Lefever are quite expensive and usually sell for several times as much as those in 20, 16 and 12 gauges. Guns from those makers are especially nice, since their frames are properly scaled down in size for the .410 shell. In autoloaders, I am quite fond of the old Remington Model 11-48 because it is a bit lighter then the Model 1100. I would really like to see Franchi introduce a .410 on its 28-gauge 48AL receiver. The Japanese-built Winchester Model 23 double in .410 is another nice little bird gun of yesteryear, but it too has become quite expensive. My friend Doug Kennemore owns several and seldom uses anything else for hunting quail. Another friend and skeet-shooting pal Ronnie Gillis was in the market for a .410, and upon my recommendation bought a Browning Citori with 30-inch barrels. It has become his favorite gun for shooting plantation quail.

Some of the nicest .410 doubles made today come from various Spanish makers. My No. 1 grade AyA in 28-gauge weighs only 5-1/2 pounds, and it handles like greased lightning. I was tempted to send it back to the factory for the fitting of a set of .410-bore barrels until I was told that doing so would cost about as much as I paid for the gun. Someday I'll probably buy a .410-bore AyA 453 with 28-inch barrels. The Italians also turn out a nice .410 or two each year. The Game Gun from Perazzi with its receiver properly scaled to size is one of the best handling .410s I have ever touched, but it is sinfully expensive. The Rizzini over-under is also made in Italy, and while it is not quite as dynamic in the hands as the Perazzi, it handles nicely enough considering that it costs considerably less.

One of my favorite .410s is a 1950s-vintage Browning Superposed Lightning. It started out as a 20-gauge gun, but I sent it to Briley for the installation of lightweight insert tubes in .410 and 28 gauge. Soon after having the tubes installed, I used the gun on a quail hunt in Florida with Tom Shepherd. I shot it as a .410 but had the birds been flushing wild I would have had the option of switching to 20 gauge by simply removing the tubes. I also like that old Superposed for shooting doves as the additional out-front weight of the Briley tubes makes it swing smoothly on passing shots.

I also enjoy hunting with a Winchester Model 42 pump gun. Mine is the skeet version with ventilated rib and Cutts Compensator. The only two choke tubes I have for it are Spreader and Full, but someday I will get my hands on Improved Cylinder and Modified tubes as well. Without doubt, my all-time favorite .410 is a 1930s vintage double built by Iver Johnson and called the Skeet-er. If I mentioned how many quail I have killed with that gun, you would not believe me so I won't.

While annual sales figures for the .410 shotshell and guns chambered for it will never come close to matching those of the 20 and 12 gauges, it seems to be rapidly growing in popularity among quail and dove hunters, especially in the Southeast. What the world now needs is a premium-grade loading of the three-inch shell with 11/16 ounce or perhaps even 3/4 ounce of high-antimony shot. Nestling the shot in a buffer material might also be worthwhile. So would the use of the same extremely hard No. 7-1/2 and No. 8 shot we already have available in 12-gauge target loads made for trap shooting.

The .410 has been described as a toy and a wounder of game, but this is true only for those who take shots beyond its effective range. One of the biggest mistakes made by those who first try the .410 is attempting to stretch its reach much beyond 30 yards. Thirty long paces may not sound like much, but you'd be surprised at how many game birds are taken each year at no greater distance. I am reminded of a hunt for sharptail grouse and Hungarian partridge on the vast plains of north-central Montana. My hosts were Ryan Busse and Dwight van Brunt, both of Kimber. Their friend Jim Chilton was also there. Dwight was shooting the Kimber Augusta in 12 gauge, while Ryan had chosen a 20-gauge Winchester Model 23 given to him by his father many years before. Jim had his 12-gauge Browning Citori. I brought along my 28-gauge AyA and a .410-bore Weatherby Athena. Since I had not previously hunted with the AyA, I mostly used it while neglecting the .410. So Jim Chilton decided to give it a try. After taking several sharptails with one shot each with my handload with 3/4 ounce of No. 7-1/2 shot, he was totally addicted. Which came as no surprise to me since it is almost always what happens when someone who knows how to shoot tries the right load in the right gun chambered for the .410 shotshell.

Favorite .410 Handloads

Case: Remington 2-1/2" STS plastic
Primer: Remington 209P
Powder: 2400
Powder Charge: 13.0 grains
Wad: Remington SP410
Shot Charge: 1/2 ounce
Velocity: 1200 fps
Notes: Clay target load

Case: Winchester 2-1/2" AA plastic
Primer: Winchester W209
Powder: Hodgdon Lil' Gun
Powder Charge: 12.2 grains
Wad: Winchester WAA41
Shot Charge: 1/2 ounce
Velocity: 1200 fps
Notes: Clay target load

Case: Remington 3" plastic
Primer: Remington 209P
Powder: Hodgdon H110
Powder Charge: 17.0 grains
Wad: Remington SP410
Shot Charge: 5/8 ounce (bismuth)
Velocity: 1225 fps
Notes: Nontoxic load for upland hunting

Case: Remington 3" Super-X plastic
Primer: Winchester W209
Powder: Winchester 296
Powder Charge: 15.0 grains
Wad: Winchester WAA41
Shot Charge: 11/16 ounce
Velocity: 1200 fps
Notes: Hunting load

Case: Federal 3" plastic
Primer: Winchester W209
Powder: Hodgdon H110
Powder Charge: 16.5 grains
Wad: Winchester WAA41*
Shot Charge: 3/4 ounce
Velocity: 1200 fps
Notes: Hunting load

Case: Remington 3" Express plastic
Primer: Remington 209P
Powder: Winchester 296
Powder Charge: 17.0 grains
Wad: Remington SP410*
Shot Charge: 3/4 ounce
Velocity: 1225 fps
Notes: Hunting load

*Shotcup petals shortened enough to make room for 3/4 oz. shot charge

Taking a limit of scaled quail with the .410 may be the ultimate wingshooter's challenge.

.410-Bore Effective Pattern Diameters
(Four Different Guns)

Choke	Choke Constriction (Inch)	Range (Yards)	Pattern Diameter (Inches)	Effective Pattern Pellet Density
Spreader	.000	15	19	Excessive
Skeet	.006	15	15	Excessive
Improved Cylinder	.009	15	10	Excessive
Light Modified	.011	15	10	Excessive
Full	.028	15	8	Excessive
Spreader	.000	20	23	Excellent
Skeet	.006	20	17	Excessive
Improved Cylinder	.009	20	18	Excessive
Light Modified	.011	20	15	Excessive
Full	.028	20	13	Excessive
Spreader	.000	25	27	Excellent
Skeet	.006	25	23	Excellent
Improved Cylinder	.009	25	20	Excessive
Light Modified	.011	25	22	Excellent
Full	.028	25	20	Excessive
Spreader	.000	30	31	Too thin
Skeet	.006	30	25	Too thin
Improved Cylinder	.009	30	24	Excellent
Light Modified	.011	30	21	Excellent
Full	.028	30	22	Excellent
Skeet	.006	35	30	Too thin
Full	.028	35	24	Too thin

NOTES: "Excellent" indicates adequate density for multiple pellet strikes on birds as small as quail throughout the effective pattern diameter. "Excessive" indicates more pellet strikes than required for clean kills. "Too thin" indicates consistent patchiness with one or more holes in patterns large enough to miss or wound a quail. Winchester Super-X with 11/16 oz. of No. 7-1/2 shot used. Test guns were a Cutts Compensator-equipped Winchester Model 42 with Spreader choke, Iver Johnson Skeet-er with Skeet choke, Weatherby Athena with IC, Light Modifed and Full chokes.

CHAPTER 16

My Love Affair with the 28 Gauge

The No.1 grade AyA double in 28 gauge I used to bag this sharptail grouse handles like it is a part of me. Its 26-inch barrels are choked Improved Cylinder and Modified.

Like many other wonderful ideas in shotguns and shotgunning, the 28-gauge shotshell was born in England sometime during the late 1800s. One of the first gunmakers to chamber guns for it was Greener. It seems that the 28 immigrated to America around 1905, when Parker and Remington began chambering double-barrel shotguns for it. Several shell lengths have been available since the original 2-1/2 inch version loaded with black powder and 5/8 ounce of shot was introduced. It took awhile before American ammunition manufacturers decided how long the shell should be

and how much shot it should throw. As late as the 1930s, Winchester and Peters loaded the 2-7/8 inch shell with 3/4 ounce of chilled shot, while the U.S. Cartridge Co. stuck with a 2-1/2 inch shell with 5/8 ounce of shot in its Climax family of field loads. American manufacturers eventually standardized on the 2-3/4 inch shell with 3/4 ounce of shot, although other loadings have been available. Federal once offered a field load with 7/8 ounce of shot, and Winchester continues to produce its Super-X loading with a full ounce of shot. I have used the Winchester load a great deal,

The flight of a ptarmigan shown just above the horizon in the patch of sky between the two trees at right was terminated by an ounce of No. 7-1/2 shot fired from my 28-gauge Model 12 at the very moment Gary Gracey snapped the photo. As that bird begins to fall I have already pumped a fresh shell into the chamber and am swinging on a second ptarmigan that can be seen flying about three feet to the left of the first one. Look directly to my left and you will see the white-feathered wings of five more birds as they begin to flush from the Alaska tundra. What excitement!

and it effectively squeezes 20-gauge performance from 28-gauge guns. Up until the 1960s, Remington and Winchester also loaded a half-ounce slug, which was only 1/8 ounce lighter than the slug loaded in the 20-gauge shell.

I did not discover what a great little number the 28 gauge is until I started shooting skeet on a regular basis. The 12-gauge Krieghoff 32 over-under I bought for that game came with Purbaugh subgauge tubes in .410, 28 and 20, and it took me no time at all to decide which was more fun to shoot. In addition to finding the 28 to be quite gentle on my shoulder, I found I could break just as many clay targets with it as with the 20 and 12 gauges. I don't shoot many skeet tournaments anymore, but back when I did shoot a few each year, I often shot the 28 not only in its event, but in the 20- and 12-gauge events as well. I also shot the 28 in skeet doubles when about everyone else was shooting the 12 gauge there. I would occasionally try the 12 or the 20, but neither improved my score. Sometimes I would shoot much worse with the 12, most likely due to its heavier recoil.

A number of excellent 28-gauge target loads are available today, all with 3/4 ounce of shot. Those loaded with extremely hard shot are excellent choices for use in the field so long as the birds being hunted are not too large to be taken with the smaller shot sizes. I have used the Remington Premier STS load with No. 9 shot on woodcock and found it to be quite effective. That same load with No. 8 shot is also one of my favorites for quail

and doves. Winchester AA ammo loaded with those same two shot sizes also does an excellent job in the field. I have not hunted with 28-gauge target loads by Federal, Kent and others, but I know of no reason why they would not work quite well on the smaller game birds. Something else the 28-gauge has going for it is a day's supply of shells weighs very little and takes up almost no room in the pocket of a hunting coat.

Some who have written about the 28 through the years would have us believe it possesses some sort of magical properties that allow it to perform better in the field than its modest shot charge would appear to be capable of. When we consider that most skeet shooters break about as many and sometimes even more targets with the 28 as with the larger gauges, it is easy to see why this might appear to be true. I just checked the averages of the top 10 skeet shooters in the world in an annual report published by the National Skeet Shooting Association and found that their overall average for a combined total of over 60,000 registered targets during a 12-month period was .9965 percent for the 12 gauge, .9960 percent for the 20 gauge, .9949 percent for the 28 gauge and .9949 percent for the .410. In other words, each time one of those shooters shot at 100 targets, he or she averaged breaking over 99 percent of them regardless of which shotshell was being used.

But, you say, those guys are like machines and could break about as many targets with their eyes closed. This is more true than not, but even when we move far-

Phyllis is quite fond of 28-gauge guns. They are usually trim and light and their recoil is mild. Many women shoot them better than guns of larger gauges.

ther back in the pack and look closely at average shooters like you and me, the comparisons do not change a great deal. A couple dozen C-class shooters I picked at random from the same NSSA report averaged .9060 percent with the 12 gauge, .9127 with the 20 gauge, .9148 percent with the 28 and .8968 percent with the .410. Like the top guns who shoot thousands upon thousands of targets each year, average guys and gals, many of whom shoot fewer than 1,000 registered targets each year do as well with the 28 as they do with the 20 and the 12.

I know why I shoot clay targets as well and often better with the 28 than with the 12. I also know it has absolutely nothing to do with magic. It has everything to do with recoil and its effect on the human body. Anytime I go to the gun club and shoot no more than a couple of practice rounds of skeet, I will sometimes break a few more targets with the 12. But, when I shoot a four-gun tournament in which 500 targets are shot in two or three days, I always end up with a better score when shooting the 12-, 20- and 28-gauge events with a 28-gauge gun. I also shoot the doubles event as well or better with the 28 gauge. Up to a certain point I shoot the 12 quite well, but

then my mind begins to wander. I lose my concentration. I lift my head when shooting. I think about my score. I commit those and other sins that spell doom for the skeet shooter.

So how does my performance with various gauges on the skeet field compare to what happens when the birds I am shooting wear feathers and make noise when they fly? In skeet, most targets are broken inside 30 yards, and as long as game birds are no farther away than that when I pull the trigger, I shoot 28-gauge guns just as well in the field as guns chambered for the 20, 16 and 12 gauges. Regardless of whether I am hunting a bird as large as ringneck pheasant or as small as a woodcock, I will average no more shots per bird with the 28 than I will with a larger gauge. On hunts where the days and miles are especially long and tiring, I often shoot better with the 28 because most of the guns I own are considerably lighter than those of larger gauges. Increase the range on out to 40 yards and beyond and I am ready and willing to leave the 28 at home and hunt with something bigger. But on hunts where most birds get up within 30 yards of where I am standing, I'll take the 28 gauge every time. I will also end the day less fatigued and with just as many birds in my bag.

The first 28-gauge hunting gun I added to my battery did not start out as a 28-gauge gun. A few years before my father died, he decided that I should own his 1960s vintage Browning Superposed in 20 gauge. After shooting it for several years I sent it to Briley and had lightweight full-length inserts in .410 and 28 gauge installed. A pair of those tubes adds 10 ounces to the gun, much of it up front so they actually improve its handling, especially on passing shots at birds. I have shot the little Browning more as a .410, but the 28-gauge tubes enjoy their share of my attention as well. If I had to pick one gun from my battery for the rest of my dove shooting, it would be the Superposed with its two pairs of Briley tubes.

Another of my favorite 28-gauge shotguns weighs 5-1/2 pounds. A Winchester reproduction of the Parker, it came in a leather case and its 26-inch barrels are choked "Quail-1" and "Quail-2." According to my Brownells gauge, bore diameter of both barrels is .552 inch, and they are constricted .002 and .007 inch. My friends at Briley Manufacturing would describe the choke in the right barrel as a bit lighter than Light Skeet and the left barrel as Improved Skeet. The Parker has a straight grip and a beavertail forearm, a combination I really like on a small-gauge bird gun. Its single trigger was built and installed by the Miller brothers shortly before they sold out to Doug Turnbull. On close-range shots, the little gun seems to have a mind of its own and hits more often than it misses, but increase the distance from muzzle to bird much beyond 25 yards, and patterns delivered by its open chokes become a bit too thin. For quick shots just off its muzzles, it is pure magic. I cannot imagine ever owning a better ruffed grouse gun.

As much as I love the Browning and the Parker, I will have to admit the love of my life in 28-gauge shotguns was built around 1990 by the Spanish firm of AyA. A No. 1 grade sidelock, it has 26-inch barrels at a time when longer barrels are the fashionable thing to be seen afield with, but that doesn't keep me from shooting it as well as any shotgun I have ever owned. Its barrels are choked .006 and .015 inch, about as close as you can get to Improved Cylinder and Modified for the 28 gauge. Weighing a mere 5-1/2 pounds, the little double carries like a fistful of feathers, springs to shoulder like it is a part of me and points as naturally as my finger. The very first bird I killed with it was a Hungarian partridge on the plains of north-central Montana. I dropped the bird stone dead with my first shot at 32 long paces. During that same trip, the gun also worked nicely on early-season sharptails that were polite enough to allow the AyA and me to get within 35 yards or so before taking wing.

When fired in most guns, the Winchester one-ounce 28-gauge load delivers denser patterns at all ranges than 3/4 ounce loads. This is because of its higher pellet count.

Another of my favorite shotguns in 28 gauge is the Browning reproduction of the Winchester Model 12. If your interest is in collecting guns, the original Winchester Model 12 in 28 gauge is the one to buy if you can afford it. If, like me, you buy guns for using, then the Browning reproduction is every bit as good. As often happens to those of us who tend to procrastinate too long, I did not get around to buying one until after Browning's Japanese manufacturer stopped producing them. The price had gone up a bit, but considering how well it is built, it was still a bargain. Made in grades I and V, an engraved receiver with gold-filled pointers and flushing game birds identifies mine as the latter. They say only 3,999 others like mine were built. At 7-1/4 pounds, it is a bit heavy when compared to my other 28-gauge guns, but I have carried the sleek little pump gun in many places, including Alaska, and lived to tell about it. Call it the 28-gauge Winchester Model 12 I once wanted but could not afford to buy.

A Franchi 48AL is another 28-gauge shotgun I would hate to have to give up. I fell in love with it while hunting chukar and Hungarian partridge at Pintail Point, a fabulous hunting resort located on the eastern shore of Maryland. I had never before held the gun in my hands, and yet I bagged 17 birds with 21 shots, six of which were doubles. I had to have that gun! A deluxe-grade gun with fancy, hand-selected wood and highly polished blued steel, it weighs only a couple of ounces over 5-1/2 pounds and fits me perfectly. The Franchi has a 26-inch barrel, and while its manufacturer identifies the screw-in choke I use most often as Improved Cylinder, it is closer to Light Modified with its .013 inch of constriction. I liked the little 48AL so much, I went out and bought another just like it except in 20 gauge.

I shoot skeet and sporting clays with my bird guns for off-season practice, but I use a Krieghoff 32 over-under with 28-inch barrels when shooting the few tournaments I manage to attend each year. A 1950s vintage gun, it still has its original Purbaugh subgauge inserts in 20, 28 and .410. With either set of tubes installed, it weighs 9 pounds. Combine its weight with the mild recoil of the 28-gauge shell and you have a shotgun that can be shot all day long, day after day, with no discomfort whatsoever. I have used the K32 on several high-volume bird shoots in South America, usually with a pair of Briley 20-gauge tubes installed because 20-gauge shells are easier to come by south of the border than 28 gauge. On a hunt in Old Mexico, I also took along a pair of 28-gauge tubes from Briley and a few shells loaded with an ounce of Federal's Tungsten-Polymer shot. Three of us shot my 28-gauge handload against Federal 20-gauge Tungsten-Polymer loads and could tell no difference between the two when shooting teal over decoys.

At 7-1/2 pounds this Browning/Winchester Model 12 is the heaviest 28-gauge shotgun I own. It is also my lucky ptarmigan gun.

I am extremely fond of the 28-gauge shotshell for upland wingshooting, especially when it is chambered in a gun built around an action properly scaled to its size. The ideal weight for a 28-gauge double to be used for shooting flushing birds is 5-1/2 to no more than six pounds. For pass-shooting doves and such, a double weighing around 6-1/2 pounds with just a bit of weight-forward balance is about right for me.

As a rule, pumps and autoloaders weigh a bit more. The Remington Model 870 usually runs around 6-1/2 pounds, and the Model 1100 from the same company will weigh about another half pound. I have a 28-gauge Model 1100, and it weighs two ounces shy of seven pounds on my postal scale. If I had a wife, a daughter or a son who wanted to hunt but was sensitive to recoil, I would buy him or her a 28-gauge Model 1100. It delivers 20-gauge performance from a lighter gun, and when its gas-operated action is combined with the low level of recoil of the 28-gauge shell, you have an extremely comfortable shotgun to shoot. An exception in weight is the Franchi 48AL I mentioned earlier; it weighs only a bit more than 5-1/2 pounds.

As for barrel length, I have shot 28-gauge doubles that were as short as 26 inches and as long as 29 inches. If the gun fits me and if it feels right, I usually shoot it quite well regardless of the length of its barrels. If not, I probably won't shoot it all that well. I like a 26-inch barrel on pumps and autoloaders. Anything shorter makes the gun too whippy, and anything longer spoils its handling qualities.

I could just about fill another book with my adventures with the 28 gauge. For starters, I have taken all six species of quail with a Weatherby Athena chambered for the little cartridge. With that gun, I bagged valley and mountain quail in California, scaled, Mearns and Gambel in Arizona and bobwhite in too many states to mention. I will always remember the mountain quail hunt in the Sierra Nevadas with Bob and Mary Koble. Then there was the glorious week Mike Schwiebert and I spent hunting valley quail. The Arizona hunt with friends Brad Ruddell, Bryan "Murph" Murray and Roxie Kelso for scalies, Mearns and Gamble also ranks up there with the best of them, even though I am still picking out cactus spines, and those three walked my legs down to bloody stumps. But there have been other 28-gauge guns and other 28-gauge hunts. Like the time Ryan Busse and I left our footprints over a big chunk of Montana while hunting sharptail grouse and Hungarian partridge. It was the maiden hunt for my No. 1 grade AyA, and I don't mind saying I shot it well. Then there was the hunt along Lake Illiamna in Alaska, when the caribou forgot to show up. It mattered not one whit to me because I'd rather shoot ptarmigan than hunt caribou any day, which is exactly what I did with my 28-gauge Model 12 pump gun. Like I said, I could fill another book, and maybe I will do just that someday.

A good 28-gauge gun is right at home in Gambel quail country—if you can run fast enough to get a shot.

28-Gauge Effective Pattern Diameters
(Weatherby Athena)

Choke	Choke Constriction (Inch)	Range (Yards)	Effective Pattern Diameter (Inches)	Pellet Density
Skeet	.003	15	22	Excellent
IC	.008	15	18	Excessive
Lt Mod	.015	15	13	Excessive
Mod	.018	15	12	Excessive
Full	.028	15	10	Excessive
Skeet	.003	20	25	Excellent
IC	.008	20	20	Excellent
Lt Mod	.015	20	16	Excessive
Mod	.018	20	13	Excessive
Full	.028	20	11	Excessive
Skeet	.003	25	28	Too Thin
IC	.008	25	25	Excellent
Lt Mod	.015	25	20	Excellent
Mod	.018	25	16	Excessive
Full	.028	25	14	Excessive
Lt Mod	.015	30	25	Excellent
Mod	.018	30	23	Excellent
Full	.028	30	22	Excellent
Lt Mod	.015	35	31	Too Thin
Mod	.018	35	30	Too Thin
Full	.028	35	26	Excellent
Full	.028	40	31	Too Thin

NOTES: "Excellent" means adequate density for multiple pellet strikes on birds as small as quail throughout the effective pattern diameter. Excessive indicates more pellet strikes than required for clean kills. "Too Thin" indicates consisten patchiness with one or more holes in patterns large enough to miss or wound a quail. Remington Express with 3/4 Oz of No. 7-1/2 shot used. Interchangeable, screw-in chokes were furnished by Weatherby and Briley.

FAVORITE 28-GAUGE LOADS

Case: Remington STS
Primer: Remington 209 STS
Powder: Universal Clays
Powder Charge: 13.5 grains
Wad: Remington PT28
Shot Charge: 3/4 ounce
Velocity: 1200 fps
Notes: A favorite for skeet and sporting clays

Case: Winchester AA
Primer: Winchester 209
Powder: Green Dot
Powder Charge: 12.5 grains
Wad: Winchester WAA28
Shot Charge: 3/4 ounce
Velocity: 1200 fps
Notes: A favorite for skeet and sporting clays

Case: Remington STS
Primer: Remington 209 STS
Powder: Herco
Powder Charge: 14.0 grains
Wad: Remington PT28
Shot Charge: 3/4 ounce
Velocity: 1300 fps
Notes: Excellent high-velocity field load

Case: Federal Gold Medal
Primer: Remington 209 STS
Powder: Universal Clays
Powder Charge: 13.5 grains
Wad: Remington PT28
Shot Charge: 3/4 ounce (bismuth)
Velocity: 1200 fps
Notes: Excellent duck load out to 30 yards

Case: Federal Gold Medal
Primer: Remington 209 STS
Powder: HS-7
Powder Charge: 19.0 grains
Wad: Remington PT28
Shot Charge: 7/8 ounce
Velocity: 1200 fps
Notes: Duplicates 20-gauge performance

CHAPTER 17

The Unsinkable 20 Gauge

Any hunter of the uplands who owns an over-under like this Weatherby Athena in 20 gauge is all set for about 99 percent of the shooting he will ever do.

Speaking from a purely practical point of view, the 20 gauge is all the shotshell needed for about 99 percent of the shotgunning 99 percent of shotgunners do. There are few things within the realm of hunting and clay-target shooting that cannot be handled by a gun chambered for the 20 gauge, if the gun fits its owner and he knows how to shoot. Many other shotgunners have the same opinion. The ammunition companies sell about twice as many 20-gauge shells each year as the 16, 28, and 10 gauges and the .410 bore combined. This makes it second in popularity only to the 12 gauge. The British are usually credited with inventing the 20, but it was perfected and popularized in America. One of the first shotguns of American

make to be chambered for it, and most likely one of the reasons for its start in this country, was the Winchester Model 12. Described by Winchester as the "Perfect Repeater" (which it just about was), it was introduced to the market in 12 and 16 gauges in 1912. The 20-gauge Model 12 was first offered with the old 2-1/2 inch chambering in 1913, but its chamber eventually got lengthened for the 2-3/4 inch shell.

Even though Winchester has probably done more than any other company to promote the 20-gauge through the years, Remington may have been first to offer guns chambered for it. As best as I can determine, Remington's first 20-gauge was a single-shot introduced in 1893 and called the Model 1893. The first 20-gauge repeater built by Remington was a sleek little pump gun offered in no other gauge and called the Model 1917. One thing Remington has never done, and this will come as a surprise to many shooters, is offer the 20-gauge chambering in a company-designed, double-barrel shotgun. Beginning back in 1874 with the Model 74 (in 10- and 12-gauge only) and counting through the Model 332 over-under, Remington has introduced 10 different side-by-side and over-under doubles, and not a single one of them has been offered in 20 gauge. My crystal ball says that will eventually change, but I have no intention of holding my breath until it does.

Quite a few guns were chambered for the 2-1/2 inch version of the 20 gauge, and American ammunition companies did not get around to offering the 2-3/4 inch shell until about the mid 1930s. Catalogs published in 1932 by Winchester, Remington, Western and Peters show only the 2-1/2 inch shell available, and it was loaded with either 7/8 ounce or one ounce of shot. Catalogs published by those same companies in 1938 show the 2-1/2 inch shell still available, but by that time it had been joined by its 2-3/4 inch replacement loaded with a full ounce of shot. The longer shell was also available with a 5/8-ounce round ball as well as a new 5/8-ounce rifled slug designed by Karl Foster. The 2-1/2 inch shell was eventually dropped, but its 7/8-ounce shot charge lives on today in the 2-3/4 inch shell.

The performance of the 2-3/4 inch shell received a big boost when the baby magnum version loaded with 1-1/8 ounces of shot was introduced during the 1950s. Other good news came along during the same decade. Beginning in the 1940s, Winchester executives John and Spencer Olin had been shooting ducks on the Mississippi flyway with Model 21s chambered for the 3-inch shell loaded with 1-3/16 ounces of shot, and while the company could have one-upped the competition by introducing it commercially a bit sooner, they chose to wait until 1953 to do so. When the new shell did emerge, its shot charge had been increased to 1-1/4 ounces. That caused lots of excitement because for many years 1-1/4 ounces of shot was considered just the ticket for shooting ducks at long range with a 12-gauge gun. The Winchester Model 21 was the first production gun to be chambered for the new 3-inch shell, and the Browning Superposed was either second or close to it. During the 1950s, the 20 gauge was available with three different shot charges, 7/8, 1 and 1-1/4 ounces, and so it would remain until 2002 when Federal introduced its new turkey load with 1-5/16 ounces of shot.

Today, the 20 gauge is offered in a variety of loadings capable of handling almost anything anyone might want to do with a shotgun. Beginning with skeet

Like many other hunters, Mike Schwiebert considers a good 20-gauge double to be the ultimate quail gun.

and the close- to medium-range shooting of rabbits, squirrels and various game birds, we have various loads with 7/8 ounce of shot. Target loads such as the Gold Medal from Federal, Remington's Premier STS and the Winchester AA are quite popular among skeet shooters, and the excellent pattern quality delivered by their extremely hard, high-antimony shot makes them some of the very best loads available for hunting as well. My favorite medicine for bobwhite quail and mourning dove is the Remington STS load with an ounce of No. 8 shot. The Winchester AA shell loaded with an ounce of No. 7-1/2s is just the ticket for bigger birds, such as chukar and Hungarian partridge. A grouse-hunting friend of mine shoots the Remington target load with an ounce of No. 9 shot during the early season when shots are generally quite close. He likes it so well, he bought a lifetime supply just in case Remington ever decides to change it.

When hunting wild pheasants with the 20 gauge, I generally stick with premium-grade ammunition and the heavier shot charges available. For early-season hunting with a double, I often load an ounce of No. 7-1/2 shot in the first barrel and a 3-inch magnum with 1-1/4 ounces of No. 6s in the second barrel. Later in the season, when

Of the autoloaders sitting in my gun rack, two Franchi AL48s in 28 and 20 gauges are my favorites for upland hunting. The 20-gauge gun shown here weighs a mere 5-1/2 pounds.

birds have a tendency to flush farther away from the gun, I usually load both barrels with 3-inch shells loaded with No. 6 shot. I seldom shoot the 2-3/4 inch baby magnum shell with its 1-1/8 ounce shot charge. It is usually no faster than various 3-inch loads and not as fast as most 2-3/4 inch loads.

During a pheasant hunt in Nebraska, I loaded the bottom barrel of a Weatherby Athena with Remington's 2-3/4 inch Express load with an ounce of No. 7 1/2 shot at 1220 fps. Resting in its top barrel was the Remington Premier 3-inch turkey load with 1-1/4 ounces of No. 6 Hevi-Shot shot at 1185 fps. The barrels of the Weatherby were choked Improved Cylinder and Modified. That, my friend, is one deadly combination for a double-barrel shotgun, and it will hold its own out to 40 yards with just about anything that can be stuffed into the 2-3/4 inch 12-gauge shell. Recoil is certainly there in a light gun, but considering the number of shots most of us take on pheasants each day, few should be bothered by it. During a trip to California, I had exactly 1-1/2 days to hunt mountain quail, and I needed to be prepared for everything from birds that flushed just off the muzzle of my shotgun to those that got up at over 40 yards. The combination I have just described for pheasant worked equally well there.

The mandatory use of steel shot on waterfowl

had caused the 20 gauge to virtually disappear from duck blinds all across America. The 20-gauge is available with steel shot, but its limited capacity keeps pellet count with the larger shot sizes lower than many hunters think it should be. The introduction of new nontoxic shot made of materials as dense as lead has changed that. For older guns that were not designed to handle steel, Kent's Tungsten-Matrix and bismuth shot from Bismuth Cartridge are the answers. I have used both in my Westley Richards, not only on ducks, but also on pheasants in areas where nontoxic shot has to be used on upland game as well. Anything that can be done with lead shot can be done with those two. Bismuth and Tungsten-Matrix are also quite popular for use in modern guns by hunters who are willing to pay what they cost in order to deliver lead shot performance from a nontoxic shot. Both are quite good, and I have used them in the field with complete satisfaction, but when it comes down to making the 20 perform like the 12 in a duck blind, Remington's Hevi-Shot cannot be beat. It is far superior to any 12-gauge steel shot load I have tried, and that includes the 3-1/2 inch shell.

I bought my first 3-inch 20 in 1966 from Pepper's Feed & Seed in Easley, South Carolina. I remember the year because it is when the first 20-gauge Model 101 over-unders left the Winchester factory. My father had bought a 12-gauge Model 101 the previous year, and we both liked it so much I told Old Man Pepper I wanted the first one in 20-gauge he could get his hands on. A few weeks later, I became the owner of a field grade with 26-inch barrels choked Improved Cylinder and Modified. I have no idea how many thousands of rounds I have fired in it, but counting all the quail hunting, mourning dove shooting and crow plinking it has suffered through, along with trips to South America, the little gun has seen a great deal of use. Knock wood but it has yet to break a single part. I only wish I could hop aboard a time machine and travel back to 1966 so I could buy two more in 28 gauge and .410 for $293.95 each!

It might be of interest to note that some guns simply do not like the 3-inch shell and will actually deliver denser patterns at long range with 2-3/4 inch ammo loaded with a lighter shot charge. A Beretta over-under I tested placed more shot in a 30-inch circle at 40 yards with Federal and Remington 2-3/4 inch ammo loaded with an ounce No. 6s than with any 3-inch load with 1-1/4 or 1-5/16 ounces of the same size lead shot. The only way I could get that gun to shoot worth a darn with 3-inch ammo was to switch to Remington factory load with 1-1/4 ounces of No. 6 Hevi-Shot and replace the Full choke I had been using with one marked Modified. My Browning Superposed Lightning is another gun that does not deliver decent patterns with 3-inch ammo. I suspect it has to do with shot size and the bore of the 20 gauge is simply too small in diameter for optimum performance with 1-1/4 ounces of No. 6 lead shot. I have yet to find a gun that does not shoot decent patterns with 3-inch ammo loaded with 1-1/4 ounces of No. 6 Hevi-Shot.

Something else I have noticed is the top barrels of some over-unders shoot considerably higher at 40 yards with 3-inch ammo than with 2-3/4 inch ammo. When shooting 2-3/4 inch shells, both barrels of my Weatherby Athena deliver 60/40 patterns at 40 yards. The bottom barrel shoots about the same with 3-inch ammo but, depending on the brand of ammo used, the top barrel consistently delivers patterns that measure about 70/30 with the longer shell. There is one exception. The top barrel of that gun shoots about 60/40 with Remington ammo loaded with 1-1/4 ounces of Hevi-Shot.

I do believe the typical 20-gauge gun is more finicky about loads than the typical guns in 12 and 16 gauge. I have worked with many 12s and 16s that really did not indicate a great difference in the quality of the patterns they delivered when tested with a variety of loads, so long as the quality of the ammo was the same. Quite often, I find that 20-gauge guns indicate strong preferences in what they are fed. I recall pattern-testing two guns on the same day, a Weatherby Athena over-under and

Whether in an autoloader or a double, the 20 gauge with its variety of loads is close to ideal for most upland gunning.

a Westley Richards side-by-side. I was using 2-3/4 inch ammo loaded with No. 7-1/2 shot. The Weatherby delivered its best patterns at all distances from 25 to 40 yards with Remington Express ammo, and it shot worst with Federal's Gold Medal target load. It was just the opposite with the Westley Richards. Patterns delivered by it with the Remington ammo were mediocre at best, but it absolutely loved the Federal load.

Some 20-gauge guns will shoot patterns of the same quality with either standard-velocity or high-velocity ammo, but I do occasionally run across one that prefers one over the other. Soon after adding a Remington 11-87 to my battery, I checked it out with both types of loads. It turned in better performance at the pattern board with the Remington Express High Velocity load than with Remington's standard Express load. Both were loaded with an ounce of No. 7-1/2s, but with a velocity of 1300 fps, the high-speed load is 80 fps faster than the standard-speed load. One might logically assume that the high-velocity load delivered better performance because it is loaded with copper-plated shot, but that cannot be, since a Weatherby Athena I hunted with actually shot better with the slower of the two loads.

I own several guns in 20-gauge, and most of them are favorites. One is a 1940s vintage double built by the English firm of Westley Richards. The little gun weighs only 5-1/2 pounds. Its 28-inch barrels have four points of choke to the right and 14 points to the left. As is typical for classic British game guns, it has two triggers, a straight wrist and a splinter forearm. Another is a Remington Model 1100 LT-20 skeet gun. Once my father's favorite quail gun, it has a 25-1/2 inch barrel with

Its 5-1/2 pound weight and excellent balance make the 20-gauge Westley Richards I used to bag this sharptail grouse a marvelous upland gun. It has 28-inch barrels choked Skeet and Modified.

.003 inch of choke constriction. The Weatherby Athena I used to bag the grand slam of American quail is a favorite as well. I have 28-gauge and .410 barrels for that gun, and since I have also taken all six species of quail with them, I have officially taken three grand slams with the same gun in three different chamberings. Then we have the Winchester Model 101 I described in the previous paragraph. I have actually hunted more with that gun than with either of the other three because I have owned it longer. For several years, it was about the only thing I used when hunting quail and doves and shooting crows. When hunting flushing birds such as quail and pheasant, I shoot those four guns about the same, but anytime I find myself sitting on the edge of a dove field, I almost always shoot either of the over-unders better than the muzzle-light autoloader. I also enjoy shooting a Browning Superposed Lightning with Briley subgauge tubes in .410 and 28 gauge. A gun I shoot as well on flushing game

birds as any I have ever owned is a Franchi 48AL. It weighs 5-1/2 pounds and has a variety of screw-in chokes. I actually have a matched pair of those guns, the other in 28 gauge.

It is easy to see that I really don't I need another 20-gauge shotgun, but if I were to add another to my battery tomorrow, it might just be a trim little autoloader built by Benelli and called the Legacy. The very first time I ever held one of those guns in my hands I pulled off several shots I am not sure I could repeat. One shot was at a Hungarian partridge that obviously thought it was a ruffed grouse. How my charge of 7-1/2s managed to make it through all those vines, limbs and twigs neither Steve McKelvain nor I will never know. It was one of those rare days when I felt like I simply could not miss, and I didn't very often. The Legacy I used had a 26-inch barrel choked Improved Cylinder and it fit me like a glove.

The 20-gauge is the first shotshell I ever hand-

A light 20 gauge gun is the ideal choice for use in mountain quail country.

loaded. Back in those days, I used a single-stage reloader. I also used cardboard and felt wads, since the one-piece plastic wad column was a couple of years away from making its debut. I now load all the ammunition I use for shooting clay targets, most of it in the Remington Premier STS hull. I usually stick with 7/8 ounce of No. 9s for skeet, and an ounce of No. 8s for 16-yard trap. Depending on the target presentation, I use one or the other of those loads in most of the sporting clays shooting I do with the 20 gauge. One of the best loads I have come up with for shooting quail and doves out to 30 yards or so was developed only a few years ago for my Westley Richards double. Listed among the loads at the end of this chapter, it virtually duplicates 28-gauge performance in the 20-gauge hull and is extremely comfortable to shoot. I had the load tested for chamber pressure while visiting my friends at the Primex powder factory in Florida, and it registered an extremely mild 8,000 psi average for five

shots in their pressure gun. This is 3,000 to 4,000 psi milder than most factory ammunition is loaded to. The heaviest handload I use in that gun is the 7/8 ounce load shown with Hodgdon's Longshot in my favorite load chart. It generates less than 10,000 psi, and yet the shot charge exits the muzzle at a rather speedy 1250 fps.

Some of the best shooting I have ever done with the 20 gauge, and most certainly some of the best I have seen anyone else do, with it took place down in Uruguay in 2002. Eddie Stevenson and Scott Hanes of Remington had invited Nick Sisley and me along to wring out new ammunition loaded with Hevi-Shot on waterfowl. We were also there to give prototypes of Remington's new 12-gauge Model 332 over-under its first workout, but since we had a supply of Hevi-Shot ammo in both 12 and 20 gauges, Nick and I had brought along Model 11-87 autoloaders in 20 gauge. On the second morning of our duck hunt, I teamed up with Eddie while Nick and Scott

I used a Browning BPS and the Winchester 3-inch 20 gauge turkey load with 1-1/4 ounces of No. 5 shot to take this Osceola gobbler while hunting in south Florida with Eddie Salter. One shot at 36 yards did the trick.

shared a blind about 50 yards to our right. Eddie and Scott were shooting 12-gauge guns, and Nick and I were shooting the 20s and 1-1/8 ounces of No. 6 Hevi-Shot. Everyone made fantastic shots that day, but the real surprise to all of us was how far those 20-gauge guns reached out and clobbered ducks. I had brought a laser rangefinder with me, so the yardages we wrote down were exact and not estimated. With the 20-gauge guns, we killed many ducks out at the 50-yard marker, and no small number at 60 yards. I am sure Nick killed a few even farther

out than that! If you do not believe that, you certainly will not believe this: The barrels of our guns were choked Improved Cylinder.

In addition to being one of the best wingshots I know, Ryan Busse uses the 20 gauge on everything from Kansas bobwhites to South Dakota pheasants. I have hunted sharptail grouse and Hungarian partridge with him a lot, and birds seem to be drawn to him like a magnet. But not always early in the day. I remember breaking for lunch on an especially beautiful Montana day, when I was one bird short of the eight-bird limit. I was hunting with my 20-gauge Westley Richards. Ryan had not fired a shot all morning, but he made up for it after lunch by bagging six birds in less than an hour. He sticks with an ounce of No. 7-1/2 shot, and has come to prefer the high-velocity loads at 1300 fps from Remington and Estate. Ryan uses one gun on everything that flies: a Winchester Model 23 given to him by his father many years ago. It has 26-inch barrels and is choked Improved Cylinder and Modified. One look at that gun, and you know it has been used hard and used a lot.

As 20-gauge ammunition goes, I cannot think of a single thing we need, but I can think of something I would like to see added to the shotgun lineup. The relatively light guns we have are ideal for lots of walking in the field, but they are too light for a lot of shooting. This is why I would like to see someone offer a 20-gauge autoloader built on the 12-gauge receiver. Remington is the likely candidate, since the very first 20-gauge Model 1100s were nothing more than 12-gauge guns with 20-gauge barrels, but I would not object to seeing another company such as Benelli or Franchi take the leap today. I believe every skeet shooter in the country would buy one, not to mention the thousands who travel to South America each year for a bit of high-volume bird shooting. Those who own over-under and side-by-side doubles in 12 gauge can convert them to 20-gauge with a pair of subgauge tubes from Briley, but the autoloader fan has no such choice. Clarence Purbaugh used to convert 20-gauge Model 1100s built on the small frame to .410 and 20 gauge, and I see no reason why a 12-gauge autoloader could not be converted to 20 gauge. A good gunsmith who knows shotguns could surely do it, but it would likely be far more expensive than buying a factory gun.

A great little shotshell, the 20 gauge. Those who know it well often love it with a passion. A friend of mine who is big on trim and lightweight guns for upland shooting says if it cannot be done with the 20, he had just as soon leave it for someone else to do. He is quite safe in saying that because as time goes on, it becomes more and more difficult to find something the 20 gauge cannot handle. And quite well at that.

A FEW FAVORITE 20-GAUGE HANDLOADS

Case: 2-3/4" Remington STS
Primer: W209
Powder: International Clays
Powder Charge: 11.5 grains
Wad: Win WAA20
Shot Charge: 3/4 ounces
Velocity: 1100 fps
Notes: Low-recoil, 28-gauge equivalent

Case: 2-3/4" Remington STS
Primer: Rem 209P
Powder: International Clays
Powder Charge: 14.0 grains
Wad: Win WAA20
Shot Charge: 7/8 ounces
Velocity: 1200 fps
Notes: Excellent for hunting and clay targets

Case: 2-3/4" Remington STS
Primer: Rem 209P
Powder: Longshot
Powder Charge: 17.6 grains
Wad: Remington RXP20
Shot Charge: 1 ounce
Velocity: 1250 fps
Notes: Excellent high-velocity hunting load at low chamber pressure

Case: 2-3/4" Remington STS
Primer: Rem 209P
Powder: Blue Dot
Powder Charge: 24.0 grains
Wad: Rem SP20
Shot Charge: 1 ounce
Velocity: 1200 fps
Notes: Favorite quail load

Case: 2-3/4" Remington STS
Primer: Remington 209 STS
Powder: Blue Dot
Charge: 22.0 grains
Wad: Remington SP20
Shot Charge: 1-1/8 ounces
Velocity: 1175 fps
Notes: Excellent trap load

Case: 3" Remington Premier
Primer: Win 209
Powder: HS-7
Powder Charge: 25.0 grains
Wad: Rem RXP20
Shot Charge: 1-1/4 ounces
Velocity: 1250 fps
Notes: Excellent long-range pheasant load

CHAPTER 18

The Saga of Sweet 16

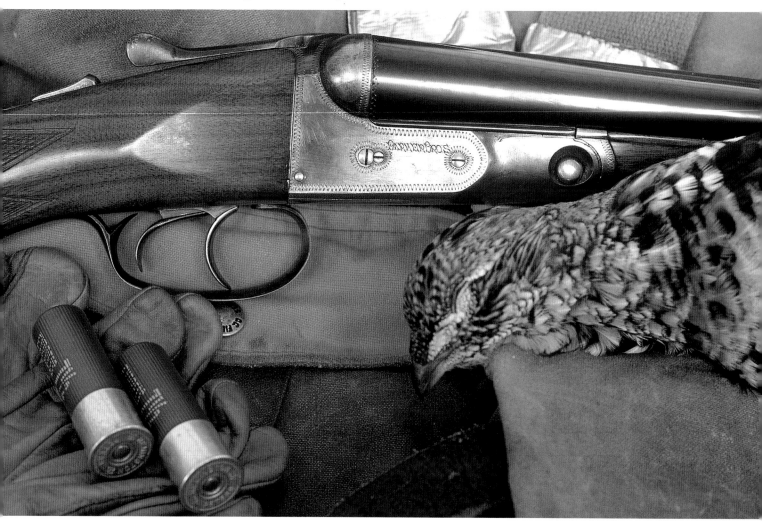

A vintage double like this Parker is sometimes less expensive because the 16-gauge is not as popular as other gauges. This makes it an excellent buy.

Like Rodney Dangerfield, the 16-gauge shotshell gets no respect anymore from hunters anywhere. This has not always been the case. During the late 1950s, *American Rifleman* published a comparison chart based on shotgun sales numbers obtained from the major manufacturers. At the time, 52 percent of the scatterguns sold in the United States were in 12 gauge, with the 16 gauge in a strong second place at 24 percent. Imagine that: 24 of every 100 shotguns bought by American hunters were in 16 gauge. Guns in 10, 20 and 28 gauge along with the .410 accounted for the remaining 24 percent. I have no idea how many 16-gauge guns now leave factories around the world each year, but based on the amount of ammunition sold in the United States, they have to represent a very small drop in a

very large bucket. According to Linda Powell of Remington, the 16-gauge represented only 2.6 percent of total shotshell sales for her company during 2001.

While growing up in the Deep South, I had no way of knowing how the 16 ranked in any national popularity poll, but I did notice that lots of local hunters carried guns chambered for it. At the time, my father's favorite shotgun was a 16-gauge L.C. Smith double, and he used on everything from bobwhite quail to cottontail rabbits to whitetail deer to the occasional chicken-stealing hawk. Old "Elsie's" 26-inch barrels were choked Improved Cylinder and Modified. I can even recall the shot sizes he preferred — No. 8s for quail and doves and 4s for everything else. I am saddened by the fact that those grand old days along with every single one of the coverts Dad and I hunted together are long gone, and while the 16 gauge is still with us, it is but a ghost of what it might have been.

So what killed Sweet Sixteen? A number of things, actually, but mainly it got crowded from the trough by the bigger 12 gauge on one side and the smaller 20 gauge on the other. Throughout decades of hunting seasons, the ammunition companies devoted large quantities of both time and money to the development of uncountable loads for the 12 and 20, while at the same time all but totally neglecting the 16. It is now possible to buy the 12-gauge shell in three lengths with loads ranging from low-recoil, one-ounce powder-puffers to shoulder-bruising, 2-1/4 ounce turkey-crushers. The 16 is still available only in 2-3/4 inch length and its load options of one, 1-1/8 and 1-1/4 ounces of shot are the same today as they were half a century ago.

The 20 gauge moved ahead primarily because it was available in trim, lightweight guns properly scaled to size, whereas many 16s were nothing more than heavy 12-gauge guns wearing 16-gauge barrels. Few wanted to carry a 12-gauge gun that shot like a 16-gauge gun. The development of plenty of new loads helped the 20's cause, too. It is now available in 2-3/4 and 3-inch lengths with various shot charges including mart-special 3/4 ounce field loads, 7/8 ounce for clay target and quail loads to a 1-5/16 ounce turkey load. When nothing but shot charge weights are compared, the 20-gauge shell of today is capable of doing anything that could be done with the 12-gauge shell in days of old, but the 16 will do very little more than it ever has.

For many years, I was convinced that the 20-gauge shell was the equal of the 16 gauge when both are loaded with the same shot charge. A great deal of pattern testing has changed my mind. In most guns, the 20-gauge loaded with an ounce of shot will pattern as well as the typical 16-gauge gun loaded with the same amount of shot. Increase the shot charge to 1-1/8 ounces in both, and while some 20-gauge guns will deliver pattern quality as high as the 16 gauge, not all are capable of doing so. When moving up to 1-1/4 ounces of shot, many of the 20-gauge guns I have tested delivered poor results at the pattern board, while most 16-gauge guns I have worked with shot beautiful patterns.

Something else a 16-gauge gun has going for it is that it will almost always handle the larger shot sizes better than the typical 20-gauge gun. Most 20-gauge guns pattern nicely with shot no larger than No. 8, and I have

Michigan hunters Bud and John Louck consider a good 16-gauge gun just the ticket for ruffed grouse.

worked with a few that performed quite well with 7-1/2s, but it is the rare 20 that will produce uniform patterns with anything larger. Most 16-gauge guns are capable of delivering excellent patterns with all popular shot sizes up to No. 4. Some will handle even larger pellets. I once decided to work up a long-range sage grouse load for my L.C. Smith, one to be used late in the season when the birds are more likely to flush with a bit of distance between them and the gun. Needing only a few rounds, I robbed No. 2 copper-plated shot from some Federal 12-gauge Premium ammo I had on hand. I then replaced the 1-1/4 ounces of No. 4 shot in Federal's Premium 16-gauge ammo with the No. 2 shot, and headed to the pattern board. At 40 yards, the Modified barrel placed an average of 71 No. 2s in a 30-inch circle for an average of about 65 percent. Pattern uniformity was beautiful. Few 20-gauge guns will shoot that well with anything larger than No. 7-1/2 shot.

Many years ago, the 16-gauge shell was offered in 2-1/2, 2-9/16, 2-5/8, 2-3/4 and 2-7/8 inch lengths. I have also heard of an experimental 3-inch shell, but I have never seen one. In the old days, 16-gauge fans could choose from quite a variety of ammunition. For those who owned 16-gauge skeet guns built by Remington, Winchester, Iver Johnson and others, several companies peddled target loads with an ounce of No. 9 chilled shot. Trap loads with 1-1/8 ounces of No. 8s were also available. Hunters who owned guns choked a bit too tightly for close-range shooting (and many did) could buy shells

A good 16-gauge gun will handle 99 percent of the upland hunting 99 percent of hunters do.

loaded with special wads that caused the shot charge pattern to open up more quickly. Remington called its version the Scatter Load, Peters ammo was marked "Spreader Load," over at Winchester it was known as Brush Load, and ruffed grouse hunters who dropped by the local hardware store to buy a box of Western shells asked for the Thicket Load. Shot-charge options available in standard field loads back in the bad old days stopped at 1-1/8 ounces, but by the time the 1950s rolled around, both Winchester and Remington were offering 1-1/4 ounce loads as well. Available shot sizes ranged from No. 9 for clay targets to No. 1 buck, the latter a long-time favorite among Deep South hunters who pursued deer with hounds. Back then, ammunition was priced the way common sense says it ought to be, which made 16-gauge ammo less expensive than 12 gauge and .410 shells cheapest of all.

Federal, Remington, Winchester and Kent offer a decent variety of 16-gauge loads. They, along with Bismuth Cartridge, are the places to go for nontoxic loadings, steel for those who own guns young enough to handle it, Tungsten-Matrix and bismuth for those of us who often hunt with vintage guns. My father's old L.C. Smith kicks a bit harder now than it did back when I was a teenager, so when using it on quail, doves and ruffed grouse early in the season, I prefer the various 7/8 ounce and one ounce loads with their relatively light recoil. The softest-kicking factory load I have tried came from

Polywad. Loaded in the 2-1/2 inch shell, it pushed 7/8 ounce of shot along at a leisurely 1175 fps. I have also shot Westley Richards 2-1/2 inch ammo loaded with the same shot charge, but since its throttle is pushed forward to 1300 fps or so, it is not as comfortable to shoot in lightweight game guns. The Gamebore one ounce load I tried was also a soft-kicker, but it patterned rather poorly in my L.C. Smith. At one time or another, 16-gauge ammunition made by other companies such as Fiocchi, Baschieri & Pellagri and Sellier & Bellot has been available on the American market. The various 7/8 ounce loads are quite comfortable to shoot in lightweight doubles, but some may not reliably operate the Remington 1100, Browning A-5, Remington 11-48 and other autoloaders.

About the heaviest loads I care to use in my L.C. Smith on a regular basis are those loaded to 1300 fps or so (2-3/4 dram equivalent) with 1-1/8 ounces of shot. I have used the Remington, Federal and Winchester loads with No. 7-1/2 shot and found all to be quite effective on a variety of game birds, but the Remington and Federal loads pattern best in my old double. Heavier loads are available, but they can be uncomfortable to shoot in anything but the gas-powered Remington Model 1100 autoloader. Firing more than a few rounds of the Federal 3-1/4 dram load with its 1-1/4 ounces of shot at 1260 fps in a lightweight gun gives me a terrible headache, although I can tolerate it on a couple of late-season pheasant hunts each year. Kent's 1-1/4 ounce loading of No. 5 Tungsten-Matrix also kicks like the Dickens in a lightweight gun, but it is an excellent nontoxic duck load.

There was a time when I had little reason or desire to handload 16-gauge shotshells, but each time one of our ammunition manufacturers decides to drop another loading from the list, I am forced to spend more time at the reloading bench. One of my favorites is a light-recoil recipe with 7/8 ounce of lead shot that works beautifully on quail and doves out to about 30 yards. I have also used it to break a few clay targets on the skeet field. Shotcup capacity of the Remington plastic wad has to be reduced for the light shot charge by the insertion of a .125-inch, 28-gauge felt wad before the shot is dropped in and the case crimped. Average muzzle velocity is around 1050 fps, making it one sweet-shooting load for doubles and pump guns. My L.C. Smith delivers beautiful patterns with it, too. The downside is it may be too light to operate autoloaders such as the Remington 1100 and Browning A-5. When shooting ducks over decoys with vintage 16-gauge guns, and when chasing after upland game in areas where nontoxic shot is required, I sometimes use a recipe with an ounce of bismuth shot. Shown at the end of this chapter, it was developed by my friends at Hodgdon Powder Company.

Remington builds its 16-gauge Model 870 on the 12-gauge receiver. It is a nice gun but it would be even nicer if it were built on the smaller and lighter 20-gauge receiver.

Not as many guns are available in 16 gauge as during days of yesteryear, but some are still out there. Every gun company who was anybody in America used to offer their own version of the Sweet 16, but most were discontinued long ago. Remington dropped the chambering from its Model 870 pump gun in 1980 and then brought it back in 2002. How long it will remain in production is anybody's guess. Ithaca still keeps the 16 gauge alive in the Model 37 pump gun. I have no idea how many companies have built 16-gauge slide-action shotguns, but I wish I had bought the Remington Model 31 I took home on a trial basis some years back. A Tournament-grade gun with fancy wood and checkering, it had a 28-inch vent-ribbed barrel and the smoothest action of any pump gun I have ever held in my hands. There is absolutely nothing wrong with the Remington 870, so long as you have no objection to hunting with a 12-gauge gun chambered for the 16 gauge. One of the best shots on Texas quail I have every hunted with used nothing but a battle-scarred old Model 870 and handloads with 1-1/8 ounces of No. 7-1/2 shot.

As repeating shotguns go, the Winchester Model 12 is the nicest 16 gauge ever made. It is built on the same frame size as the 20- and 28-gauge Model 12s, and that alone makes it lighter than the same gun in 12 gauge. But there is more. The barrel walls of the 20- and 28-gauge guns are considerably thicker at their chamber ends than the 16-gauge barrel, and this makes Model 12s in those two chamberings heavier than one in 16 gauge. A friend of mine has Model 12s in all four gauges, and you only have to handle them once to feel how much lighter the 16-gauge gun is than the other three.

One of the made-in-America prizes is an exact recreation of the Ithaca N.I.D. side-by-side double built by Ithaca Classic Doubles of Victor, New York. Then we have the freshly manufactured Fox doubles from Connecticut Shotgun Mfg. Company. Kimber has yet to offer a side-by-side shotgun, but if and when that company decides to build one scaled to proper size for the 16 gauge, you can bet it will be a dandy. A side-by-side double called the Anson and built by the Spanish firm of F.lli Poli is especially nice, since it is built on a 20-gauge frame. I am also quite fond of AyA guns built on the small frame. Although I have yet to see one, a 16-gauge Athena from Weatherby's custom shop would be nice to own. Other manufacturers and importers also offer side-by-side 16s, some affordable, some not. They include Griffin & Howe, Gardone, Grulla, Merkel, Westley Richards, Holland & Holland, Famars, Dakota, Bertuzzi, Garbi, Arrieta, Lebeau-Courally and Rizzini.

As for vintage doubles of American make at prices that won't break the bank, the Fox Sterlingworth

Hungarian partridge and sharptail grouse taken with Dad's old 16-gauge L.C. Smith double.

troduced the 16-gauge chambering in the Model 1100 with a vent-ribbed barrel.

Of the few 16-gauge guns I own, my favorite is a field-grade L.C. Smith with 26-inch barrels. Built in 1949, it was purchased by my father during that same year. Dad bought the gun new from Bruce Smith, who owned a farm-supply store called Smith's Feed & Seed. At the time, Bruce was one of only two gun dealers located in my hometown of Liberty, South Carolina. Dad used the gun for all of his upland hunting until a 20-gauge Browning Superposed won his heart around 1967. The receiver of the L.C. Smith wears only a small trace of its original case coloring, and most of the bluing on its barrels has faded to a brown patina. Its bores measure .658 inch, a bit tight since .670 inch is standard for the 16 gauge. Dad always said the barrels were choked Improved Cylinder and Modified, but actual constrictions of .008 and .023 inch put them closer to Improved Skeet and Improved Modified. Patterns thrown by the left barrel are a bit snug for most of the hunting I do, and while I really should have it opened up a bit, I will probably leave it as it was when Dad hunted with it. The gun weighs exactly 6-3/4 pounds.

Unlike some older L.C. Smith's, mine does not have excessive drop in its stock. The gun fits me so nicely, I shoot it about as well in the field as any shotgun of any type I have ever owned. I had not hunted with it for several years, when I received an invitation from my friend Ryan Busse to hunt sage grouse, Hungarian partridge and sharptail grouse with him in Montana. In addition to Ryan, there were his Brittany, Ruark, and his German shorthair, Clancy. Allen Remley also accompanied us. That was the first time the old L.C. Smith had left South Carolina since either Dad or I had owned it. While hunting sharpies and Huns, I used Remington Express cartridges loaded with 1-1/8 ounces of No. 7-1/2 shot at 1295 fps, and since most birds were taken inside 40 yards, I could not have chosen a more perfect load.

Anyone who has hunted the Hungarian Partridge knows it can be quite unpredictable, and it may fly in about any direction when flushed. Most game birds tend to fly with the wind, especially if it is blowing quite hard, but not Mr. Hun. I have seen them fly for several yards directly into a wind so strong, I could hardly stand against it, and then rocket off in another direction. Their tendency to fly in whatever direction they might please has set the stage for some of the fanciest shooting I have ever pulled off in the field. A few of those shots happened with Ryan Busse looking on from about 30 yards away. I dropped an outgoing Hun with the right barrel of the L.C. Smith as the birds flushed from a 10-foot-tall windrow of Siberian pea (or Caragana, as local ranchers call it). I then swung on a second bird flying toward my left and grassed

built on a 20-gauge frame is my favorite, with the field grade L.C. Smith in a very close second place. I have a friend who owns a Fox ejector gun with 30-inch barrels built during the 1920s, and he is very careful about keeping it under lock and key when I am around. Some of the very best buys on the used-gun market are field-grade Parkers and L.C. Smiths, as they are usually priced lower than the same guns in 12 or 20 gauge. As the over-under goes, a number of Browning Citoris have been built in 16 gauge, but they are becoming quite scarce. My favorite 16-gauge autoloader is the Remington 11-48, although the Browning A-5 in its Sweet Sixteen configuration is also well worth owning. There was a time when the rarest 16-gauge autoloader ever built was the Remington Model 1100 with a ventilated rib on its barrel. Plain-barrel Model 1100s were quite common, but for some reason Remington had built very few 16s with ribs riding atop their barrels. This changed in 2003 when Remington rein-

An ounce of shot is plenty for early season hunting of pheasant but later in the year 1-1/4 ounces can be none too much.

it with the left barrel. Huns often flush in concert, but the occasional straggler will allow those of us who hunt with doubles a third shot. Just as I lowered my gun to reload, another bird flushed from about 50 yards out and began flying almost directly toward me. Quickly breaking down the gun (while silently wishing it were equipped with automatic ejectors), I replaced the spent case in the right barrel with a fresh round, closed the gun, swung on the bird just as it passed to my left and dropped it in a shower of feathers. The shot was exactly as presented from station one low house on the skeet field, except the bird was about 20 yards out as it attempted to pass me by. Try making that shot in skeet, but don't load your gun until after you call for the bird, and you will experience the shot I made on one very unlucky Hun. I am sure Dad nodded his head in approval as he looked down on that beautiful Montana day and saw me bag a species of bird he never got to hunt with his old L.C. Smith.

FAVORITE 16-GAUGE HANDLOADS

Case: Remington Express Plastic
Primer: Winchester 209
Powder: Hodgdon Universal Clays
Powder Charge: 17.0 grains
Wad: Remington SP16*
Shot Charge: 7/8 ounce
Velocity: 1050 fps
Notes: Excellent low-recoil load for quail, dove and skeet

Case: Federal Classic Plastic
Primer: Federal 209A
Powder: Alliant Herco
Powder Charge: 22.0 grains
Wad: Remington SP16
Shot Charge: 1 ounce
Velocity: 1250 fps
Notes: Favorite ruffed grouse load

Case: Remington Express Plastic
Primer: Remington 209P
Powder: Hodgdon Universal Clays
Powder Charge: 18.0 grains
Wad: Remington SP16
Shot Charge: 1 ounce (Bismuth)
Velocity: 1200 fps
Notes: Great for ducks over decoys

Case: Winchester Super-X Plastic
Primer: Federal 209
Powder: Hodgdon HS-6
Powder Charge: 27.0 grains
Wad: Remington SP16
Shot Charge: 1-1/8 ounces
Velocity: 1225 fps
Notes: Best all-purpose 16-gauge load for everything from quail to pheasants

Case: Federal Classic Plastic
Primer: Federal 209
Powder: Alliant Blue Dot
Powder Charge: 25.0 grains
Wad: Remington SP16
Shot Charge: 1-1/4 ounces
Velocity: 1200 fps
Notes: Left-barrel load for L.C. Smith when hunting pheasants

*Shotcup capacity reduced by inserting a .125-inch, 28-gauge felt wad prior to dropping shot

CHAPTER 19

The All-Around 12 Gauge

Regardless of whether it is used in a side-by-side double like the one this fellow is hunting with or in another type of gun, the 12-gauge is our most popular shotshell.

I absolutely love the 28-gauge shotshell, and I put more rounds through guns chambered for it each year than for any other. Some of my all-time favorite hunts have been with .410-bore guns, and life would not be the same without them. If I had to give up all of my shotguns except for a couple, one would be chambered to either the 16 or 20 gauge. Then we have the 10 gauge; it is my favorite for hunting waterfowl with steel shot simply because an autoloader chambered for it is more comfortable to shoot than guns chambered for the 3-inch 12-gauge shell. But as fond as I am of all the others, I must

admit the 12 gauge is the most useful simply because it is by far the most versatile. You name the game, and the 12 is capable of playing it quite well. It can be made to duplicate the performance of the lightest target load available in the 28 gauge, the heaviest field load available in the 10 gauge and everything in between. Some shotshells are capable of performing equally well at various points within the shotshell performance spectrum, but no other shotshell is capable of covering everything as well. The 12 is king of shotshells, and it will remain so as long as birds are available for the hunting and clay targets are

Because of the great variety in factory loads, a 12-gauge autoloader is an excellent choice for the shotgunner who prefers to do all of his hunting with one gun.

there for the breaking.

Through the years the 12-gauge shell has been available in a number of lengths including 2-1/2, 2-5/8, 2-3/4, 2-7/8, 3, 3-1/8, 3-1/4 and 3-1/2 inches. The 2-3/4 inch is the most popular today, although many duck and goose hunters prefer the 3-inch shell because its greater capacity allows the use of heavier charges of steel shot. The 3-inch shell is preferred by no small number of turkey hunters, but the 3-1/2 incher is becoming popular there as well.

Many older guns, especially those of foreign manufacture were reamed for the 2 and 2-1/2 inch shells. For this reason, both continue to be loaded by various English companies as well as small American specialty shops such as Polywad. My Fox Sterlingworth originally had 2-5/8 inch chambers. I once tried Gamebore 2-inch ammo in an old English-built gun, and it worked okay there, but I could never get the Fox to shoot decent patterns with it. So I used a reamer from Brownells to lengthen its chambers to 2-3/4 inches and also lengthened its forcing cones at the same time. I probably should have left well enough alone with that one. Prior to modifying the chambers of that gun I tried

2-3/4 inch shells in it and observed no sign of excessive chamber pressures. Patterns shot with 2-3/4 inch shells back then were every bit as good those the gun now delivers, and if the longer forcing cones have made it more comfortable to shoot, my shoulder is too insensitive to detect it.

A shotgun chambered for the 12-gauge shotshell is the single most useful firearm anyone can own, and this includes rifles and handguns as well. It would not be my first choice for hunting elk, but I would rather do so with a 12-gauge slug gun than attempt to hunt ducks or quail with a rifle in .300 Magnum. A handgun is more easily concealed for defensive use, but when it comes to home protection, a shotgun with its magazine filled with the right loads is a better choice. And plenty of loads are available since most ammunition manufactures offer more options in 12 gauge than for all the others combined. In Remington's lineup, for example, I see 163 12-gauge offerings compared to 45 for the 20 gauge and 26 for the 10, 16, 28 and .410 combined. Shot charge options from Remington, Federal, Winchester and others range from target loads with 24 grams (slightly less than 7/8 ounce) to a whopping two ounces

Dwight Van Brunt seems overjoyed to have taken this
brace of sharptail with his 12-gauge Kimber over-under.

for bumping off a turkey gobbler a long range.

We all know the 12 gauge is capable of killing
game farther away than is possible with the smaller
gauges because it is capable of holding more shot. What
some shotgunners don't realize is the fact that it is not
unusual to see 12-gauge guns deliver better pattern performance at all ranges with cheap ammunition. The soft
shot found in economy-grade shotshells is easily
deformed during firing, and the shorter the shot column, the fewer the number of pellets that will suffer setback deformation and further damage as the charge
squeezes through the forcing cone of the barrel. Very
little difference will be seen at the pattern board when
guns in 12 and 16 gauge are compared with 1-1/8 ounce
shot charges, but considerable differences will often
become evident when the 20 and 28 gauge enter the
comparison. The smaller the gauge, the more it will
benefit from the use of the hardest shot available, and
when soft shot is used in all, the 12 with its shorter shot
column will often deliver the best patterns.

I don't hunt with the 12 gauge as much as with
the smaller gauges, but I hunt with it enough to own a
few favorite guns. If I had to single out a favorite I
would have a tough time deciding between a Remington
Model 3200 and a Fox Sterlingworth, the latter of 1920s
vintage. Both guns have 30-inch barrels choked
Modified and Full, so they are seen at their best for
long-range shooting at pheasant and waterfowl.

The gun I have used to bag more game than
any other in 12 gauge is one of the first Model 11-87
autoloaders built by Remington. It has seen action all
over America and in several foreign countries as well. I
have 26- and 28-inch barrels for it, and while I shoot
both about the same on pheasant, I prefer the longer
barrel when hunting ducks and geese. Once on a high-

volume duck shoot in South America, my old Model
11-87 was about the only autoloader in our group of
hunters that did not experience mechanical problems.

The 12-gauge gun I have put the most rounds
through is a 1950s vintage Krieghoff Model 32 over-under
with 28-inch barrels. I originally bought it for shooting
registered skeet and it came cased with Purbaugh subgauge tubes in .410, 28 and 20. I am not a serious skeet
shooter, so even when competing in the 12- and 20-gauge
events I most often shoot that gun in 28 gauge simply
because I break just as many targets and it is so comfortable to shoot. I also have a pair of 20-gauge Briley tubes
with a variety of screw-in chokes for that gun and have
used it on several dove and duck shoots in Old Mexico.

One thing is certain: Every shotgun manufacturer who is anybody makes shotguns in 12 gauge.
There was a time when the typical 12-gauge gun was
considerably heavier than those in the smaller gauges.
This still holds true for most pumps and autoloaders,
but the use of aluminum receivers by Browning,
Beretta and Franchi has resulted in 12-gauge over-
unders that are as light as and sometimes even lighter
than some guns of that type in 20 gauge. The 12-gauge
Franchi Alcione Titanium is rated at a few ounces
under 7 pounds, which is more than half a pound
lighter than the standard Alcione of the same gauge.
Still, few 12-gauge shotguns handle and feel as nicely
as guns of smaller gauges. Given one of my better days
in a field full of ringneck pheasants or prairie chickens,
I will shoot my 12-gauge Fox as well as my 16-gauge
L.C. Smith, but the slim and trim lines of the Elsie
make it more pleasurable to carry. Toward the end of a
10-mile hike after sharptail grouse, my 20- and 28-
gauge guns feel even better, and this is why you will
see me toting them in the field more often than the
larger gauges.

I seldom ever hunt quail with a 12-gauge gun,
but when birds are flushing wild, I often take along light
target loads with either an ounce or 1-1/8 ounces of No.
7-1/2 or No. 8 shot. Target loads don't always pattern
better than premium-grade field loads, but they do so
often enough to prompt me to try them first. When trying out a new gun, I'll head to the pattern board with a
supply of Federal Gold Medal, Remington STS and
Winchester AA ammo and let the gun decide which will
be used. If I had to pick two loads that have consistently
delivered the prettiest patterns out to 30 yards in a variety of guns, they would be Federal Gold Medal with an
ounce of No. 8s at 1180 fps and Remington Premier STS
Low Recoil with 1-1/8 ounces of No. 7-1/2s at 1100 fps.

The various trap loads loaded with 1-1/8
ounces of No. 7-1/2 shot are some of the very best med-

Brad Ruddell with Gambel quail taken with the assistance of his equally happy guide, Roxie Kelso.

icine I have ever used for long-range shooting on various game birds such as sharptail grouse and prairie chickens. Those loads contain extremely hard, high-antimony shot, so it is not unusual to see them deliver better patterns than premium-grade field loads with buffered, copper-plated shot. Examples are the Federal Gold Medal in either a paper or plastic shell, the Remington STS Premier and the Winchester AA. Of those I have tried, Remington's STS Nitro Sporting Clays load with a muzzle velocity of 1300 fps seems to be the most effective once the range increases beyond 30 yards. I have used that same load with No. 8 shot for late-season dove shooting, and it worked equally well there. I would really like to see this one become available with 1-1/8 ounces of magnum-grade No. 6 shot. What a terrific pheasant load that would make! I also have some experience in the game fields with Remington's STS Nitro 27 Handicap load, and while it, too, is loaded with 1-1/8 ounces of No. 7-1/2 or 8 shot, it patterns a bit better from some guns than the sporting clays load. This is probably due to its lower velocity of 1235 fps. Federal Gold Medal Extra-Lite is loaded to

only 1100 fps, and while it does not deliver as much punch at long range as the faster loads, its soft recoil makes it a delight to shoot.

I use factory ammunition for most of the hunting I do with 12-gauge guns, but I handload almost all of my ammo for clay target shooting. I do this not because handloaded shells are better, but because handloading allows me to shoot about twice as much for the same amount of money. Handloading also enables me to come up with specialty loads not offered by the various manufacturers. Most factory loads containing less than an ounce of shot are loaded to high velocity, and that increases recoil. One of my favorite low-recoil recipes for shooting skeet, sporting clays and 16-yard trap pushes 7/8 ounce of shot along at a leisurely 1150 fps. It is extremely comfortable to shoot, even in light-weight guns. That load also works quite well on doves and quail out to about 25 yards, but it does not build up enough steam to operate some autoloaders. Attempting to use it in a Beretta 391 or Remington 1100 never fails to turn them into single-shots, but my Remington Model 11-87 has never missed a beat during the firing

J.B. Hodgdon and I bagged these ringnecks with a handload containing International Clays and 1-1/8 ounces of No. 6 shot.

of several thousand rounds. Team up so light a load with a relatively heavy gun like my 7-1/2-pound Fox Sterlingworth or my 8-1/2 pound Remington 3200, and you have a combination that can be shot all day long with no stress or strain.

I often use the 7/8 ounce handload for 16-yard trap, and for the first shot in trap doubles but I prefer 1-1/8 ounces of high-antimony No.7-1/2 shot for handicap distances and for the second shot in doubles. The smaller No. 8 shot is probably about as good for breaking clay targets at long range, but the guns I shoot in trap seem to throw better patterns with 7-1/2s. I shoot trap singles with a Remington 90-T with a 32-inch barrel choked .035 inch. For doubles, I switch to a Remington 3200 with 30-inch barrels choked .020 and .040 inch. When shooting trap for fun, I am just as likely to shoot my Fox Sterlingworth and usually break about as many targets with it as with the other two. Its 30-inch barrels are choked .020 and .041 inch.

When shooting sporting clays with the 12 gauge, I use a Krieghoff 32 or a Remington Model 11-87. Both guns have screw-in chokes. For the easier shots, I shoot my 7/8-ounce handload through either Skeet or Improved Cylinder choke. For extremely long shots I switch to my long-range trap load with 1-1/8 ounces of No. 7-1/2 shot and seldom use more choke than Modified.

I have no scientific proof of this, and I realize my opinion flies in the face of popular reasoning, but many years of shooting have convinced me that when gun weight, shot charge weight and velocity are the same, a fixed-breech gun in 12 gauge kicks harder than one chambered for a smaller gauge. In an eight-pound gun, the 12 gauge loaded with an ounce of shot at 1200 fps seems to recoil more than when the same shot charge is fired at the same velocity from a 20-gauge gun of the same weight. Shoot an ounce of shot at 1200 fps in a 28-gauge gun weighing 8 pounds, and it will be a bit more comfortable to shoot than the 20-gauge gun. Other factors are at play here, but as a rule, it takes a few grains more powder to push an ounce of shot at 1200 fps from the 12 than from the 20, and the heavier the powder charge burned, the heavier is recoil. The 28 burns a bit less powder than the 20.

I have no idea why this is true, but I would not be surprised if it also has to do with the fact that as shotshell head diameter (or surface area) is increased, so is the amount of backthrust against the standing breech of a double-barrel shotgun. Think about it for a moment. A load that generates 11,000 pounds per square inch of chamber pressure is pushing against an area half that size with only half as much pressure. Since the head diameters of the 16- and 20-gauge shells are smaller than that of the 12 gauge, and the 28 gauge is even smaller yet, it

Crow shooter Paul Hammer uses a secret weapon to bring them within range of his 12-gauge Remington 870.

stands to reason that rearward push during firing is less with the smaller gauges. Regardless of whether I am on the right track or full of beans I will say this: My Krieghoff 32 weighs exactly the same with its 20- and 28-gauge tubes, and it is noticeably more comfortable to shoot with one ounce of 28-gauge ammo than with an ounce of shot in the 20 gauge. When weighted to weigh exactly the same, as it is when either pair of those tubes is installed, that gun kicks harder with one-ounce 12-gauge loads than with one-ounce 20-gauge loads.

Most shooters are not aware of this phenomenon because shotguns in the smaller gauges usually weigh less than those in 12 gauge. When the same shot charge at the same velocity is fired in both, the 12 gauge can actually be more comfortable to shoot because it is heavier. But when guns weigh the same, my shoulder says the smaller the gauge, the lighter is recoil.

Through the years, I have enjoyed a number of great hunts with various 12-gauge guns. The very first time I hunted turkeys with a Remington Model 870

Special Field, I bagged two mature gobblers with two shots. I still own that gun, and I have since taken many more turkeys with it. With its 21-inch barrel and weight of around seven pounds, it is my favorite for hunting the big bird in rugged mountain country where the only two directions you walk are straight up and straight down. It is also a darned good ruffed grouse gun, although I have used it very little for that.

Another great turkey gun I will never forget is the Benelli autoloader I used while hunting in western Kentucky with Harold Knight. The gun wore an extended-grip stock from a Benelli police gun, and while I did not care for it at first, I eventually learned to like it very much, and not because I took two gobblers with it during that hunt. As I discovered, its stock made it more comfortable to shoot with heavy loads than the same gun with a stock of more conventional shape. I also discovered that I could shoot a gobbler with one hand while resting the forearm of the gun atop my knee as I sat on the ground with my back against a tree.

On two of my best waterfowl hunts, both in Uruguay, I used a Remington Model 11-87 autoloader and a Remington Model 332 over-under. I was there with the Model 11-87 to field test Kent's new nontoxic waterfowl ammo loaded with Tungsten-Matrix shot, shortly before it was approved for use in the United States. The Model 332 I used was one of the first half-dozen guns built, and in it I used ammo loaded by Remington with Hevi-Shot.

Some of my best upland bird hunting with the 12-gauge took place in the sandhills of Nebraska. I was hunting with my Fox Sterlingworth and a new load Remington had just introduced as Express High Velocity Extra Long Range. It was loaded to 1325 fps with 1-1/4 ounces of shot and, wow, was it deadly. Using No. 6s on prairie chickens and No. 4s on pheasant, I made a couple of the longest shots I have ever made on game birds.

Another memorable 12-gauge adventure came to be known as the Great 12-gauge Huntathon. Hatched by Jim Bequette, the idea was for me to take a variety of game all over the country with various loads made by one of the major ammunition companies. Its purpose was to illustrate to readers of *Shooting Times* magazine that the company had all the hunting bases covered with its vast variety of loadings. I used the same autoloading shotgun on everything. The adventure got kicked off in Idaho where I shot chukar, pheasants, Hungarian partridge, bobwhite quail and probably a few other things I don't remember. Then it was off to other states for ducks, geese, sharptail grouse and mourning doves. I even installed a scope and a rifled barrel on the gun and took a nice whitetail buck with it. Of all the hunts we made for that series, one stands out as the most fun by a country mile — hunting cottontail rabbits with Allen Corsine's pack of beagles.

FAVORITE 12-GAUGE HANDLOADS

Case: Remington STS Plastic
Primer: Remington 209 STS
Powder: Hodgdon Clays
Powder Charge: 16.0 grains
Wad: Winchester WAA12L
Shot Charge: 3/4 ounce
Velocity: 1200 fps
Notes: Duplicates standard 28-gauge load.

Case: Remington STS Plastic
Primer: Remington 209 STS
Powder: Hodgdon Clays
Powder Charge: 15.5 grains
Wad: Winchester WAA12L
Shot Charge: 7/8 ounce
Velocity: 1150 fps
Notes: Excellent low-recoil load*

Case: Remington STS Plastic
Primer: Remington 209 STS
Powder: Hodgdon International Clays
Powder Charge: 22.0 grains
Wad: Winchester WAA12L
Shot Charge: 7/8 ounce
Velocity: 1325 fps
Notes: Duplicates performance of 24-gram international target loads

Case: Remington STS Plastic
Primer: Remington 209 STS
Powder: Hodgdon International Clays
Powder Charge: 24.5 grains
Wad: Winchester WAA12L
Shot Charge: 7/8 ounce
Velocity: 1400 fps
Notes: Extremely fast but does not pattern well in some guns

Case: Federal Gold Medal Plastic
Primer: Remington 209 STS
Powder: Hodgdon Clays
Powder Charge: 17.5 grains
Wad: Winchester WAA12L
Shot Charge: 1 ounce lead
Velocity: 1125 fps
Notes: Low-recoil load*

Case: Federal Gold Medal Plastic
Primer: Winchester 209
Powder: Alliant Red Dot
Powder Charge: 20.0 grains
Wad: Winchester WAA12L
Shot Charge: 1 ounce
Velocity: 1290 fps
Notes: High-velocity load

Case: Remington STS Plastic
Primer: Remington 209 STS
Powder: Accurate Nitro 100
Powder Charge: 16.0 grains
Wad: Remington Figure-8
Shot Charge: 1-1/8 ounces
Velocity: 1125 fps

Case: Winchester AA Plastic
Primer: Winchester 209
Powder: Alliant American Select
Powder Charge: 17.0 grains
Wad: Remington STS Plastic
Shot Charge: 1-1/8 ounces
Velocity: 1150 fps
Notes: Another great low-recoil load*

Case: Remington STS Plastic
Primer: Winchester 209
Powder: Hodgdon International Clays
Powder Charge: 21.0 grains
Wad: Remington Figure-8
Shot Charge: 1-1/8 ounces
Velocity: 1250 fps
Notes: Deadly on pheasants

Case: Winchester AA Plastic
Primer: Remington 209
Powder: Alliant Green Dot
Powder Charge: 21.0 grains
Wad: Winchester CB3118-12A
Shot Charge: 1-1/8 ounces (with Polywad Spred-R insert)
Velocity: 1200 fps
Notes: Excellent spreader load with No. 7-1/2 and smaller shot

Case: Remington STS Plastic
Primer: Remington 209 STS
Powder: Alliant Herco
Powder Charge: 25.0 grains
Wad: Remington SP12
Shot Charge: 1-1/4 ounces
Velocity: 1225 fps
Notes: Great long-range pheasant load

Case: Remington STS Plastic
Primer: Remington 209P
Powder: Hodgdon HS-6
Powder Charge: 30.0 grains
Wad: Remington RP12
Shot Charge: 1-1/4 ounces (bismuth)

Velocity: 1225 fps
Notes: Favorite waterfowl load for Fox Sterlingworth

Case: Federal Gold Medal Plastic
Primer: Winchester 209
Powder: Hodgdon HS-7
Powder Charge: 35.5 grains
Wad: Winchester WAA12R
Shot Charge: 1-3/8 ounces
Velocity: 1225 fps
Notes: Excellent patterns from several guns

Case: Federal Gold Medal Plastic
Primer: Remington 209 STS
Powder: Alliant Blue Dot
Powder Charge: 33.0 grains
Wad: Remington SP12
Shot Charge: 1-1/2 ounces
Velocity: 1200 fps
Notes: Very effective on turkey gobblers

Case: Federal Hi Power Plastic (3")
Primer: Winchester 209
Powder: Hodgdon HS-6
Powder Charge: 32.5 grains
Wad: Winchester WAA12F114
Shot Charge: 1-5/8 ounces (bismuth)
Velocity: 1200 fps
Notes: Favorite waterfowl load for Winchester Model 12 Heavy Duck Gun

Case: Federal Hi Power Plastic (3")
Primer: Winchester 209
Powder: Alliant Blue Dot
Powder Charge: 33.0 grs
Wad: Remington SP12
Shot Charge: 2 ounces
Velocity: 1150 fps
Notes: Favorite turkey load for 3-inch guns

Case: Remington Plastic (3-1/2")
Primer: Winchester 209
Powder: Alliant Blue Dot
Powder Charge: 38.0 grains
Wad: Remington SP12
Shot Charge: 2-1/4 ounces
Velocity: 1150 fps
Notes: Great turkey load for gas-operated autoloaders.

*Will usually operate the Remington Model 11-87, but port pressure is usually too low to operate some of the other autoloaders.

CHAPTER 20

Long Live The Mighty 10 Gauge

Some inexpensive 10-gauge doubles imported into America have been less than desirable but this AyA Matador was not a bad gun for the money.

The 10 gauge used to be what the 12 gauge is today. It is now everything developers of the 3-1/2 inch 12-gauge shell hope it will eventually prove to be. Is the young upstart equal to the old-timer? It depends on the type of shot being used. When both are loaded with the smaller sizes of steel shot, patterns fired by one can hardly be told from those fired by the other. Switch to the larger sizes of shot such as BB, BBB and T needed when hunting geese, and it is not at all unusual to see the 10 gauge deliver better patterns than the 12. This is one reason why I prefer the 10 gauge for waterfowling. Another reason is its availabil-

ity in the Remington SP-10 shotgun. Push a maximum charge of steel from the muzzles of some shotguns chambered for the 3-1/2 inch 12-gauge shell, and you'd best hang onto your bridgework. Push the same amount of shot from the muzzle of the SP-10, and you'll want to shoot it again and again. The difference is in the weight of the guns. The SP-10 will tip the scale at 10 to 11 pounds, a bit much for toting in chukar or quail country, but just right for pushing a handful of steel shot skyward from a duck blind. If a better gun has ever been built for pass-shooting waterfowl at long range, I have yet to discover it. Once you get all that

The Remington SP-10 is the gun I often reach for when using steel shot.

out-front weight in motion, the momentum won't allow you to suddenly get lazy and stop your swing without proper follow through. You can miss a duck or goose with the SP-10, but you have to try really hard in order to pull it off.

Switch to lead shot or soft nontoxic shot such as Tungsten-Matrix and bismuth, and the pendulum swings even farther in favor of the 10 gauge. When teamed up with the right choke the 3-1/2 inch 12 will shoot patterns dense enough to saturate the head and neck of a turkey gobbler out to 45 yards, but beyond that distance, patterns start losing density at an extremely rapid rate. I have heard that some guns will make it to 50 yards while others are effective on out to 60 yards, but I have yet to have the opportunity to test one. I have spent enough time at the pattern board and in the field with guns of all gauges to conclude that whatever the average 3-1/2 inch 12-gauge gun will do at 45 yards, a good 10-gauge gun will do at 55 yards. I have shot some choke and load combinations that produced uniformly dense patterns out to an honest 65 yards. That, by the way, just happens to be four yards farther than the longest shot I have ever made on a turkey gobbler. I was shooting the Remington SP-10 wearing a Briley choke with .040 inch of constriction. I was also using Remington's Premier load with 2-1/4 ounces of No.

5 shot. The bird was killed dead in its tracks.

The 10 gauge has been around for a very long time and was quite popular when muzzleloaders were the latest in shotguns. But it was not the biggest shotgun around, since the 4 and 8 gauges were also popular among waterfowlers. The British still load the 4 gauge with three ounces of shot, and the 8 gauge with two ounces. In the United States, the development of smokeless powder and choke-bored barrels put both in their graves during the early 1900s, but the 10 gauge managed to hang on. It has been available in a number of lengths, including 2-1/2, 2-5/8, 2-3/4, 2-7/8, 3, 3-1/8, 3-1/4 and 3-1/2 inches, but now only the 3-1/2-inch version is loaded by American manufacturers. Back in its blackpowder days, the 10-gauge shell was commonly loaded with 1-1/4 ounces of shot, which, interestingly enough, is now standard for the 3-inch 20-gauge shell. Availability of a smokeless-powder version of the 1-1/4-ounce load was eventually developed, and it was not until the 1920s that shot charge weight for the 2-7/8 inch hull was increased to 1-5/8 ounces. A muzzle velocity of 1,285 fps was considered rather speedy in those days. During the 1930s, Western Cartridge Company increased the payload to two ounces and then later to 2-1/4 ounces, giving the 10 gauge a 1/4 ounce advantage over the 3-inch 12 gauge. The Big Ten held

Many decades ago a 10-gauge double was the waterfowl gun by which all others were measured.

onto that edge until the 1990s, when the 3-1/2 inch version of the 12 gauge with its 2-1/4 ounce shot charge was introduced.

Remington offers quite a variety of 10-gauge loadings. They include 2-1/4 ounces of No. 4 and 6 lead at 1210 fps, 1-3/4 ounces of T, BBB, BB, 1 and 2 steel at 1260 fps and 1-3/4 ounces of No. 2 and 4 Hevi-Shot at 1300 fps. Over at Federal, we have two ounces of No. 4, 5, and 6 lead at 1300 fps, 1-3/8 ounces of Tungsten-Iron at a speedy 1450 fps, and 1-3/8 ounces of steel BBs and BBBs at 1425 fps. Winchester offers two ounces of No. 4, 5, and 6 lead at 1300 fps, 1-3/8 ounces of BBB, BB and No. 2 steel at 1450 fps, and another steel shot loading with 1-3/4 ounces of No. 1, 2, 3 and BB at 1260 fps. At this point, it might be appropriate to interject the fact that when all things are equal, including shot charge weight and velocity, the 3-1/2-inch 12-gauge shell develops higher chamber pressures than the 10-gauge shell of the same length. This is why the extra-long 12-gauge shell has a reputation for being much harder on guns than the 10 gauge.

There are still places in the Deep South where hunters go after deer with shotguns loaded with buckshot, and for this nothing is better than the 10 gauge. A good example is the Savannah River Site near Jackson, South Carolina, where hundreds of orange-clad hunters gather each year to participate in organized deer hunts with hounds. I hunted there once and found it to be quite a spectacle. The most popular 10-gauge load among those deer hunters is 18 double-ought pellets at 1100 to 1150 fps, a recipe offered by both Federal and Winchester. That same load is used in other parts of the world as well. A few professional hunters in Africa use 10-gauge guns loaded with buckshot anytime they have to go into the thick brush to finish off a leopard wounded by a client. They say nothing else is as devastating at close range. Federal also offers a deer and black bear load with a 1-3/4 ounce Foster-style slug at 1280 feet per second. It delivers close to a ton of energy at 50 yards with a .78 caliber slug weighing 766 grains, and it is quite capable of punching a mighty big hole through anything that gets in its way. I once shot a whitetail buck at about 70 yards with that load, and it dropped so quickly from my sight, I thought I had missed.

I believe Winchester built the first repeating shotgun in 10 gauge. In 1887, that company introduced a

The 10-gauge shotshell is effective turkey medicine but the weight of most guns chambered for it makes it a better choice for waterfowling.

John Browning-designed lever-action shotgun called the Model 1887. Offered in 10 and 12 gauge, its tubular magazine held four rounds. After making about 85,000 Model 87s, Winchester ceased its production in 1901 and replaced it with smokeless-powder version of the same gun but called it the Model 1901. The Model 1901 was manufactured in 10 gauge only, but never became very popular, and fewer than 14,000 were built during almost 20 years of production.

The finest 10-gauge guns created by the hands of American craftsmen were side-by-side doubles. Several American companies including Remington and Parker built them, but when it came to turning out both quality and quantity, Ithaca led the race. Guns chambered to 10 gauge always cost a bit more than the same grades built in smaller gauges. During the 1930s, the least expensive 12-bore field-grade Ithaca sold for $43, while the same gun in 10 gauge cost an additional $10.80. Other options ran the same, regardless of gauge: $8.50 for a nonselective single trigger, $21.60 for a single-selective trigger, $2.25 for a rubber recoil pad, and $1.10 for an ivory front sight instead of brass. Ithaca also offered its higher grades in 10 gauge: the No. 2 at $73.05, the No. 4 Ejector Gun at $130 and the top-of-line No. 7 Ejector at $379.20. Among other nice things, that gun had highly figured walnut, beavertail forearm, ventilated rib, gold-plated trigger and elaborate engraving on its receiver. For a bit more money, Ithaca

would choke one of its guns to a customer's specifications. If a customer wanted the right barrel of his gun to deliver 55 percent patterns at 40 yards with Winchester Super-X loaded with 1-5/8 ounces of chilled No. 6s, and the left barrel to produce 70 percent patterns at the same range with Super-X loaded with 1-5/8 ounces of No. 4s, Ithaca craftsmen would spend hours painstakingly reaming and shooting and then reaming and shooting some more until those exact percentages were achieved. The most famous 10-gauge Ithaca was first owned by Major Charles Askins and then by Elmer Keith after Askins died. Both were impressed by its performance, opinions well documented in books and magazine articles written by them.

After Ithaca stopped manufacturing doubles, the responsibility of supplying American hunters with 10-gauge shotguns fell on the shoulders of foreign companies. A number of inexpensive side-by-side and over-under doubles were imported into the United States. One of the finest was a side-by-side built by Krieghoff, a German firm better known for its K32 and K80 over-unders. There were also a few clunkers in the bunch, but some of the inexpensive doubles were not all that bad. The Matador, a 10 gauge side-by-side built by the Spanish firm of AyA, might have been the best of the low-priced bunch. While no more than a brief glance told you it was not built by Purdey or Westley Richards, I killed enough

Some duck hunters remain convinced that a 10-gauge gun is capable of delivering better patterns than a gun chambered for the 3-1/2 inch 12-gauge shell.

ducks and geese with that gun to make me wish I had bought a couple back in the 1960s when they sold for around $200. Decades later, during the 2001 season, I hunted ducks on the Missouri River, and one of the other hunters had brought along a 10-gauge Matador as a spare gun. Shooting a few ducks with it brought back plenty of good memories of times we will never again see. I need another shotgun like I need higher taxes, but if ever I bump into a 10-gauge Matador at a fair price, I might just take it home with me.

Because Ithaca was an early leader in the production of American 10-gauge guns, it was only fitting that the same company (under different ownership) would be the first to introduce a successful repeating 10 gauge. Introduced in 1974 as the Mag-10, its 12-pound weight, along with its gas operation, tamed 10-gauge recoil like it had never been tamed before. Tommy Hamrick, a friend of mine and an avid duck hunter, has hunted a lot with his Mag-10 — and I do mean a lot. Back when the Ithaca autoloader was front-page news, lead shot was still being used on waterfowl, so its designers did not have to contend with steel shot. Once the use of steel shot was mandated, Tommy started feeding it to his Mag-10, but finally quit after the extremely hard shot had ironed most of the choke from its barrel. Installing a screw-in choke designed for use with steel shot would put the old gun back in the duck blind, but that may never happen since my friend has now switched to a 20-gauge autoloader and seldom shoots anything but Remington's Hevi-Shot.

Ithaca began experiencing financial difficulties during the early 1980s and eventually ceased production of the Mag-10. But the idea of a comfortable-to-shoot shotgun chambered for the big shotshell was just too darned good to die. Remington bought manufacturing rights to the Mag-10 from Ithaca, but after several of its design weaknesses were uncovered, the decision was made to basically dump it and come up with a totally new gun — which is exactly what happened. After almost 1-1/2 years of design work, Remington unveiled its new SP-10 in 1989. That was only two years after steel shot became mandated for waterfowl hunting in the United States, so Remington's timing could not have been better. Until the 3-1/2 inch version of the 12-gauge shotshell came along some years later, the SP-10 was the benchmark by which all other waterfowl guns were measured. And believe me, when the typical 12-gauge gun loaded with steel shot was pitted against the SP-10, it did not measure up all that well. All of the 5,000 SP-10s built during 1989 were described by Remington as limited-edition guns and are easily identified by their LE89 serial number prefix. The serial number of my gun is LE89-0529, so it was probably built during the first or second month of SP-10 production.

As I write this, popularity of the 10 gauge is on the decline. This is due to the fact that guns chambered for the 3-1/2 inch 12-gauge shell are more versatile. All things considered, the 10-gauge gun simply cannot be beat for use on waterfowl with steel shot, but that's about

Back when the Remington SP-10 had just been introduced I used one to bag a few ducks on the Alaska Peninsula. Just behind me, the Ocean River is dumping its icy waters into the Bering Sea.

the limit of its usefulness. When a gun chambered for the 3-1/2 inch 12-gauge shell is teamed up with a variety of loads containing shot charges weighing from 1-1/8 to 2-1/4 ounces along with a good slug load, that one gun can be used for everything from upland wingshooting to waterfowling to deer hunting to trap shooting. It may not be ideal for all those applications, but it is better suited for shooting quail at close range and for carrying for many

miles each day during a South Dakota pheasant hunt than the heavier 10-gauge gun. As 10-gauge guns I would want to hunt with go, only the Remington SP-10, Browning BPS and Browning Gold 10 are still with us, and I am not sure they will be around for very long.

One of the most enjoyable waterfowl hunts I have ever been on took place on the Alaska Peninsula not long after the SP-10 was introduced. I was there to hunt moose, and since I managed to bag a nice bull fairly quickly, I needed to use up the remaining days on something else. The hunt was sponsored by Remington, so in addition to the rifles we used when hunting moose, a number of shotguns and plenty of ammunition for them was on hand. I don't recall whether I spent more time hunting ptarmigan with a 12-gauge Model 11-87 or waterfowl with the SP-10, but I do remember spending about every hour of daylight each day chasing one or the other. Wildman Lodge, the place I called home during those 10 days, was located on the west side of the peninsula and only a few miles from where the Ocean River pours its waters into the Bering Sea. I really got to know Remington's SP-10 on that hunt. I had already taken several turkey gobblers with the one I had back home, but had not used the big gun a lot on waterfowl prior to the Alaska trip. I shot Remington ammo with 1-3/4 ounces of No. 2 steel shot and could hardly believe how much more effective it was on ducks than the 12-gauge gun I was accustomed to using on waterfowl.

Long live the 10 gauge. May its voice never grow silent in America's marshlands.

FAVORITE 10-GAUGE HANDLOADS

Case: Remington SP Plastic
Primer: Remington 209 STS
Powder: Hodgdon HS-7
Powder Charge: 41.0 grains
Wad: Remington SP10
Shot Charge: 2 ounces (bismuth)
Velocity: 1200 fps
Notes: Outstanding long-range waterfowl load

Case: Federal Plastic (with Paper Base Wad)
Primer: CCI 209M
Powder: Alliant Blue Dot
Powder Charge: 42.0 grains
Wad: Remington SP10
Shot Charge: 2-1/4 ounces
Velocity: 1150 fps
Notes: Fantastic turkey load

Case: Winchester Polyformed Plastic
Primer: Winchester 209
Powder: Hodgdon HS-7
Powder Charge: 43.0 grains
Wad: Remington SP-10
Shot Charge: 2-1/4 ounces
Velocity: 1200 fps
Notes: 60-yard gobbler killer

Case: Remington SP Plastic
Primer: Remington 209 STS
Powder: Alliant Blue Dot
Powder Charge: 42.5 grains
Wad: Remington SP10
Shot Charge: 2 ounces
Velocity: 1210
Notes: Duplicates 12-gauge 3-inch turkey load

CHAPTER 21

The Upland Gun

The upland gun is about a good dog, a good shotgun and at least one prairie chicken that cooperates before a long day ends.

I greatly enjoy spending a day in the marshes with a good waterfowl gun. I am also quite fond of any gun capable of reaching out and putting the brakes on a big turkey gobbler. Skeet guns, trap guns and sporting clays guns are also my cups of tea. I like about any type of shotgun you can think of, but my true love is the upland gun.

The really big soft spot in my heart is for the upland gun because it is about a covey of quail flushing from a brush pile and then making a beeline toward the swamp they have called home for as long as I can remember. It is about the cackling protest a gaudy old ringneck pheasant makes as it scares me half to death

while lifting its heavy body toward the sky with strong beats of its wings. The upland gun is about the flush of ruffed grouse I never saw, the whistle of a mourning dove's wings, the penetrating brown eyes of a curious bird called woodcock. It is about briar patches and cottontail rabbits and beagles named Sam, Bell and Sue. It is about mountain quail country too steep to climb in a day, sharptail grouse country too big to see in a lifetime and chukar country too scary for me to be in. It is about endless treks after Hungarian partridges and lung-bursting sprints after scaled quail. It is about blued steel, hand-checkered walnut, fine leather gun cases and an open bottle of Hoppe's No. 9. The upland gun is also about pointing dogs, tattered hunting coats, muddy boots, Jack-frost mornings and the smell of burning gunpowder. But best of all, the upland gun is about spending many wonderful days afield with some of the best people I have ever known.

Ask any shotgunner to describe the ideal gun for hunting upland game, and his answer will be greatly influenced by what and where he hunts. The hunter who spends his time flushing ruffed grouse from the Appalachian mountain thickets of West Virginia is likely to have different ideas about the subject than the fellow who hunts sharptail grouse on the plains of Montana. Someone who hunts ringnecked pheasants in Nebraska corn fields will probably describe the upland gun a bit differently than the fellow who spends all of his time hunting bobwhite quail in Georgia or South Carolina.

Regardless of who uses them, where they are used or what they are used for, all really good upland guns have one thing in common – they fit their owners well enough to allow them to shoot quickly and to consistently hit what they are shooting at. The deer hunter who sits in a tree stand and aims his slug gun like a rifle at a buck can get by with a stock that does not fit him all that well, because he usually has plenty of time to make his body conform to the gun. The same goes for the turkey hunter who wraps himself around the stock, takes careful aim and fires at a gobbler while it is standing still. A hunter who takes most of his ducks and geese by pass shooting is not greatly handicapped by gun that does not fit him perfectly. But give an ill-fitting gun to a ruffed grouse hunter who must shoulder his gun, make his swing and squeeze off a shot at a mere glimpse of a bird within a couple of heartbeats and he is likely to miss more often than he hits. One of the best ways to find out whether or not a gun fits is to shoot a few rounds of skeet or sporting clays from the old low-gun start position. Anyone who can consistently break 22 or 23 out of 25 targets is shooting a gun that fits them rather nicely. If you can break all targets thrown at station eight using the low-gun start, you should never let the gun in your hands out of your sight.

Jack O'Connor once described the ideal upland gun as short of barrel and light of weight. For some applications, I will agree even today. The ideal ruffed grouse gun should be light enough to be carried in one hand while the other hand is busy parting thick brush. The gun should also be short enough to maneuver through places you sometimes wish you had never entered. Killing a ruffed grouse requires the quickest shooting of any hunting I have tried, and for this reason I believe the ideal gun for it should be light enough to be carried in the ready position for long periods of time

The upland gun is about a stock that fits its owner as well as the one on my old L.C. Smith fits me.

without tiring out the arms. I have also hunted bobwhite quail and California quail in thickets where he who delays his shots for more than a second or two will go home with an empty game bag.

One of the best ruffed grouse guns I own is a Winchester reproduction of the Parker in 28 gauge. It has 26-inch barrels, and since it is only 42-1/2 inches long overall, it is rather handy for carrying in thick places. The little gun weighs only 5-1/2 pounds, so I can carry it all day long in the toughest, roughest, steepest country you can find without realizing it is in my hands until trigger-pulling time rolls around. I can get off an accurate shot rather quickly with several of my guns, but I am just a shade quicker with the little Parker because it is so light and it fits me so well. I have never timed myself when shooting a grouse or quail in the woods with that gun, but beginning from the low-gun start position, I can break the low-house target from station seven in skeet in well under a second. I mention this not to boast of my blazing speed with a shotgun, but to

The upland gun is about sharptail grouse country too big to see in a lifetime.

emphasize what can be done with a lightweight gun that fits an owner who occasionally practices with it.

Upland guns used for hunting other birds in other places can be heavier, but where a lot of walking is involved, 7-1/2 pounds is about as heavy as many hunters will want to go. I just weighed several of my guns and came up with the following, beginning with the lightest and working up; 20-gauge Westley Richards, 5-1/2 pounds; 28-gauge AyA No. 1, 5-1/2 pounds; .410-caliber Iver Johnson Skeet-er, six pounds; .410-caliber Winchester Model 42 and 20-gauge Browning Superposed Lightning, 6-1/4 pounds; 20-gauge Winchester Model 101, 6-1/2 pounds; 16-gauge L.C. Smith and 20-gauge Remington Model 11-87, 6-3/4 pounds; 28-gauge Remington Model 1100, six pounds, 15 ounces; 20-gauge Model 1100 ST-20 and 12-gauge Model 870 Special Field, seven pounds; 12-gauge Fox Sterlingworth and 12-gauge Remington Model 870, 7-1/2 pounds.

I work out at least three times each week, year-around, and I have been doing it for many years, so when hunting season rolls around, I am in good enough shape to walk up to 10 miles per day if my feet don't

blister up. I enjoy hunting with a lightweight gun, but it is not something I really have to have. I have carried my Fox Sterlingworth for many miles while hunting prairie chickens and pheasants, and it is no lightweight. I shoot it so well and enjoy hunting with it so much, I seldom notice its weight, even toward the end of a long day in the field. Still, even I will have to admit that my 16-gauge L.C. Smith is even more fun to carry, and if my 28-gauge AyA would handle everything under all conditions, some of my other doubles would suffer from even more neglect than they already do.

As autoloaders go, I prefer the 20- and 28-gauge chambering because the typical gun of that type in 12 gauge is a bit on the hefty side for long treks afield. And besides, there are not many jobs in the uplands that cannot be handled by the two smaller shells. Whereas it is not uncommon to see 12-gauge autos weighing upwards of eight pounds, very few in 20 gauge will exceed seven pounds. The lightest 20-gauge gun I own is a Franchi 48AL at 5-1/2 pounds. I also have the same gun in 28 gauge, and while the Franchi catalog rates it at about three ounces lighter, mine is actually two ounces heavier than my 20-gauge 48AL.

The upland gun is about valley quail taken in coverts other hunters have overlooked or passed by.

Both have 26-inch barrels. I shoot them as well on flushing birds as any shotguns I have ever owned. Franchi also makes an extremely light 12-gauge autoloader. Called the Model 612 Sporting, it weighs around seven pounds. Whereas the 48AL is recoil-operated, the Model 612 is gas-operated.

Autoloaders such as the Weatherby SAS, Browning Gold, Beretta AL391 and Remington Model 11-87, all in 12 gauge, tip the scale at 7-3/4 to eight pounds. Incidentally, the 12-gauge Remington Model 11-87 is usually a bit lighter than the Remington Model 1100. At 7-3/4 pounds, my Model 11-87 with a 28-inch barrel is a quarter pound lighter than my Model 1100 with a 26-inch barrel. A 20-gauge Model 11-87 I hunted with in Uruguay weighed almost a quarter pound less than my old Model 1100 in the same gauge.

When it comes down to ease of carry, some of the slide action shotguns have a lot going for them. The lightest pump gun I own is a .410-caliber Winchester Model 42; it weighs only 6-1/4 pounds. The Remington Model 870 Wingmaster in either 12 or 16 gauge will vary a few ounces from gun to gun due to differences in the densities of their wood stocks, but the typical gun

will usually weigh around 7-1/2 pounds. The 12-gauge Browning BPS, Ithaca Model 37 and Winchester Model 1300 weigh about the same as the Model 870. A Model 870 Special Field I occasionally hunt ruffed grouse with has an English-style buttstock and a 21-inch barrel. It weighs exactly seven pounds. The Model 870 in 20 or 28 gauge will average anywhere from six to 6-1/2 pounds. The Winchester Model 12 is considerably heavier. A 28-gauge gun sitting in my gun rack weighs 7-1/4 pounds, and a 12-gauge Model 12 belonging to a friend is only an ounce shy of eight pounds. Any Model 12 almost always feels lighter than it actually it because it is balanced so well. The Benelli Nova is also a rather heavy pump gun, and this is one of the reasons why it has become popular among waterfowl hunters who shoot heavy loads. The one I had on consignment for a while wore a 26-inch barrel and weighed an ounce over eight pounds on my postal scale.

The double-barrel shotgun is tough to beat in the uplands for a number of reasons. One is weight. Lightweight 12-gauge over-unders with aluminum receivers made by Franchi, Beretta and Browning weigh considerably less than most 12-gauge pumps and

The upland gun is about chukar country too steep to climb.

autoloaders. The Alcione Titanium in 12-gauge from Franchi is rated at a couple of ounces less than seven pounds with 28-inch barrels, while the 20-gauge version doesn't miss 6-1/2 pounds by very much. I once hunted chukar with the 20-gauge gun and shot it quite well. The fact that lightweight 12-gauge over-unders can be punishing to shoot with heavy loads is a moot point since light to medium loads will handle most upland gunning with room to spare.

One of the nicest-feeling and best-balanced 12-gauge over-unders I have hunted with is the Remington Model 332. It weighs 7-1/4 pounds with 28-inch barrels, and it fits like it was custom made just for me. I also like the aluminum-framed over-under made by Franchi. It is called Veloce, which means fast in Italian. I used one in 28 gauge while hunting planted Huns and chukars in Maryland, and even though its John Browning-style safety and barrel selector gave me fits at times, I hated to come home without it. I did not get around to weighing the gun, but it is rated at 5-1/2 pounds. The 20-gauge version weighs about a quarter pound more. Without doubt, the classiest over-under I have ever shot belongs to a friend with whom I once hunted ducks in Uruguay. Made by the English firm of Holland & Holland, its price back then was close to $30,000.

Of the over-unders now sitting in my gun room, a Winchester 101, a Browning Superposed Lightning and a Weatherby Athena are favorites for most of the upland hunting I do. The Winchester weighs 6-1/2 pounds, the Browning weighs 6-1/4 pounds and the Weatherby weighs 6-3/4 pounds. All are in 20 gauge and they have 3-inch chambers. The barrels of the Winchester measure 26-1/2 inches long, the Weatherby has 28-inch barrels, and while the barrels of the Browning actually measure 26-3/8 inches, their official length according to Browning is 26-1/2 inches. The Weatherby and the Browning have a variety of Briley screw-in chokes ranging from Skeet to Full. The Winchester is choked Improved Skeet and Light Modified. I also have Briley subgauge tubes in .410 and 28 gauge for it, and they too have a variety of screw-in chokes. The Weatherby Athena is actually a three-barrel set with extra 26-inch barrels in .410 and 28-inch barrels 28 gauge.

The Model 101 was the first double-barrel shotgun I ever bought with my own money. The Superposed once belonged to my father and was one of his favorite quail guns. Crossing too many barbed-wire fences and bucking too many briar thickets had taken a terrible toll on its finish, so I sent the gun to Browning for refinishing soon after it came into my possession.

The Weatherby Athena holds the distinction of taking the grand slam of quail with all three sets of its barrels. With that gun in .410, 28-gauge and 20-gauge, I have bagged valley and mountain quail in California, scaled, Mearns and Gambel quail in Arizona and bobwhite quail in too many states to mention. Anytime I need to reach out farther than those two guns are capable of and want to stick with the over-under, I usually use my old Remington Model 3200. Its 30-inch barrels are choked Modified and Full.

As much as I enjoy hunting with the over-under, I will have to admit the side-by-side is where my heart is. To me, the side-by-side double looks and feels exactly the way an upland gun is supposed to look and feel. Unfortunately, a good one of current production usually costs more than an equally good over-under. As I write this, a No. 1 grade AyA like the one in 28 gauge I own will set you back close to $8,000, but you don't have to spend that kind of money to own a good side-by-side. The AyA 453 drops game birds with equal efficiency, and while not as handsome as the higher grades, it is handsome enough and it costs about one-fourth as much. There was a time when shotguns built in Spain did not enjoy the best of reputations among American hunters, but this is no longer true.

While side-by-sides built by firms such as AyA, Armas Garbi and Arrieta fall a bit short of the best British game guns in fit, finish and attention to other minor aesthetic details, they are just as durable (if not more so), they handle just as nicely and they cost much less. Buying a British double in the same class as my AyA would set you back anywhere from $30,000 to $40,000. English-built doubles made years ago can sometimes be bought for a lot less money than a new one would cost. My 1940s-vintage 20-gauge Westley Richards is valued at less than $10,000 on the used gun market. Last time I looked, Westley Richards was charging about three times as much for the same gun, and the delivery time was about two years.

Through the years, a number of cheap knock-about doubles have been available at bargain-basement prices, and among other things they lack the handling qualities of better guns. A good rule of thumb to keep in mind is this: In order to come up with a side-by-side double that looks and feels the way a gun to be used for upland hunting should, you will likely have to pay no less than two to three times as much for it as you would pay for a top-quality autoloader such as the Remington Model 11-87, Benelli M1 Field, Browning Gold and Beretta AL391. From there, the sky and your line of credit at the bank are your only limitations. As new side-by-sides go, you cannot go wrong with those built

The upland gun is about pausing for a moment to drink in the beauty of a small chunk of America.

by reputable Spanish manufacturers. In that same league is the Highlander from Franchi. Guns built by the German firm of Merkel are also quite nice. As the few side-by-sides now being made in America go, the one I would most like to own is the Fox built by Connecticut Shotguns. The Ithaca built by Ithaca Classic Doubles is also nice.

If I were to start shopping for a side-by-side double tomorrow, I would look long and hard at guns that are no longer in production. A 12-gauge Fox Sterlingworth in excellent condition can be bought for less than a good gun of current production, and it is often a better investment. The field grade L.C. Smith usually brings a bit less money than the Fox, while the Winchester Model 21 usually runs about three times the price of a good autoloader. Always take a close look at stock dimensions before buying an old double, as some have excessive drop at the comb and heel. But not all do. My Fox Sterlingworth was built during the mid-1920s, and its stock dimensions are no different than those on my modern guns. The same applies to other vintage doubles in my battery.

I would hate to have to give up all but one among my side-by-side guns because I own several that I am quite fond of. I could, however, boil it down to just half a dozen. My favorite woodcock gun and the one I usually reach for when hunting liberated pheasants, quail and chukar on commercial preserves is a .410-bore Iver Johnson Skeet-er. It has .006 inch of choke in both barrels. For shooting quail and ruffed grouse at fairly close range, I am very partial to a 28-gauge Parker. It has two points of constriction in its

right barrel and seven points in its left. For longer shots at quail, sharptail grouse, chukar and Hungarian partridge it becomes a tossup between my 28-gauge AyA and my 20-gauge Westley Richards. The Spanish gun is choked .006 and .018 inch, while the English gun is choked .004 and .014 inch. I also enjoy shooting mourning doves with those two. Another favorite, and one that I shoot as well as any gun I have ever owned, is a 16-gauge L.C. Smith. Anytime pheasants, sharptail grouse and prairie chickens are flushing wild, I'd just as soon have my 12-gauge Fox Sterlingworth as any gun I have ever shot. Choked .020 and .041 inch, it is capable of reaching out and dropping birds much farther away than I have any business shooting at them.

Regardless of whether its barrels are oriented north and south or east and west, the double has an advantage or two over other types of shotguns. Probably most important, it allows the hunter to instantly choose between two different chokes. I have hunted in times and places where one shot might come inside 20 yards, while the next might be out around 40 yards. Having an open choke instantly available for a close shot and a tighter choke on tap for a longer shot without having to remember what button or lever to move in which direction is something you can have only with a double with two triggers. A pump or autoloader equipped with a variable choke device such as the old Poly Choke offers the same options, but they are not instantly available and no pheasant or quail will wait around long enough for you to twist the device from one constriction to another.

The upland gun is about ruffed grouse country ablaze with autumn colors.

I should mention that the only way to utilize the two-choke option of a double to its fullest is to have a gun with two triggers. Most of the barrel selectors on side-by-sides and over-unders are OK if you have plenty of time to prepare for the shot, as sometimes happens when pass-shooting waterfowl and doves. Most selectors are worthless when a quail explodes from the broom sedge and you must get off a shot before it disappears behind a thick wall of brush. Fooling around with a barrel selector at a time when you should be concentrating on the target can be a mistake, and it is often too much for the human brain to handle. This is why the barrel selectors of most guns are seldom, if ever used by their owners. An exception is the one on the Remington Model 3200. When its safety lever is in the middle position, the gun is on safe. Flicking the tail of the lever to the left with your thumb takes the gun off safe and allows the bottom barrel to be fired first with a pull on the trigger. Flicking the lever to the right of center also takes the gun off safe but it allows the top barrel to be fired first. The design works equally well for right- or left-hand-ed shooters, and anyone who takes the time to become accustomed to it will find it to be as good as having two triggers on a gun. It might be even better, since it offers the best of both designs, instant choke selection as with double triggers, and the constant length of pull of the single trigger.

When all have barrels of the same length, the double is shorter overall than the pump and autoloader, and this can make it handier to use under some conditions. This is due to the shorter receiver of the double. My Fox Sterlingworth has 30-inch barrels, and yet it is 1-3/4 inches shorter overall than my Remington Model 11-87 autoloader with its 28-inch barrel. My 28-gauge Parker double and 28-gauge Remington Model 1100 both have 22-inch barrels, but the Parker is almost three inches shorter. The over-under is usually a bit longer overall than the side-by-side because its receiver is a bit longer, but the difference is seldom enough to write home about. My Remington Model 3200 is less than an inch longer than my Fox Sterlingworth, and my Browning Superposed is exactly one inch longer than my Parker.

CHAPTER 22
Guns and Loads for Waterfowl

The paradise duck is one of the most handsome of waterfowl. I took this one in New Zealand with Adrian Moody's old BRNO shotgun.

There was a time long ago when most duck and goose hunters favored the double-barrel shotgun. Some of the old doubles not only became as famous as their masters, they managed to outlive them as well. A 12-gauge gun called Bo Whoop by its owner, Nash Buckingham, naturally comes to mind. Built around a Fox action by Philadelphia barrel maker Burt Becker, its 32-inch barrels were chambered for the 3-inch shell and choked Full. Buckingham acquired the 10-pound double in 1926,

and as all such stories about waterfowl guns should read, it earned its name in a Mississippi river duck blind. I'll let Buckingham's hunting partner, Colonel H.P. Sheldon, take it from here.

"Nash had blinded up in a dense thicket of willows along the edge of a clear channel some 150 yards from my own stand. A pair of mallards traveling high and in hurry went over Nash. Both collapsed and after a moment of complete silence the double boom of the big gun came rolling roundly over the marshes. It

Sunrise over the Missouri River.

sounded exactly like two solo notes from the bass horn in a symphony orchestra, and I mentioned it to Nash when we got back to the lodge. 'Bo Whoop, Bo Whoop'." The Becker-built Fox owned by Buckingham went on to become the most famous gun in waterfowling history. (Actually, there are two Bo Whoops, but that's another story for another time.)

Then there was the 10-gauge Ithaca originally owned by Major Charles Askins. If the name is not familiar to you, Askins was a well-known firearms writer who had collaborated with Burt Becker in the development of the Fox HE grade waterfowl gun, or Super-Fox as it was also called. Askins' 10-bore Ithaca was later owned by writer Elmer Keith, who wove it into the fabric of several of his hunting stories. That gun had 32-inch barrels choked Full, and both Askins and Keith swore it would deliver patterns bordering on 100 percent at 40 yards. Keith wrote about killing ducks out to 80 yards with Western Super-X shells loaded with two ounces of No. 2 Lubaloy, and since most who hunted with him considered him to be one of the finest long-range waterfowl shots of his time, he most likely did just that. I never had the pleasure of seeing Elmer and his old Ithaca in action, but I once sat with him in a pit at Remington Farms and watched in amazement as he reached into the heavens with a 3-inch Model 1100 and brought Canada geese down

from heights I dared not attempt.

Like so many of us who enjoy waterfowling with double-barrel shotguns, Keith, Askins and Buckingham were actually throwbacks to a time that no longer existed. As Bob Hinman so aptly put it in his book *The Golden Age of Shotgunning*, the double's reign as king of America's marshes and uplands came and went during the last three decades of the 19th century. Even though American gun makers such as Parker, Ithaca, L.C. Smith, Fox and Lefever continued to make the finest doubles ever built in this country as late as the 1930s, their decline in popularity had begun in 1897, the year the first truly successful repeating shotgun was introduced by Winchester. The new Model 97 pump gun was cheaper than a good double, more durable than a cheap double and its magazine capacity allowed it to be loaded on Sunday and shot all week. None of this went unnoticed during an era when the number of Americans who hunted to eat still outnumbered those who hunted solely for the love of sport.

The slide action is still an excellent choice for waterfowling. It is less expensive than the double and the autoloader, and for this reason when I see my old Model 870 lying in the bottom of a duck boat all covered with mud, I don't get too excited. The pump is the lightest repeating shotgun available, and this is important to the hunter who must carry a load of decoys and

Thanks to the availability of soft nontoxic shot such as bismuth and Tungsten-Matrix, I am once again able to hunt geese with my 1920s-vintage Fox Sterlingworth.

other gear a long way across the marsh. Under the worst of conditions, the pump is more reliable. Drop an autoloader, a double and a pump into a barrel of mud and the pump is the one most likely to come out shooting. When the pump and autoloader are properly maintained and cared for, they can be quite reliable, but when all are exposed to an entire season of wet-weather hunting, the pump is less likely to choke up in the middle of a mallard attack. Its action is less complex and it has fewer parts than the autoloader. The action of the pump gun is also easier to get into than the double. This makes the gun easier to clean after it has been rained on.

While the slide action is still quite popular among waterfowlers, I would not be surprised if someone told me the semiautomatic has surpassed it in popularity. I am sure some buy the autoloader because they think it can be fired faster, but probably more choose it because most gas-operated models reduce perceived recoil, and this is important when shooting heavy duck loads. Soon after the 3-1/2 inch version of the 12-gauge shell was introduced, I tried it in an inexpensive pump gun that weighed about 7-1/2 pounds. It took only a few rounds before I decided I would stick with the 2-3/4 and 3-inch shells. Later, I tried the heaviest 3-1/2 inch waterfowl loads available in a gas-operated autoloader weighing 8-1/4 pounds and found recoil to be tolerable.

One of the things that makes the gas gun more comfortable to shoot is its heavier weight. Another is its ability to lengthen or prolong the recoil curve. A gas-urged autoloader doesn't reduce actual recoil, but it does reduce perceived recoil, and that is what is important to the shooter standing behind it.

The double-barrel shotgun is making somewhat of a comeback among waterfowlers, but today it is the over-under rather than the side-by-side. The double also comes with a few advantages. When barrel lengths are the same, it is shorter overall than the pump and autoloader, and this makes it easier to handle in the cramped quarters of some duck blinds. Two barrels also offer the option of two different chokes, an open choke for the duck that cups its wings and drops into your decoys, and a tighter choke for the duck that tries to sneak by out at 40 yards. The double also allows a duck hunter to switch loads more quickly when a flock of geese decide to fly within range. I know a fellow who loads steel shot in one barrel and a Remington shell loaded with Hevi-Shot in the other. If a duck or goose flies within 30 yards of his blind he blasts it with less expensive steel shot. If a bird is farther away than that he downs it with Hevi-Shot. Having to break its barrels down for reloading does make the double less handy in a blind than the pump and autoloader, but this is offset by the fact that it does not ricochet spent cases off the side of your shooting partner's head.

A Currier and Ives morning on Maryland's eastern shore.

which is their durability and their reliability under harsh conditions.

Some of the doubles I own were not built for use with steel shot, so I use loads with either bismuth or Tungsten-Matrix shot in them. My favorite is a 12-gauge Fox Sterlingworth with 30-inch barrels. I shoot is as well as any gun I own. It also holds the record for making the longest shot I have ever made on a very unlucky Nebraska duck. My old Remington Model 3200 also works quite nicely on ducks and geese. I like that gun a lot, and while I can break a few more clay targets at trap with it than with the Fox, I shoot the Fox better in the field. I also enjoy using a 16-gauge L.C. Smith, and even though its barrels are choked rather loose at .010 and .025 inch, it does an excellent job on ducks out to 35 yards or so. For it, I handload bismuth shot or, if I don't have time to load shells, I simply use Kent ammunition with Tungsten-Matrix shot. One of these days, I will buy a good side-by-side double in 10 gauge. Sometime back, a friend let me shoot a few ducks with his and I really enjoyed it.

As a rule, waterfowlers don't place as much importance on how a gun looks as those who hunt upland game. In fact, some of the homeliest shotguns I have seen were being used by duck and goose hunters. There is absolutely nothing whatsoever wrong with that, and maybe decades of hunting bobwhite quail with handsome guns has spoiled me, but I am convinced a gun does not have to be ugly to kill ducks. This may be why I so greatly enjoyed hunting mallards in flooded timber at Wingmead sometime back with a Weatherby Athena, one of the best looking over-unders around. It may also be why I love to shoot ducks over decoys with my 20-gauge Westley Richards and my 16-gauge L.C. Smith. Ducks shot with those guns don't die any deader than those shot with guns that have no personality, but for me at least they are much more fun to shoot.

The development of nontoxic shot with densities comparable to that of lead is responsible for bringing the smaller gauges back into duck blinds all across America. Back when lead could still be used on waterfowl, one of my favorite guns for use on ducks in flooded timber was a 20-gauge Winchester Model 101. After steel shot became mandated, I switched to 12-gauge guns, but the availability of bismuth shot from Bismuth

When hunting with heavy steel shot loads, I prefer the autoloading shotgun because it is more comfortable to shoot. Remington built the two guns I have used most. One is a Model 11-87 with a 28-inch barrel. That gun had a 26-inch barrel when I first added it to my battery, but I switched it out for a 28-incher after discovering how much better I averaged with it on passing shots. The other autoloader I use a lot was one of the first SP-10s built by Remington in 1989. For the Model 11-87, I have a collection of Rem Chokes of various constrictions. I also use several chokes made by Remington in the SP-10, but Briley made my favorite choke for goose hunting. The extended type, it has .030 inch of constriction, which is Light Full for the 10 gauge.

If I were to buy a semiautomatic for hunting waterfowl tomorrow, I would look long and hard at what Benelli has to offer. I shot ducks and geese on the eastern shore of Maryland with the M1 Field and the Super Black Eagle, and could not decide which I liked best. Benelli autoloaders are quite popular among waterfowlers for a number of reasons, not the least of

Guns and Loads for Waterfowl **161**

Even when wearing all the clothes I could walk in I still got chilled to the bone on this goose hunt.

Cartridge and Tungsten-Matrix from Kent has caused me to swing back to the smaller gauges for quite a bit of my waterfowling.

I have hunted ducks in Alaska with a 28-gauge Winchester Model 12 and a handload with an ounce of No. 5 bismuth. It is surprisingly effective out to about as far away as I shoot most of my ducks. During one those trips, my guide was shooting a 12-gauge gun with the cheapest "mart special" steel shot ammo he could find. Most of the ducks that flew within 35 yards of my gun died on the spot when I hit them, whereas my guide was having one heck of a time bringing his first one down. Turning to me he said, "You are a much better wingshot than I." I replied that the difference was in the ammunition we were using, and not the shooters. To prove it, I asked him to swap guns with me, and he immediately started killing ducks. The only things I got for my trouble while shooting his gun were a few feathers.

I have also used the 28-gauge on ducks in Old Mexico but I used a handload with an ounce of

Tungsten-Polymer shot, which was being made by Federal Cartridge at the time. I took my Krieghoff 32 and Briley tubes in 28 and 20 gauges so I could compare the effectiveness of the two shotshells on waterfowl. After using up all my 28-gauge cartridges, I switched to Federal 20-gauge factory ammo loaded with 1-1/8 ounces of Tungsten-Polymer. We were shooting mostly teal inside 35 yards, and I could tell no difference between the 28 and the 20. For that matter, I also shot Federal 12-gauge ammo loaded with the same type of shot and did no better with it than with the two smaller gauges.

Remington loads the most effective 20-gauge waterfowl medicine I have ever used. Soon after that company adopted Hevi-Shot, four of us headed to Uruguay to wring it out on ducks. We were there to field test three prototypes of the Remington Model 332 shotgun, but we also brought along 20-gauge Model 11-87 autoloaders. I flew from my home in Simpsonville, South Carolina, to Miami, Florida, and eight hours, about 130,000 pounds of jet fuel and some 4,000 miles

Nick Sisley awaiting the next flight of ducks in a flooded rice field somewhere in northern Uruguay.

later, we were in Buenos Aires, Argentina. Another 30-minute flight had us in Montevideo, the capital of Uruguay. From there, we drove north in an Argentine copy of the British Land Rover until we came to Chuy, a small village located only a few miles from where Uruguay borders with Brazil.

We headquartered at Fort San Miguel, a magnificent structure built entirely of hand-carved stone with walls almost two feet thick. The massive door to my private room had been hewn from a local eucalyptus tree and was hinged on pieces of hand-forged iron. We were there in August, and even though temperature seldom dropped below 45 degrees Fahrenheit, the huge fireplace in the main hall felt nice and cozy after a day's hunt. Our tired but happy group was always greeted by a table running over with homemade sopre-salta sausage, ripe olives, local cheese and other appetizers. The wine was made from grapes grown in Uruguay. The olives came from trees just down the road. Then it was on to a main course with enough wonderfully prepared grass-fed beef to cause any vegetarian to go screaming into the night.

Our routine stayed about the same each day: up at 4:30 a.m. for a breakfast of bacon and eggs, freshly cooked breads, hand-squeezed orange juice and coffee grown, roasted and brewed as only it can be done in South America. Then it was off to the duck blinds for more shooting in one morning than many waterfowl hunters experience in a lifetime. Our blinds mostly con-

sisted of a few branches broken off from whatever bushes happened to be handy and stuck into the mud along the edge of a flooded field. The birds didn't seem to mind. Just at daybreak, before the ducks started flying, flocks of ibis, with bills drooping like melted wax flew over in steady ribbons of jet-black. We shot more different flavors of teal than I had seen before: cinnamon, speckled, range, silver, pink and Brazilian. The Brazilian gets my vote as the most beautiful of all teal and one of the more magnificent of the world's ducks. The "Pacasso," or rosy-billed pochard, was also represented in great numbers and made up about half of the birds we took. Quite beautiful in flight, the rosey is often described as South America's mallard because the two are about the same size and it is so common there. We also bagged the occasional spoonbill, southern widgeon, yellow-billed pintail, shoveler and whatnot.

The farmer who owned one 14,000-hectare field we hunted had been unable to harvest most of his crop of rice before unseasonable monsoons put it out of reach in about three feet of water. Like a giant magnet, it had attracted ducks by the hundreds of thousands, perhaps even by the millions. We rode in on a two-wheel trailer pulled by a four-wheel-drive tractor made by the Swedish company of Valmet and driven by Miguel, a quiet fellow who could probably show anyone a thing or two about being tough. As we entered the shooting area, wave after wave of ducks lifted in concert from the water's surface, slowly circled us a time or two and then set back down to continue their feast. I have hunted waterfowl in about every state in the United States where they are hunted, and on three other continents as well, and never had I seen anything that came close to that day in a rice field in Uruguay.

On the second day, I shared a blind with Eddie Stevenson of Remington while Scott Hanes, also of Remington, and Nick Sisley shot next door. Nick and I were using 20-gauge Remington Model 11-87 shotguns with 28-inch barrels choked Improved Cylinder. Our ammo was Remington Premier with 1-1/8 ounces of No. 6 Hevi-Shot. Much to everyone's amazement (especially mine), Nick and I consistently killed ducks out to a laser-ranged 60 yards with that combination. If you find such a statement of fact impossible to believe, I fully understand because if I had not actually been there, done it and seen it with my own eyes, I would not have believed it either. Each time I reached far into the heavens and brought a duck cartwheeling to earth, I sang a little song that said it all: "Give me a lifetime supply of Hevi-Shot, and I'll never shoot the 12 gauge again." Scott Hanes got the entire performance on video, although I doubt it will ever make the Top 40.

CHAPTER 23

Gunning for Gobblers

The electronic sight on this Benelli turkey gun is the thing to have for precision shooting at long range.

I can easily recall a time when most hunters owned one shotgun, and they hunted everything with it. I grew up in the Deep South where the 16-gauge side-by-side double was quite popular, although it was outnumbered by single-barrel guns in 12 gauge. Guns owned by most farmers got used on everything from quail, doves, cottontail rabbits, turkey and deer to the occasional chicken-stealing hawk. To say that times have changed dramatically is rather an understatement. It is now quite common for a hunter to own an entire battery of specialized shotguns, one for upland wingshooting, another for waterfowling, another with a rifled barrel for deer and yet another reserved for turkey

hunting. If the shotgunner also enjoys shooting clay targets, he or she might even have three or four more guns, one for skeet, a couple for trap and another for sporting clays. Manufacturers have capitalized on this trend by designing use-specific firearms, and nowhere is it more evident than in the proliferation of guns built specifically for those who hunt turkeys. In addition to featuring all the bells and whistles that many hunters are convinced they must have, turkey guns are available with various types of actions.

The single-shot shotgun is most often seen in the hands of youngsters accompanied by their fathers, but it offers a few advantages for grownups, too. To begin with, it is the least expensive of all shotguns. Lightness of weight also makes the single-shooter nice to carry over hill and dale, but at the same time its lightness can cause the gun to be uncomfortable to shoot with heavy loads. If I hunted turkey with this type of gun, I would probably choose the 20 gauge and wait until a gobbler stepped inside 30 yards before pulling the trigger. If I decided to go with the 12 gauge, I would stick with 2-3/4 inch loads and leave the longer magnums for those who hunt with autoloaders.

The biggest shortcoming of the single shot is it holds only one shell, and that makes it rather slow for follow-up shots. I can count on one hand the number of gobblers I have had to shoot more than one time and still have most of my fingers left over, but it can happen and when it does, having a quick second shot on tap can save the day.

Then we have the bolt-action shotgun. The first thing that comes to my mind when thinking about the old bolt gun is we see even fewer of them used by turkey hunters than single shots. This is probably not as it should be, since most turkey guns are aimed rather than pointed, and the bolt action feels just fine for that. A bolt-action like the Savage Model 210F Master Shot turkey gun has several things going for it, not the least of which are its affordable price and relatively light weight. Mounting a scope or electronic sight is easy, since its receiver is also drilled and tapped at the factory. As for shortcomings, I can think of only two at the moment – the bolt-action is not as fast on a follow-up shot as the pump, auto or double, nor is it as suitable for other types of hunting as those guns. But most hunters find it faster than the single shot, and few who know how to operate it would let a wounded gobbler get away.

Everything considered, I believe the slide action comes about as close to being the perfect turkey gun as we are likely to ever get. It costs less than the autoloader and equally important during those long days afield, it is considerably lighter. I just weighed a Remington 870 with a 28-inch barrel, and it went exactly 7-1/2 pounds on my postal scale. Most semiautomatics run at least a pound more, and some are even heavier than that. I have not weighed all of the slide-action shotguns available, but according to a few catalogs in my file, the Benelli Nova weighs eight pounds, the Browning BPS weighs 7-1/2 pounds and the Ithaca Model 37 weighs 7-1/4 pounds. Those weights are for 12-gauge guns.

Had I written this book before World War II, I would probably say the pump gun is more reliable than the auto, but it has been so long since I have had any problems with a modern and properly maintained shotgun of that type, I no longer consider reliability to be a

I used a 12-gauge Benelli with the SteadyGrip stock to bag this eastern gobbler in the hills of Kentucky.

good argument either way. Drop both into the mud from a duck blind and the pump gun is more likely to come out shooting, but under normal conditions I consider reliability to be a tossup between the two.

I own several pump guns, but the two I have used most to hunt turkeys are Remington 870s. One is a Special Purpose Magnum with a 26-inch barrel, bead-blasted metal finish and dull-finished wood. It wears a quick-detachable carrying sling, a Burris electronic sight with a three-minute dot, and it shoots fantastic patterns out to 70 yards with Remington ammo loaded with Hevi-Shot. My second favorite turkey gun is a Model 870 Special Field with a 21-inch barrel. With the exception of its carrying sling, it is no different now than it was the day I bought it. I occasionally hunt gobblers in extremely steep mountain country where the only two directions to be walked are straight up and straight down and thick woods rule out shots much beyond 25 yards. The snub-nosed 870 is my pick of the litter for that. At seven

A double-barrel shotgun like this Remington Model 332 offers a turkey hunter the instant availability of two different chokes, tight for long-range shooting and loose for shots at close range.

pounds, it is the Winchester 94 of turkey guns.

The pump gun is more fun to carry because it is lighter, but the autoloading shotgun is more fun to shoot because is does not kick as hard. We have only to look at the number of models and variations of autoloaders available from various manufacturers to see that it is the king of turkey guns. There are important reasons why this is true. At the top of the priority list, as far as I am concerned, the modern gas-operated autoloader is more comfortable to shoot with heavy loads than any other type of shotgun. During our lifetime, we experience a number of unforgettable events, and the first time I fired a shotgun chambered for the then-new 3-1/2 inch 12-gauge shell is one of mine. The gun was a pump weighing about 7-1/2 pounds, and since I am still trying my best to forget the experience, I will say no more. I later tried the extra-long shell in a Browning Gold autoloader, and the pain soon went away. Even after spending about an hour pattern-testing that gun and Winchester 3-1/2 inch magnum loads from the sitting position, my shoulder still felt fine. Within the next two days I bagged two big spring gobblers with two shots from that combination. In addition to its ability to soften recoil, the

autoloader is tough to beat anytime a follow-up shoot is needed.

I enjoy hunting turkeys with a double-barrel shotgun, but not many are bagged with doubles each year because most hunters overlook obvious advantages in its design. The traditional way to bag a gobbler these days is to aim for its head and neck as it stands flat-footed on the ground. Since the target is not very large, small shot ranging in size from No. 4 to No. 6 is used for adequate pattern density. This might surprise a turkey hunter who is still looking forward to his 50th birthday, but there is absolutely nothing wrong with shooting a turkey on the wing. Through the years I have had several opportunities to do so, but I held my fire because the size of the shot in my gun was too small. No doubt, the smaller shot sizes are capable of penetrating the neck bone and skull of a gobbler at reasonable distances, but they do not offer enough penetration for a body shot, and that's where a flying bird is likely to be hit. The target will probably be flying away from the gun, so the shot must be heavy enough to break wing bones and penetrate a lot of bird before reaching its vitals. This is where the double-barrel has the edge over any other type of shotgun. Fine shot loaded in one barrel can be used to head-shoot a standing gobbler while No. 2 shot in the other barrel (in states where it is legal) is reserved for shooting an airborne gobbler.

Here is another advantage turkey hunters often overlook in the double: Some of the special turkey chokes now being used throw patterns about the size of a coffee cup inside 25 yards, making it extremely difficult to hit the head and neck of a turkey at close range if the bird is walking along rather than standing still. During the past few years, I have had numerous turkey hunters tell me this has happened to them. A double with one barrel choked extremely tight for long shots and the other choked Improved Cylinder or Modifed solves that problem.

While this book is mostly about modern guns, I can't resist the opportunity to mention how much fun hunting gobblers with a muzzleloader can be. Anyone who studies turkey hunters knows they can be neatly divided into three categories. First there are those who are new to the game. Those fellows are likely to choose the most powerful guns and loads available simply because bagging a gobbler is their No. 1 priority (and how well I remember the feeling). Next we have the group of hunters who have been in the game for a long time. Those guys and gals have bagged many gobblers and want to bag many more because they can never get enough. They, too, are likely to choose the most effective firepower available.

Sauntering along behind those two groups are hunters who have put their shares of drumsticks on the table and are looking for ways to add a bit more challenge to the game. Some are at a point in life where they get much more enjoyment out of successfully guiding others who have yet to kill a gobbler than actually pulling the trigger themselves. I am a member of this group – most of the time. Anytime I need to bag a gobbler for a story, I take along all the firepower available and then some, but when I am hunting on my own time, I often use something that shifts more of the advantage back to the bird.

The ultimate challenge in turkey hunting is to bag a mature gobbler with bow and arrow, but since I seldom hunt with stick and string anymore, one of my concessions to the primitive movement is hunting turkey with a muzzleloader. The side-by-side double I hunt with is called the T&T (Turkey & Trap), and Navy Arms once imported it from Italy. It has 28-inch barrels and, quite important in a turkey gun, its right barrel has been fitted with an extremely tight Briley screw-in choke. My favorite turkey load for it starts with 90.0 grains of Pyrodex RS, over which I seat a couple of .125-inch cardboard overpowder wads followed by a half-inch fiber cushion wad. Then comes 1-1/4 ounces of high-antimo-

All good turkey guns and loads have the capability of delivering extremely tight patterns at long range. John Fink of Remington shot this pattern at 40 yards while demonstrating the penetration of No. 6 Hevi-Shot on a steel plate.

ny No. 6 shot held in place by a paper overshot wad. When loaded in that manner, that gun shoots tight enough to saturate the head and neck of a gobbler out to 40 yards, but I get a bigger kick out of waiting until the bird is no more than 25 paces from the muzzle before pulling the trigger. A muzzleloader with more open choke constriction can be sent to the Houston, Texas, firm of Briley for the installation of screw-in chokes. Briley offers chokes slightly belled at the muzzle for the easy insertion of wads.

I also enjoy hunting turkey with a Knight TK2000. A single-barrel gun, it is capable of handling 100 grains of Pyrodex RS and 2-1/2 ounces of shot. This allows it to reach out farther than my double-barrel muzzleloader. The patterns it delivers with its Extra-Full choke are plenty good for ventilating the head and neck of a gobbler out to 50 yards.

These days, the well-dressed turkey hunter totes a shotgun with a camo finish, and while it is a nice thing to have, no hunter has to have it in order to kill a turkey. Just look around and see for yourself the next time you are in the woods. Notice how many items do not have a camo pattern, and yet they blend in quite naturally with the scenery. To a turkey, a shotgun in a hunter's hand is nothing more than another dark-colored sapling or tree limb so long as neither hunter nor gun shines nor moves. I am convinced a turkey is no more likely to be spooked

Linda Powell and her guide, Gary Roberson, know how effective the Model 11-87 autoloader and Hevi-Shot can be on a big Rio Grande gobbler.

by a shotgun with a matte blued finish on its metal and a dull satin finish on its wood than one with the fanciest camo finish available. If you like a camo-colored gun and intend to use it for nothing but turkey and waterfowl hunting, then by all means buy it. If you really don't care for camo and are shopping for an all-purpose shotgun to be used for hunting quail, rabbits and for shooting clay targets in addition to turkey hunting, you will be more socially accepted in some crowds with the matte-finished gun. I don't own a single shotgun with a camo finish, and if that has ever prevented me from bagging a gobbler, I am unaware of it.

There was a time when I wanted nothing more than front and middle beads on the top rib of a turkey gun for sighting at the head of a distant bird. Aligning two beads in a figure-eight configuration with the top of the middle bead snuggled against the bottom of the top bead is still precise enough if the gun shoots where it is pointed and if range does not greatly exceed 40 yards. All too often, though, a shotgun does not place the center of its pattern where the two beads up top say it should, and when that happens some type of sight capable of being adjusted for windage and elevation is a good solution. Adjustable sights allow a shotgun to be sighted in just like a rifle, and considering the extremely small patterns some guns of capable of shooting, this can be extremely important.

Iron sights consisting of a front bead combined with a fully adjustable open sight or peep sight out back are good answers out to about 45 yards. The peep sight with an extremely large aperture is better because its adjustments are more precise, although it is not as good as the open sight at the crack of dawn when ambient lighting conditions are poor. As I proved while hunting black bear on Vancouver Island with a Marlin Model 336CB in .38-55 Winchester wearing a Marble's tang sight, wearing shooting glasses with yellow lenses is the way to go when using a peep sight in poor light.

For turkey guns capable of reaching beyond 45 yards, the electronic sight and the scope are the ways to go. As for choosing between those two, both have their advantages. As a rule, an electric sight is lighter and shorter than a scope, but not by much if the scope is one of the compact models. The Burris Compact in 4x magnification weighs 7.8 ounces compared to that company's SpeedDot electronic sight at five ounces. Should you decide to take a shot at a turkey on the wing, the electronic sight with its huge field of view and noncritical eye alignment has the edge. If you take a poke at the head and neck of a gobbler standing more than 40 yards from the muzzle of your gun, the ability of the telescopic sight to increase image size gives it the edge. Some scopes are available with special reticles designed specifically for the turkey hunter, and while all probably work quite well, the duplex-style offered by everyone is probably just as good. I like a three-minute dot in an electronic sight because it is big enough to use at extremely close range and covers only about 1-1/2 inches of the target at 50 yards. The disadvantages of the scope and electronic sight? Either adds more weight to a shotgun than iron sights, and both have a tendency to spoil the handling and feel of a shotgun by making it top-heavy.

When it comes to choosing between the scope and electric sight, I have no preference but I seem to get around to using turkey guns wearing the latter more often. The importance of using something other than twin beads for sights on a turkey gun first got my undivided attention during a hunt in western Kentucky with Harold Knight of Knight & Hale Game Calls. On the afternoon of my arrival, I was issued a Benelli autoloader along with a supply of Remington shells loaded with 1-5/8 ounces of No. 6 Hevi-Shot. I was then driven to an area where our hosts had set up a benchrest. The shotgun had .055 inch of choke and wore a Burris SpeedDot 135 with a three-minute dot. While making sure the gun was perfectly zeroed at 30 yards, I was amazed at how many pellets I was placing into the head and neck of paper turkey targets. Out of curiosity, I began to increase the distance from me to the target in five yard increments until I began to run low on ammo at 70 yards. Then and there, two things really got my attention. For one, at 70 yards I was still putting at least 17 Hevi-Shot pellets into the head/neck zone of the target. For two, had it not been for the electronic sight, I could not have held close enough beyond 40 yards to accomplish such a feat. Later that week, I killed two gobblers, one laser-ranged at 59 yards.

While a heavy 10- or 12-gauge gun loaded with an extremely heavy shot charge is the traditional turkey medicine, I see a movement toward lighter guns and smaller gauges among some of the more experienced hunters. This is due in large part to the development of special turkey loads and extremely tight chokes for the 20 gauge. The trend got its start when it finally dawned on the arms and ammunition makers that 12-gauge turkey guns kicked too hard and were too heavy for youngsters and some women. The idea picked up even more momentum when other hunters discovered the advantages of a lighter gun for hunting in mountainous country.

Single-shot, slide-action and autoloading shotguns offered in 20 gauge by manufacturers such as New England Firearms, Remington, Benelli, Browning, USRAC/Winchester and Beretta are entirely suitable for turkey hunting, and some even come with a camouflage finish. Ammunition developed specifically for bringing home a turkey dinner is also available. Remington and Winchester offer the 3-inch 20-gauge shell loaded with 1-1/4 ounces of lead shot, and Federal has upped the ante a bit more by offering a 1-5/16 ounce loading. When teamed up with an Extra Full choke with about .030 inch of constriction, a properly patterned gun and a hunter who knows how to shoot, either load is capable of saturating the head and neck of a gobbler out to 35 yards. The most effective 20-gauge combination I have tried is Remington Premier ammo loaded with 1-1/4 ounces of No. 6 Hevi-Shot and the special .040-inch choke developed by Remington for use with that type of shot.

CHAPTER 24
Hunting with the Muzzleloading Shotgun

When I bought this 12-gauge double-barrel muzzleloader it was being imported by Navy Arms. Similar guns in 10, 12 and 20 gauge are now available from other sources.

The older I become, the more I enjoy hunting with old guns or guns the designs of which came about many years ago. Only a few months prior to writing this, I took a very nice black bear while hunting on Vancouver Island of British Columbia with Tony Aeschliman of Marlin. The Model 336 lever action in .38-55 Winchester I used wore a Marble's tang sight, and it reached 43 yards down the side of a mountain to drop the bruin in its tracks. A few months prior to that trip, I bagged a nilgai on the King Ranch in south Texas with my old Winchester Model 71 lever action in .348 Winchester, and that animal also dropped in its tracks.

That rifle was equipped with a Williams receiver sight. I have long since forgotten much of the game I have bagged with modern firearms, but you can bet I will always remember those and others I have taken with vintage guns.

I also enjoy hunting with muzzleloading shotguns, but it is something I did not get around to trying until I was in my 30s. The very first game I bagged with one was an Eastern turkey gobbler. The gun I used was made by the Italian firm of Pedersoli and imported by Navy Arms. It no longer is available from that company, but Dixie Arms and Cabela's offer sim-

I took my first turkey gobbler with a muzzleloader quite a few years ago.

ilar shotguns in 12 and 20 gauges. My double is called the T&T (Turkey and Trap), and while it was supposed to be choked Full in both barrels, its chokes actually measured .019 and .025 inch, which put them closer to Modified and Improved Modified. Bore diameters are a bit tight with the right barrel measuring .715 inch and the left .717 inch. The Italian factory worker who soldered the two barrels together must have dipped a bit too deeply into the sauce the night before, because the tighter choke was in the right barrel, just the opposite of where it is supposed to be on a side-by-side double.

The barrels of my 12-gauge double were choked too tightly for some of the wingshooting I wanted to do with it and too loose for turkey hunting. So I finally got around to sending it to Chuck Webb at Briley for the installation of screw-in chokes. I wanted to experiment with not only the old-fashioned card and fiber wads but with modern plastic wads as well, so I requested that the chokes be beveled at the muzzle so they would easily accept the latter. Two of the chokes have constrictions of .003 and .035 inch or Light Skeet and Full, as the Briley catalog describes them. With .012-inch of constriction, one of the other two chokes falls about midway between Light Modified and Modified. Since the fourth choke has no choke at all it, is classified as Cylinder Bore. That par-

ticular choke has never performed acceptably in my gun, and most patterns fired with it look like a large doughnut with not a single pellet strike in the inner eight inches of pattern center. The other chokes perform as expected. The Light Skeet and Light Modified chokes work fine for skeet shooting and for shooting quail, sharptail grouse, chukar and Hungarian partridge. The more open of those two chokes is also an excellent choice for use on ruffed grouse. Modified is great for 16-yard trap, and it along with Full are what I use when shooting trap doubles. I also use Full choke when hunting spring gobblers and when going after pheasants late in the season. When loaded with 80.0 grains of Hodgdon's Triple-7 powder and 1-1/8 ounces of No. 6 shot, that choke will absolutely saturate the head and neck of a turkey gobbler out to 40 yards.

Both single- and double-barrel muzzleloaders are still being manufactured. Since the double barrel offers the advantage of a second shot, it is my first choice for wingshooting. It is also much better balanced for that type of shooting than the single barrel. A 12-gauge double with each of its barrels loaded with a single ball weighing around 500 grains is not a bad choice for use on deer, black bear and wild boar. A ball small enough in diameter to fit tightly inside the shotcup of a plastic wad works very nicely and it is held in place by a thin overshot wad. Muzzle energy of

This Knight TK2000 single-barrel muzzleloader will handle heavier charges of shot and powder than most doubles. That, along with its ability to shoot extremely tight patterns at long range, makes it a favorite of turkey hunters.

the old "punkin ball" load, as it was once called, can be as high as 1500 foot-pounds when a heavy charge of powder is used. Because of the accuracy limitations of the shotgun's smooth bore, shots should be restricted to a maximum of about 50 yards.

The double-barrel muzzleloader is a bit heavier than the single-shooter, but at 7-1/4 pounds, my Navy Arms 12-gauge gun is not too heavy to carry all day long in the field. Due to their inefficiency when compared to smokeless powder, black powder and its substitutes require the use of extremely heavy charges. My double has to digest 60 grains of FFG powder (80 grains bulk measured) in order to push a 1-1/8 ounce shot charge along about as fast as it is pushed by only 20 grains of smokeless powder in my Fox Sterlingworth. While it might seem that the use of so much powder in the muzzleloader would result in an uncomfortable level of recoil, I do not find this to be true. Recoil from the old front-stuffer comes as a slow push whereas it is more of a quick shove with smoke-

less powder in a modern gun. Doubles are also available in 10 and 20 gauge, some suitable for use with steel shot. My gun was not built to handle steel, so I load it with Bismuth shot when using it on waterfowl.

Some turkey hunters prefer the single-barrel muzzleloader because those built with an extremely thick barrel wall can be safely used with heavier charges of powder and shot. According to its manufacturer, the Knight TK2000 is capable of handling 120 grains of FFG black powder and 2-1/2 ounces of shot. I know some hunters who load it even hotter than that, but since the gun weighs only 7-1/2 pounds, 100 grains is about all the fun my shoulder wants to handle. The Knight muzzleloader also feels more like a rifle than a good double, and that along with its excellent trigger and adjustable sights, makes it a favorite of turkey hunters. The one I worked with would not quite deliver pattern percentages as high as some modern guns equipped with extremely tight chokes, but it did exceed 80 percent at 50 yards with 2-1/2 ounces of

This photo was taken by Dennis Macnab only a split second before I dropped an Oregon pheasant with my 12-gauge double. Snowflakes had just begun to fall.

No. 6 shot, and that is plenty good for turkey hunting. The 12-gauge muzzleloader barrel offered by Thompson/Center for its Encore will also turn a turkey gobbler every way but loose.

Most manufacturers of muzzleloaders recommend maximum loads for their guns. Some, and my Navy Arms double is a good example, have the maximum charge stamped somewhere on their barrels. According the maker of my gun, I should not exceed 89.0 grains (or 3-1/4 drams) by volume of black powder or black-powder substitute or 1-1/4 ounces of shot in it. I no longer use black powder in muzzleloading shotguns. Soon after Hodgdon introduced Pyrodex RS and Pyrodex Select, I switched to them because they are easier to find than black powder. Then when Triple-7 in FFG granulation came along, I switched to it mainly because it leaves less residue in the barrel and that makes the gun easier to load after a few shots. It also smells more pleasant. The cloud of smoke Triple-7 produces seems to be just enough thinner on a still day to enable me to better tell whether or not I hit my target. But not always. Only a day before I wrote this, I killed a cottontail rabbit while hunting with Jackie Rogers and his pack of little 13-inch bea-

gles. I shot the bunny while it was on the run at about 30 yards and was not absolutely sure I had hit it until the smoke cleared and I saw it kicking its last. Triple-7 has its advantages, but the residue it leaves behind will cause rust to start forming just as quickly as Pyrodex and black powder, so any gun using it should be thoroughly cleaned at the end of each hunting day.

The old card and fiber wads remain the best choices for use in some muzzleloaders. For easy loading in a tight barrel, the edges of the overpowder and cushion wads should be lightly lubed with Natural Lube 1000 from Thompson/Center or Wonder Lube 1000 Plus from Ox-Yoke Originals. I actually use two overpowder wads. After pushing the first wad into the bore about 1/4 inch, I place a dab of lube on its surface. I then place a second overpowder wad over that one, and when they are rammed home, a thin coat of lube oozes from between them and is applied to the bore. Applying lube to the edge of the cushion wad makes it easier to ram home, but just as important, the coat of lube seems to go a long way toward reducing powder-fouling buildup in the bore.

Modern plastic wads work fine in some guns if they fit tightly in the bore, but other guns refuse to

The smoke pouring from the right barrel of my double on an extremely humid morning was generated by 80.0 grains of Hodgdon Triple-7 powder. Almost hidden from view by the smoke, the pheasant appears much closer than it actually was because the photo was taken with a telephoto lens.

I seat the plastic wad directly atop the powder charge, pour in the shot charge and then cap everything off with an overshot wad. The gun shoots beautiful patterns when loaded in that manner.

I hunt only with muzzleloaders of recent manufacture. Some antique guns with Damascus barrels may not be safe to shoot, so anyone who owns one is wise to have a qualified gunsmith determine whether or not it should be shot or hung on the wall. Many of the older guns as well as modern reproductions of them have no choke constriction in their barrels, but they can still be about as effective as modern breechloading guns out to 20 yards or so. In the old days, the barrels of some of the better guns had jug-style chokes. In that type of choke, the constricted section of the barrel is far enough back from its muzzle to allow the muzzle to be flared for the easy insertion of wads.

Some modern muzzleloaders come with screw-in chokes, but if the chokes are tightly constricted, they have to be removed before the wads can be pushed down the barrel during loading. That setup is probably OK for turkey hunting, since a gun usually does not have to be loaded very often during a hunt. Having to remove the choke each time the gun is loaded is a royal pain in the neck if the gun is used for hunting rabbits, for wingshooting or for shooting clay targets. Knight Manufacturing solved the problem with its TK2000 shotgun by threading the outside of the barrel at its muzzle and screwing on a jug-style choke with a flared muzzle. It works great, even when plastic wads are used. Improved Cylinder, Modified and Full constrictions are available, and they are easily switched. The Knight system is a good idea for a single-barrel gun, but it will not work on a double. The best solution I have found for the double is to send it to Briley and have it fitted with screw-in chokes with beveled muzzles. I finally got around to having that done to my 12-gauge double, and my only regret is I should have had it done many years earlier.

It is not unusual to see a muzzleloader shoot higher pattern percentages and deliver more uniform pellet density than a breechloading shotgun when both are loaded with the same shot charge. This was first discovered by shotgun manufacturers at the turn of the 20th century, when the breechloader was just beginning to really take off. I won't go into all the reasons why this is true, but I believe the main factor is lack of a forcing cone in the barrel of a muzzleloader. The chamber of a modern shotgun has to be larger than the bore diameter of its barrel. Since the shotshell contains wads that are the same diameter as the bore, the outside diameter of

deliver decent patterns with them regardless of how good the fit is. Modern breechloading shotguns are designed to handle chamber pressures as high as 12,000 LUP (lead units of pressure). Since muzzleloaders operate at chamber pressures in the 5,000 to 6,000 pounds-per-square-inch range, pressure is not high enough to cause the base of some plastic wads to obturate enough to completely seal off the bore. When this happens, propellant gas escapes around the wad during firing, causing both velocity and pattern quality to suffer. Gas blow-by becomes even more of a problem when the gun is used during winter, since cold temperatures can harden the plastic wad and cause it to resist obturation even more. The plastic wad can still be used to decrease pellet deformation by loading it either on top of a regular over-powder wad or atop the cushion wad, but even then it does not always improve pattern quality. The Navy Arms double I hunt with has never delivered patterns as good with plastic wads as with the old card and fiber wads. On the other hand, when loading the Knight TK2000 turkey gun, I use plastic wads sold by Knight and made specifically for the use of shot charges as heavy as 2-1/4 ounces in that gun. Using no overpowder wad, the cartridge has to exceed bore diameter. The tapered transition section of a barrel from its chamber to its primary bore is called the forcing cone. It serves to funnel the shot charge from the chamber and into the main bore. As the speeding shot charge collides with the angled wall of the forcing cone during firing, some of the lead pellets are severely deformed by the impact. Since the wads, powder and shot are loaded directly into the barrel of a muzzleloader, no forcing cone is needed and as a result, bore diameter is the same from breech to the choked area at the muzzle. Considering this, it stands to reason that so long as the shot charge is protected by the shotcup of a modern plastic wad, fewer pellets suffer deformation when they are fired from a muzzleloader. The lower the number of deformed pellets in a shot charge, the better is pattern quality when lead shot is used.

One of the neat things about hunting with a muzzleloader is you can switch loads in the field as conditions dictate. Let us say you are hunting pheasants in open country, and since most shots are beyond 30 yards, you need plenty of choke and all the pattern density you can get. For those conditions, you are loading your gun with modern plastic wads and 1-1/4 ounces of shot. Later in the day, the birds you find along a ditch overgrown with brush and tall weeds have a tendency to flush inside 20 yards. Screwing in more open chokes will increase pattern size for those close shots, but so might switching to card and fiber wads. You may also want to back off on the powder charge or shot charge for less recoil on those close shots. Or perhaps you have been using No. 4 shot for long-range shots at pheasants and would like to switch to No. 7-1/2s for that covey of Huns old Rover just bumped. It is also possible to duplicate loads commonly used in the smaller gauges. As examples, 3/4 ounce of shot at 1200 fps is a 28-gauge equivalent load, while 11/16 ounce duplicates the 3-inch .410. I often duplicate the 20 gauge with my 12-gauge gun by loading it with 7/8 ounce or one ounce of shot. Any of this comes as easy as pie when you are toting a muzzleloader.

Hunters who are seriously into the traditional side of shooting muzzleloaders use horns and flasks for carrying their powder and shot in the field. Those who are less serious about looking like Daniel Boone use cylindrical plastic chargers designed to hold powder in one end and shot in the other. They are available from Knight, Thompson/Center and others. I always have a good supply of plastic 35mm film canisters on hand, so I use them. A small pouch worn on my belt has two compartments. One holds a supply of canisters

The hunter who goes afield with a muzzleloader does not give up a lot in the way of downrange performance to someone who uses a shotgun of more modern design. But is does take him longer to reload.

with pre-measured charges of powder, while canisters in the other side contain pre-measured shot charges. Another compartment holds the various wads needed. A capper filled with percussion caps goes in a small zippered pocket on the side of the pouch. Back when I shot Pyrodex, I also took along a supply of cotton patches and a small bottle of solvent so I could swab barrels every dozen shots. I simply swished a patch lightly dampened with solvent to and fro in each barrel a few times and then dried them out with a fresh patch before loading up. I find this to be unnecessary when shooting Triple-7.

The small brass powder measure sold by Michael's of Oregon and other suppliers of muzzleloader accessories can be used to measure shot. It is especially handy when a lot of pattern-testing needs to be done. A plastic 35mm film canister works great as a dipper, and when the shot is being poured into the measure, its mouth can be pinched to form a narrow trough for no-spill pouring. The measure I use came from Michael's, and when it is set halfway between its 80- and 85-grain graduations, it will hold 1-1/8 ounces of shot. When set just past the 70-grain mark, it holds an ounce, and when set on 90, it holds 1-1/4 ounces of shot. All of this is easily determined with the powder scale owned by those of us who load metallic cartridges so long as you keep in mind that one ounce of shot weighs 438 grains (7,000 divided by 16) and 1/8 ounce of shot weighs 55 grains (438 divided by 8). By the same token, 1/16 ounce of shot weighs 27 grains (438 divided by 16).

As it is with modern shotguns, a muzzleloader should be tested at the patterning board to make sure it is shooting where it is being pointed. I prefer what target shooters call a flat-shooting gun or one that places the center of its pattern dead on my hold point at 16 yards. I can live with a gun that shoots 60/40 or one that places 60 percent of its pattern above where I am holding, but that's the highest-shooting gun I want for hunting. If your muzzleloader is not shooting where you want it to, try different powder charges behind various shot-charge weights and you might find a combination that puts it closer to where you are looking. If that doesn't work, the best bet is to have eccentric chokes installed by Briley. Some guns also have certain preferences in shot sizes. The only way you will know for sure which your gun prefers is to try several in it. As a rule, any good muzzleloader is capable of delivering excellent patterns at muzzle velocities in the 1000 to 1200 fps velocity range.

Hitting or missing with a muzzleloader is no different than with a modern shotgun, with one exception. Due to the comparatively slow lock time of some guns, completing the swing with proper follow-through is even more important than when shooting a modern shotgun. This is why shotgunners who have plenty of experience and who are excellent shots seldom experience a single problem when making the transition from modern shotgun to muzzleloader. It is also one of the primary reasons why those who make all the classic mistakes of shotgunning often find flying targets quite difficult to hit with the muzzleloader.

Rules of safety that apply to modern breechloaders also apply to the muzzleloader, but there are a few others to keep in mind as well. While hunting with a double, you may fire only one of its barrels and then need to reload it before carrying on. Always remove the percussion cap from the loaded barrel before beginning your reloading procedure on the barrel you have just fired. Other rules are equally important. Always make sure your finger is off the trigger when cocking the hammers, and do not walk around with the hammers cocked. With practice, you will learn to cock the hammers in one smooth motion as you shoulder the gun for firing. If you have the hammers cocked over loaded barrels and decide to

decock them, make sure you pull the correct trigger when lowering a hammer with your thumb. Removing the caps from both nipples before attempting to lower the hammers is not a bad idea. Just as important as all the rest, always keep those muzzles pointed in a safe direction.

To avoid double-charging a barrel of a double-barrel gun, you should adopt a certain loading procedure and stick with it. Do it long enough and it will become an ingrained habit that will kick into the proper sequence even when you are attempting to reload the gun with a covey of quail flying all around your head. When loading a double from scratch, I pour a powder charge into one of its barrels. I then start an over-powder wad into that barrel but I leave it where I can see it rather than pushing it home with the ramrod. Next I pour a powder charge into the other barrel, insert an over-powder wad and ram it as well as the over-powder wad in the other barrel all the way home. Both barrels are now loaded with powder. I follow the same procedure when loading shot. I pour a charge of shot down one of the barrels and I then place an over-shot wad into that barrel, but I do not push it home. Then a shot charge goes into the second barrel and its over-shot wad as well as the one in the first barrel are rammed home. Both barrels are now fully loaded, but more important, each contains only one charge. Placing caps on the nipples is the last thing I do. When shooting skeet, trap or sporting clays with a muzzleloader, you should never cap its nipples until you are standing on a station and it is your turn to shoot. Both hammers should be in the half-cocked position as they are being capped.

If you fire only one barrel, make sure you are reloading only that barrel and you are not double-charging the barrel you did not fire. Placing a cotton cleaning patch partially into the muzzle of the loaded barrel while you are loading the other barrel is not a bad idea, but don't forget to remove it prior to firing the gun. When only one barrel of a double is fired several times, recoil can cause the shot charge in the other barrel to shift forward a bit and create an airspace between it and the cushion wad. Firing that barrel can result in a bulge in the barrel. This can be avoided by using the ramrod to make sure the shot charge in the unfired barrel is fully seated each time the fired barrel is reloaded, but it does not always work. The best bet is to alternate firing the two barrels. And I repeat – remove the percussion cap from the loaded barrel before you start loading the barrel you have fired.

The ramrod can be used as a guide to remind you whether or not a gun is loaded. It can also be used to reveal a double-charge of powder or shot or both.

Hunting cottontail rabbits with the old front-stuffer is more fun than the law should allow.

Steve Puppe bagged this Merriam's gobbler in Montana with a Knight TK2000 muzzleloading shotgun in 12 gauge. He used 2-1/2 ounces of No. 5 shot and a heavy charge of Hodgdon Triple-7 powder.

Because it is only slightly longer than the bore, very little of the ramrod will protrude from the muzzle when the barrel contains no powder or shot. After loading your new gun for the first time and before placing a cap on its nipple, drop the ramrod into the barrel and make a mark on it adjacent to the muzzle of the barrel. A couple wraps of tape will work if the ramrod cannot be marked. If ever you drop the ramrod into the barrel and the mark is more than a quarter-inch above the muzzle, you have screwed up in your loading procedure and something that should not be in there is in there. To unload that barrel, make sure the

cap is off the nipple and use a screw-like ramrod attachment called a bullet puller or worm to pull the over-shot, filler and over-powder wads from the barrel. Available from any supplier of muzzleloader accessories, a worm looks like a wood screw and when rotated, its point is sharp enough to bite into or "worm" its way into a wad. Another ramrod attachment called a patch puller works better on a fiber cushion wad if it is too soft for the worm to hang onto as you attempt to pull it from the barrel.

Someone who hunts with a modern breechloading shotgun enjoys certain advantages in the field over his chum who hunts with a muzzleloader, but the edge is not as big as some might think. The biggest disadvantage to hunting with a front-stuffer is it cannot be reloaded as rapidly as a modern gun. This is why it works best if your hunting partner is also carrying muzzleloader. I once used my 12-gauge double while hunting wild pheasants, chukar and California quail with Jeff Patterson and Mike Schwiebert. I bagged as many birds as they did with their modern autoloaders, but I was often embarrassed by their insistence on holding up the hunt until I could reload. On a number of occasions, I insisted that they hunt on while I reloaded, but like true gentlemen, they would have none of that. I took my first California quail with a muzzleloader on that hunt.

As far as the actual hunting goes, slowness in reloading the gun seldom matters when hunting rabbits with beagles. If the target is not down and out after you empty both barrels, having additional shots on tap will seldom make a difference in the outcome anyhow. Same goes for pass-shooting a dove or duck: If you miss with both barrels of a double, you probably would not be much better off with a pump or autoloader since we all know that third shots miss more often than they hit. There are times, though, like in the midst of a covey of flushing quail, when you might find yourself wishing for a gun capable of being reloaded more quickly. Even then, I am not sure it really matters. A Texan I know hunts bobwhite and scaled quail with nothing but 20-gauge double-barrel muzzleloaders, and he gets his limit just as often as his pals who use modern guns. It might take him a bit longer, but he takes home just as many birds. Most of us who hunt with muzzleloaders do so for the same reason we hunt with handguns and lever-action rifles with open sights – it puts more of the hunt back into hunting. Another reason I enjoy taking a front-loader to the field is the older I get, the more importance I place on having fun and the less importance I place on how heavy my game bag is at the end of the day.

A Few Favorite 12-gauge Loads
(Powder charges measured by volume and not weight)

Shotgun: Knight TK2000, 26-inch Barrel

Primer: Remington 209 Premier STS
Powder: Pyrodex RS
Charge Weight: 110.0 grains
Wad: Knight Plastic
Over-Shot Wad: Knight
Shot Charge: 2-1/4 ounces
Velocity: 1020 fps
Notes: Excellent 50-yard turkey load

Shotgun: Thompson/Center Encore, 24-inch Barrel

Primer: Remington 209 Premier STS
Powder: Hodgdon Triple-7
Charge Weight: 100.0 grains
Wad: Knight Plastic
Over-Shot Wad: Knight
Shot Charge: 2-1/4 ounces
Velocity: 1050 fps
Notes: Excellent 50-yard turkey load

Shotgun: Navy Arms T&T, 28-inch Barrels

Cap: Remington No. 11 percussion
Powder: Pyrodex RS
Charge Weight: 70 grains
Over-Powder Wad: .125" card (2)
Cushion Wad: .500" fiber
Over-Shot Wad: .030" card
Shot Charge: 3/4 ounce
Velocity: 1210 fps
Notes: Excellent 28-gauge equivalent low-recoil load for clay targets and quail

Cap: Remington No. 11 percussion
Powder: Pyrodex RS
Charge Weight: 90 grains
Wad: Winchester WAA12L
Shot Charge: 7/8 ounce
Velocity: 1250 fps
Notes: Great for quail and dove

Cap: Remington No. 11 percussion
Powder: Pyrodex Select
Charge Weight: 90.0 grains
Over-Powder Wad: .125" card (2)
Cushion Wad: .500" fiber
Over-Shot Wad: .030" card
Shot Charge: 1 ounce
Velocity: 1225 fps
Notes: Excellent 20-gauge equivalent load for dove and quail

Cap: Remington No. 11 percussion
Powder: Pyrodex RS
Charge Weight: 90.0 grains
Over-Powder Wad: .125" card (2)
Cushion Wad: .500"
Over-Shot Wad: .030" card
Shot Charge: 1-1/8 ounces
Velocity: 1080 fps
Notes: Works great on all birds including pheasant

Cap: CCI No. 11 Magnum
Powder: Hodgdon Triple-7 (FFG)
Charge: 80.0 grains
Over-Powder Wad: .125" card (2)
Cushion Wad: .500" fiber
Over-Shot Wad: .030" card
Shot Charge: 1-1/8 ounces
Velocity: 1100 fps
Notes: Excellent clean-burning hunting load

Cap: Remington No. 11 percussion
Powder: Pyrodex RS
Charge Weight: 90.0 grains
Over-Powder Wad: .125" card (2)
Cushion Wad: .500"
Over-Shot Wad: .030" card
Shot Charge: 1-1/4 ounces
Velocity: 1010 fps
Notes: Works on turkey gobblers out to 40 yards.

CHAPTER 25
The Shotgun Stock and How It Should Fit

A splinter forearm like the one on this No. 1 grade AyA double Phyllis is about to shoot looks nice but the half-beavertail style would do a better job of protecting her fingers from hot barrels.

In the beginning, firearms were called hand cannons and they had no stocks, but as time passed, a piece of wood was added in order to make things a bit easier on the brave soul who had enough nerve to fire one. As decades came and went, the stocks on various types of firearms eventually began to take on a shape now familiar to all shooters. The most beautiful shotgun stocks were and still are carved by masters of the trade at prestigious old English firms such as Holland & Holland, Purdey, Westley Richards and Boss. Side-by-side doubles in the higher grades turned out during days of yesteryear by Parker, Fox, L.C. Smith, Lefever and Ithaca were quite nice indeed, but American makers of yesteryear never really managed to capture the grace and beauty of the English stock. The differences are often so subtle, they are difficult if not impossible to describe with either words or photographs, and yet they are immediately sensed and felt, even by someone who picks up a best-grade English double for the very first time.

Stock fit is more important in a shotgun than in a rifle. Whereas a rifleman usually has plenty of time to

The stock on the Remington Model 90-T trap gun Bob Stoner is holding is adjustable for length of pull and comb height.

wrap himself around the stock and force his body to confirm to its dimensions before taking a shot at a deer, the shotgunner has to get off a shot at a flushing quail or grouse in no time flat. For this reason, he must have a stock that fits reasonably well. If the stock does not fit him, he is likely to shoot high, low or over toward Aunt Hattie's hen house.

To understand why stock shape is important, you must first understand the four-point relationship between the shotgun and the human body. Think of a table with four legs; weaken one of those legs or saw one leg shorter than the other three, and the table becomes unstable. The same applies to shotgun fit. Beginning with two of those support points, the shotgun is designed to be firmly supported up front at its fore-arm by one hand and at the grip by the other hand. Some shooters control the swing of a gun with the hand out on the forearm, while others control it with the hand holding the wrist of the stock. Others apply equal amounts of pressure with both hands. In describing the way I swing a shotgun, I would have to say that I control it just as much with one hand as with the other. This may be all right or it may be all wrong, but it seems to work for me. Regardless of which of your hands does what, I believe the key word here is consistency in the amount of pressure applied from shot to shot.

Then we have the third contact point. When a stock fits the shooter properly his face makes firm but

comfortable contact with the comb of the stock. Comb height is a very critical stock dimension and it is easily measured. Simply rest the shotgun upside down with its rib on the flat surface of a table. Then with the portion of the rib that contains the sight or sights hanging over the edge, measure the distance from the top of the table to the stock at its comb and heel. Correct comb height will vary from one shooter to another due to differences in the shapes of their faces. If the comb is too low for a shooter, he will find himself looking into the rear of the receiver when he shoulders the gun. If it is excessive in height, he will see too much of the rib. I like to see just a bit of rib when shooting any shotgun. When shooting a gun with two beads, I prefer to see a figure-eight sight picture with the top of the middle bead resting snugly against the bottom of the front bead. Understand that when I use the term sight picture in a discussion of shotguns, I mean it is used only to confirm gun fit and alignment. A shotgun should be pointed at flying targets and not aimed; the bead or beads atop the barrel mere-ly serve as reference points for eye to barrel alignment before a shot is taken on the clay target range. When a shotgun is fired in the field, the shooter's eye should ignore any sights sitting on top of the barrel and con-centrate solely on the target.

The most punishing shotgun stocks ever built have too much drop at the heel. Since excessive drop there positions the center of the butt far below the axis

The correct length of pull for me may not be correct for Steve Otway but 14-1/4 inches is a workable length for many shooters.

of the bore, a gun with such a stock rears up and pounds the shooter in the face each time it is fired. Add more drop than needed at the comb, and you've got a real torture instrument, especially when heavy loads are fired in the gun. The exact dimensions will vary from shooter to shooter, and my correct measurements may not be right for someone whose face is thicker or thinner, but a shotgun stock with 1-1/4 to 1-3/8 inches of drop at its comb and from 2 to 2-1/2 inches at its heel is about right for me. As a number of skeet and trap shooters have discovered, having a stock with the same amount of drop at its comb and heel is not a bad idea. When shooting a gun with a straight comb, the distance between the center of the eye and the top of the barrel remains the same regardless of whether you crawl the stock and place your cheek as far forward as possible, or you place it farther back. Considering the fact that we normally place our cheek farther forward when wearing light clothing during summer and farther back when wearing heavy clothing during winter, a straight comb makes as much sense on a hunting gun as it does on a gun used for shooting clay targets. The next time I have one of my bird guns restocked, I will specify a drop of 1-3/8 inches at its comb and heel.

Because the eye of the shooter serves as the rear sight on a shotgun, excessive comb height can cause the gun to shoot too high. By the same token, not enough comb height for a particular shooter can cause the gun to shoot low. Actually, the gun itself is shooting neither high nor low, but having the eye positioned too far in either direction will prevent the shooter's hold point and point of impact of the shot charge from converging at game-shooting distances. The combs of stocks on guns used for shooting trap and skeet are often mechanically adjustable for height. My Remington Model 90-T came from the factory with that type of stock. Drop at comb and heel of the stocks of the Weatherby SAS and Beretta 391 can be changed by utilizing special shims or spacers that come with those guns.

The easiest way to increase comb height on a nonadjustable stock is to build it up with an adhesive-backed layer of relatively soft rubber designed for just that purpose. Available from Brownells with names like Kick-Eez, Cheekeeze and Scope-Eze, they come in about any thickness needed from 1/16 inch to 1-1/8 inches. Made of a soft, spongy material, they also do a good job of soaking up a bit of the recoil before it

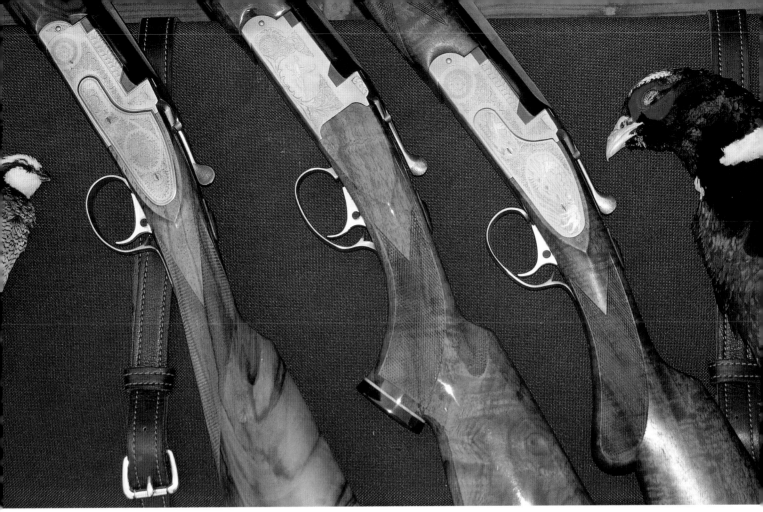

The three commonly seen grip styles are from left to right; straight or English, full-pistol and half-pistol.

reaches the shooter's cheek. To determine which thickness to order, first measure comb height. Then build up the comb by tightly wrapping it with layers of newspaper held in place by masking tape until your eye is seeing the sight picture you want. Now measure the height of the built-up comb, subtract the original comb height from what you get, and you have the additional height needed. Stick-on comb elevators are not terribly expensive, so you might want to buy several in different thicknesses and experiment a bit before deciding on the exact comb height for you.

It should be easy to remember that for each 1/16 inch the comb is lowered or raised, pattern point of impact will be lowered or raised by about an inch at 16 yards. In other words, if your gun is shooting five inches too low at that distance, increasing comb height by 5/16 inch should put the center of the pattern quite close to your hold point.

Some gunsmiths bend wood stocks to increase comb height. A synthetic stock can be built up with layers of fiberglass fabric and glue, and then repainted. A material called Bondo, which is used in great quantities at automobile-body repair shops, can also be used, but since it is quite heavy, it can spoil the balance

of a gun. I have seen wood stocks that were modified by sawing out the existing comb, inletting a higher section of wood into the stock and then dressing it down to the desired height.

Before leaving the subject of comb height, I must comment on those who incorrectly assume that just because a shotgun is old it will have too much drop in its stock. This is not always the case, simply because some makers of doubles offered the customer options that differed from standard off-the-shelf stock dimensions. And the option was not always restricted to the higher grades of guns. During the 1930s, Fox charged $3.50 extra to increase or decrease drop by as much as 3/8 inch in the stock of its $39.50 Sterlingworth. My Sterlingworth was made in 1924, and the drop at comb and heel of its stock are precisely the same as for the stock of one of my Remington Model 1100s, and it was made about 80 years later. Drops at comb and heel on the stock of my Iver Johnson Skeet-er are exactly the same as for those two guns, and it was built during the 1930s. I once shot quail with a couple of 1930s-vintage Parkers belonging to Art Wheaton and Jay Bunting, and the comb height of their stocks was just right for me. Continuing on with our discussion of the relationship

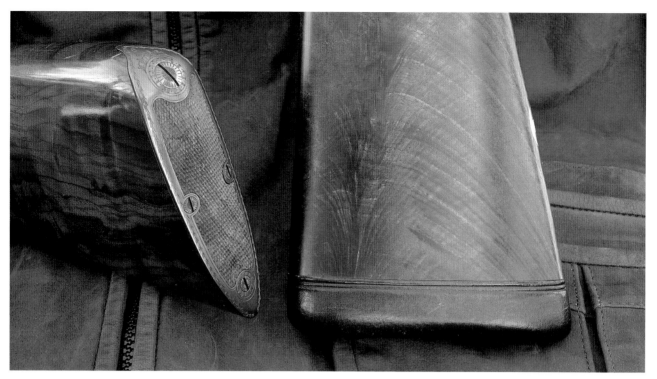

The Parker at left has a skeletonized buttplate and hand-cut checkering covering the wood left exposed by its open areas. The leather-covered recoil pad on the AyA double at right is equally handsome and more practical on a field gun.

between the shooter and his shotgun stock, the fourth important contact point is between the shoulder and the butt of the stock. In addition to making firm contact with the shoulder, the butt should be angled so as to fit squarely against the shoulder. If only the heel or the top of the butt contacts the shoulder firmly, the stock has too much down-pitch. The amount and direction of pitch in a stock or the angle of its butt in relation to the centerline of the barrel is important. Depending on how the owner of a shotgun is built and his shooting style, a stock should either have neutral pitch or its barrel or barrels should be pitched only slightly downward. Down-pitch in a stock can be measured close enough by placing the butt of the gun flat against the floor of your home, sliding the gun toward a wall until the top of its breech makes contact with the wall and then measuring the distance between the wall and the top of the barrel at its muzzle.

If when measuring the pitch of a gun with the just-described method you find that its muzzle makes contact with the wall before the top of the receiver does, that gun has up-pitch in its stock. In this case, it is likely that only the toe or the bottom of the butt will make firm contact with your shoulder. This can cause the butt to slip downward and off your shoulder when the gun is fired. Seeing a hunting gun with up-pitch in its stock is rare but it does exist. The No. 1 grade shotgun made by the Spanish firm of AyA is a custom-

order gun, and the previous owner of mine ordered it with about 3/4 inch of up-pitch in its stock. That may not sound like much, but each time I shot the gun, its butt ended up beneath my armpit, regardless of how tightly I pulled it against my shoulder. I had David and Cathy Yale out in Yellow Jacket, Colorado, install one of their beautiful leather-covered recoil pads and asked that the stock be shortened just enough at its toe to introduce two inches of down-pitch. I now shoot that gun quite well.

It is common to see English-built doubles with cast-off in their stocks. This places the centerline of the stock a bit to the right of the centerline of the top rib for a right-handed shooter. Cast-on is just the opposite, and you will see it in a stock built for a left-hander. Neither is easy to measure, but best as I can determine, my Westley Richards has half an inch of cast-off. So what's it good for? Cast-off enables the shooter to align his eye with the center of the rib without rolling his face over the comb of the stock. Most Americans are so accustomed to shooting in that manner, they could care less about whether the stock is bent one way or the other, but anyone who tries a stock with the proper amount of cast is likely to be sold on it. Will it ever become popular on shotguns built in the United States? It already has on some guns. The Weatherby SAS and Beretta 391, both autoloaders, come with special shims that allow their owners to not only introduce cast-off or cast-on into their stocks, but to change the drop at comb and heel as well. I doubt if the cast-off option will ever become available as an integral part of the stock in the United States. Since stocks would have to be bent one way for right-handed shooters and the other way for southpaws – and since just the right amount of either for one shooter might be too much or too little for another – I don't see it ever happening to mass-produced shotguns. Custom guns are another matter entirely.

Incidentally, it is not unusual to see adjustable buttplates or recoil pads on guns used by those who shoot trap and skeet rather seriously. Such a device allows the vertical angle of the pad or plate to be adjusted to fit the shooter. Since it allows the toe of the stock to be angled outward and away from the body, this gizmo is especially popular among both men and women who have rather large chests.

As someone who has never fired a shotgun might logically assume, length of pull is the distance from the butt of the stock to the trigger. The factory stocks on most of today's single-trigger guns usually measure around 14 inches, but I've measured some as short as 13-1/2 inches. Pull length to the front trigger of a double-barrel gun with two triggers is usually a bit longer. A half dozen doubles I measured ranged from 14-1/8 to 14-1/4 inches. While many shooters easily adapt to the typical factory stock, those with long arms might find some of them a bit short. Adding a recoil pad is one way to lengthen the stock. If a stock is a lot too short, gluing a piece of matching wood to the butt and then capping it off with a pad or plate can lengthen it. Done properly, this modification does not look at all bad, but it can be quite expensive. Many of the English doubles in 20 and 28 gauges and .410 caliber were built specifically for women and youngsters, so their stocks are often quite short. Many have had their stocks professionally lengthened by the addition of a piece of matching wood before being exported to the United States so they will be more appealing to Americans who love small-gauge guns.

Installing a recoil pad or replacing an existing pad with a thicker one are quicker and less costly ways of making a stock longer. Installing a lace-on leather pad is quicker and easier yet. Even better is to use the same type of pad, but with a Velcro fastener. When preparing for a duck and pigeon shoot in Uruguay, I found the stock of the 20-gauge Remington 11-87 I would be using a bit short for the light clothing I planned to wear. So I strapped on a leather pad and increased length of pull from 14 to 14-1/2 inches, and the stock fit me perfectly. The nice thing about that type of setup is you can use the pad when shooting in light clothing and then later remove it when you need a shorter stock for shooting in winter garb.

Keep in mind that installing a recoil pad can change the balance of a gun to the point where the added weight may need to be compensated for by removing a few ounces from somewhere else at the rear or by adding a bit of weight up front. This is usually done on a fine double by hollowing out its buttstock or, if that has already been done, by adding a bit of lead inside its forearm. Brownells sells various types of weights that either clamp to the barrel or fit inside the magazine of a repeater. Another type replaces the magazine caps of various pumps and autoloaders. The one I find to be most useful clamps to the barrel and comes with four-, six- and eight-ounce steel weights. When outfitting the Remington Model 11-87 I mentioned earlier for its trip to Uruguay, I tried different weights just in front of its forearm and ended up going with the half-pounder. In addition to compensating for the added weight of the recoil pad out back, it added a few more ounces up front, and that made the gun swing smoother on passing shots. Increasing the weight of the gun also reduced perceived recoil.

Women and youngsters with short arms sometimes find a factory stock too long. This is an easy problem to solve because any gunsmith who knows his stuff can shorten a stock to any reasonable length. But all women do not require short stocks. My wife, Phyllis, stands 5-feet-8 in her stocking feet, not exactly short as female shooters go, but still four inches shorter than me, and yet she considers many factory stocks too skimpy. She prefers a pull length of 14-1/4 to 14-1/2 inches, which just happens to be about right for me as well.

They say one of the best ways for a shooter to determine his correct stock length is to have a professional stock maker take the measurements with a special try-gun. I have had this done on a couple of occasions, and while I am not sure I learned a whole lot, the procedure did make me feel important. But since guys who take all those measurements aren't exactly lurking behind every bush, the next best way is to visit gun shops and try various shotguns on for size. Once you find one that feels just right, either buy it quick or take note of its stock dimensions and keep them where you can find them.

An old stock maker's trick of determining if stock length is correct is to rest the butt of the shotgun inside the forearm of a shooter to see whether or not his trigger finger reaches the trigger. As theory has it, if the crooked finger extends beyond the trigger, the stock is too short. If his finger falls short of reaching the trigger, the stock is too long. It is not uncommon to see this method ridiculed by some of today's self-proclaimed experts, but even they might be surprised at how close it comes to the correct measurement for a large number of people. Far from exact, it might not work on uncommonly tall or extremely short people, but it quite often works for average-size folks like me. Although I can shoot shotguns with either shorter or longer stocks I feel most comfortable with one that measures 14-1/4 inches. That just happens to be what I get when measuring my arm by the old stock maker's method. When shooting in light clothing during warm weather, I can use a stock measuring closer to 15 inches, but anything longer is too long for me.

It is important to note that hunters who are concerned with quick shots at game birds need shorter stocks than trap and skeet shooters who shoulder their guns before calling for the target. It is equally important to remember that a stock that fits perfectly when the shooter is wearing thin clothing may be too long when the same shooter is bundled in heavy clothing. The stocks on my favorite waterfowl guns measure 14 to 14-1/4 inches, and I would not want them to be any longer when I am wearing everything I can get my hands on in a duck blind in December. While hunting both waterfowl and upland game birds with a variety of shotguns through the years, I have come to the conclusion that I shoot much better if a stock is a bit too short than if it is a bit too long.

The butts of most shotgun stocks made in America today are fitted at the factory with soft rubber recoil pads. The very best at soaking up the pain from a hard-kicking gun I have tried is the R3 pad from Remington. The Pachmayr Decelerator is also quite good. A recoil pad with solid sides is best because it doesn't collect mud and other field debris like a pad with openings in its sides is inclined to do. In addition to soaking up some of the recoil, a rubber pad prevents the butt of a gun from slipping when it is set down on a hard surface. For that same reason, some pads won't slide smoothly across clothing worn by the shooter, and this can present a gun-mounting problem for some. There are a couple of things that can be done to solve the problem. Grinding a bevel into the top edge of the pad often helps. Another way to skin the cat is to make the pad as slick as owl grease by coating its surface with Slick-EEZ from Brownells. I have never experienced this problem because of something my father taught me at a very young age. When mounting a shotgun, I push it forward as I begin lifting it and I don't begin pulling it back toward by

shoulder until it has almost reached its shooting elevation. This out-up-in motion can be accomplished quite smoothly, and it prevents the butt of the gun from dragging against my clothing. It also enables me to shoot guns with considerable variations in length of pull with no problem, even when wearing heavy winter clothing. Some call it the Churchill method of mounting a gun, but neither my father nor I had ever heard of the chap back in those days.

The butts of some guns are covered with natural horn or hard rubber. Some high-grade guns have skeletonized steel plates with the exposed areas of the wood hand checkered. This is often seen on Parker doubles. Some butts are not covered at all, and the entire area is checkered. With or without the skeleton plate, a checkered butt looks quite nice, but it is easily damaged in the field. Bump the butt against something hard, and the toe may splinter off and ruin the stock. At the very least, you have dinged those nicely pointed diamonds in the checkering pattern. Even if the checkering is sharp, it has more of a tendency to slip on the shoulder than a rubber or leather pad. I protect the checkering on the butt of my Westley Richards by covering it with a strap-on leather pad, but its stock is short enough to allow me to do so. The butt of my Parker is also checkered, but a strap-on pad would make it too long, so I use it as is and hope for the best when using it in the field.

When it comes to materials used to cover the butt of a stock, the leather-covered recoil pad is the classiest of all. Extremely difficult to make (and expensive for that reason) it gives a fine gun an even more elegant look. I had never owned one until the purchase of a 28-gauge AyA double with up-pitch in its stock gave me a good excuse for doing so. A leather-covered pad can be special-ordered on fine doubles made in England, Spain and probably in a few other countries as well, but only a small handful of craftsmen in the United States are both willing and capable of taking on the job. David Yale and his wife, Cathy, most certainly are. After David fits the pad to the stock and carefully shapes it, Cathy spends many long hours applying its leather covering. I chose a one inch Pachmayr Decelerator covered with calfskin for my AyA, but other brands of pads and other types of leather are also available. A good leather pad is expensive because its installation is so labor-intensive, but few things look better on a high-grade gun.

The three styles of grips commonly seen on shotgun stocks are the straight or English-style, as it is also called, the half grip and the full pistol grip. Since the full pistol grip is the most popular among American shooters, it is the one seen on most guns built in America. Clay tar-

Scoring over 90 percent in skeet while pulling targets for myself tells me a gun like this 28-gauge Franchi 48AL fits me reasonably well. Here I am standing at station two with my eyes on the high house from which the clay target will emerge.

get shooters are especially fond of it because they believe it is better for controlling the gun with their trigger hand than a stock with a more open grip. Some shooters also find it to be more comfortable than other styles of grips. On some trap guns, the radius of the grip is quite tight, and the grip extends far below the belly of the stock. One of the more famous is the Etchen grip, which was developed and popularized by champion trapshooter Fred Etchen. The stocks of most pumps and autoloaders have the full pistol grip, although a few like the Remington Special Field, Franchi 48AL and Browning BPS Upland have been built with straight grips.

Then we have the half pistol grip. It is called that because its radius is about halfway between that of the full pistol grip and no radius at all, as seen in the straight grip. The half pistol grip was first made pop-

ular in the United States by the Browning A-5 and then later by the Browning Superposed. Several other doubles such as the Weatherby Athena, some variations of the Browning Citori and the Italian-built Rizzini as imported into the United States by Sigarms and others have gone a long way toward making it even more popular today. If all the data on how the shotgun stock of a game gun is supposed to be shaped were fed into a computer, it might spit out the half pistol grip stock as the best. That style gives the hand more room for movement when shooting a gun with two triggers, and it offers the trigger hand a bit more control of the gun than does the straight grip. A Weatherby Athena three-barrel set in 20, 28 and .410 I have been shooting has that style of grip, and I really like the way it handles and feels.

When it comes down to sleekness and beauty, nothing else comes close to a side-by-side double in 20 or 28 gauge with twin triggers and a straight wrist. The British long ago popularized the straight grip by incorporating its grace into the lines of fine doubles, and it simply cannot be beat on a gun with two triggers. Some say it gives the hand more room for to and fro movement when shooting a gun with two triggers, and while this is quite true, I like it because it makes the rear trigger easier to reach first. Due to its rather tight radius, the full pistol grip on my Fox Sterlingworth feels a bit cramped when a far-flushing bird makes me reach for the rear trigger first in order to utilize the tighter choke. This never happens with the English-style grip. The straight grip also encourages lifting of the shooting elbow for better control of the gun on going-away shots. If you sawed through the straight grip of an English-built double (or a Spanish copy of same) and looked at its cross-section, you would likely see it as diamond shaped. This is how the grips of my Westley Richards and AyA doubles are shaped. As popular thinking among British stock makers has long had it, the diamond-shaped wrist does a better job of preventing the gun from twisting in the hand than an oval-shaped grip. Whether or not this is actually true cannot be proven by me, but I'll have to admit it looks nice on a game gun. At the very least it is probably stronger.

The grips of gun stocks vary considerably in circumference. As a rule, lightweight game guns with straight wrists are the trimmest. I just measured my 20-gauge Westley Richards and it went 4-1/16 inches around the wrist. A 28-gauge Winchester/Parker I love to hunt quail with measures exactly the same. Since my .410 bore Iver Johnson Skeet-er also measures 4-1/16 inches, I am inclined to believe that's how a straight grip should measure on a small-gauge double. My 28-gauge AyA is even smaller at 3-15/16 inches, and it feels as good in my hands as the others. On average, the grips of upland guns built in America as well as those built elsewhere but for the American market are a bit fatter than those on lightweight game guns. The same can usually be said of other styles of grips. The half pistol grip of a 20-gauge Weatherby Athena I recently checked went a hair over 4-9/16 inches. The full pistol grip of a 28-gauge Remington Model 1100 also measures 4-9/16 inches, while the grips of my 20- and 28-gauge Franchi 48AL shotguns are the same at 4-7/8 inches.

I like trim wrists on the small-gauge guns I use for upland wingshooting, but guns that are likely to get bounced around in the bottom of a duck boat should have heavier grips for greater strength. At 4-11/16 inches, a 10-gauge Remington SP-10 in my battery is probably about right for rough-duty waterfowl armament. It is thick enough to resist breakage but not so thick as to feel uncomfortable in the hand. I also believe the stock on a gun used solely for clay target shooting should be none too trim, since a larger grip seems to enable the trigger hand to soak up a bit of the recoil before it reaches the shoulder. It may not amount to much, but when you are shooting hundreds of rounds of heavy loads in a single day, every little bit helps. The grips on my Krieghoff 32 and Remington 3200 measure 4-3/4 inches, and I would not want them to be any smaller. Actually, if the grip is shaped properly, it can be quite large yet feel okay. The grip on my Winchester Model 42 skeet gun measures exactly five inches in circumference, and while I'd just as soon it were thinner, it does not feel all that bad because of its oval shape.

The extended grip as seen on shotguns designed for law enforcement and military use earns zero marks in appearance, but for some applications it makes a lot of sense on a hunting gun. This style of grip is popular on police guns because it makes the gun easy to handle and control with one hand while the other hand is busy with things like operating a portable radio or opening a door. Since the hand grasping the grip absorbs a bit of the recoil before it reaches the shoulder, a gun wearing a stock with an extended grip can be a bit more comfortable to shoot than one with a stock of more conventional shape. I first discovered this while hunting spring gobblers in Kentucky with Steve McKelvain of Benelli and Harold Knight of Knight & Hale Game Calls. The Benelli autoloader I was hunting with wore an experimental buttstock from the company's police gun, and while pattern-testing it

from a benchrest, I could not help but notice how comfortable it was to shoot with heavy 3-1/2 inch turkey loads. Benelli management thought they had something new until one of the guides who worked at the hunting camp brought out a shotgun he had been using for several years for all of his hunting. The fellow was a right-hander, and his left hand had suffered permanent damage from an accident. The stock he had installed on his shotgun had an extended grip, and it enabled him to control it mostly with his right hand. Several of the other guides described him as one of the best shots in the county on quail and doves

The forearms on shotguns have come in many sizes and shapes through the years, but the most popular are the splinter, the semi-beavertail and the full beavertail. My Westley Richards and AyA doubles have splinter forearms, and I absolutely love the way they look. The splinter is a fine choice for any type of shooting where shots do not come often enough to heat up the barrels to the point where they become uncomfortable to touch. But since the small sliver of wood does not wrap around the outside edges of the barrels enough to prevent the fingers from touching them, it is not the best design for fast and steady shooting. I often shoot low-gun skeet at a rapid pace by pulling for myself, and when I shoot 25 rounds in only a few minutes, the barrels can become quite hot. The beavertail-style forearm is better for that kind of shooting because it prevents my fingers from making contact with the hot barrels. Since it is wider and fuller, I also find the beavertail to be a bit better for controlling the swing of a gun, especially on hard left-to-right and right-to-left passing shots like those we see in a dove field, from a duck blind or at stations three, four and five in skeet.

The forearm on my Parker is a semi-beavertail, and I consider its dimensions perfect for a 28-gauge gun. Including its forearm iron, it is 10-1/4 inches long. When viewed from the side and measured from top to bottom, it is 1-1/4 inches at its deepest point at the rear and 3/4 inch deep at the front. The edges of the forearm curve around the sides of the barrels and stop just short of their top surfaces. Widest at the rear, it measures two inches there and tapers to about 1-3/4 inches at the front. Regardless of how hot those barrels might become, that piece of checkered wood keeps my fingers out of harm's way. The forearm on my Iver Johnson Skeet-er is also the semi-beavertail style. To be perfectly candid, size, shape and style are not really all that important so long as a forearm feels good to the owner of the shotgun and he is happy with it. There is one style that I do not like. Since I often position the fingers of my left hand around the front

The SteadyGrip stock on the Benelli turkey gun I used to bag a Kentucky gobbler while hunting with Steve McKelvain made the gun quite comfortable to shoot with heavy loads.

edge of the forearm on an over-under shotgun, those with a schnabel up front are quite distracting to me.

Opinions vary from shooter to shooter on how the stock of a shotgun should look and feel. What suits me best may not be someone else's cup of tea. I am also convinced that the shooter who claims one style of stock is better than all the others has not taken the time to try good examples of the various styles. The stock on the Remington Model 332 over-under not only appeals to my eye, it fits me like a glove and handles like greasy lightning. Everything considered, it might seem logical for me to say its classic styling is best. But I won't because the Weatherby Athena with its straighter comb also appeals to my eye, fits me like a glove and handles like greasy lightning. Two completely different designs and yet I like one just as well as the other.

To see how well your shotgun fits you, shoot it at a couple of sheets of newspaper stapled to heavy cardboard. A piece of wrapping paper measuring around 40 inches square is better, but if I tell you to use

that, you probably won't go to the trouble of rounding it up. Using a big felt pen, mark an aiming point about 4 inches in diameter in the center of the paper. Carefully measure back 16 yards from your new patterning board and place another sheet of newspaper flat on the ground. If the wind is blowing, you will need to anchor it with several rocks. Now back off another 10 yards, load your shotgun and start walking slowly forward with your eyes focused on the center of the target. Just as you reach the piece of paper lying on the ground, shoulder the gun and fire at the target. Do not rush the shot, but you don't want to take careful aim either. Simply focus on the mark you made on the paper, bring the gun smoothly to your shoulder and pretend you are shooting at a quail. After firing a half dozen rounds at the same sheet of paper in that manner, go take a look at it. If the mark on the paper is dead center of the patterns you fired, the gun fits and you have what is commonly called a flat-shooting gun. If about 3/5ths of the pattern is above the spot on the paper, the gun is shooting a bit high, but it is still quite

Because the wingshooter usually has very little time to shoulder his gun and get off a shot at a flushed bird, stock fit is more important on a shotgun than on a rifle.

acceptable for most wingshooting. Trap shooters would call it a 60/40 gun, since it is placing 60 percent of its pattern above your hold point. If the gun is shooting higher than that, you may shoot over the next chukar you take a crack at as it dives off into a canyon. If the gun is placing more than half of its pattern below the spot on the paper, it is shooting too low, and that is as bad if not worse than a gun that shoots too high. A close look at the patterns will also tell you if your gun is shooting too far left or right.

I have a quick and easy way of finding out whether or not a gun fits me really well. After verifying that it is shooting where I look at the pattern board, I shoot rounds of regular skeet, but rather than allowing someone else to pull the targets for me as is usually done, I loop the pull cord through my belt and pull for myself. While holding the pull buttons in my left hand, I hold the gun by its grip with my right hand and with its butt resting against my waist. After pushing the appropriate button with my left hand, I start the swing by pivoting my entire body, grasp the forearm with my left hand as I shoulder the gun, complete my swing through the clay target and pull the trigger. The real test

comes at station eight with its in-your-face shots from the high and low houses. Everything happens so quickly, my subconscious does not have time to force my body into conforming to an ill-fitting gun.

So how do I know if the gun fits? When I break more than 90 out of 100 targets, the gun is for me. When I do that and break all eight targets at station eight, I get out my checkbook. Several of my guns seldom ever fail to pass that test with flying colors. One is a 20-gauge Westley Richards double. Another is a Weatherby Athena over-under I have hunted with a lot. A couple of others are 28-gauge guns, a Winchester reproduction of the Parker and a No. 1 grade AyA. I can also do it with my Browning Superposed Lightning, either in 20 gauge or when it is wearing its Briley tubes in 28-gauge or .410. The first time I tried it with a 12-gauge Remington Model 332 with 28-inch barrels, I broke 94 out of 100 and I missed not a single bird at station eight. I can also pull it off with a 12-gauge Remington Model 1100 skeet gun with a 26-inch barrel and a 28-gauge Model 12 pump gun with a barrel of the same length. The same goes for a matched pair of Franchi 48AL autoloaders in 20 and 28 gauge.

SHOTGUN STOCK DIMENSIONS
(Inches, as measured by the author)

	Gauge/ Caliber	Barrel Length	Drop at Comb	Drop at Heel	Length of Pull	Pitch
AyA No. 1	28	26	1-1/4	2	14-1/4*	2
Browning/Win. M12	28	26	1-3/8	2-3/4	14	2-1/2
Browning Superposed	20	26.5	1-3/8	2-1/8	14-1/4	2
Fox Sterlingworth	12	30	1-1/2	2-1/2	14-3/8*	1-1/4
Franchi 48AL	28	26	1-3/8	2-1/8	14-3/8	1/2
Franchi 48AL	20	26	1-3/8	2-1/8	14-3/8	5/8
Iver Johnson Skeet-er	.410	26	1-1/2	2-1/2	14-1/4*	2-1/4
Kimber Over-Under	12	30	1-1/4	2-1/4	14-3/4	1-1/2
Krieghoff 32	12	28	1-5/16	1-7/8	14-1/8	3/8
Winchester/Parker	28	26	1-1/4	2-1/4	14-1/4	2
Remington Model 11-87	12	26	1-1/2	2	14	3-3/8
Remington Model 1100	20	26	1-1/2	2-1/2	14	1-1/2
Remington Model 1100	12	26	1-5/16	2	14	3
Remington Model 332	12	28	1-3/8	2	14	1-1/4
Remington M3200 Field	12	30	1-3/8	2	14-1/8	1-3/8
Weatherby Athena	.410	26	1-3/8	2-1/8	14-1/4	1-3/4
Westley Richards	20	28	1-3/8	2	14-1/8*	1-1/4
Winchester Model 42	.410	26	1-1/2	2-1/4	14	5/8
Winchester Model 101	20	26	1-3/8	2-5/16	14-1/8	1-3/4

*To the front trigger of a twin-trigger gun

CHAPTER 26

All About Shotgun Barrels

The forcing cone in this sectioned Remington barrel is the tapered section between the mouth of the fired shotshell in the chamber and the base of the purple wad positioned at the beginning of the bore. (Courtesy of Ed Schoppman, Remington Arms)

Whereas a barrel made for a rifle is nothing more than a straight bar of steel with a rifled hole through its center and a chamber reamed out at one end, the shotgun barrel is a bit more complex. The chamber is made larger than the main bore so it will accept a shell, or cartridge, as the British say. Since the shotshell is considerably larger in diameter than the bore, some means must be provided to enable the shot charge to travel from the shell to the bore during firing without allowing a lot of propellant gas to escape around the base of the wad. This is accomplished by gradually reducing the section just forward of the chamber down to bore diameter. Called the forcing cone, this short-tapered portion of the bore allows the shot charge to make its way smoothly from the shotshell to the primary bore of the barrel. From that point on out to the muzzle, we have the main or primary bore. Choke

can be introduced by reducing bore diameter at the muzzle or as is more common today, by threading its interior surface for the acceptance of interchangeable chokes with varying degrees of constriction.

The gauge designations we use today go back to an age when the bore size of a firearm was indicated by the weight of a round ball that would fit inside its bore. A gun that used a lead ball weighing 1/12 pound was called a 12 gauge. Another way to explain it is to say that twelve balls of the correct size for the gun weighed 1 pound. Others came by their names in the same way; a 10-gauge gun used a lead ball weighing 1/10 pound, it was 1/16-pound for the 16 gauge, and a 20-gauge gun took a ball weighing 1/20 pound. While this does not tell us a lot about the actual size of a barrel, you will have to admit, "12-gauge" rolls off the tongue much more smoothly than ".729-inch," which is

Some modern barrels like the one on this 16-gauge Remington Model 870 are cold-formed by the hammer forging method of manufacture.

the nominal bore diameter for that gauge in America. A gun chambered for the .410 shotshell is an exception to all of this, since its bore diameter actually is .410 inch. This is why the .410 should always be referred to as .410 caliber or .410 bore and never .410 gauge, which it most certainly is not. Had the .410 been named like the others, it would be called 67 gauge.

A chart at the end of this chapter contains bore diameters commonly used by American manufacturers, but as you can see in another chart made up of actual bore diameters for a number of barrels I have measured, the dimensions can vary from barrel to barrel. This is due to a dimensional tolerance range used within the industry. Since modern plastic wads do such a great job of sealing off the bore during firing, bore diameter can

vary far more than is commonly seen in mass-produced barrels with absolutely no ill effect on shotshell performance. With the introduction of the plastic wad, some American gun makers began to bore their barrels to slightly larger diameters than in the past, but since the old fiber and felt wads are still commonly used throughout Europe, many guns built outside the United States still have rather tight bores. The bores of my Italian-built 12 gauge muzzleloading shotgun measure .715 inch, and since the over shot and filler wads I use in it measure .740 to .750 inch, they fit tightly enough to do an excellent job of sealing off propellant gas during firing. Until recently, barrels made in Italy by Beretta seldom measured larger than .725 inch, but times are changing. The Xtrema autoloader introduced to American shooters by Beretta during 2002 has a nominal bore diameter of .731 inch, and one I measured was even a bit larger. The bores of most barrels now made by Remington will average somewhere in the neighborhood of .729 inch although those made by that company for some of its clay target guns will run as large as .735 inch.

Up until the tail end of the 19th century all shotgun barrels were made completely by hand. Thin, narrow strips of iron and steel were heated red-hot, twisted together and then pounded around a mandrel, the diameter of which roughly determined the diameter of the bore. Finish-reaming and polishing the bore and hand-striking or turning down the exterior of the barrel to its final dimensions in a lathe completed the job. Some barrel makers referred to the process as Damascus, while others called it laminated. Every writer who knows how to spell the word shotgun eventually gets around to warning his readers about the dangers of shooting guns with Damascus barrels, and this is quite true in some cases. The Damascus barrel earned its reputation for weakness from cheap $12 doubles sold by the hundreds of thousands by dozens of American companies during the 19th and 20th centuries. Chuck Webb of Briley Manufacturing is convinced that a top-quality Damascus-barreled double built by one of the reputable English makers is safe to shoot so long as two important rules are followed. The gun must have recently passed English proof testing, and the loads used in it must not generate higher chamber pressures than the gun was designed for. Several English firms still load shells of various lengths to mild pressures for use in the older guns.

Shotgun barrels are made in a couple of different ways today. Some start as solid bars of steel of the same length as the finished barrel. After the bar is drilled and reamed to form the bore, a lathe is used to

Double-barrel shotguns cost more than repeaters for several reasons; two barrels cost more to make than one and properly regulating a pair of barrels so their patterns converge at 40 yards is time-consuming. A top-quality double usually requires some hand-fitting of its barrels while the repeater does not.

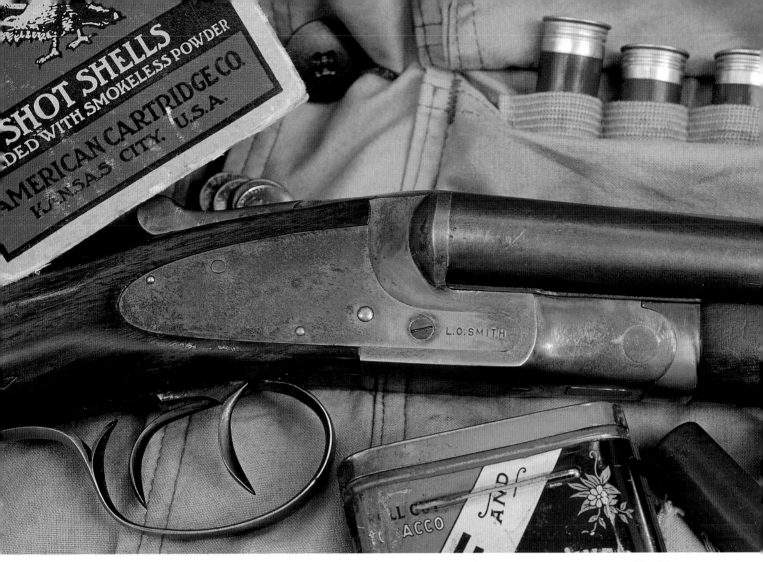

Many old guns have barrels with extremely tight bores. The barrels of this L.C. Smith measure .655 inch, considerably smaller than the .670 inch standard for that gauge.

turn down its outside surface to the desired size and shape. A special reamer is used to ream the chamber and forcing cone. The muzzle of the barrel is squeezed inward to form the desired amount of choke constriction or it is threaded for the use of screw-in chokes.

Many of today's barrels are hammer-forged, a process first introduced in America by Weatherby during the 1950s. In this process, a section of thick-walled tubing considerably shorter than the finished barrel is used. A mandrel is inserted into the tube and it is then placed into a machine that actually hammers it to final shape with a great deal of noise and commotion. While watching this process at the Remington factory, I was simply amazed at the number of Model 870 and Model 11-87 barrels that could be made in a very short time. One advantage to hammer forging is it takes only a few seconds to make a barrel, and that keeps cost down. Another advantage is the chamber, forcing cone and bore are all formed at the same time. Giving it a final polishing and cutting threads at its muzzle for screw-in

chokes completes the bore of the barrel. After a ventilated rib is electronically welded on and the barrel receives its blued finish, it is ready to become an important part of a shotgun.

The barrels of a double-barrel shotgun are more expensive to make, because of the time it takes to join them together and to regulate them. Positioning the exact centers of the barrels closer together at the muzzle than at the breech causes shot charges fired from the two barrels to converge at some predetermined distance, usually 40 yards. If this were not done, the left barrel of a side-by-side double would shoot to the left of where the gun is pointed, and the right barrel would shoot to the right. In the case of the over-under, its lower barrel would shoot low, and its upper barrel would shoot high.

In addition to having a ventilated rib riding atop its top barrel, the typical over-under has side ribs or filets that fill in the space between its barrels. A few guns like Remington's Model 32 and Model 3200 do

Some hunters would consider the 26-inch barrels on the double Phyllis is hunting with too short. If a gun fits the shooter, barrel length usually doesn't matter unless it is uncommonly long or short.

not have the side ribs, and I like the look, especially on a target gun. This is an idea thought to have originated with Scottish gun builder Alex Martin. Some of the side-by-side doubles built by the Birmingham, England, firm of A.A. Brown & Sons have no top or bottom rib. The only one I have ever examined had a short swamped rib at the breech and a bracket holding the barrels together at their muzzles. Otherwise, nothing but empty space separated the two barrels. Eliminating the ribs between the barrels of a double gives a manufacturer the option of making the walls of the barrels a bit thicker for greater strength without increasing the weight of the gun. Or barrel-wall thickness can remain the same for a lighter gun.

An interesting feature of the old Remington 32, one inherited by its German clone, the Krieghoff 32, is its floating bottom barrel. Rather than fastening the barrels rigidly together at their muzzles, a slip-ring type bracket is fastened to the top barrel, and the bottom barrel is suspended within it. The arrangement allows inde-

pendent to and fro expansion and contraction between the two barrels as they heat up and cool down during firing. Clay-target shooters consider this a good thing, since in skeet and in the singles game of 16-yard trap, the bottom barrel is often fired until it becomes quite hot, while the top barrel remains cooler. The Remington Model 3200, which I rank among the 10 best over-unders ever built by anybody in the entire world, has the same type of barrel hanger.

Top ribs on both side-by-sides and over-unders are supposed to lead the eye to the muzzle, but those of us who grew up on inexpensive guns without ribs know it is something we really do not have to have. Ribs have come in many heights, shapes and widths through the years. As might be expected, a flat rib has a flattened top surface, often covered with serrations to reduce glare. If you have already guessed that the surface of a concave rib is concaved, you are correct. The sides of the Churchill-style rib are sharply angled, and this makes its flat top surface about half as wide as those on most ribs. Just the opposite of that is the old Broadway version of the Browning Superposed trap gun. Gaze along the top of its rib and you will think you are looking down a six-lane highway. The ribs on some trap guns are so high, the sight of one never failed to remind the late Don Zutz of the Golden Gate bridge. A good example is the rib on the Krieghoff unsingle. On the other hand, the ribs of some side-by-sides are so low you don't even know they are there, even when looking along the top of their barrels. The swamped rib on my Westley Richards is like that, and the British are right about it being a great idea on a game gun. Then we have solid ribs and ventilated ribs.

The ventilated rib looks racy on a modern gun, but it is not without its shortcoming. Rust likes to hide out in its nooks and crannies, and the vents can be difficult to keep free of weeds, seeds and other debris in the field. We have become so accustomed to seeing ventilated ribs sitting atop the barrels of shotguns, it is doubtful if anything except a single-shot knockabout would sell without it. Even that type of gun has been available with a rib. The old Winchester Model 20 and the new Stoeger Hunter single shots have very nice ventilated ribs. About the only thing I do not like in the way of ribs is the extremely high ventilated type on a side-by-side double. A friend of mine has a fairly late-production Winchester Model 21 with such a rib, and every time I look at it, I get the creeps.

Shotguns have been made with many different barrel lengths through the years. Contrary to what many shotgunners believe, an extremely long barrel does not shoot a lot "harder" than a shorter barrel. Most of the modern powders loaded in shotshells today produce about the same velocity when burned in a 26-inch barrel as they do in a 32-inch barrel. When deciding what barrel length to buy, you should first decide what the gun will be used for. There was a time when 26 inches was the most popular length for the barrels of doubles used for upland wingshooting, but the trend has now moved toward those measuring 28 inches. The 26-inch barrel is still popular on pumps and autoloaders because their receivers are much longer than the receivers of side-by-sides and over-unders. My 20-gauge Westley Richards double has 28-inch barrels and measures 44 inches overall, 2 inches shorter then my Remington Model 1100 skeet gun with its 25-1/2 inch barrel. My 20-gauge Weatherby Athena over-under also has 28-inch barrel, and while its receiver is a bit longer than that of the Westley Richards, it is still almost an inch shorter overall than the Model 1100 with its shorter barrel. Some guns handle better with barrels of different lengths, even though they share the same type of action. When I am having a good day, I shoot my 12-gauge Remington 11-87 quite well when it is wearing its 26-inch barrel, but I shoot it with its 28-inch barrel a bit better. It is just the opposite with a 20-gauge Model 11-87; I hit more birds and break more clay targets with its 26-inch barrel than with its 28-inch barrel.

When pass-shooting waterfowl and doves, I lean toward longer barrels. Once I get the extra weight up front moving along smoothly, I am less likely to become lazy and stop my swing too early. I like the feel of 28- or 30-inch barrels on a double, while 28 inches seems about right for me on most pumps and autoloaders. The over-under I shoot most often in skeet has 28-inch barrels, while the barrels on my Remington Model 3200 trap gun measure 30 inches. I shoot a single-barrel Remington 90-T in trap doubles, and it has a 32-inch barrel. Most of the top sporting clays shooters use barrels measuring 28 inches and longer, but I find that I score about as well in that game with two 28-gauge doubles wearing 26-inch barrels. One is Winchester's reproduction of the Parker, and the other is a No. 1 grade AyA. Shooters love to argue about barrel lengths, but if a gun fits me and I occasionally practice with it on clay targets, its barrel length does not seem to matter a whole lot. My favorite doubles have 26-, 28- and 30-inch barrels, and since all fit me like my old bedroom slippers, I shoot them equally well.

One of the more common changes gunsmiths make to barrels is enlarging the diameter of their bores. This, by the way, is not exactly a new idea. The British experimented with oversized bores during the 19th century, and the A. H. Fox company was offering overbored barrels as early as the 1920s. Major Charles Askins, who collaborated with barrel maker Burt Becker in the development of the Fox HE-grade waterfowl gun, once wrote that the first of those guns built had bores measuring .750 inch rather than .729 inch, which is standard for the 12 gauge. Fox also built 20-gauge guns with .626-inch bores rather than the standard .615 inch. In those days, the bores were made oversized because they were thought to handle heavier shot charges more efficiently than bores of standard diameter. Today, the modification is especially popular among target shooters who are convinced of its ability to reduce perceived recoil.

Once referred to as overboring and now more commonly called backboring, it simply means the bore is reamed out to a larger diameter than the old standards. Bore size of a 12-gauge barrel is increased from the usual .729 inch to as much as .740 inch, although somewhere around .735 inch seems to have become the norm. Backboring has also caught on among some of the manufacturers who make guns for clay target shoot-

Bore and choke diameters are easily measured with a gauge from Brownells. The bores of this 28-gauge double checked out at slightly over .545 inch.

ing. The bores of my Remington Model 3200 trap gun are .735 inch in diameter, and my Krieghoff 32 measures .739 inch. The late Washington state gunsmith Stan Baker experimented with even greater extremes by reaming out 12-gauge barrels to diameters as large as is commonly seen in 10-gauge barrels. Such grossly oversized bores seem to work okay except when cold weather hardens the plastic wad in shotshells and prevents its base from obturating sufficiently to completely seal off the bore during firing.

Whether or not backboring a barrel actually does reduce perceived recoil is something I cannot swear to, but I will say that some of the hardest-kicking guns I have fired had extremely tight bores. On the other hand, my Remington Model 3200 and Kreighoff Model 32 have oversized bores, and yet I do not find them to be any more comfortable to shoot than my Fox Sterlingworth, and its bores are rather tight. One of my Remington Model 1100 shotguns weighs two ounces more than one of my Model 11-87s, and its bore diameter is .007 inch larger. I have shot those two guns side by side with the same loads, and if the one with the larger bore kicks noticeably less, you cannot prove it by me.

The only thing that will convince me beyond doubt that backboring actually works as advertised is to see someone come up with some type of instrument or device that accurately measures actual recoil before and after the modification. Until then, I will remain quite skeptical of its ability to do anything other than possibly improve pattern quality a bit. When all is said and done, that alone may be enough to ask for.

There are those who believe another popular bore modification also reduces recoil. Shotguns built during the age of card and fiber wads usually have forcing cones measuring about half an inch long. A short forcing cone allows the shot charge to make its trip from chamber to bore with a minimal loss of propellant gas. The development of the plastic wad and its ability to better seal off the bore made the use of longer forcing cones practical. Using a special reamer to lengthen the forcing cone to about 1-1/2 inches gives it a milder angle, and this is said to allow the shot charge to make a smoother and more gradual transition from chamber to bore. A few gunsmiths who perform this operation claim it reduces recoil. I remain somewhat of a skeptic here, too. They also swear it cuts down on pellet deformation with lead shot, and I will go along with that.

When I bought my old Fox Sterlingworth it had 2-5/8 inch chambers and extremely short forcing cones. One afternoon when I needed something to do, I used a special reamer from Brownells to lengthen its forcing cones and to extend its chambers out to 2-3/4 inches. I did it mainly because I wanted to shoot 2-3/4 inch shells in the gun, and I figured any reduction in recoil would be a bonus. If that gun kicks any less now than it did before its surgery, my memory is too short and my shoulder is too insensitive to notice. I have also been unable to see any improvement in pattern quality, but that may be because the gun was already delivering beautiful patterns before the modification. If actual truth were known, a lot of this barrel modification stuff is a mental thing. If a shooter is convinced that backboring a barrel and lengthening its forcing cone reduces recoil, his brain will relay that message to his shoulder, and he will become convinced the gun kicks less than it did before the modifications were made.

A few of today's barrels are chrome-plated at the factory, but most are not. Whether or not this is good or bad depends on who you are and your point of view. A chrome skin inside the barrel prevents rust, so it is a good thing for the shooter who does not clean his gun very often. But because chrome plating the entire length of the bore makes modifications such as overboring, forcing-cone lengthening and threading a barrel for screw-in chokes more difficult for a gunsmith to perform, it will cost the owner of the gun more to have the work done. For this reason, there are those who will not buy a gun with a chrome-plated bore. I am not inclined to have a lot of modifications made to the barrel of a shotgun so I can live with or without chrome. I do like to see it in the chamber, since that's where rust is most likely to form inside a barrel, but anywhere else I can take it or leave it.

Then we have the question of steel shot. The barrels of some older guns, especially doubles, were not made to handle steel, and anyone who is foolish enough to use it in a fine old gun made by Parker, Fox, Ithaca, L.C. Smith, Browning and a number of others is risking damage to its barrels. During the 1970s, Winchester technicians discovered that the firing of only 500 rounds of ammunition loaded with steel shot in barrels with Full choke constriction increased bore diameter at the muzzle by as much as .003 inch. And the barrels they used were made of modern steel, which is much tougher than some of the steels used by gunmakers during days of yesteryear. If the barrel wall is quite thin at the muzzle (as is the case for many of the older doubles), bulging can be detected with a diameter increase as small as .001 inch.

Some believe the installation of screw-in chokes made of a special steel hard enough to withstand the ravages of steel shot will make any shotgun suitable for use with any type of shot. This may be true out at the muzzle, especially if an extended choke is used, but many of the older barrels are quite soft. Since steel shot is considerably harder than some of the steels used to make barrels in the old days (and even harder than some of the steels used today), there is always the danger of a few pellets escaping from within the confines of the plastic shotcup and scoring the bore. What it all boils down to is the availability of nontoxic shot such as Bismuth and Tungsten-Matrix leaves us with no sensible reason for risking damage to an older gun by feeding it steel shot. If in doubt about whether your gun is suitable for use with steel, contact its manufacturer. If the maker of the gun is no longer in business and no one else can say for sure, play it safe by not using steel.

NOMINAL BORE DIAMETERS

10-gauge — 0.775-inch	16-gauge — 0.670 inch	28-gauge — 0.550 inch
12-gauge — 0.729-inch	20-gauge — 0.615 inch	.410 bore — .410 inch

SHOTGUN BORES MEASURED BY THE AUTHOR

Gun	Gauge or Caliber	Actual Diameter (Inch)	Gun	Gauge or Caliber	Actual Diameter (Inch)
Briley Subgauge Tube	.410	.405	Remington Model 1100	16	.657
Iver Johnson Skeet-er	.410	.398	Browning Citori	12	.712
Weatherby Athena Over-Under	.410	.406	Browning Citori Top-Single	12	.715
Weatherby Orion Side-By-Side	.410	.406	Fox Sterlingworth	12	.728
AyA No. 1 Grade	28	.547	Investarm/Kimber	12	.725
Browning Superposed	28	.535	Krieghoff Model 32	12	.739
Franchi 48AL	28	.555	Remington M870 SF	12	.725
Krieghoff M32/Purbaugh tube	28	.549	Remington M870 SP	12	.724
Winchester Model 12	28	.553	Remington 11-87	12	.728
Winchester Parker Reproduction	28	.552	Remington Peerless	12	.729
Weatherby Athena Over-Under	28	.545	Remington Model 1100	12	.735
Franchi 48AL	20	.627	Remington Model 3200 Field	12	.729
Krieghoff M32	20	.614	Remington Model 3200 Trap	12	.735
Remington Model 1100	20	.623	Remington Model 332	12	.730
Remington Model 11-87	20	.611	Ruger Red Lab	12	.724
Winchester Model 101	20	.615	SKB M685 Trap	12	.725
Weatherby Athena Over-Under	20	.618	Winchester M37 Steelbilt	12	.731
Westley Richards	20	.618	Winchester Model 1897	12	.726
Browning A5	16	.658	Remington SP-10	10	.776
L.C. Smith	16	.655	AyA Matador	10	.772

CHAPTER 27

Handloading Shotshells

All the 28, 20, and 12-gauge shotshells I use for clay target shooting are loaded on progressive machines like these from Dillon, RCBS and Ponsness-Warren.

Those of us who reload metallic cartridges do so for a number of reasons, not the least of which is the opportunity to develop a handload specifically for a particular firearm and to possibly tailor the load for a specific application. And while some reloaders probably end up spending more money on ammunition than those who shoot factory cartridges, they enjoy a greater number of squeezes on the trigger for each dollar spent.

The reasons for reloading shotshells are fewer in number, but important just the same. At the very top of the list is the lesser cost of reloads versus factory ammo. Prices of shotshell components will vary from area to area, but a bit of prudent shopping along with purchasing in relatively large quantities will bring prices to a reasonable level. I seldom stock up with fewer than 5,000 primers and wads and an 8-pound canister of powder, and if the price is right, I'll skip a few lunches and buy even more. So how much money do I save by loading my own? The 1-ounce 12-gauge reloads I use on clay targets usually run about a dollar per box less than the least expensive promotional ammo sold at "mart"

prices, and they contain a higher grade of shot to boot. Even at discount prices, premium-grade target loads like Remington's Premier STS, Winchester's AA and Federal's Gold Medal can run upwards of three times the cost of a box of my handloads, while top-level hunting loads, especially waterfowl loads with nontoxic shot, will set you back even more.

Skeet shooting and sporting clays are where the most money is saved by reloading, simply because the 28 and .410 are used in both, and because of their lower volume of sales, factory target loadings of those two cost about 20 percent more than 12- and 20-gauge loads. But since the two smaller shells use less powder and lighter charges of shot, they actually cost less to reload than the 12 and 20. I can put together a box of 28-gauge 3/4 ounce skeet loads in Remington Premier or Winchester AA hulls for about a dollar less than for 12-gauge loads, which is one of the reasons I shoot a lot of 28-gauge shells in practice. Boiling it all down to brass tacks and ammunition cost, I can shoot about three rounds of skeet with reloads for the same price as one round with factory ammo.

Saving money is by no means the only logical reason to consider reloading those empty hulls you've been tossing in the waste can. Reloading your own will allow you to come up with some very useful loads not offered by the ammunition companies. A good example is the 7/8 ounce 12-gauge load, which is available in factory ammo, but not always in the combinations we sometimes need. I use this shot weight in handloads for most of my skeet shooting, for 16-yard trap, for gimmie targets in sporting clays, and for a great deal of my upland wingshooting. Several companies offer 12-gauge loadings with that shot charge as well as the similar 24-gram charge, but all are available only in three shot sizes: 7-1/2s, 8s and 9s. They are fantastic target loads, and those loaded with No. 8 shot are great for hunting bobwhite quail with a good dog. But the pheasant hunter who wants a light-kicking load for tight-holding birds, or perhaps the beagle man who loves to chase cottontails, is out of luck because no such load is offered with larger shot. Loading your own shotshells gives you the option of using just such a recipe.

Something else about the 7/8 ounce 12-gauge load is that most U.S. ammo companies push it to a nominal muzzle velocity of 1325 fps, and the Europeans move it out it even faster. Since such blazing speed is not actually needed for most of the applications for which that shot charge is so well suited, I prefer to back off on the throttle to the 1150-1200 fps levels for a very noticeable reduction in recoil. One of my favorite mixtures is the Winchester 209 primer, Winchester WAA12L wad, 18.3 grains of Hodgdon Clays and 7/8 ounce of shot, all stacked into the Remington Premier or Federal Gold Medal hull. Muzzle velocity averages around 1200 fps in the 28-inch barrels of my Krieghoff K32. Shooting that load in a gas-operated autoloader such as Remington's 11-87 has about the same effect on my shoulder as shooting the 3/4-ounce 28-gauge shell in a standard-weight gun. The down side to such a light load is it doesn't generate high enough gas pressure to operate the Remington Model 1100, Beretta 391 and some of the other autoloaders.

Here is another example of a special load made possible by my reloading machine. When my father died a few years back, he left me all of his hunting guns, one of which is a very nice 6-3/4 pound L.C. Smith in 16 gauge. The handsome little double is in excellent shape and still as tight as the day he bought it during the late 1940s, but it kicks like a Missouri mule when fed heavy loads. I realize that having Elsie's forcing cones lengthened and also having her barrels backbored might reduce perceived recoil a bit, but I prefer to hunt with the piece just as it was when Dad hunted with it. So out

A reloading manual like this one from Hodgdon is the very first item a beginning handloader should buy.

of necessity, I tried several one-ounce handloads until I came up with something that was kinder to the shoulder. The load I finally settled on consists of the Federal plastic case, Federal 209A primer, 14.5 grains of Nitro 100 and the Remington SP16 plastic wad column with its shotcup capacity reduced slightly by the insertion of one 28-gauge, .125-inch-thick card overpowder wad beneath the shot charge. Velocity averages just over 1100 fps in a 26-inch barrel, and not only does the load make the little double a delight to shoot, but pattern uniformity is excellent. Out to 30 yards or so, I find the L.C. Smith to be just as effective on bobwhites and mourning doves as it is when I feed it harder-kicking loads with heaver shot charges. I am also experimenting with 7/8 and 3/4 ounce loads for that particular gun, something I could not do if I did not handload.

Now for one last of many good reasons I have to reload my own shotshells. Sometime back, I bought an old Winchester Model 1897 pump gun in 12 gauge. I had planned to use it in cowboy action shooting, but strayed in another direction instead, so the old corn sheller sat neglected in the corner for several months. Then a couple of friends invited me on what they described as an "old-timer's" quail hunt, referring to the shotguns to be used and not the hunters. They went on to mention that anyone who brought a gun introduced after World War I was likely to get his pant legs hosed down by the bird dogs we would be hunting with. My old 97 Winchester qualified in vintage, but its full-choked barrel made it less than ideal for dropping a bobwhite at 20 yards and still having enough left to eat. So I cooked up a spreader load by decreasing the powder charge of one of my regular 7/8 ounce loads by one grain and placing a Polywad Spred-R insert atop the

Reducing velocity by handloading reduces recoil without sacrificing performance on close- to medium-range shots at game birds.

shot charge just prior to fold-crimping each shell. The end result was a load that delivered Improved Cylinder patterns from a Full choke barrel and allowed me to get by with a long-range duck gun on close-range quail.

Whether or not you should start reloading shotshells depends more on how much shooting you do than anything else. If you shoot no more than a case or two of shells each year, it is difficult to justify the purchase of even the most inexpensive reloader available unless you need to come up with a special load as I have for my L.C. Smith double and Winchester pump gun. On the other hand, if you shoot a lot, then you're just the kind of fellow the makers of shotshell reloaders and reloading components are looking for.

The three basic types of shotshell reloaders are single-stage, manual-progressive and auto-progressive. All have a number of stations, each of which accomplishes one or more steps of the reloading cycle. When using a single-stage machine, the operator loads one shell at a time and must move the case from station to station for each of the loading operations. If the machine has five stations, its handle will have to be cycled at least five times in order to produce one loaded round. In addition, some single-stage reloaders require the operator to manually insert each individual case, wad and primer into the machine, and he must also operate the powder and shot charge bars. In other words, producing

a single shotshell can require well over a dozen movements of the hands.

In contrast, the auto-progressive reloader produces a loaded round with each cycle of its operating handle. It does this by simultaneously performing all operations while each of its stations contains a case with one or more operations performed at each station. In addition, most progressives also dispense primers as well as the powder and shot charges automatically, and the new five-station Dillon SL 900 even feeds cases in the same manner.

I reload all of my shotshells on Ponsness Warren, RCBS and Dillon reloaders, so to give you some idea of how an auto-progressive works, I'll describe what happens with each complete cycle of the Dillon. On the down-stroke of its handle, the machine transfers a primer from its reservoir to station two, orients a case base-down from another reservoir, feeds a case into station one where it is resized and deprimed, drops a powder charge into a primed case at station two, seats a wad and drops the shot charge into another case at station three, starts the crimp on a fully loaded case at station four, completes the crimp and slightly tapers the mouth of a finished shell at station five. On the return up-stroke of the operating handle, the shell plate automatically rotates (or progresses) clockwise by one station and in doing so, ejects a loaded round from station five and into a collection bin. The upstroke also seats a primer at station two and tilts out the wad holder at station three. In other words, the machine produces a ready-to-shoot round with each complete cycle of its operating handle.

The manual-progressive reloader also performs all reloading operations simultaneously, but unlike the auto-progressive, which automatically rotates the shell holder, its shell holder must be manually rotated after each cycle of the operating handle. The MEC 8567 Grabber is this type of reloader, and while it is a bit slower than a fully automatic machine, it is also a bit less expensive.

There once was a time when most of the experts recommended single-stage reloaders for beginners, but today's top-of-line progressives are so much more foolproof than those of yesteryear, I'm not sure this is still good advice. Errors, mistakes and blunders can be made with either type, so my advice is to buy the one that best suits your needs, follow written instructions carefully, remain totally conscious of what's going on when using the machine, and enjoy burning up those reloads at the range or in the field.

The was also once a time when the single-stage reloader was the best bet for those who spend a lot of their time developing loads, and this is still true of progressives that do not allow easy removal and insertion of cases or partially loaded shells at each station. But since machines such as RCBS Grand, Dillon RL-900 and Ponsness Warren Platinum 2000 allow that to be done, they are just as suitable for load development as a single-stage machine.

Which reloader to choose usually boils down to the size of one's budget and annual shotshell consumption. Assuming no stoppages, one of the inexpensive single-stage machines can turn out about 125 rounds or five boxes of shotshells per hour. Someone who reloads mainly for hunting and perhaps a round or two of skeet or sporting clays each month can live happily ever after with a single-stage reloader. I know this to be true because that's exactly what I used for many years. Then I grew more interested in the clay target games and found myself spending more and more time popping caps in not only skeet and sporting clays, but trap as well. This led to a need to reload the 12, 20 and 28 gauges as well as the .410, and it soon became obvious that I had outgrown my single-stage reloaders. I then switched to auto-progressives, all capable of producing an easy 400 to 450 rounds per hour, and began to spend a lot more time shooting and a lot less time reloading. Still, I continue to load the 16-gauge on a single-stage machine simply because I don't shoot it enough to make

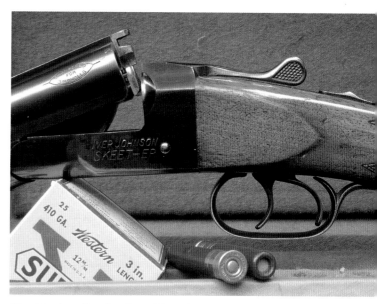

If not for handloading I would not be able to shoot 3/4-ounce loads in the three-inch .410 shell.

switching to a progressive worthwhile. I also load the .410 on a single-stage machine, but would switch to a progressive if I could find one that worked satisfactorily with the tiny shell.

The number of times a shotshell case can be reloaded is influenced by number of things with its type of construction at the top of the list. The old paper shotshells were good for very few reloads, but some of the modern plastic hulls will withstand many firings. Even among plastic cases, reloading life varies considerably with compression-formed cases of one-piece construction such as the Remington Premier, Federal Gold Medal and Winchester AA usually good for more reloadings than other types. As described in Hodgdon's *Shotshell Data Manual*, a 12-gauge Remington Premier hull was loaded and fired 15 times and even though splits appeared in its crimp fold during the last firing, the shell still produced the same velocity as it did on its first firing. Just as remarkable is the fact that maximum velocity variation throughout the 15 firings was a mere six feet per second. Though quite interesting, such a test took things to the extreme. Usually I dispose of Winchester AA, Remington Premier and Federal Gold Medal hulls after reloading them eight to 10 times.

As a rule, and this applies to all types of plastic cases, 12, 16, 20 and 28-gauge hulls will hold up to many more firings than .410 hulls. Most of the time, .410s are ready to be discarded after the third or fourth firing. They say this is due to the higher chamber pressures to which the .410 is loaded, but the 28-gauge also churns up higher pressures than the 12 and 20, and I am still shooting some Winchester AA hulls of that gauge after half a dozen loadings.

CHAPTER 28

Patterning the Shotgun

Except for a couple of patchy areas, this particular load delivered patterns of acceptable density and uniformity at 40 yards when fired in my 12-gauge Fox Sterlingworth. More important, pattern center landed dead on my hold point.

Some big-game hunters I know are real perfection-ists when it comes to making sure their rifles are perfectly sighted in prior to opening day of the season. They fuss, they fret and they carefully twist the windage and elevation adjustments on their scopes until their rifles place a bullet precisely where they want it to go. Several of those fellows also hunt a great deal with shotguns, and if a single one of them has ever gone to the trouble of pattern-testing his gun, he has done a good job of keeping his secret hidden from me. I am greatly puzzled by this because knowing exactly where a shotgun places the center of its pattern and the quali-ty of the pattern it throws with various sizes of shot is every bit as important to me as being familiar with where my deer rifle places its bullet.

A couple of hours at the pattern board will reveal many things about a shotgun. It will tell you where your gun is placing the shot charge in relation to your hold point, and this is an important thing to know. Fire a round at the patterning board or plate from 16 yards, but rather than taking careful aim, quickly shoulder the gun and shoot, same as you would do in the field. Shoot the same target four more times, and the heaviest concentra-tion of pellets will indicate where the pattern center is impacting in relation to your point of hold. Ideally, the center of the pattern will be dead on your hold point, in which case you have what clay target shooters call a flat-shooting gun. This is about perfect from a gun used for wingshooting. For targets that usually gain elevation as they fly away from the hunter, quail and pheasant being examples, most hunters can get by with a gun that shoots a bit high, but it should not place over 60 percent of its pattern above the hold point. If the pattern measures, let us say, 30 inches in diameter, about 18 inches would be above the hold point while 12 inches would be below it. One of my hunting guns shoots closer to 70/30, and I shoot it quite well on flushing birds but for pass-shooting I do better with a flatter-shooting gun.

A close look reveals that the gun I used to shoot this pattern placed the center of the pattern high and left. My hold was on the red circle in the center of the target.

Take it from one who has learned from experience, all shotguns do not shoot where the eye is looking as it gazes over the top of the barrel. Years ago I bought a Browning reproduction of the Winchester Model 12 in 28 gauge and decided to shoot a few rounds of skeet with it before I had time to check it out at the pattern board. I did not do so well. When shooting from stations where the birds are launched at hard angles from left to right or from right to left, I smoked most of them, but when shooting at easy going-away shots from stations one and seven, I missed more birds than I hit. It was especially frustrating since I seldom ever miss shots from those stations with other guns. A few minutes at the pattern board proved to be a real eye opener as the gun was placing the right-hand edge of its pattern to my hold point. The fact that it was shooting its entire pattern to the left of where I was looking explained why I missed those easy shots at station seven, where the low-house target travels almost directly away from the shooter. I was holding dead on as I usually do, but the shot charge was missing to the left.

The Browning is but one of several shotguns I have worked with that shot where it wanted to rather than where I wanted it to. Here is another example: One of the firearms manufacturers invited me on a wingshooting adventure in South America and sent me a 20-gauge autoloader to take along. Since we would be using a new load, I decided to wait until ammunition samples arrived before testing the gun. To make a long story short, with departure time less than two weeks away and the shotshells yet to arrive, I decided to go ahead and check out the gun with ammunition I had on hand. As I had done earlier with the Browning pump, I decided to shoot a round of skeet with the gun before heading to the pattern board. I am not a bad shot at skeet, and seldom break fewer than 23 targets out of 25. Quite often I run 25 straight. During my first round of skeet with the 20-gauge autoloader, I broke exactly three birds. The other fellows in my squad could hardly believe their eyes. A few minutes at the pattern board revealed why I missed more often than I hit. At 20 yards, the gun was placing all but about the top inch of

Attaching an electronic sight to a shotgun is a method commonly used by turkey hunters to get sighted in.

its pattern below my hold point. As I eventually figured out, the screw-in choke threads at the muzzle of its barrel were terribly misaligned with the bore of the gun. Lucky for me, I had time to round up a new barrel before departing for my hunt.

Changing loads will sometimes shift pattern point of impact by a small amount. One of my favorite waterfowl guns is a Remington Model 11-87. It shoots a bit higher with high-velocity steel-shot loads than with slower loads. Changing the drop or pitch (or both) of the stock can also modify pattern point of impact in relation to your hold point. This is due to the fact that the shooter's eye serves as the rear sight of a shotgun. Lowering the comb of the stock with a wood rasp lowers the position of the eye in relation to the muzzle of the barrel and makes the gun shoot lower. By the same

token, increasing comb height by the application of layers of adhesive-backed moleskin (available from any pharmacy) will cause it to shoot higher. Applying layers of moleskin to the left side of the comb will cause the gun to shoot farther to the left (for a right-handed shooter) while removing wood from the same side of the stock will cause it to shoot to the right. Using this method to shift windage by a great deal is actually less than desirable, since the eye will probably no longer be aligned with the center of the rib.

While the cures I have described may be all some shotguns need, others require more drastic measures. Back when few pumps and autoloaders came without ventilated ribs, it was common for gunsmiths to adjust pattern point of impact by carefully bending the barrel in the proper direction. A barrel with a ventilated rib can also be bent, but since a portion of the rib may have to be taken loose from the bar... ...ered back in place, it ...e operation, one not ...lling to take on. For ...ns, bending the bar- ...gun has never been

...) see turkey hunters ...quipping them with ...ngshooters consid- ...esirable or practi- ...ing pump gun I ...d in a very satis- ...rrel, along with ...to indicate how ...off, to Briley ...ation of eccen- ...in chokes. ...of the barrel ...weaked just ...f impact by ...sired direc- ...reat and it ...rn quality. ...versatility ...te set of ...rom .005 ...nstalled. ...k from ...ard and ...nother trip to Houst... ...d. Briley had transformed a gun ... ...it with into one I now hit with n...

While I am on the subject of chokes, I should also mention that some of the thousands of older guns still in use with variable-choke devices such as the Cutts Compensator have a tendency to shoot off toward Aunt Nettie's hen house because they were installed incorrectly. The Cutts on my Winchester Model 42 is dead on the money, but I once shot a Winchester Model 12 wearing a similar type of gizmo once offered by Weaver, and it put the center of its pattern several inches to the right of my hold point. I decided to not buy that particular Model 12, but I probably should have since its affliction could have been easily corrected by a good gunsmith.

Time spent at the pattern board can also reveal a shotgun's preference in loads. Just as deer rifles often shoot more accurately with some loads than with others, so it goes with shotguns. I remember testing a

I took this gobbler at 59 yards while hunting in Kentucky with Harold Knight. Incredibly tight patterns delivered at long range by the Benelli shotgun and Hevi-Shot along with a Burris electronic sight made the shot both possible and feasible.

Beretta Xtrema autoloader, and as is often the case with shotguns, I found pattern quality to range from mediocre to excellent with the various steel shot loads I had on hand. Shot distribution throughout the patterns fired with the loads it liked best was quite uniform, with very few open patches big enough to allow a bird to fly through. Patterns fired with loads the gun did not like showed dramatic patchiness in pellet distribution.

Wringing out the Beretta revealed yet another benefit to pattern testing I have long been aware of. Like many shotguns are prone to do, it shot its most uniform patterns when certain shot sizes were matched up with certain choke constrictions. The clear winners in steel shot for that particular gun were No. 2s pushed through Improved Modified choke (.025 inch of constriction) and BBBs matched up with Light Modified (.015 inch). All guns do not shoot their best with those same combinations. A Remington 11-87 I have used on waterfowl hunts from Alaska to Uruguay also likes No. 2 steel, but it throws its best patterns with Full choke, which in that gun measures just under .035 inch of constriction. It also likes BBBs in heavy goose loads, but prefers to push them through only .007 of constriction, a choke usually described as Light Skeet. Another of my favorite duck guns is a 1924-vintage Fox Sterlingworth with 30-inch barrels. It has 20 points of choke in its right barrel and 41 points in its left. That gun simply refuses to shoot decent patterns with Kent's No. 6 Tungsten-Matrix shot with either barrel, and yet patterns delivered by it with No. 4 Tungsten-Matrix are as good as they get out to an honest 50 yards.

Loads should also be tested to see how the effective diameters of the patterns they deliver are affected by changes in choke constriction, shot sizes and load quality at the various ranges at which game is commonly taken. If most of your shots are at close range and the effective pattern diameter delivered by your gun/choke/ammo combination measures smaller than 25 inches at 25 yards, you should seriously consider switching to a choke with less constriction. Moving to the opposite extreme, if the effective pattern diameter of your long-range load measures much greater than 40 inches at 40 yards, you might need to tighten up the choke in order to deliver adequate pellet density at that range.

Evaluating Patterns

Shotgun and shotshell manufacturers customarily test their products by shooting patterns at 40 yards and then drawing a 30-inch circle around the highest concentration of holes in the paper. The holes within that circle are then counted and compared with the number of pellets in the test load in order to arrive at the pattern percentage. For example, if the shell being tested is loaded with, let us say, 1-1/2 ounces of No. 2 shot, it should contain approximately 187 pellets, since that size runs about 125 pellets per ounce (see charts at the end of this chapter). If 130 holes are counted inside our 30-inch circle, we arrive at 70 percent, which indicates the gun/load combination is delivering Full choke performance. By the same token, 112 holes (60 percent) counted would indicate Modified choke, and 102 holes would indicate Improved Cylinder. Since patterns fired with the same gun/choke/load combination can vary from one to the next, the manufacturers usually fire a minimum of 10 patterns and average them for the final result.

All of this is well and good and quite useful for those who desire to compare the performance of their chokes and loads to the industry standards. Seeing how a choke and load are performing at long range is something every shotgunner should be interested in, but it does not tell those who take game at closer ranges everything they need to know. A Michigan grouse hunter who drops most of his birds inside 25 yards could not care less about how many pellets land in a 30-inch circle at 40 yards. Same goes for the fellow out in California who hunts valley quail in thick brush, and the Illinois hunter who shoots all of his ducks over decoys at close range. Those guys are more interested in how big a pattern a choke/load combo delivers at ranges as close as 10 to 15 yards. And since those hunters most likely plan to eat any birds they shoot, they also need to know which chokes and loads deliver patterns dense enough to kill cleanly at close range but not so dense as to grind birds into puffs of feathers. Sessions with a pattern board will reveal that and much more.

Regardless of whether I am after mallards with No. 2 shot or Canada geese with triple-Bs, I prefer to limit my shooting to about 30 yards when using steel shot. For this reason, most of my pattern testing with steel takes place inside that range. When testing ammo loaded with nontoxic shot of higher density such as Remington's Hevi-Shot, Tungsten-Iron from Federal and Kent's Tungsten-Matrix, I might move the pattern board on out to 40 yards and sometimes a bit farther. But when it comes to the use of steel, I am more interested in how a load performs at ranges where it is most effective. Switching to lead shot, I kill most of my quail inside 25 yards. and the majority of the woodcock I manage to intercept with a swarm of shot usually hit the ground about 20 yards from where I am standing. When pattern-testing guns and loads for hunting those birds, I am not very interested in how they perform at greater distances.

But there are times when and places where game birds are taken at longer distances. Late-season pheasant hunting is a good example. To determine how far away a particular choke/load combination will deliver patterns of adequate density, start by shooting paper at 20 yards and then back off from the pattern board in 5-yard increments, shooting patterns at each range. Once you see the percentage of shot inside a 30-inch circle drop below 60 percent, you have exceeded the maximum range for that particular combination. Actually, 70 percent is not a bad minimum to stick by.

Sighting in the Turkey Gun

Always use a steady rest when zeroing a turkey gun. Start at 10 yards and make sight adjustments until the shot charge is striking the target dead on your line of sight. If the gun has open sights, just remember to move its rear sight in the direction you want the center of the pattern to

Ammunition manufacturers pattern-test their loads at 40 yards but knowing how his gun and load performs at much closer ranges is more important to this hunter. He will have to drop the bird he is about to flush inside 20 yards, before it disappears into heavy brush.

move in relation to your line of sight. In other words, if the gun is shooting low and to the right, move the rear sight up and to the left. Arrows on the windage and elevation adjustment turrets of scopes and red dot sights indicate in which direction the knobs should be turned.

After zeroing the gun at 10 yards, start backing off in 10-yard increments and shoot additional patterns at each distance. Use a steel patterning plate or paper measuring about 40 inches square to verify that the highest concentration of shot pellets and your line of sight coincide at various distances. After this is done, you can switch to the smaller head/neck turkey profile targets to determine the maximum range of the choke/load combination you are using.

You have exceeded the maximum range of a particular combination when it fails to consistently place no less than a dozen pellets into the head/neck area of the target. It takes only one pellet through the brain or spine of a gobbler to drop it for keeps, but it is possible for all pellets to miss those targets. When that happens, multiple pellet strikes will usually deliver enough energy to keep the bird down long enough for the coup de grace.

The most common question I am asked about turkey guns is, "How high are you supposed to hold when shooting at long range to compensate for pellet drop?" The answer is not at all. Even when using the tightest chokes available, pellet dispersion is still great

A double that delivers large patterns with one barrel and tight patterns with the other is an excellent combination for Gambel quail.

enough to compensate for distance, and a dead-on hold at long range will result in one very dead turkey if the gun was properly zeroed to begin with.

Setting Up a Pattern Board

The ammunition manufacturers do their pattern-testing in underground tunnels filled with all sorts of expensive equipment, but such an elaborate setup is not required in order to produce the results the average shotgunner should be interested in. Plain paper measuring 40 inches or so wide can be purchased at most paper-supply houses, although unused scrap paper of about the same width is available from some hometown newspaper publishers. Simply attach a sheet of paper to a rigid backboard with a heavy-duty staple gun, and you are ready to shoot your first pattern. Heavy cardboard works fine as a backboard, although 3/4 inch plywood will last longer. Regardless of which is used, it should be attached to a couple of wooden stakes measuring

about 4-1/2 feet in length and driven into the ground to prevent wind from blowing the target over. For an even sturdier and more permanent setup, mount the plywood to pressure-treated 4x4s with their ends sunk at least a foot into the ground. The backboard will eventually be shot to pieces, so attaching it to its posts with bolts or screws instead of nails makes it easier to replace. A portable target frame made of two inch PVC plastic pipe can be used, but the slightest breeze will tip it over unless its base is firmly anchored with concrete blocks or other heavy objects.

I use a 40x40-inch steel patterning plate for a lot of my testing. The plate is not as useful as paper targets for evaluating pattern percentages, but it tells me where the center of a pattern is impacting, how large in diameter the pattern is and how uniformly pellets are distributed within the pattern. Most of the time, those things are all I really want to know, and it is much quicker than using paper targets. When preparing for the first shot, I use a felt paint roller to cover the face of the plate with a mixture of white paint pigment and motor oil. While holding on the center of the plate, I fire a round, evaluate the pattern and then use the roller to erase those pellet hits before firing the next round. Some shooters prefer to use paper targets because they can be filed away at home. A friend of mine who prefers the speed and convenience of the patterning plate accomplishes basically the same thing by hanging a small identification number on each of his patterns and shooting each one with a digital still camera. Using the reference numbers along with his laptop computer, he files away what load was used to shoot each pattern. Due to the danger of pellets bouncing back and striking the shooter, a steel patterning plate should not be used for testing loads with shot harder than lead. This includes steel shot and Hevi-Shot.

APPROXIMATE NUMBER OF LEAD SHOT PER LOAD

Shot Charge (ozs)	Shot Size									
	9	8	7-1/2	6	5	4	3	2	1	BB
1/2	293	205	173	112	86	68	53	44	35	30
5/8	366	256	216	139	108	85	66	55	44	37
11/16	402	281	237	153	118	94	73	61	49	41
3/4	439	307	259	167	129	102	80	66	53	44
7/8	512	358	302	195	151	119	93	77	62	52
1	585	409	345	223	172	136	106	88	71	60
1-1/8	658	460	388	251	194	153	120	99	80	67
1-1/4	731	511	431	279	215	170	133	110	89	74
1-3/8	804	562	474	307	237	187	146	121	98	82
1-1/2	878	614	518	335	258	204	160	132	107	89
1-5/8	951	665	561	362	280	221	173	143	116	97
1-3/4	1024	716	604	390	301	238	186	154	125	104
1-7/8	1097	767	647	418	323	255	200	165	134	112
2	1170	818	690	446	344	272	213	176	143	119
2-1/8	1243	869	733	474	366	289	226	187	152	127
2-1/4	1316	894	756	492	378	307	240	196	161	134

APPROXIMATE NUMBER OF STEEL SHOT PER OUNCE

Shot Size	Pellets Per Ounce
F	40
T	52
BBB	61
BB	72
No. 1	103
No. 2	125
No. 3	153
No. 4	190
No. 5	243
No. 6	315

NOTE: To calculate the number of pellets in a 1-1/4 ounce shot charge, multiply the above numbers by 1.25. For a 1-1/2 ounce charge, multiply by 1.50, etc.

INDUSTRY STANDARD PATTERN PERCENTAGES

Choke	Percentage
Cylinder	40
Skeet	50
Improved Cylinder	55
Modified	60
Improved Modified	65
Full	70

CHAPTER 29
Maintaining the Shotgun

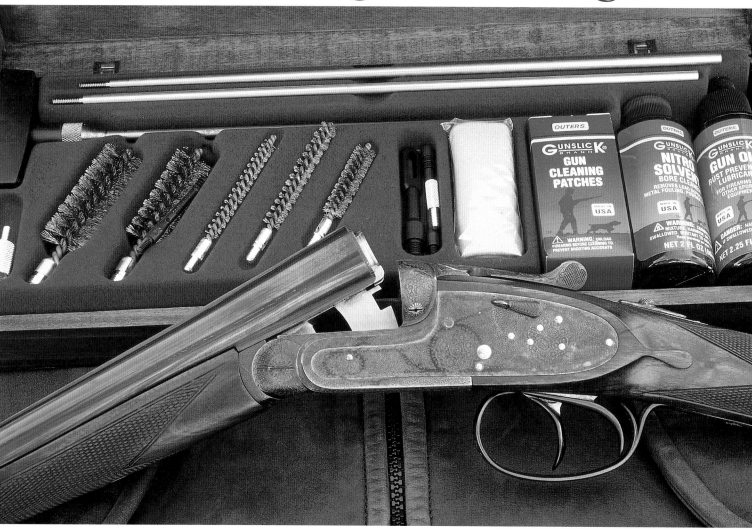

Every shotgun owner needs a good cleaning kit.

Back in the old days, when all shotshell hulls were made of waxed paper and wads were either cardboard or felt, shotgunners had to be concerned only with keeping the bores of their shotguns free of propellant fouling and leading. The fouling was nothing more than a residue left by the burning powder, and the leading was caused by pushing unprotected lead shot through the barrel at high speed. Scrubbing the bore with a brush dipped in solvent loosened the powder fouling enough to allow it to be swept away with a cotton patch. Most shooters knew that if the powder fouling was left in the bore, it would accelerate rusting by absorbing moisture from the air, but some were not aware that moisture could make its way beneath the thin lead deposits and remain there even after the bore had been cleaned. Applying a good oil to the bore did not always prevent

rust from forming, simply because it could not reach those areas covered by the lead deposits. This is one of the reasons why it is not unusual to look down the bore of an old shotgun and see some areas that are nice and shiny while other areas show random pitting.

Leading was once a problem because the old paper wads used in shotshells allowed the shot to scrub hard against the wall of the barrel as it traveled on its way. It is now virtually a thing of the past because the shotcup of the plastic wad column commonly loaded in shotshells prevents the shot from making contact with the barrel. The leading of shotgun bores continues to be a problem only when Foster-style slugs are used, and if the lead streaks are not kept under control, accuracy can fall off rather quickly. The quickest way to remove leading from a shotgun barrel is the same now as it was back in the bad old days: simply wrap 0000-grade steel wool around a bore brush of the correct size, and scrub it out. Another way to get the lead out is to coat the bore liberally with a bore solvent formulated to migrate beneath the lead to loosen its grip on the barrel and allow it to soak for about 15 minutes. Even when using a solvent, you can't beat a good scrubbing with four-ought steel wool for whisking away lead, and it won't harm the barrel.

The introduction of the plastic wad is one of the most important advancements ever made in shotshells, and while it solved several problems, it also created another. The plastic wad does a great job of preventing lead fouling, and it usually prevents steel shot from scoring the barrel, but it can leave behind streaks of plastic residue in the bore. Just as moisture lurking beneath lead deposits can cause rust, so it goes with the deposits of plastic. The buildup is often difficult to see when looking down the bore, but the accumulation usually starts at the forcing cone of the barrel with the firing of the first round and gradually makes its way on out to the muzzle. The plastic continues to build up as more and more rounds are fired, and in addition to allowing rust to form, it can cause pattern quality to suffer. I have seen guns used by trap shooters that had not been thoroughly cleaned for several thousand rounds; when their owners finally got around to cleaning them with solvent, long slimy strings of plastic came out of their bores.

Several things greatly influence how quickly plastic builds up, and one is the wad used. I handload all my practice ammunition, and the wads I use are the cheapest money can buy. Even though they plastic-foul a barrel quicker than some of the more expensive wads, they produce excellent patterns in my guns, and since I clean their barrels quite often, I am able to keep the fouling under control. But factors other than the quality of the wad used can cause severe plastic fouling. When left in the bore during firing, some gun oils seem to cause both powder and plastic fouling to accumulate at a more rapid rate than others. This is why some competitive shooters either start each shooting session with a dry bore or with the bore coated with solvent rather than oil. Another thing that accelerates the plastic buildup is a rough bore. I shoot skeet, sporting clays and most of my trap with a Krieghoff 32 over-under, and normal bore cleanings with the use of nothing more than a brush and solvent every 200 rounds or so keep its bore absolutely free of all types of fouling. In contrast, I once owned a SKB trap gun, and its bores were rough enough to cause severe plastic buildup after no more than a few rounds of trap. The bores of another of my doubles are extremely smooth, but its

The Oliver tractor and my L.C. Smith double have been around for about the same number of years. The tractor no longer runs, but proper maintenance has kept the gun active in the field.

screw-in chokes are a bit rough so that's where plastic builds up fastest.

What you have just read about plastic shotshell wads also applies to the plastic sabots of slug loads. In addition to leaving streaks of fouling in a smoothbore barrel, they can also deposit plastic in the rifling of rifled barrels and rifled screw-in chokes. Allowing the residue to build up excessively can eventually affect accuracy. The method for removing plastic fouling from a rifled barrel is the same as for the smoothbore, but the use of steel wool makes me nervous since frequent cleanings over many years could possibly round off the sharp corners of the rifling. Since it is softer than steel wool, 00-grade bronze wool (from Brownells) wrapped around a bore brush is a better choice for cleaning rifled barrels. Possibly even better is to simply stick with a solvent designed to zap both plastic and propellant fouling.

A screw-in choke can be left in the barrel for cleaning, but if the plastic buildup is severe, it is sometimes easier to remove the choke for a good scrubbing. When cleaning a choke in this manner, I wear heavy rubber gloves to protect my hands from the bore brush and the solvent. Never clamp a choke in a vise for cleaning, as doing so can collapse it out of round just enough to prevent it from being screwed back into the barrel. A screw-in choke should be occasionally removed so its threads as well as the threads in the muzzle of the barrel can be cleaned with solvent. The threads are easily cleaned with

The chambers of shotgun barrels should be thoroughly cleaned to prevent rusting caused by plastic shotshell hulls.

an old toothbrush, a parts cleaning brush or a brush designed just for that purpose from Midway, Briley Manufacturing and others. This step is important because as the barrel heats up during firing and then cools down, condensation can form around the threads, and if the choke is left in long enough for rust to form, it can become impossible to remove. After the threads of the choke and barrel are cleaned, they should be thoroughly dried with a paper towel and then lightly coated with a heavy grease or thick oil available for that specific purpose. Anything is better than nothing, but products formulated to withstand high temperatures and available from Birchwood Casey and Briley are the ones to use. Lubricants developed to prevent the breech plug of a muzzleloader from seizing work equally well. They are available from a number of sources, including Knight and

Thompson/Center. I like to remove the choke or chokes from a field gun for a complete cleaning and lube job every half-dozen or so hunts, but if the gun gets rained on, I do it as soon as possible after that hunt. Doing so will prevent the choke from seizing in the barrel.

Another giant step forward in the evolution of the shotshell was the development of the plastic hull. If exposed to wet weather, the old paper-hull shells would absorb moisture and swell up to the point where they refused to enter the chamber of a shotgun. Their reloading life was quite short, too, but they did smell great on a cold morning just after being fired. Cartridges with plastic hulls are far more weatherproof and they last through many reloadings, but soon after they came into common use, shotgunners began to notice rusting in the chambers of their guns even after a thorough cleaning.

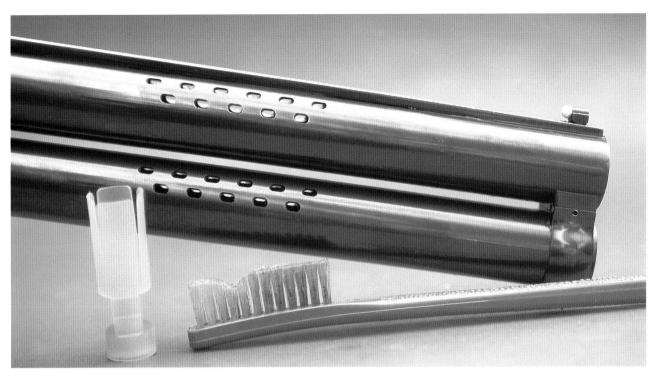

Solvent and a brush will remove plastic wad fouling from the ports of a muzzle brake.

It has yet to be revealed why this happened, but as one popular speculation had it, when the shells were handled, the acids in skin oil from the hands caused a chemical reaction on the surface of the plastic hull, and this left a residue in the chamber when the shell was fired. As was eventually discovered, simply pushing an oily rag through the chamber did not prevent rusting caused by the new plastic hulls.

Plastic shotshell hulls made today have been improved to the point where they don't seem to cause rusting in the chamber of a gun like those made years ago, but I am convinced they are still more inclined to do so than the old paper-hull shells. I have no scientific proof of this, but I believe slight traces of the wax introduced into paper hulls during their manufacture was transferred to the chamber of a gun during firing and that protected the metal from rusting when perspiration and skin oils were transferred from hand to gun by the shell. But even when using plastic hulls, chamber rusting is no longer a problem so long as that area is given a good scrubbing when the bore is cleaned.

To recap what I have gone over in this chapter, I'll describe in a nutshell how I clean the barrel of a shotgun. When possible, I always clean a barrel from its chamber end. After removing it from the receiver, I clamp it horizontally in a padded bench vise and secure a large Ziploc sandwich bag over its muzzle with a rubber band. The plastic bag catches dirty patches and prevents solvent from dripping onto my workbench. I then attach a cotton patch to the tip of my cleaning rod, dip the patch in bore solvent and push and pull it to and fro through the barrel several times in order to apply a liberal coat to the bore. When I use the word liberal, I mean just that; I want the bore to contain enough solvent to drip out the end if its muzzle when it is tipped downward.

If the solvent is formulated to lift plastic from the bore, it will usually do its job in no more than a minute or so, and that's about how long I usually allow it to soak. Using a cleaning rod or wooden dowel, I then push a section of paper towel through the bore to whisk away as much loosened fouling as possible. I next dip a snug-fitting bore brush into the solvent and make about one complete trip through the barrel for each 10 rounds fired, but never less than a couple dozen trips even if only a few rounds have been fired. During this step, I dip the brush in solvent several times to make sure the bore is getting a good soaking. Again, I want the bore to be dripping wet. After allowing the bore to soak a minute or so, I then push a section of dry paper towel through the bore.

How clean is clean enough? A friend of mine spends about half an hour scrubbing the barrels of his Browning over-under until the patches come out snow white, but so much effort really isn't necessary. It probably makes him feel better, but less cleaning will suffice. The procedure I have described above takes less than 10 minutes for any shotgun, and it prevents rusting of the bores.

How often the action of a shotgun should be field-stripped and cleaned is greatly dependent on the weather conditions to which it is subjected.

The barrels on a couple of my shotguns have been ported to reduce muzzle jump, and the ports treat a plastic wad the same way an old fashioned kitchen grater treats a piece of lemon rind. Each time a wad speeds by, the ports shave off a bit of plastic and leave a buildup that should be removed during the bore-cleaning process. An old toothbrush or parts cleaning brush dipped in solvent works fine for cleaning out the ports, although a special brush designed specifically for this purpose is available from Brownells.

The final step in cleaning the bore of a shotgun barrel is the application of a rust inhibitor. Guns with stainless steel barrels or chrome-plated bores are more resistant to rusting, but even they should be protected in the same manner. Most solvents will prevent the formation of rust for a short period of time, and that's what I apply to guns that will be used within a few days after cleaning. Seldom does a week go by when I don't shoot several rounds of clay targets, so the bores of my skeet gun usually get nothing more than a light coat of solvent. Anytime I do leave oil in the bore of a competition gun, I remove it with solvent before firing it because some products can cause powder and plastic fouling to build up quicker than no oil at all. The bores of hunting guns that see frequent use do get a light coat of protective oil, and when preparing guns for long-term storage – an entire summer between hunting seasons, for instance – I like to apply a thin coat of rust-inhibiting grease such as RIG to their bores. The grease is removed with solvent before the gun is fired.

While I have mainly dealt with the maintenance of shotgun bores here, we must not overlook the fact that keeping the action clean and in proper working order is equally important. The actions of some pumps and autoloaders are so easy to field strip and put back together, there really is no excuse for anything short of first-rate care. The Browning Gold Hunter, Franchi 48AL, Benelli Nova and Beretta 391 are good examples, as are Remington's Models 870 pump gun and 11-87 and 1100 autoloaders; simply push out the pins located just above the trigger guard in their receivers and then pull out their entire fire control assemblies. With the trigger removed, it is easy to reach inside the receiver and loosen up any accumulation of dust, dirt

The threads of screw-in chokes and barrels should be kept clean of propellant fouling and coated with an anti-seize lubricant.

and crud with an old toothbrush and a bore solvent.

The inside of the magazine tube and its follower spring on a pump or autoloader can become quite dirty, so that area should not be overlooked. In some autoloaders, carbon has a tendency to build up on the magazine tube beneath the forearm, and it should be kept under control. After everything inside the action of a pump or autoloader is clean and dry, I like to spray on a very thin coat of combination rust inhibitor and lubricant. It is okay to apply a thin coat of rust inhibitor to the exterior of the magazine tubes of gas-operated autoloaders, but the tubes of recoil-operated guns like the Franchi 48AL and Browning A-5 should be wiped clean with a dry cloth or paper towel and left dry.

Each time the barrels of a double-barrel shotgun are cleaned, the hinge points between its barrels and receiver should also be cleaned and coated with a good oil or grease designed specifically for that job. Other points on a double that should be lubed are the forearm underlug on its barrel, any exposed locking bolt surfaces and the contact areas between the rear of the forend iron and the front of the receiver. Just prior to shooting a double in one of the clay target games where it will be opened and closed many times during a day, I also like to apply a very thin film of grease to its standing breech. A gun used for high-volume bird shooting in South America should be treated the same.

How often the action of a shotgun should be field stripped for cleaning is dependent on what it is subjected to. Under conditions normally encountered when hunting upland game and wingshooting, an annual cleaning at the end of each hunting season will usually suffice. If the gun is used regularly for hunting waterfowl and subject to getting wet, more frequent cleanings may be in order. As a rule, the actions of pumps and autoloaders are more inclined to accumulate dust, dirt and water than double-barrel shotguns, but even they should be disassembled and cleaned as needed. Some over-unders are fairly easy to take apart, while others, along with most of the better side-by-sides, are best left to an experienced gunsmith. The Remington Model 332 is an easy one. Using a 7/16 inch socket wrench on a long extension to remove its stock exposes most of the parts inside its receiver for cleaning. Perazzi, Krieghoff and most Beretta over-unders are also easy to get into. Doubles used for a lot of clay target shooting should be cleaned and lubricated internally about every 10,000 rounds.

CHAPTER 30
Hunting Birds on Commercial Preserves

Commercially grown Hungarian partridges like this pair bagged by Brad Ruddell fly about as well when released on private preserves as they do when they hatch and grow up in the wilds.

I have no idea how many commercial hunting preserves are now operating in the United States but hundreds are listed each year in *Black's Wing & Clay* guide. Georgia alone has almost 50, and Illinois, South Dakota and Kansas have over 50 each. There are close to 40 hunting preserves in California. The state with the most places to shoot is Texas with over 80. The states with the fewest number are Delaware and Hawaii with only one each. Some people are under the impression that hunting preserves thrive only where there are lots of people and not much land for them to hunt on, but this is far from true. States like Montana, Wyoming, Colorado, Idaho, New Mexico, Nebraska, South Dakota, North Dakota and Oklahoma with their sparse populations and wide-open spaces are literally dotted with them.

There are those among us who turn up their noses at the mere thought of hunting pen-raised game

birds on a commercially operated preserve. All I can say to them is they should thank their lucky stars for living where they can still enjoy an abundance of wild bird hunting. I also know hunters who have tried preserves only to swear they will never do it again after experiencing the frustration of birds that either refused to fly or their flight consisted of nothing more than a halfhearted hop. Unfortunately, those fellows hung up their guns before discovering that the quality of the hunting available on some preserves can be as close as you can get to hunting wild birds without actually traveling to another state.

While hunting on quite a few preserves from coast to coast, I have discovered that they differ considerably in many ways. Just because an outfit goes by a clever name, has an expensive lodge and spends a fortune on full-color advertisements in upper-crust magazines does not guarantee the hunting there will be worth the trip. The

Located in north-central Oregon, Highland Hills Ranch offers some of the best hunting for wild chukar, Hungarian partridge and California quail I have experienced.

hunting at one of the fanciest places I have visited was so poor, I have no desire to ever go back, but someone obviously does since the outfit continues to run full-page color ads in outdoor magazines.

On the other hand, the all-around finest preserve I have ever visited in America had some of the best wing-shooting I have experienced. It is called Highland Hills Ranch. Located about 2-1/2 hours from Portland in north-central Oregon, the fabulous lodge sits in a valley alongside a nice little trout stream. If the scenery does not take your breath away, the gourmet meals served three times each day by Sandy Macnab and her staff most certainly will. The guides all dress alike in freshly ironed shirts and canvas pants. They drive shiny new Ford trucks and Chevy Suburbans, and they take their jobs quite seriously. Each of the German shorthairs and English pointers has its own private apartment inside a fancy aluminum dog box. The dogs I hunted with went by the names of JJ and Iceman, and they were some of finest I have shot over. Most of the hunting there is for wild birds, including Hungarian partridge, California quail and chukar partridge. Several weeks prior to opening day of the season, owner Dennis Macnab releases hundreds of ringneck pheasants on the 2,000-acre ranch, and by the time hunters arrive, they are as wild as their country cousins. Each pair of hunters and their guide have their own private hunting block of several hundred acres, and it is most unusual to see other hunters during the day. Management can tailor a hunt to various degrees of difficulty ranging from easy to quite challenging. Some of the wild chukar hunting takes place on canyon walls steep enough to make a flatlander like me wonder what he is doing there. I first hunted at Highland Hills during January of 2003

with my friends Mike Schwiebert and Jeff Patterson. On the first day, we used Weatherby SAS shotguns quite effectively. On the second day I switched to my 12-gauge muzzleloader and took pheasants, California quail and chukar. The only thing I could find to complain about is our stay did not last for at least a month.

A game farm does not have to be fancy or expensive to offer excellent hunting. I have found some of my best bird shooting on preserves of modest means. One such place in South Carolina uses an old converted farmhouse for a lodge and serves no lunch. Another outfit serves meals and offers rooms in a remodeled barn. The owners of those preserves funnel all of their time, money and effort into the hunting side of the business, and that makes them the places for me. One is called Sunshine Hunting Preserve, and the other is called Little River Plantation. The beat-up pickups driven by their guides are about ready for the scrap heap, but the guides and their dogs more than make up for it in the hunting. I am a regular at both places because they are close to where I live and the shooting is almost always excellent. A full day of bird shooting will not break the bank, and is easily afforded by anyone who wants to hunt as badly as I do.

Regardless of whether they are big, small, fancy or plain, really good preserves have one important thing in common: They do an excellent job of offering hunting in a natural setting, and they present game birds as close as possible to how you would find them in the wilds. Some places look like commercial operations because everything is too artificial and overly manicured. Others fail to pay enough attention to important details like not allowing empty shotshell cases to become knee-deep in the fields. With just a little imagination and positive

All good hunting preserves do not have a magnificent lodge in which to stay. While the facilities here were modest they were tidy and clean and the hunting was excellent.

thinking on the part of the hunter, a pheasant hunt on a small but well-managed preserve, whether it be in California or South Carolina, can be just as enjoyable as a hunt on a 10,000-acre farm in South Dakota. It is usually a whole lot cheaper too.

The amenities and activities available at some hunting preserves probably attract about as many shotgunners as the bird hunting they offer. Many have some type of clay target shooting on the program so the hunter can warm up and sharpen his eye a bit before heading to the field. Three of the best sporting clays courses I have shot are at South Carolina preserves called River Bend, Little River Plantation and Harris Springs. Primland, a wonderful place in the mountains of Virginia, also has excellent sporting clays. Many preserves offer lodging and hot meals, and most will clean and package the birds you shoot. Some will even clean your gun for you after the hunt! As a way of bringing new hunters into their folds, some offer special husband-wife and parent-child hunts on certain days at discounted prices. Some preserves offer a one-day basic shooting school taught by a professional instructor. Others offer cooking lessons and kennel services for dogs belonging to their clientele. Some have shops filled with hunting clothing and accessories and fine used guns.

Before taking your first hunt on a game farm, you should first decide what you are looking for in the way of a hunting experience. When making the call, be honest with yourself about your ability with a shotgun and explain up front how much hunting experience you have and the type of hunt you expect. Some preserves cater mostly to corporations that entertain overweight and out-of-shape clientele who don't even know how to load the gun they are renting, much less how to hit a quail or pheasant with it. The hunting, if you want to call it that, consists of walking a short distance from a truck and blasting away with a 12-gauge semiautomatic as half-asleep quail are booted from the broom sedge by a nervous guide. Lead flies in all directions, but most of the time most of the quail escape without a scratch. Sometimes the guide hits the dirt to avoid being shot. His dogs run yipping back to the lodge with their tails between their legs. This may be the type of place for those who have little to no hunting experience, but it is a place to be avoided by the experienced hunter.

I have been hunting for many years and consider myself to be a fair shot with a shotgun, so very few hunting preserves are capable of meeting my expectations. One of the best at putting together the only type of hunt I am interested in is John Edens of Little River Plantation. John knows me, he knows I want the toughest wingshooting he can come up with, and he does a darned good job at it. A typical "Layne-type quail hunt," as he calls it, takes place in woods, swamps and fields so thick with briars and brambles, the only other people who dare venture there are a couple of close friends who hunt with me. On top of that, we make it a .410-only hunt. The shooting is so difficult our birds-killed-to-birds-flushed ratio is about the same as when we hunt wild birds, which is exactly the way we want it to be. Dennis Macnab at Highland Hills Ranch is also one of the few preserve owners who does a great job of tailoring a hunt to the ability of the hunter. His birds fly better than those I have shot on any other preserve, simply because a large percentage of them are wild birds. All of the California quail I hunted there were wild birds, and so were many of the chukar. The pheasants were not, but since Dennis releases them several weeks prior to opening day of the season, they act and fly exactly like they were born and grew up in the wild.

A well-run hunting preserve is an excellent place to introduce a youngster, a wife, a husband or just a good friend to winghooting, simply because there is never any doubt about birds being there. The hunt should be easy enough to keep the interest and enthusiasm of the inexperienced hunter high, but enough challenging shots should be mixed in to prevent him or her from thinking all hunting is like shooting fish in a barrel. Praise the shooter when he makes a good shot and, rather than criticizing him for missing, explain why he did if you can. Make sure the new hunter walks some distance between shots at birds and with just the right amount of rough terrain thrown in for good measure, it will seem more like real hunting. Do everything you can to make him understand

A preserve is an excellent place to train a young hunting dog or to keep a trained dog fine-tuned because you know the birds will be there when you arrive.

that just being fortunate enough to be there and to see good dogs work are far more important than heading back home with a full game bag.

Some preserves offer the options of hunting with a guide and his dog or hunting alone with your own dog. Hunting on your own is less expensive since you are not paying a guide to carry your birds for you. It is an excellent way to train a young dog because birds will surely be there for Rover to find. While I am on the subject of dogs, I will mention one other thing: As a rule, you will enjoy a better hunt at a preserve where each guide either owns the dogs he uses or the preserve owns them, and the guide is responsible for their training and maintenance. Under ideal circumstances, that guide and only that guide hunts with those dogs. When dogs owned by the preserve are forced to hunt with different guides each day, the poor things often become impossible to control to the point where they can make your hunt miserable. I am reminded of a quail hunt in Florida during which the guide almost drove my hunting partner and me nuts as he screamed at the dogs to no avail each time they bumped birds far out of range of our guns.

Mondays, Tuesdays and Wednesdays are often the best days to hunt at some preserves because hunter traffic is not as heavy as later in the week, and particularly on weekends. Since those are slow days, you might receive more and better attention from management and guides. Some preserves also offer better rates on those days. At the very least, you will stand a better chance of hunting a favorite field since you may be the only person there to request it.

Some preserves offer nothing but pen-raised birds. Others offer a combination of wild and liberated birds. At Highland Hills Ranch in north-central Oregon, I hunted wild California quail, wild chukar and liberated pheasants on the same day. The pheasants flew so well, I would not have known they were not wild birds had I not been told so. At the High Desert Hunt Club in southern California, I have hunted wild valley quail in the morning and then shot liberated pheasants, bobwhite quail and Hungarian Partridge after lunch. A few days later and farther north, I went after wild valley quail and planted pheasants with Stacy Twisselman of Twisselman's Outfitters. Later in the week and even farther north, I hunted valley quail, pheasants and Hungarian partridge at Rock Springs Ranch. In South Carolina, Georgia and Alabama, I have hunted farms that contained both wild and released bobwhite quail. In South Dakota, Oregon and Nebraska, I have hunted a mixture of liberated and wild pheasants. Since the pen-raised pheasants had been released and on their own for several weeks prior to my arrival, I could not tell them from their country cousins. Both acted the same, flew the same and tasted the same.

Some released birds fly about as well as those found in the wild. This plus the fact that they are relatively easy to raise in captivity is why the ring-necked pheasant and Hungarian partridge are so popular among preserve owners. The pheasant is always a big hit among hunters where the bird is not native to their state. It is big, it is beautiful and just knowing one is about to flush from under a pointing dog's nose is guaranteed to increase the pulse rate of any wingshooter. Those that decide to flush unannounced are even more exciting. The liberated pheasant flies just as fast and can be just as bulletproof as its country cousin, but being more of a gentleman, it is more likely to hold tightly to the point of a dog and not flush until the hunter is well within shooting range. This is why many experienced shotgunners use guns in the smaller gauges when hunting them.

Of the birds I have shot on commercial preserves, I will have to rate the Hungarian partridge as the most sporting. It is a much smaller target than the pheasant and it flies about as fast as a quail. It is also as good to eat as those two birds. I have shot Huns on preserves as far west as California and as far east as Maryland, and enjoyed every minute of it. Most I have bagged acted the same as wild birds that have never enjoyed an easy meal. I also find the preserve Hun to be capable of running off with a hit that would put most birds down for the count. I will never forget shooting Huns at Pintail Point on the eastern shore of Maryland. High winds made the shooting quite challenging for Steve Otway and me. While hunting with Steve, I used a Franchi 48AL in 28 gauge.

Most hunting preserves offer several different game birds. This cheerful crew took bobwhite quail, pheasant and chukar on the same morning.

On the next day, while hunting with Joe Troiani, I carried a .410-bore Stoeger Uplander. Then on the last day I hunted with Steve McKelvain and shot a 20-gauge Benelli Legacy. We all occasionally have a day when we seldom miss, but that was the first time I had three of them in a row!

The bobwhite quail is available on more game farms than any other bird. It is exciting to hunt, it can be challenging to hit, it is good to eat and it is usually the least expensive bird to hunt. The bobwhite can also vary more in the degree of challenge it offers to the shotgunner than any bird you are likely to shoot. I have seen some that flew almost as well as their wild cousins, and I have observed others that absolutely refused to fly more than a few feet before touching down. Whether or not a quail flies as planned is greatly influenced by how it is raised, but the weather can also have a lot to do with it. Forget hunting quail on a rainy day; once their feathers get wet, they often refuse to budge, even with an English pointer breathing down their necks.

The chukar is just the opposite and will fly aggressively come rain or shine. I remember one December when Tom Latham and I had booked a quail hunt at River Bend in South Carolina. Snow started to fall pretty hard before we got there, and by the time we arrived, maximum visibility was inside a hundred feet. Realizing quail would refuse to fly in such weather, lodge owner Ralph Brendle suggested that we hunt chukar instead. Of the many preserve hunts I have been on, that was one of the most enjoyable because I love to hunt

birds while it is snowing. It was also some of the toughest shooting I have ever experienced. Tom and I were hunting with .410s, and anytime we failed to drop a bird soon after it flushed, it was quickly swallowed up by a solid wall of falling snowflakes. We were having so much fun, we forgot about the trip back home on slippery roads. (The fact that I am writing this is proof that we made it home alive.) The chukar is not as good a flyer as the Hungarian partridge, especially on windy days, but it is close enough to make it one of the best. Like the Hun, it is less expensive to hunt than the pheasant, but it usually costs more than quail.

Some preserves offer optional modes of transportation during the hunt. Some of the classier outfits located in Mississippi, Alabama, Georgia, Florida and other Southern states have fancy mule-drawn wagons built to carry half a dozen hunters in softly cushioned seats. The typical wagon has built-in boxes for the dogs, padded racks for the guns and a place for stowing cool drinks and sandwiches. It rolls along on rubber tires. The driver of the wagon does nothing else. The guide (or hunt master, if the outfit is really fancy) rides alongside the wagon on his horse. You bounce along, and when the dogs lock on point, two hunters in your group step down from the wagon, load their guns and accompany the guide to where the dogs are pointing. The birds are flushed, the hunters shoot, and they then return to the wagon. On the next point, another pair of hunters will shoot. In the old days of bobwhite quail hunting, there were pointers and there were retrievers, and no dog was expected to do both as they are trained to do today. The custom of riding through the fields in a fancy shooting wagon started back at the turn of the 20th century, when wealthy Yankees bought up thousands of acres in the Deep South and started their own private quail-hunting preserves. Some of the wagons were made of the finest of woods and leather, and their fittings were polished brass. Studebaker, the manufacturer of automobiles, built a number of them.

I prefer to describe bouncing along in a wagon as quail shooting rather than quail hunting, and while every quail hunter owes it to himself to try it once in a lifetime, it is not my cup of tea. Perhaps it is the peasant in me, but I don't consider quail hunting the real thing unless it involves lots of walking and very little riding. To me, quail hunting is getting to where you are going by truck, Jeep or other vehicle, and then hoofing it from that point on. The best view of what is going on is down at ground level with the pointers and the setters.

I can think of one time when I did welcome another mode of transportation. The old Alabama farm Jim Bequette and I were hunting had been abandoned for decades. Just about every foot of ground was covered with thick brush, vicious saw briars and blackberry vines thicker than your thumb. At first we were a bit skeptical about hunting from the backs of a couple of mules, but we changed our minds when we hit those briar patches. I was amazed at how those gentle animals were able to gingerly pick their way through the brambles without suffering a single scratch. Rather than shooting from the back of my mule as I was told I could, I dismounted each time the dogs pointed, loaded my shotgun after pulling it from a leather saddle scabbard, and walked in to flush the birds. It was a grand way to hunt quail in country where the walking ranged from difficult to near impossible, and given the opportunity, I would do it again at the drop of a hat.

One of the great things about preserves is they extend the hunting season to more than half a year. I usually do my hunting there when the regular seasons are closed. The action usually begins in September and runs through March, with the best times being from about mid-October through the end of February. Hunt much earlier and you may find the weather too warm. Head to the field much later than the second week in March, and you may find nothing to hunt but molting birds that refuse to fly. That is, if you find anything at all to hunt. The managers of some preserves end their hunting sometime in March rather than booking later hunts at the risk of having dissatisfied customers.

As for what guns are best for preserve hunting, there is absolutely no law against using the 12 gauge, and when loaded with an ounce of shot, it is not a bad choice.

A really good hunting preserve neither looks nor feels like a hunting preserve.

But many guides have told me about hunters showing up for a quail hunt with guns of that gauge and loads heavy enough to bump off a flying turkey gobbler at 60 paces. Any birds they managed to hit were ground into red mists and puffs of feathers. Most preserve birds are killed inside 25 yards, so the 20 gauge is a much better choice since it leaves more meat for the pot. Standard-velocity loads with 7/8 ounce of No. 8 shot for quail and an ounce of No. 7-1/2s for everything else are all you should ever need. If a poll were taken at hunting lodges all across the country, the 12 gauge would emerge as the most popular among once-a-year hunters, and the 20 gauge would be the first choice of regular customers, although the 28 gauge is closing in on it at a rapid pace. I would not be surprised to eventually see the 28 become the official hunting preserve shotshell among experienced hunters. Recoil is a bit lighter than the 20 gauge, and its 3/4-ounce shot charge will handle about 99 percent of the shots you will get on liberated birds. The 3-inch .410 is my personal favorite, and I use it on everything from quail to pheasant. While it too is enjoying a surge in popularity, I doubt if it will ever overtake the 28 gauge.

Commercial preserves are here to stay, but how long it will be before the average working man cannot find one he can afford to hunt on is open to question. Some outfits now cater to corporations with huge entertainment budgets that are written off as tax deductions. No small number of those companies could care less about the cost of a hunt, and the managers of many preserves have increased their prices accordingly. In doing so, they have priced all but the most wealthy of individual hunters completely out of the picture. I see this more often among the larger hunting preserves, but it is happening to some of the smaller outfits as well.

CHAPTER 31
Clothing for the Shotgunner

Lightweight vests with a blood-proof game bag and plenty of pockets like these worn by mountain quail hunters Bob and Mary Koble are ideal for hunting during mild weather.

Some hunters and shooters devote most of their conversation time to shotguns, game birds, hunting dogs and other things while overlooking the fact that a day in the field without the proper clothing can be a miserable day indeed. Reaching into the sky to bring down a flying target can be difficult when you are as wet as a drowned rat and your feet are all blistered up or feel like ice cubes. When I was much younger, I could get by with a lot less, but as several decades of hunting seasons have come and gone I have come to realize that being comfortable in the field is as important as what you came there to do.

Boots

The first rule to remember when shopping for hunting boots is never buy a pair with wedge-style soles unless you plan to wear them only on flat ground. Just try walking down a steep slope covered with pebbles, small sticks or leaves while wearing wedgies and as you pick your aching body up from the ground for the 10th time, you will come to understand why I consider them to be an invention of the devil. The soles of hunting boots should have heels for downhill traction.

Rubber-bottomed pacs like those made by L.L. Bean are the cat's meow for much of the rabbit and bird hunting I do in the Deep South. I have also worn them on early-season pheasant hunts in Nebraska, South Dakota and other states. Their leather uppers make them more comfortable to wear than all-rubber boots, and their rubber bottoms keep the feet dry when walking through grass and weeds covered with dew or when crossing a shallow stream. My feet have extremely high arches, so I have to install aftermarket innersoles with additional support in them. I actually have three styles of L.L. Bean pacs. The pair with no insulation gets worn during the early season when the weather is warm. The pair with Thinsulate insulation does a good job of keeping my feet warm at temperatures down to about the freezing point so long as I am walking, but when it really gets cold, I wear the serious pair with felt booties. I actually have two pair of booties. One is always back in camp drying out while I am wearing the other in the field. Pacs are a good choice for hunts that do not cover more than a few miles in a day, but they do not support the feet enough for long-distance walking. Or at least this is what my feet have to say about the subject.

For covering many miles per day in country with rolling hills, I have not found anything to beat a top-quality boot made entirely of leather or a combination of leather and synthetic. My favorites for wearing in warm to cool weather are non-insulated Irish Setter boots from Red Wing. Later in the season, I switch to a boot with 200 to 400 grams of Thinsulate insulation. Styles come and go, but some of my favorites through the years have been described by Red Wing as the 1955 and 2005 Generation boots. Other favorites are the Feather 846 and the Wingshoooter 854. The nine- and ten-inch versions with a Gore-Tex liner are especially good because they enable me to wade shallow creeks without getting my feet wet. As comfortable from day one as an old pair of bedroom slippers, Red Wings are the boots I wear when making 10-mile-per-day treks after sharptail grouse, prairie chickens and Hungarian partridges. I have worn them a lot when hunting mountain and valley quail in California and when hunting Gambel, Mearns and scaled quail in Arizona and bobwhites in Texas, Florida, Virginia, South Carolina and a number of other states. I have also worn them when hunting ruffed grouse in Michigan, Virginia and West Virginia, and when covering a big part of Uruguay in pursuit of perdiz.

When hunting chukar in the awful places those birds often call home, I prefer boots that have plenty of ankle support for walking around steep sidehills. I also prefer soles with aggressive tread patterns. The Vibram sole is a good choice for walking on dry ground and in rocky country. It also works in soft snow, but it is worthless on ice-covered rocks. I discovered this while hunting mule deer in the high country of Wyoming with Ron

Anyone who hunts mountain quail will appreciate sturdy boots with plenty of ankle support and an aggressive sole.

Dube. Ron was wearing boots with air-bob soles while my boots had Vibram soles. Snow had melted and then frozen into treacherous sheets of ice on rocks and boulders. While Ron's feet never slipped a single time, I hit the ground so many times just thinking about it today causes me to hurt all over.

I have since worn boots with air-bob soles more than those with Vibram soles, even during dry weather, and while they don't last as long in rocky country, I have no intention of ever turning back. One pair of all-leather boots I am now wearing came from a shop in Bozeman, Montana, called Schnee's. Possibly the very best mountain boot I have worn while chasing chukar is made by Red Wing and called the Elk Tracker. Several variations are available, but my favorite is the Model 859. Made of kangaroo leather, it has an air-bob sole and a pair weighs only four pounds. Another boot called the Model 895 Versa Track is also an excellent choice for high-country wear. A combination of leather and synthetics, it is waterproof, measures 11 inches high and it has a very aggressive sole. Weighing only 3-3/4 pounds for the pair, it is lighter than an all-leather boot. Six interchangeable cleats on each sole are easily changed, just like switching cleats on a pair of golf shoes. One set of cleats has extremely sharp stainless steel spikes, making them just the ticket for walking on ice-covered rocks. I have also worn those boots while hunting black bear among the vast logging slashes of Vancouver Island in British Columbia, and after walking on wet logs without having my feet slip from beneath me a single time, I can see why the boots of professional loggers have steel spikes. I have also worn them while hunting in the ice-covered Transylvania mountains of Romania. At first I thought the idea was just another gimmick, but the more I wear those boots, the more I like them. Using the wrench enclosed with them, I can switch cleats in less than a minute.

Most states have their official flowers, birds, trees and other things. The Carolina wren is the official state bird of South Carolina, and the yellow jessamine is its official flower. If the various states ever decide to adopt official boots, the hip boot will surely start appearing on the flag of the state of Alaska. The first time I hunted the land of ptarmigan and abundant waterfowl, I took along regular hip boots, and if not for the generosity of my guide who agreed to switch boots with me, my feet would not have made it beyond the third day. Ankle-fit hippers are the only way to go in Alaska, but they are extremely difficult to pull on in the morning and even more difficult to pull off at the end of the day. A pair I once wore was so difficult to remove, I would have left them on during the entire hunt had it not been for getting mud inside my sleeping bag at night. Since discovering the Bog-Buster hip boot from Cabela's, I have worn nothing else. When a nylon web strap across the top of the foot is buckled it fits the foot as snugly as if it were a regular ankle-fit boot. Unbuckling the strap makes the boot as easy to remove as a regular hipper. I like the Bog-Buster so well I have squirreled away a second pair in case my old ones wear out and Cabela's decides to discontinue them.

About Blisters

When I was a youngster, I could walk for miles all day long, day after day, in cheap and ill-fitting boots, and I never suffered a single blister on my feet. As I have grown older and my skin has become thinner, I am forced to take better care of my favorite mode of transportation. My problem with blisters seemed to happen overnight. One day I had no problem whatsoever, and the next day I could hardly walk. It first happened during a hunt in Alaska with Ed Weatherby, his son Daniel and Brad Ruddell. When I finally bagged my caribou, Brad and I were about 12 miles from camp and even though I had made sure the boots I was wearing were well broken in before the hunt, the heels and bottoms of my feet blistered up so badly, I had to use my rifle like a crutch in order to make it back to camp. After trying about every combination of sock and boot possible, I finally stumbled on a way of preventing those blisters.

The Cabela's Bog Busters I am wearing here on a ptarmigan hunt in Alaska is the best idea ever in ankle-fit hip boots. I like them so well I have squirreled away a spare pair.

Or perhaps I should say the solution turned out to be a combination of what I had already tried and something suggested by family friend Sandra Mullikin, who is not a physician but really should have been.

I installed gel-type innersoles in all of my boots for maximum cushioning. That alone is all I need for one-day hunts, but I have to go a step further before trying to keep up with Ryan Busse in sharptail grouse country. I first use surgical tape to secure two half-sheets of moleskin padding to the bottom of each foot. It is important to use the padding and not plain moleskin, which is thinner. Then I tape a two-inch sponge to each heel. The sponges are found in the lady's makeup department in most drug stores. After I have prepared my feet in that manner, I pick and choose among my collection of socks and liners until I come up with something that makes my feet fit tightly enough in the boots to prevent any side-to-side or front-to-rear movement, but not so tight as to restrict circulation. The combination that works best for me is a liner sock made of either silk or polypropylene worn beneath socks that are no less than 90 percent wool. When walking many miles each day, my feet simply do not like outer socks containing much more than 10 percent synthetic material, even when the weather is warm.

Pants

I can remember when I wanted to wear nothing but heavy canvas pants for upland hunting. Then I discovered pants that not only protect my legs from briars, but also keep them dry when I wade through tall grass wet with morning dew or when a rain shower catches me a long way from my truck. Several companies offer them, but the best I have tried are called Gore-Tex Upland Hunter. They are available from Cabela's. At first glance, the pants look like they would not turn away a stunted briar, but I have waded through enough buckbrush (also called mountain white thorn) while hunting mountain quail in the Sierra Nevadas of California to know their outer layer of Pinnacle Cloth will protect my legs from scratches. When things really get sticky, I wear those same pants beneath canvas chaps. That combination has done a great job of protecting me while hunting quail in the cactus country of Arizona and New Mexico.

Where things that stick into my skin are not present and the weather is dry, I'd just as soon have an old pair of cotton duck pants. Many of the pretty lightweight pants faced with nylon you see worn in mail-order catalogs by models who don't know a quail from a bull moose are okay for wearing at the gun club or on hunting preserves where the walking is usually clear and easy, but when subjected to hard use by a serious hunter, some will be ready for the rag bin before their first season of briar-busting is half over. Heavy-duty canvas work pants made by Carhartt last longer and are much less expensive. Lightweight denim jeans are one of the worst things the upland hunter can wear simply because they soak up water like a sponge and they do not turn briars.

Coats

It has to get really cold before I wear a coat while hunting upland game, especially if I am doing a lot of walking. When a sweater lined with a wind-breaking material worn over a wool shirt and beneath a hunting vest is not enough to keep me warm and toasty, I wear one of three coats. The one I have from Cabela's matches the upland pants I have described above. With its Gore-Tex liner, it is the coat I reach for when the weather promises to become a bit nasty. I've worn it on rainy days while hunting ruffed grouse on the upper peninsula of Michigan and I have worn it when hunting pheasants in the snow in South Dakota. It has never let me down. Browning also offers an upland coat with Gore-Tex, and like all other clothing I have tried from that company, it is top-notch. Another hunting coat I own and trust was made by Boyt. It does not have a Gore-Tex

Canvas pants are hard to beat when hunting in cactus country. They are even better when worn beneath heavy canvas chaps.

liner like the coats from Browning and Cabela's, but because it is heavier, it keeps me warmer when ice has formed on the barrel of my shotgun and the sky is spitting snow.

One of the things to look for in an upland coat is a game bag with a bloodproof liner that can be loaded from both front and rear. The bag should also zip open for easy cleaning. The two side pockets of the coat should be the bellows type and roomy enough to hold a day's supply of shells. Elastic shell loops on the inside of each pocket keep spreader loads or shells with different shot sizes separate from those carried loose. But make sure the bottom ends of the loops are sewn shut. The coat should have additional pockets suitable for stowing other items such as earplugs, shooting glasses and gloves. Higher up on the chest, the coat should have a couple of slash pockets with zippered flaps. When the weather is really bitter, I like to keep a couple of chemical hand warmers in there. The collar of a hunting coat should be

No longer must women hunters wear clothing made for men and boys. Phyllis Simpson is shown here wearing her fashionable yet durable Beretta upland coat and pant. A blaze orange cap or hat will complete her outfit.

made of a soft material so it doesn't chafe your neck. Either corduroy or leather works fine, although the former is better in extremely cold weather. And don't buy your coat too small. If it is cold enough to wear a coat while hunting, it is likely cold enough to wear a heavy shirt along with a sweater or vest beneath the coat.

Clothing for Ladies

There was a time when women had two choices in clothing when heading afield; they could wear street clothes that fit but were not durable enough for the field, or they could wear men's or boy's hunting clothing that did not fit. This no longer is true, as several companies now offer clothing made just for the gals. My wife, Phyllis, has two different sets of upland clothing, and both fit her quite nicely. One is the Gore-Tex Upland Hunter from Cabela's. The coat and pants look the same as those I wear, but the fit is not the same simply because unless you have lived alone in a cave all your life, you know that a woman's body is shaped differently than a man's.

Phyllis also has a shirt, pants, vest and coat made by Beretta, and they are her favorites when look-

ing pretty is as important as shooting birds. Made of a medium-weight cotton material, the various garments are reinforced with Cordura in high-stress areas, such as at the elbows of the coat and the legs of the pants. The coat has a soft leather collar, and its cuffs are trimmed with the same material. Phyllis likes the outfit so well, she has reserved the vest for casual wear with jeans. Browning also offers hunting clothing not only for women, but for kids as well. Phyllis is especially fond of the Upland Epic jacket and pant from that company.

Gloves

Several of the side-by-side doubles I hunt with have splinter forearms. When shooting clay targets at a rapid clip with one of those guns or when I am being attacked from all directions by a flock of enraged mourning doves, their barrels have a tendency to become quite hot. Wearing a glove on my forward hand prevents it from getting burned. Wearing a pair of gloves also protects the hands from briars and splinters. They are really worth their cost when several barbed-wire fences have to be crossed. For someone who is not bothered by their thickness, plain old cowhide work gloves found at most any hardware store are hard to beat for upland hunting. The camp glove sold by Michaels of Oregon is even better, since it stays soft through several years of hard use. If mine could talk, they would tell you many tales worth listening to.

Because you can feel right through them, thinner gloves made of pigskin are better for clay target shooting, especially during the heat of summer. The unlined cabretta leather shooting gloves from Browning are especially nice. Golf gloves also work for shooting if you can find them in a dark color. When hunting late-season pheasants in the snow, I wear a wool mitten faced with leather on my left hand, but I wear a thinner leather glove on right hand and keep it in a pocket of my coat for warmth when possible.

Vests For Hunting

I prefer a strap vest for most of the upland hunting I do in weather ranging from warm to cool. It can be worn over a t-shirt, a long-sleeved shirt or a sweater. The good ones are quite durable, and in addition to having a roomy game pouch out back, they have pockets big enough to hold plenty of shells along with various accessories. Someday, someone will introduce a model without metal buckles that scratch the stock of a good shotgun, but until that happens I will continue covering those on the one I use with duct tape. I do not care for elastic shell loops on the outside of a vest, but I like to have

Western hunters who go after game birds in open country should wear blaze orange, same as those who hunt wooded and brushy areas in the east. Look closely and you can see feathers flying from the pheasant this hunter has just shot. To the right is a yellow 20-gauge hull ejected from his autoloader.

them inside a couple of side pockets. I often carry several different loads for the same gun on a hunt, and the loops allow me to keep those shells separated from the ones carried loose in the pockets. The bottom end of each loop should be sewn shut to prevent shells carried in them from slipping on through and becoming mixed up with those in the pocket.

Then we have the half-vest. It is not a bad garment for early-season hunts, when the weather is quite warm. I especially like it for opening-day dove shooting and when shooting sporting clays in the heat of the summer. The half-vest is not as good as the strap vest for walking, because it tends to slip lower and lower on the waist and has to be tugged back into position every hundred steps or so. This holds especially true when its side pockets are loaded with shells and several birds are stowed in its game pocket. The weight also hangs on the waist rather than being supported by the shoulders as with the strap vest. The half-vest is, however, cooler to

wear in extremely hot weather than the strap vest. Everything you have just read also applies to what some clothing manufacturers refer to as a belted game bag.

Clay Target Shooting

When participating in the various clay target games during the hot weather of midsummer, I usually put on a light cotton shirt and wear a shell pouch on a belt around my waist. The pouch I use when shooting skeet and sporting clays was made by Remington, and it has two compartments, one for loaded shells and another for empty hulls. The same type of shell pouch also works nicely for early-season, hot-weather dove shooting. The leather pouch I use when shooting trap also has two compartments. If I am the leadoff man in a squad of trap shooters, I dump an entire box of shells into the inner compartment then place five of them into the outer compartment. Each time I change stations, I place five shells in the outer compartment. Doing so allows me to

The half-vest is an excellent choice for standing in one spot and shooting early-season doves in warm weather. But as I discovered here while hunting perdiz in Uruguay, it is less than ideal for a lot of walking.

A hat with a medium-wide brim and frequent applications of sunscreen to the face and neck offer a great deal of protection from the rays of the sun.

concentrate on my shooting without worrying about keeping a mental count on how many shells I have fired at a station. When no more shells are in the outer compartment, I know it is time to rotate to the next station. As the weather starts to cool down, I prefer to wear the type of vest owned by every skeet shooter. Mine was made by the Naples, Florida, firm of Chimere, but other companies such as Bob Allen offer basically the same thing. Made of a light cotton material, its mesh back has a pouch for empty shells. Up front, the vest has one breast pocket and four roomy cargo-style pockets, all trimmed in leather for wear resistance. The side pockets are big enough to hold a generous supply of loaded shells as well as various accessories such as shooting glasses, ear protection and gloves. I am a right-handed shooter, so the entire right side of the vest is covered with soft leather for wear and dirt resistance; the same vest made for southpaw shooters would have the leather on the opposite side.

When shooting clay targets during extremely cold weather, I wear a coat made specifically for that purpose by Browning. It is quite warm and rain-resistant, and it has pockets large enough to hold both loaded rounds and empties. The same type of coat is also available from Chimere and Bob Allen.

Hats and Caps

I never gave the subject of headgear much thought until I lay prone on a cold table while a dermatologist used what must have been the dullest knife he had to cut bits and chunks of flesh from a face that had absorbed too much sun through the years. Now I am very careful about what I wear on my head. Weather permitting, I still wear a baseball cap and plenty of sunscreen lotion, but if the sun is intense, I put on something that does a better job of shading my entire face, my ears and the back of my neck. During warm weather, it will be either a broad-brimmed straw hat or a cotton fishing cap, the latter with a neck flap and a long bill.

As the weather turns cool, I like to wear a felt hat with a three-inch brim. A wider brim seems to get in the way of my shooting, and if it is more narrow than that it does not keep the sun and rain off my face and neck. My favorite hat of this type is made from the underfur of wild rabbits, or so they say, and I like it a lot. Called the Akubra Riverina, I bought it from Noggin Tops. In addition to making me look rather dashing (or so says Phyllis), it offers excellent protection from the elements. When wearing that hat and carrying my 16-gauge L. C. Smith, I seem to always have uncommonly good luck on sharptail grouse, pheasant and Hungarian partridge.

CHAPTER 32

Sporting Clays and Skeet: Rx For Wingshooting

Shooting a round of sporting clays has been described as playing golf with a shotgun.

One hot July day, I enjoyed an excellent day of shotgunning down in Mississippi. Within moments after I had dropped a couple of rounds of Dionisi ammo into the chambers of a SIG Arms Aurora over-under, a pair of quail flushed into the air from my left. I grassed both birds, and no sooner had I reloaded my gun than two rabbits exploded from the bushes to my right. Just as I closed my gun on two fresh cartridges, more quail began to flush from the broom sedge. I managed to take all seven of the birds, but one

of those wascally wabbits bounced high in the air just as I pulled the trigger, causing me to miss by a country mile. A bit farther down the trail, wood ducks were drifting in from over the tops of tall oaks and landing in a small pond in front of me. I had to take them quickly as they darted through the only opening in the trees directly overhead.

As I left the woods to walk across an open field, I came to a place where mourning doves were darting to and fro like silver bullets. I took the incom-

A sporting clays station like this one holds very little practice value for the Eastern hunter. It does come close to simulating few shots I have taken on wild chukar while hunting among steep canyon walls of Idaho and Oregon.

ers and outgoers as easy as pie but flat-out missed the passing shots. Rounding a bend in the path, I was caught off guard as several Hungarian partridges flushed high and flew in different directions, as they are known to do. I bagged six of the eight birds. Farther on, several chukar sprang from the brink of a deep canyon and dropped into its depths. Accustomed to shooting birds that rise in flight, I shot over the first two but quickly compensated and dropped the next pair. I prefer not to talk about the shots I made on ruffed grouse that day, as those scheming birds embarrassed me in front of onlookers as they almost always do. I later made up for my poor showing there by dropping six sharptail grouse at long range with only eight shots. Then came the grand finale as eight pheasants flushed from the briars and brambles. By that point in the hunt, I was really on a roll and managed to drop seven birds in a row. I should have had number eight but lifted my head from the gun stock just as I shot. I ended up killing 86 of the 100 birds and rabbits I shot at. I easily did it all in one day, and the tab was less than it takes to fill the gas tank of my Suburban.

By now, you might be wondering where I managed to find a wingshooter's paradise filled with so many different species of game birds and with such generous bag limits. You might also be puzzled by the fact that I was legally hunting in the United States during the month of July. Actually, I wasn't hunting at all – I was shooting sporting clays at a wonderful place

called The Willows near Tunica, Mississippi. It is one of the best places I have found for keeping my shooting form in shape during the off-season. To explain in detail how sporting clays and skeet are played would use up too much space in this book, so I will merely hit the high spots. And since I will be discussing each with wingshooting practice and not tournament shooting in mind, some of the things you read may not agree with the official rules of the games.

Someone once described sporting clays as golf with a shotgun, and the description stuck because it is a good one. Whereas the skeet and trap fields you see at one gun club will be laid out exactly the same as those at all other gun clubs, no two sporting clays courses are exactly the same. It requires a bit more shooting too. Whereas a round of trap or skeet takes 25 shotshells, it is not unusual to fire 50 to 100 rounds when shooting a round of sporting. A good sporting course meanders for several miles through both wooded and open terrain, and usually has 10 to 12 different stations. Descriptive names such as "Rabbit Run," "Springing Teal," "Bobwhite Flush," "Dove Attack," "Thundering Grouse" and "Going-Away Ringneck" indicate the types of hunting shots the designer of the course has attempted to simulate at a particular shooting station. In trap and skeet, the same type of clay target is used, but targets of five different sizes and shapes are shot in sporting. Airborne targets range from the standard trap and skeet target to the mini, which is only 60mm in

Five different clay targets are thrown in sporting clays. Beginning with the white target at left and moving right, we have the rabbit, midi, standard, battue and mini.

diameter and resembles a bumblebee flying through the air. Another target called the rabbit is basically a clay disk designed to resist breakage as it rolls and bounces along the ground. Depending in the station, targets may be thrown as singles, as true pairs (both launched simultaneously) or as report pairs where the second target is launched as soon as the trap-puller hears the report of the shooter's gun on the first bird thrown.

Most wingshooters agree that sporting clays is hard to beat for off-season practice simply because it does a fairly good job of simulating some of the shots presented us in the field. But it does have its disadvantages. For one, sporting is considerably more expensive than trap and skeet. This is mainly due to the fact that setting up a tournament-quality sporting clays course is an extremely expensive undertaking. To start with, the required acreage located in an area with no neighbors to complain about the noise can run a fortune. It then takes the knowledge and expertise of a professional designer to lay out the course properly. Combine his tab with the cost of equipping each station with one or more expensive trap machines, and you are into really big money. Add trap operation and maintenance along with target cost and several other things I am sure I do not even know about, and you have a capital investment that will require many rounds of sporting clays to be shot by many paying customers before any profit can be made.

Skeet

Every hunter who owns a shotgun does not have a sporting clays facility nearby, but most gun clubs offer either skeet or trap. Many offer both. For practic-

ing shots at certain shooting angles, skeet and trap are every bit as useful as sporting. If dove hunting is your thing, shooting skeet from stations 2 through 6 will simulate about every shot you are likely to get in the field except for a sneak attack from behind. I enjoy heading west each year to hunt ringneck pheasants, sharptail grouse and prairie chickens. Since those birds are usually taken as they fly away from the gun at various angles, nothing beats trap for keeping my shooting eye sharp for them. Whereas sporting clays is the youngest clay target game to invade America, only trap has been with us longer than skeet.

The game of skeet got its start during the mid-1920s at the Glen Rock Kennels in Andover, Massachusetts. It was born simply because a group of wingshooters headed by C.E. Davis needed some way to keep their shooting eyes sharp and their gun handling fine-tuned during the off-season. The original layout consisted of a circle with a 25-yard radius and with a dozen shooting stations marked off much like the face of a clock. Positioned at 12 o'clock, the trap threw targets across the circle and directly toward the 6 o'clock station. Shooting "around the clock" as it was called back then eventually caught on and evolved into the organized sport it is today. Shooting in all directions presented a problem due to the amount of property needed for safety, so eventually only half of the clock face was used but another trap was added. The traps were positioned at what was originally 9 and 3 o'clock and what eventually became known as stations one and eight.

The new shotgun game received its first major publicity in 1926, when it was described in the *National Sportsman* and *Hunting and Fishing* magazines. A prize of $100 was offered to the person who came up with the best name for it. Among the 10,000 entries, Mrs. Gertrude Hurlbutt of Dayton, Montana, took home the money with her suggestion of "Skeet," an old Scandinavian form of the word "shoot." The National Skeet Shooting Association was eventually formed with the first national championship tournament held during August of 1935 at Cleveland, Ohio. Just over 100 shooters attended. Sad to say, many of today's clay target shooters (including skeet shooters) are not members of the National Rifle Association. They should hang their

An over-under shotgun like this Rizzini from SIG Arms is quite popular among casual sporting clays shooters but many professionals prefer the autoloader and its softer recoil.

heads in shame since the NSSA might not have survived had it not been for a no-interest loan made to it by the NRA soon after World War II.

Many gun clubs offer the option of shooting skeet on the same fields as trap, but since their disciplines differ considerably, they are not shot at the same time. Think of a skeet field layout as the bottom half of the face on a clock with shooting stations located at roughly the 9, 8, 7, 6, 5, 4 and 3 o'clock positions and with trap houses located at 9 and 3 o'clock, and you begin to get the picture. The 8th station is located midway between the two houses and in the center of the field.

In skeet, targets emerge from the left-hand house (or high house as it is called) at an elevation of 10 feet, while those thrown from the right-hand house (or low house) emerge three feet above the ground. Targets thrown from the low house travel at an upward angle for about 25 yards before curving back toward earth. Those coming from the high house fly a bit flatter and then begin losing altitude fast. Shots in skeet are much closer than in trap, with the longest at about 25 yards. In a standard round of skeet, you start with 25 shells, begin shooting at station 1 and work your way around to station 8. At stations 1, 2, 6 and 7 you will shoot a single target thrown from each of the two houses before shooting a pair thrown simultaneously from both houses. At each of the other stations, you shoot singles only for a total of 24 shots. So what do you do with the 25th shell in a box? If you miss a target prior to reaching station 8, it is used for shooting an optional target. If you have

not missed prior to reaching station 8, the extra shell is used to shoot another single target from that station. Hit that last bird, and you have experienced the holy grail of skeet shooting by "going straight" for 25 shots. Other shooters in your squad will pound you on the back. Sweet young things watching your grand performance from the sidelines will swoon. Gun companies will stand in line with juicy endorsement contracts in hand.

Five Stand

Due to its simplicity, it won't take long to explain another clay target game called five stand. As the name implies, five stand has five shooting stations located side-by-side with only a few feet separating them. For reasons of safety, each station has metal or wooden barriers that prevent a shooter from swinging his gun far enough left or right to endanger one of the other shooters. Another barrier at the top prevents him from swinging his gun too far to the rear when taking a high incoming target. Traps positioned at various distances around a half-circle throw targets in all directions. Both singles and doubles are shot. Five stand is often criticized as too simple by uppity sporting clays shooters, but it is an excellent answer for gun clubs who do not have the resources or the amount of property required to set up a sporting clays course. It is also excellent practice for the wingshooter.

The most exciting variation of five-stand I have ever shot goes by names such as flurry, duck flush, dove attack and others. It usually has only three stations and it is often shot in three-man teams. I first shot it at

A highly sociable game, gun club skeet is an excellent way to prepare for those tough passing shots often seen on a dove field or from a duck blind. While a gun is never loaded until the shooter is standing at a shooting station, the third fellow from the right should not have his hands resting on the muzzle of his gun.

the Red Rock Ranch in Colorado, but have since shot it at many other places including the Willows in Mississippi and Primland in the mountains of Virginia. The computer-controlled traps throw as many as 100 targets in every direction imaginable in a minute or two. Several targets are usually in the air at the same time. The team who allows the fewest number of targets to hit the ground unbroken wins, and a perfect score is quite rare. It is a fast and furious game, and many rounds can be fired in a very short time. Once, while shooting at the Willows, we had four three-man teams shooting the same three 20-gauge Berretta Model 391s. Their triggers would become so hot, we had to occasionally stop and allow the guns to cool down to prevent burning our fingers.

Keeping an accurate score while shooting the clay target games enables me to monitor my ability with a shotgun, but if doing so makes you uncomfortable, inform the trap boy that you do not want to keep score. Anytime you encounter a station in sporting clays that appears to be unrealistic to the point of being no practice value to you as a wingshooter, feel free to skip it and shoot two rounds at another station you do like, but only if another squad of shooters is not waiting to shoot that particular station. When shooting at stations where doubles are customarily thrown in skeet, five stand and sporting, you might want to request that all targets be thrown as singles. You'll have plenty of time to shoot doubles after learn-

ing the games and becoming more proficient at them.

So what's a good score for someone who has never shot clay targets? It depends on the shooter and the game. I once watched a friend break 22 out of 25 targets on his first ever round of skeet, but he had already been shooting doves for many years and he was good at it. I'd say a beginner who breaks half that many the first time out has absolutely nothing to be ashamed of. The same goes for trap and sporting clays; anyone who breaks 50 percent of the birds on the first try has had a good day and 30 percent is not a bad score for a first-timer. I have been shooting all three games for several years. On one of my better days, I will average higher than 95 percent at trap and skeet, but anytime I break 80 out of 100 birds at sporting clays I am happy with my performance. I break about the same percentage of targets in trap singles as I do when shooting a standard round of skeet. Because of its higher level of difficulty, I usually miss about 10 percent more birds when shooting doubles in both games. When shooting skeet, I break just as many targets with the 28 gauge as I do with the 20 and 12, as do most experienced shooters. Same goes for shooting singles in trap from the 16-yard line. With the exception of a few ridiculously long tower shots, most of the stations in sporting clays I have shot were handled quite nicely with 20- and 28-gauge guns.

Except when shooting registered targets in the occasional tournament, I use the same guns for shooting skeet and sporting clays as I do for hunting. A couple are in 12 gauge, but most are chambered for the 20, 28 and .410 shotshells. Since they are capable of handling two targets thrown at the same time, pumps, autoloaders and double-barrel shotguns are the best choices, but by shooting singles only, you can still have fun and get in plenty of practice with a single-shot gun. Skeet or Improved Cylinder choke will handle all shots in skeet and most shots in sporting. Shoot quickly enough, and Improved Cylinder will handle singles from the 16-yard line in trap but Modified is best there. I enjoy shooting singles in trap with my 28-gauge and .410-bore bird guns, and since I get on a target and pull the trigger quickly enough to break it before its is much more than 30 yards away, I find Modified choke to be about perfect for the smallbores. If you shoot an over-

Five stand is popular at gun clubs because it takes up very little space and its operation is not as labor-intensive as sporting clays can be. It is great fun to shoot with a favorite bird gun.

under or side-by-side shotgun, Skeet in one barrel and Improved Cylinder in the other is a good combination for shooting doubles in skeet and sporting clays, while the combination of Improved Cylinder and Modified is hard to beat when shooting trap doubles with a twin-barrel gun. When using a pump or autoloader, I most often choose Skeet for shooting skeet, Improved Cylinder for sporting clays and Modified for trap.

As a rule, clubs offering clay target shooting require the use of No. 7-1/2 or smaller shot, and anyone caught shooting anything bigger will be asked to leave. No. 7-1/2 and No. 8 are the two best options for trap while Nos. 8, 8-1/2 and 9 are the most popular sizes in sporting. Most skeet shooters use No. 9 shot, although the other sizes mentioned will also work in the 12 and 20 gauges. Heavy loads are not needed. Standard field loads with 11/16 ounce of shot in the .410, 3/4 ounce in the 28, 7/8 ounce in the 20, one ounce in the 16, and anywhere from one to 1-1/8 ounces in the 12 are all you need. And since we are concerned with staying in tune for hunting season rather than winning tournaments, inexpensive promotional-grade ammo available at "mart" prices is good enough. On the other hand, if you want to spend a bit more and go first class, pick up a few boxes of target loads such as the Remington Premier STS, Winchester AA and Federal Gold Medal.

The old saying, "practice makes perfect" applies to many things in life, and one of them is wing-shooting. Unfortunately, hunting seasons being as short

as they are and bag limits being as small as they are, most hunters do not have the opportunity to get in a lot of practice on feathered targets with their shotguns. Between hunting seasons, the old joints tend to rust-up from lack of use as the shotgun gathers dust in the corner. When opening day does finally roll around, the season is half over before you find your groove and begin to connect with any degree of consistency. A bit of practice during the off-season can prevent that from happening, and this is exactly why the various clay target games were created.

Shooting the clay target sports can be excellent practice for wingshooting, but only if they are approached with that goal in mind. A skeet shooter who is concerned about ringing up a good score and could care less about hunting quail, pheasant, dove, or any other game bird always shoulders his or her gun before the target is called for. This is called the high-gun start position, and since an experienced hunter does not walk around in the field with his gun held to his shoulder, it is not good practice for wingshooting. Same goes for the sustained-lead method of shooting as practiced and preached by many tournament shooters. Carefully measuring the distance between the muzzle of the gun and the target before pulling the trigger works on the skeet field, but most hunters find it to be less than ideal in the field. Shooting clay birds using the low-gun start position and then swinging smoothly through the target and pulling the trigger is the way a quail or dove is shot.

CHAPTER 33
Trap Is For Bird Hunters

Look closely in the sky at about one o'clock above the right front corner of the trap house and you can see the orange clay target I just broke with a Beretta DT10 trap gun.

ames played with shotguns have been with us for a very long time. One of the first references to trapshooting appeared in the English publication *Sporting Magazine* in 1793, making it the oldest we know about. Most historians believe the game originated in the English village of Ealing, where live pigeons were placed in shallow holes dug into the ground and covered with top hats worn by well-heeled gentlemen. This gave the game its original name of "Old Hats." When the shooter yelled "pull," a long string tied to the hat was used to pull it over on its side, allowing the bird to fly. Those early games eventually evolved into the sport of trapshooting where the top hats were replaced by metal boxes or traps.

Trapshooting immigrated to America around 1830. The first registered tournament was held in 1840 at (depending on which history book you believe) the New York Sportsman's Club or the Sportsman's club of Cincinnati, Ohio. As time went on, public sentiment toward the use of live pigeons forced the adoption of targets made of inanimate materials. Various types of targets were tried, including hollow glass balls filled with substances such as feathers and powdered charcoal, but by 1880 a 4-1/4 inch clay disc invented by Cincinnati resident George Ligowsky had proven to be the best sub-

stitute for live birds. Four years later, famous duck hunter Fred Kimble of Peoria, Illinois, introduced a composition target called the Peoria Blackbird, which more closely resembled in flight the targets used today. And so, the clay pigeon was born.

The first Grand American trap shoot was held in 1900 at Interstate Park in Queens, New York. Fewer than 100 shooters attended, which is in stark contrast to the 7,000 or so who signed up at the 100th anniversary shoot I attended in 1999. The Grand is indeed a grand spectacle and as much an annual social gathering of old friends as it is a shooting tournament. No other shoot in America comes close to matching it in size or scope. More than 100 trap fields throw over five million targets in just over a week. Trolleys pulled by John Deere tractors are constantly on the move as they shuttle competitors from one end of the site to the other. The Grand is the world's largest shooting event, and as individual-participant sporting events go, only marathon running packs more people into a day's activities. Shooters from every state in the U.S. and many foreign countries attend each year. All told, 19 different events are offered during the affair, and shooting them all requires the firing of 2,400 rounds of 12-gauge trap loads in just 10 days. Equally interesting to a hopeless firearms enthusiast like me, vendor row contains over 100 exhibitors offering everything a shotgunner could possibly want or need.

Every serious shotgunner should attend the Grand American at least once in a lifetime, but for every target broken there, thousands are turned into dust at dozens of clubs across the country. At my gun club, I often see young boys and girls shooting alongside veterans in their 60s and 70s, and it is impossible to tell which is having the most fun. Clubs offering trap and skeet often utilize the same shooting fields for both, but the electrically operated traps used to throw the clay targets are in different locations for the two games. When a shooter faces such a field, the high house skeet machine is to the left, the low house machine is to the right and the trap machine is straight ahead and dead center.

A trap field has five shooting stations spaced nine feet apart and located directly behind the trap house. The trap machine is located partially below ground level, and since the guns are pointed over it as the clay targets are shot, it is usually enclosed by a protective concrete bunker. The five shooting stations located nearest the trap are exactly 16 yards behind it. Aligned directly behind each of those stations are 11 additional stations marked off in one-yard increments back to 27 yards from the trap.

In trap, all targets are thrown away from the shooter. A target might emerge from the house in a dead straightaway direction or at various left and right angles as sharp as 22 degrees from the center of the trap house. The trap is set to throw each target in a trajectory ranging from eight to 12 feet above the ground and to a maximum distance of 52 yards from the trap house (or 68 yards from the closest shooting stations). Most traps launch targets at about 45 miles per hour, and since the machine automatically rotates in a random manner for each throw, a shooter never knows at what angle a target will be traveling as it flies from the trap house. This plus the fact that the target is rising sharply and traveling fast is what makes the game of trap challenging. Add windy conditions to make those little discs of clay perform all sorts of aerobatics, and the game becomes even sportier.

Up to five shooters can shoot in a squad, and all fire at five targets from each of the five stations for a total of 25 targets. Unlike international trap, which allows two shots to be fired per target, only one shot is allowed in the American game. Each shooter rotates to the next station between each five-round string, and this allows a shooter to take the same number of shots from each station during a complete round of trap.

The three events contested in trap are called Singles, Doubles and Handicap. At most registered tournaments, no fewer than 100 targets are shot in each of the

Shooting trap is good practice for some wingshooting since the clay targets travel up and away from the shooter as this pheasant is doing.

events. In the Singles event, everyone shoots four rounds consisting of 25 targets each from the 16-yard line, but due to the Amateur Trap Association classification system, each shooter is competing against others of the same skill level (assuming no sandbaggers). Here's how the system works: Each time a shooter enters a registered shoot, whether it be at his local gun club or at a major event such as the Grand, his scores are sent to ATA headquarters, where a computer keeps a running tally on his performance. The five classification levels range from AA class, made up of those who have proven capable of consistently breaking 97 percent or more of their targets, to D class, which is mostly made up of beginners who average breaking fewer than 88 percent of their birds.

The Doubles event is the youngster of the game, as it was not introduced until 1911. The same type of shooter classification system is used here as for the Singles event. A round of Doubles plays the same as Singles, except two targets are thrown simultaneously, which is why most shooters find it to be quite challenging. Really serious tournament shooters often shoot about the same percentages in Doubles as in Singles, while recreational shooters usually average about 10 percent lower scores in Doubles. I personally consider Doubles the most fun because it simulates shots at a pair of flushing game birds rather than the single bird of the other two events. Most beginners find the first shot of a pair to be quite easy to break as it always travels straight away from the gun, but since the other bird is launched at a sharp angle to the left or right, it has been known to make even the most experienced trappers cry out in frustration. The two most common mistakes made by inexperienced shooters here are taking too much time on the first shot and lifting the head from the gun stock as the eyes search for the second bird. Take the first target

In addition to being my favorite trap gun, the Remington Model 3200 is one of the finest over-under shotguns ever built for clay target shooting.

quickly, keep "wood-on-wood" while swinging smoothly through the second target, and both birds will disappear into puffs of dust.

A third event called Handicap represents yet another attempt at leveling the playing field for all shooters. In a nutshell, each time an ATA member shoots 1,000 registered targets, his performance is evaluated and he is assigned a handicap yardage based on the percentage of targets he broke. Scoring an exceptionally high number of points or a class win in a registered tournament can also result in an increase in handicap yardage. As a rule, beginners start shooting from the 20-yard line until they become classified, at which point they are moved closer or farther away depending on how well they shoot. As a shooter's performance continues to improve, he is moved progressively farther back from the trap, but never more than 27 yards away.

When shooting Singles from the 16-yard line, a quick shooter will usually break each target before it has traveled much more than 30 yards from the muzzle of his gun. This means that in a round of Handicap trap, a 20-yard shooter is breaking birds at about 34 yards from the muzzle of his shotgun, while the target is around 41 yards away from the 27-yarder handicapper as he pulls the trigger. Slower shooters might break those same targets at respective distances of 40 and 50 yards. As intention has it, a relatively inexperienced competitor who is

shooting from one of the closer markers has as good a chance of winning all the marbles as a veteran shooter standing back at the 27-yard line simply because of the considerable differences in their target distances. To make the game even more appealing to a larger number of shooters of various skill levels, the organizers of some registered shoots award prizes to the high scorers among short-yardage and long-yardage Handicap shooters. This allows the top shooter among the 20- to 23-yard group to bask in the limelight same as the winner of the more accomplished 24- to 27-yard group.

Some shooting sports consist of many long hours of standing around waiting to shoot, intermixed with an occasional few minutes of actual shooting, but due to the fast pace of trap, you get off quite a few shots in a very short time frame. It takes a full squad of five experienced shooters only 12 to 15 minutes to shoot a complete round of Singles or Handicap, and it is not unusual to complete an entire 100-target event in less than two hours. This includes short breaks taken between each of the four 25-shot rounds.

The majority of today's serious trappers, particularly those who participate in registered matches, use over-unders made by Browning, Krieghoff, Perazzi and Beretta. While those guns are not as comfortable to shoot as gas-powered autoloaders, they are thought to be more durable and less likely to break down during an important tournament. Barrels as long as 32 inches are favored by many, and anything shorter than 28 inches is seldom seen. My favorite gun for shooting doubles is a Remington Model 3200 with 30-inch barrels choked Modified and Full.

Some use the same over/under for all three events, but a large number of shooters switch to specialized single-barrel guns made by Browning, Krieghoff and Perazzi when shooting Handicap. Some have barrels as long as 34 inches. Most of the time, I shoot trap just for fun with my hunting guns, but anytime I decide to really get serious about my Handicap score, I switch to a single-barrel gun once available from Remington and called the 90-T. It has a 32-inch barrel and is choked Full. The single-barrel gun with its extremely long barrel is quite popular because it tracks targets smoothly, its out-front weight encourages proper swing-through and yet it is not as heavy as an over/under with two barrels of the same length. Single-barrel trap guns have been around for most of this century and were once made by Lefever, L.C. Smith, Ithaca, Parker, A.H. Fox and other makers of fine doubles.

One of the great things about the clay target games, and this includes trap, is a special gun is not needed if you shoot for fun and practice as I most often do. Anyone can have a great time breaking clay targets with the same shotgun they use for wingshooting, rabbit hunting, waterfowling or whatever. According to the Amateur Trap Association, about 90 percent of the hundreds of thousands who shoot trap each year are recreational shooters who never enter a registered tournament. Most use the 12 gauge, but those who shoot for the pure fun of it find the 16, the 20 and even the 28 quite effective for 16-yard Singles. I especially enjoy shooting 28-gauge and .410-bore guns from 16 yards, and anytime I get on the target quickly enough, I usually break it. Any good scattergun, regardless of whether it be a double-barrel, autoloader, or pump gun, is quite suitable. While a repeating shotgun is needed for Doubles, shooting an inexpensive single-barrel offers all the firepower needed for Singles. A repeater with interchangeable screw-in chokes is actually better, as it will work quite well in all three events, although beginners should stick with 16-yard Singles and Doubles and save Handicap shooting for later.

Any trap shooter would have you believe his game is tougher than skeet. Ask any skeet shooter which of the clay target games is more difficult, and he probably won't even mention trap. To me, the level of difficulty is the same. Here is an example. The Greenville Gun Club has been holding its Toys for Tots shoot during the month of November for many years. You bring a toy, pay 10 bucks and shoot regular skeet, skeet doubles, regular trap and trap doubles. Trophies are awarded to the three shooters with the highest scores, and ties are broken by shooting a round of scrap (trap from the skeet stations). When competing against about 60 other shotgunners in the most recent shoot, I used a Krieghoff Model 32 in skeet and a Remington Model 3200 in trap. I shot a perfect score in regular skeet and missed three targets in skeet doubles. I shot a perfect score in regular trap and missed four targets in trap doubles. In other words, when shooting both games on the same day, my scores were virtually identical. It turned out to be a darned close match. Wally Fillinsky beat me by one target for first place overall and I nudged out Paul Hammer by one target for second place.

Some of my friends who shoot skeet or sporting clays and who also hunt with shotguns consider their game to be better practice for a wingshooter than trap. I don't totally disagree with their opinion, but I don't totally agree either. I believe it depends on what is being hunted and the types of shots presented. No doubt about it, stations two through seven in skeet do a better job of duplicating the crossing shots we often get in a dove field or from a duck blind. But when it comes to going-away shots on pheasants, quail, sage grouse and other flushing birds at various angles, trap is better practice than skeet. There are also those who believe a variation of regular trap called wobble trap is the most difficult of all due to the extreme angles traveled by the targets. Wobble trap is probably better practice for wingshooting, but on a windy day, I find it to be easier than regular trap because a quick shooter can break the targets closer to the gun.

I don't shoot a lot of registered targets, but I once decided to try my luck at the South Carolina state trap shoot. During the last couple of months prior to the tournament, I headed to the trap field twice each week. Each time I went, I tried to shoot 50 singles from the 16-yard line, another 50 from anywhere between the 21- and 27-yard lines, and the same number in doubles. Never in my life had I shot so much trap. I found myself enjoying it so much, I continued shooting regularly right on up until only a few days prior to my first bird hunt of the year. During the next few months, I had the opportunity to hunt pheasants, sharptail grouse, prairie chickens and Hungarian partridge on several occasions in a number of Western states. I don't recall ever shooting so well in the field. Time and again I shouldered my gun, remembered to keep wood on wood, pulled the trigger as the muzzle swung past the target and watched a bird bite the dust. It was exactly the same as I had been doing for months on the trap field.

CHAPTER 34

Safety and Etiquette

Keeping an eye on your hunting partner at all times and having him know where you are is much easier when blaze orange clothing is worn.

L iberal-minded parents who read this will be horrified when I mention that during my childhood, I was not only disciplined when it was needed, but I was also taught good manners. One of the many things Mother taught me was to never pick up any object while in someone else's home without first being given

permission from the owner to do so. My father was a hunter, so it was only natural that I learned firearms safety and etiquette from him. One of the first lessons I learned took place the same day he gave to me my first shotgun. It is a lesson I have never forgotten. We lived on a small farm with the nearest neighbor several miles

The hunter who is approaching the pointing dog from its left will shoot birds that flush to the left of an imaginary line extending forward from the center of the dog's nose. The hunter on the right will take birds flying on his side of the safety boundary.

away, so it was not unusual for Dad to "target practice" with his .22 rifles and shotguns in our back yard. Before I was allowed to take a gun hunting, he took me out one fine summer day, sat a big fat watermelon atop a pasture fence post and told me to shoot it from about five yards with his 16-gauge L.C. Smith. I should have known something was up when I noticed he had moved some distance behind me after handing me the gun. As I washed away the sticky juice in the little creek behind our house, Dad pointed out that a careless shooter could do to a fellow hunter or to a good hunting dog what I had just done to the watermelon. Believe me when I say it is a lesson that has stayed with me.

I am a firm believer in wearing plenty of blaze orange, even when hunting game birds such as pheasants and sharptail grouse on the open plains. Being seen at all times by your hunting partner, and being able to see your hunting partner at all times, is extremely important. When hunting during warm weather, I wear a blaze orange cap and a strap vest trimmed in the same color. If the sun is hot enough to cause me to wear a hat, and it is not orange, I make it a point to wear an orange shirt. For hunting in extremely cold weather, I have a couple of heavy hunting coats trimmed in orange. When I am

hunting ruffed grouse, quail or other birds in heavily wooded or brushy terrain, I constantly glance over to see where my hunting partner is. Anytime brush becomes so thick we lose sight of each other, I insist that we occasionally yell back and forth until we both once again see orange glowing in the distance. Never fire a shot in thick brush without knowing exactly where your hunting partner and the dogs are located.

When on a guided bird hunt, two shooters is ideal and three shooters are getting a bit crowded for safety sake. Having a fourth member of the party tagging along is awkward and just gives the other hunters something else to keep up with when shooting. Quail guides on some hunting preserves will offer to flush the birds when a dog goes on point, but I always decline the invitation and politely ask the guide to stay a couple of steps behind as the other shooter and I stay on our side of the dog while walking in to flush the birds. By hanging back a short distance, the guide is out of harm's way when the birds flush either straightaway or to the left and right. When you and your shooting partner walk in to flush the birds, it is safest if you take only those birds that flush to your side of an imaginary line drawn straight out from the dog's nose. Never attempt to take birds that peel back over your head

When three people are hunting flushing birds together, one should position himself out of the way just behind the dog and watch with unloaded gun while the other two hunters shoot. Throughout the hunt the three hunters will take turns shooting and observing. Note that Phyllis who is left-handed is correctly positioned on the right-hand side of the dog while Gina, a right-hander, is on the dog's left-hand side.

when the guide is standing behind you. If birds do fly to the rear, a good guide will note where they landed and they can later be hunted up as singles. I once observed a guide hitting the dirt as both of his hunters wheeled around and blasted away over his head, but I have yet to meet a quail I needed to shoot badly enough to try such a mindless trick.

Taking turns shooting is the fair thing to do when flushing singles. Never push the safety to its off position until you begin to shoulder your gun for a shot. The safety on a new pump gun used by a fellow I hunted quail with a time or two was so tight, it was extremely hard to operate. He had the bad habit of pushing it off as we were walking in to flush a covey of birds and the loud "click" it made was not only distracting, it made me quite nervous. I finally told him to get the safety fixed or find himself another hunting partner.

Never shoot at a low-flying bird. To do so while hunting flushing birds can put the dog or dogs at risk. Shooting at a low flyer is also a quick and easy way to get invited to leave a dove field. One of the few times I have been seriously peppered with shot came as a result of another hunter's inability to resist temptation. Six of us were standing around a small Nebraska duck pond, and while not enough distance separated us for total safety, the outfitter who dumped us out left us with no other choice. I thought about leaving, but since everyone was in plain

view of everyone else, and since the other shooters were experienced hunters like me, I figured it unlikely that anyone would do anything foolish. But someone did. The shooting had slowed to a crawl when a lone duck decided to fly through the gauntlet of guns. "Low bird," I thought to myself, "no one would dare shoot at it." How wrong I was. Just as the bird reached a point where it was directly between us and only a few feet above the water, another hunter who was a part-time gun writer and who had a radio talk show suddenly disengaged his brain, engaged the trigger of his gun and sent almost two ounces of steel 2s flying straight toward my guide and me. The guide screamed in protest at the fellow's stupidity, but fortunately he escaped unscathed.

Except for a single pellet that brought blood from one of my fingers, and several other pellets that bounced harmlessly off my chest waders, I also escaped with no serious damage. But it could have been much worse since I was wearing no eye protection. In our haste to beat daylight that morning, I had left my shooting glasses back at the guide's pickup truck and foolishly chose to not return for them. For many years now, I have made it a point to wear shooting glasses anytime I hunt or I am just out shooting, and have even written about its importance on a number of occasions. Failing to practice what I preached that one time could have cost me my eyesight. Which brings up another important rule: Regardless of where you are shooting, whether it is on the clay target range, in the uplands or in a duck blind, always were safety glasses. I have no idea why, but waterfowl hunters are the absolute worst at not wearing eye protection.

Another close call I won't soon forget took place at Wingmead, a wonderful old plantation not far from Stuttgart, Arkansas. Five of us were standing shoulder to shoulder in a duck blind, when the writer on the far end from me stood the butt of his fully loaded 12-gauge Fox double on the wood floor of the blind and rested its muzzle against the front railing. Nick Sisley was standing to my right, between that shooter and me. Hearing a loud commotion, I looked around to see the Fox lying on the floor with its muzzles pointed directly at the rest of us. Caught up in the excitement of the moment, the owner of the gun had allowed it to slide off the railing. Considering how hard it landed I wonder to this day what prevented both barrels from cutting a swath through our legs like a load of grapeshot fired from a cannon. Anytime you are in a blind with other hunters, it is best to hold onto your gun unless the railing you lean it against is deeply notched to prevent its barrel from slipping sideways.

Blinds and stands are drawn in some types of shotgunning and, as will just about always happen, some will produce better shooting than others. I am reminded of the fellow who stood all by himself in a blind on the edge of a South American lagoon. His position enabled him to cut off all the ducks before they made their way to the other three shooters. Birds were arriving in singles and pairs, and the chap spent the entire morning piling them up while the other hunters did little more than watch. Not once did he offer to switch blinds with any of the others. The same thing often happens on a dove field with one or two shooters enjoying all the action while others twiddle their thumbs. The fair and sportsmanlike thing for the gunner in the hot stand or blind to do is shoot for awhile and then offer to switch with another less-fortunate shooter.

Another time while hunting pen-raised Hungarian partridge as guests of one of the ammunition companies, several of us were assigned to a single guide and his two dogs. There were far too many hunters in our group, and while it was one of those situations where not shooting would have been wise, it would also have been rude to our hosts. Upon my suggestion, we took turns shooting in pairs while all others in the group kept a safe distance behind with unloaded guns. The plan worked fine with the exception of one shooter who conveniently failed to understand the routine and had to be practically jerked to the back of the line each time his turn was up.

Never criticize another man's dog. This is something I have been guilty of just once and I will always

Always allow a dog to retrieve a bird and return it to its owner, even if you shot the bird. To interfere is to not get invited on another hunt.

regret it. I was hunting with a friend who owned a young and inexperienced German shorthair. I have no idea how many miles of Montana prairie we covered each day, but it was a lot, and on top of that, the weather was unseasonably hot. On a number of occasions my friend's dog insisted on working too far ahead of us, and in doing so it bumped covey after covey of Huns long before we were close enough to shoot. One day, when I was especially hot and tired, I criticized the dog rather than keeping my mouth shut as any gentleman should have done. The owner of the dog obviously holds no hard feelings, because he and I have since hunted together on several occasions, but you can bet I learned my lesson.

When hunting birds that covey up and the dog goes on point near you while your partner is a good piece away, it is impolite to flush the covey and shoot without giving him time to walk over and join in on the fun. But this applies only if circumstances allow. Such good manners are not always possible when hunting birds that do not hold tight to the point. In that case, the one who gets there first should go ahead and shoot if they flush before the other hunter arrives. Hungarian partridges can be this way, although I have hunted them when they held as tightly as a covey of frozen quail.

When hunting over a dog belonging to someone else, don't forget to ask beforehand if it is okay to shoot birds that are flushed without being pointed by the dog. Some dog owners believe shooting birds that were not pointed is a good way to teach a good dog bad habits, and

As any safety-minded hunter should, Jim Chilton breaks down his double-barrel shotgun anytime he is not in the act of hunting.

even though I don't totally agree, I do respect their opinions when in the field. Always allow the dog to retrieve a dead bird when you see it lying on the ground close by, even if old Rover is looking and sniffing in the wrong place. I once watched a hunting show on TV during which the loud-mouthed star and his 12-gauge Browning A5 not only hogged most of the shots from his partner, the fellow seemed to take great joy in beating his guide's four-legged retriever to downed birds. As Phyllis would say, his behavior was most disgusting.

The safest way to carry a loaded gun while hunting with a partner is muzzle toward the sky. The position is similar to the old military port arms carry, except the muzzle of the gun is angled a bit more right or left depending on which shoulder it will be shot from. Another version of the same carry has the butt resting in one hand while the other hand holds the gun against the chest. The Indian carry with the gun resting in the crook of one arm is not only comfortable, it is quite safe as long as the muzzle always points away from your hunting partner. That type of carry works great for one of my quail hunting buddies and me since he is left-handed and I shoot from the right shoulder. When walking in to flush birds, he approaches from the right-hand side of the dog, and I approach from the other side. In that type of situation, I often lower the muzzle of my gun, since it is easier to hit a rising bird by swinging the gun up than when

swinging it down. Even then, however, I am very careful about not pointing the gun at something I do not want to kill. Some bird hunters like to carry a shotgun resting upside down on top of their shoulder with its muzzle to the rear. It is a safe way to tote a gun so long as its muzzle is always angled upward and no one is walking behind you. Problem is, some hunters tend to be rather forgetful, and I have lost count of the number of times I have looked up to see muzzles either pointed directly toward me or I see them swept in my direction as the hunter turns his body.

When approaching a fence by yourself, unload your gun and lay it on the ground on the other side before attempting to cross over. When hunting with a partner, let him or her hold your unloaded gun while you cross. After you are over the fence, your partner should hand both unloaded guns to you before attempting to join you. One of the really great things about a double-barrel shotgun is it is so easy to break down and unload before crossing over an obstacle in the field, and it encourages those who use doubles to do just that. Autoloaders like the Browning A-5 and Franchi 48AL with their magazine cutoffs are about as handy. Regardless of the type of gun you hunt with, you should adopt the habit of never loading it until you are 50 yards away from your car or truck. At the end of the day, you should pause again at the 50-yard boundary and completely unload your gun.

If you hunt with guns of more than one gauge as I do, be sure to thoroughly empty your hunting coat or vest of shells each time you switch guns. It is not unusual for me to hunt with guns of different gauges during the same day. On my first hunt for mountain quail with Mike Schwiebert, he decided it would be neat for me to do something no one else had probably ever done before: take my very first limit with guns in .410, 28, 20 and 12. I managed to do just that, but you can bet I was especially careful about matching up the right ammo with the right gun. If a 20-gauge shell is accidentally loaded into a 12-gauge gun, it will move far enough forward in the barrel to allow a 12-gauge shell to be chambered and fired behind it. Firing the gun will result in a ruptured barrel and possible injury to not only the shooter, but also any bystanders who might be standing close by. I am sure many hunters are aware of the danger of a 12/20 mix-up, but not as many know about other equally hazardous combinations. The same thing can happen if a 20-gauge or 16-gauge shell is chambered in a 10-gauge gun. The same applies to a 28-gauge shell chambered in a 16-gauge or 20-gauge gun. A .410 shell will usually zip right through a 28-gauge barrel if it has an open choke, but its rim will hang up at the muzzle if a barrel is choked tightly enough. I'll say it once more — anytime you go hunting, make doubly sure the shells you have on board are the correct size for the gun you are carrying.

I don't care what they say, turkey hunting is the most dangerous of all shooting sports. Anytime a bunch of hunters roam the woods dressed in camouflage clothing and sounding like the bird they desire to kill, someone is bound to do something stupid. Since a hunter is supposed to identify the sex of the bird before taking the shot, turkey hunting should be one of our safest sports, but there are always a few careless fools in the woods who have no qualms about breaking the law regardless of the cost. I would not be opposed to seeing a law added to the books that charges anyone who shoots another hunter in the woods with second degree murder and locking him away forever, but this will never happen in a society where individuals are not always held responsible for their actions. A few rules worth remembering may go a long way toward making your next turkey hunt a safe one when sharing the woods with other hunters.

When setting up to call, always sit with your back against the trunk of a tree wider than your shoulders. This may prevent some yo-yo from sneaking in and shooting you in the back. Never set up behind a screen of brush with your backside exposed or in a spot where you are closely surrounded on all sides by thick brush. Never attempt to stalk to within shooting distance of a turkey. I know a fellow who tried sneaking up on a big gobbler by

Spring gobbler hunting can be a hazardous sport but by taking certain precautions the hunter can make it as safe as possible.

crawling along the ground, and he came close to getting shot by another hunter who just happened to be working the same bird. Never wear anything colored red, white or blue, and this includes that patch of white t-shirt I see exposed at the unbuttoned neck of your camo shirt. Always wear plenty of blaze orange when toting a dead turkey in the woods. My camo turkey hunting vest has pullout panels in blaze orange, and you can bet they get used anytime I am not actually set up and calling a bird.

If you use a decoy, place it at least 30 yards away from where you are sitting, and position it directly between you and a large tree. Doing so should keep you out of the line of fire should another hunter decide your decoy is fair game. Always wear shooting glasses when turkey hunting. Some years ago, a hunter in my home state was permanently blinded in both eyes when another hunter shot him in the face from about 40 yards. The victim had decided to take a smoke break, and the package of cigarettes he pulled from his pocket and put to his mouth was red in color. Had the victim been wearing top-quality shooting glasses, he likely would be able to see today.

I especially enjoy guiding a hunter who has never killed a turkey, and when I do, I never allow him to load his gun until we are setting up to call. If a gobbler hangs up and we decide to move, I may allow him to keep his gun loaded, but he must carry it butt-forward when walking behind me single file.

Some people are timid about speaking up when they see someone breaking a rule of safety, but I most certainly am not. I'd rather be unpopular than dead.

CHAPTER 35

Shotgun Miscellany

The installation of Briley 20-gauge subgauge tubes in this 12-gauge Krieghoff increases its versatility.

Subgauge Tubes

Subgauge tubes slip into the barrels of side-by-side, over-under or single-barrel shotguns and increase their versatility by allowing the firing of shells of a smaller gauge (or gauges) in the same gun. The two pairs of Briley tubes I have for my 20-gauge Browning Superposed Lightning allow me to also shoot .410 and 28-gauge shells in it. For my 12-gauge Krieghoff over-under, I have tubes in .410, 28 and 20. My Remington Model 3200 is a 12-gauge gun, but its insert tubes enable me to shoot 20-gauge and 28-gauge shells in it as well. A quail-hunting pal of mine has .410 and 28-gauge tubes for his 16-gauge Winchester Model 21.

Skeet shooters have been using subgauge tubes in over-unders since the 1960s, but they still have not caught on in a big way among hunters. Available from several sources, they come in two basic types. Short tubes measuring only a bit longer than a shotshell are okay for casual recreational shooting and dog training, but for serious hunting and clay target competition, the pattern quality they deliver falls far short of the capability of full-length tubes manufactured by the Houston, Texas, firm of Briley. Briley's units are easily installed, just as easily removed, and the ejectors of the gun operate the ejectors of the tubes. Made of extremely lightweight materials, the custom-fitted Ultra Light tube weighs only five ounces. At seven ounces, the Companion tube is a bit heavier, but it is also less expensive. A gun has to be sent to Briley for the fitting of Ultra Light tubes, but this is not necessary with Companion tubes, since they are made to be used in a number of guns of the same gauge. As an example, I switch the same pair of 20-gauge Companions back and forth between three of my 12-gauge doubles, a Fox Sterlingworth side-by-side and two over-unders, a Remington Model 3200 and a Weatherby Athena. Top-quality subgauge tubes will usually last as long as the gun they are used in. Those I have for my Krieghoff skeet gun were made back in the 1960s, and even after digesting over half a million rounds of target loads, they are still going strong.

Briley presently offers 20-gauge, 28-gauge and .410-bore tubes for 12-gauge guns. The company also offers 28-gauge and .410 tubes for 16-gauge guns and .410 tubes for 28-gauge guns. Each pair of tubes comes with two screw-in chokes in constrictions of your choice. Ideally, the tubes match the length of the barrels they are used in, but you can get by in guns with barrels that are a bit longer. For example, I use 28-inch tubes in guns with 28- and 30-inch barrels. An extra-long wrench available from Briley allows chokes to be switched or checked for tightness when tubes a bit shorter than the barrels are used.

A gun with an inertia-style single trigger built by Beretta, Browning, Perazzi and others may require minor adjustment within the fire-control system, so the light recoil of .410-bore target loads will reset it reliably, but this is something Briley can handle for a small fee. The modification is not required when 20- and 28-gauge tubes are used due to their higher levels of recoil. Nor is it necessary on doubles with mechanical-type single triggers or any gun with double triggers.

Buying a pair of tubes for a gun already sitting in your gun cabinet can be considerably less expensive than buying another gun. For example, adding a 20-gauge Franchi Alcione to your battery will set you back three times as much as buying a pair of 20-gauge Companion tubes from Briley for the 12-gauge Alcione you already own.

Installing tubes in a double increases its weight, and this is a good thing for high-volume shooting since heavy guns don't kick as hard as light guns. Not long back, I tried my best to defend the country of Mexico from hoards of mourning doves, and since I knew I would be shooting several hundred rounds each day, I took along a 12-gauge over-under with 20-gauge tubes. I shot it all week with no stress or pain. When I'm not shooting a gas-powered autoloader, my favorite gun for shooting either doves or ducks in Uruguay or Argentina is a 12-gauge double with 28-gauge tubes. On the negative side, adding tubes to an upland gun that already borders on being a bit too heavy for use in country requiring lots of walking is not a good idea.

The old saying, beware the hunter who owns only one gun because he probably shoots it well, rings true for subgauge tubes since they allow you to find one gun that fits you and your shooting style and then use it in different gauges. When hunting liberated quail, chukar and pheasant on commercial preserves with my 20-gauge

The Texas firm of Americase ships its fine gun cases all over the world.

Browning Superposed Lightning, I install its .410-caliber tubes. When hunting doves and wild quail with that same gun, I often rely on its 28-gauge tubes for bringing home dinner. For late-season hunting of wild pheasants, I switch the gun to its 20-gauge mode and head to the field with a pocketful of magnum loads. Subgauge tubes do change the balance of a gun, but this is not always bad. Installing tubes in the barrels of my Superposed Lightning adds just enough weight out front to make it swing smoother on passing shots in a dove field.

Last but not least, because subgauge tubes are capable of handling modern loads, installing a pair in a double with Damascus barrels is an excellent way to return an old-timer to action in the field. A pair of 28-gauge tubes a friend of mine bought from Briley enables him shoot modern factory shells while hunting with a 1890s-vintage Parker in 12 gauge that belonged to his grandfather.

The Really Good Gun Case

A good shotgun needs a good gun case, and the best I have tried are made by Americase. Their catalog contains dozens of cases of various configurations, but if you do not see what you are looking for, simply sketch out what you need and they will build it for you. Of those I own, the fanciest was made to hold my Krieghoff skeet gun, its three sets of subgauge tubes, a variety of screw-in chokes and all the other goodies that belong to that gun. Another case I own was built specifically to hold my Remington 90-T trap gun, and its cover even has my name on it. I use another one for transporting various over-under and side-by-side hunting guns. Gun cases

A good spreader load like this one from Magnum Performance Ballistics will deliver Improved Cylinder patterns from a shotgun choked Full.

made by Americase are so strong, they cause airline baggage handlers to cry out in frustration.

Easy Ways for Reducing Recoil

One of the quickest and easiest ways to reduce recoil is to combine the smallest gauge available with the lightest load that will get the job done. Placing something soft between you and the gun also helps, and increasing gun weight doesn't hurt anything either.

Once, while preparing for a hunt in Uruguay, I knew that I would be shooting more shells in a week than some hunters shoot in a lifetime, so I wanted something that would be kind to my shoulder. The gun I chose was Remington Model 11-87 in 20 gauge. A gas-operated gun, it is quite comfortable to shoot. I chose a 28-inch barrel because it is an ounce or two heavier than a shorter tube. But I did not stop there. Even with the longer barrel, the gun was a bit muzzle-light for pass shooting, so I attached a 10-ounce weight to its barrel, just forward of the magazine cap. (Special weights designed just for that purpose are available from Brownells.) A strap-on leather recoil pad added a few more ounces to the gun and also added even more cushioning to the factory pad. Loaded with three shells, the little gun ended up weighing exactly eight pounds, which is exactly what the 12-gauge

Model 11-87 weighs. The gun felt like a 12 gauge, hit like a 20 gauge and recoiled about like a 28 gauge. Needless to say, it was very comfortable to shoot. Even though I fired hundreds of rounds in only a few days, I suffered no soreness in my shoulder or neck. But the really nice thing about it all is nothing I did to the gun was permanent; after returning home, I easily transformed it back into the lightweight, quick-handling quail gun it originally was.

The Spreader Load

Back when the skeet shooter was not allowed to shoulder his gun until a clay target emerged from one of the trap houses, he had to break some of the targets at longer range than is the case today. For this reason, the guns used in the old days were often choked a bit tighter than the modern skeet gun. It was not unusual to see a double choked "Skeet-In" (about Improved Cylinder) for incoming targets and "Skeet-Out" (about Light Modified) for the outgoers. When shooting doubles from stations 1, 2, 6 and 7, the first target was broken farther away than the second, and for this reason some of the guns had the tighter choke in the right or first barrel. This is just the opposite of what is usually seen in guns built for hunting. Some skeeters considered the chokes in their guns to be a bit too tight for high- and low-house shots at station eight, where the birds were only a few feet from the muzzle when they are broken, so ammunition manufacturers responded by developing loads containing special wads that caused the pattern to open up to a larger diameter at close range. Some companies included two spreader shells in a box of 25, but during the 1930s Remington packed half a dozen into each box of its Kleanbore Nitro Club ammunition. The six spreaders were loaded in brown-colored shells while the rest were green.

Although originally intended for skeet shooting, it was not long before hunters discovered the new loads would cause a Full-choked gun to shoot Improved Cylinder patterns. That made their waterfowl guns more suitable for shooting quail and grouse at close range in brush and timber. The ammunition companies soon got around to offering the same type of load to hunters. Remington called its version the Scatter Load. Over at Winchester it was the Brush Load, and the boys at Peters called theirs the Spreader Load. If you preferred Western ammunition, you asked for the Thicket Load. They worked quite nicely too. As a rule, when a good spreader load is fired in a gun with a Full choke, it will deliver patterns about as large in diameter as a regular load fired in a gun choked Improved Cylinder. Patterns shot with the spreader load are seldom as uniform as those shot with regular loads, and they often suffer from patchiness. Still, they usually are good enough for close-range work, which is why they were created in the first place.

The common use of interchangeable chokes pretty much put the spreader load out of business, but it is still in demand by those of us who shoot older guns with fixed chokes. During the 1990s, Orvis offered 12-, 16- and 20-gauge loads that utilized flattened or disc-shaped lead shot to open up the pattern. It was advertised as capable of delivering a pattern twice as large in diameter as loads with round shot, but unfortunately it is no longer available. Last time I looked, Fiocchi offered a spreader, but due to the small shot sizes available, it is best suited for shooting clay targets and birds no larger than quail, doves and woodcock. The Spred-R loads from Magnum Performance Ballistics are available with larger shot.

As I mention in the chapter on handloading, special wads are available for putting together spreader loads. If you need only a few shells, lead shot flattened with a hammer and loaded into a regular plastic wad will perform about the same. I have experimented by hand-loading flattened shot in the 12-gauge shell with some rather interesting results. I used No. 7-1/2 shot flattened by hand with pliers to make sure the pellets were uniform in thickness, but it was a very slow process. The pancake-

A weight attached to its barrel along with padding added to its comb and a strap-on recoil pad made this Remington Model 11-87 extremely comfortable to shoot with heavy three-inch waterfowl loads.

shaped pellets ended up with an average thickness of .075 inch. The load I used consisted of Remington components: 2-3/4inch STS Premier case and Figure-8 plastic wad along with 1-1/8 ounces of shot. I first pattern-tested a load containing all flattened shot. Then I tested a load containing 9/16 ounce of flattened shot poured on top of 9/16 ounce of round shot. Finally I tested a load containing 9/16 ounce of round shot poured on top of 9/16 ounce of flattened shot. I found the results of those tests to be rather interesting.

All loads were fired in three guns, a Fox Sterlingworth with .041 inch of constriction, a Remington Model 3200 with .040 inch and a Remington Model 11-87 with .003 inch of constriction. The two double-barrel guns are choked Extra-Full by today's standards, while the autoloader has a Skeet choke. Since the idea behind the spreader load is to enable a hunter to use a tightly choked gun for close-range shooting by increasing the diameter of the pattern it delivers, I did all of my testing at 20 yards. I first measured pattern diameters delivered by the three guns with Remington Premier STS factory ammo loaded with 1-1/8 ounces of high-antimony shot, and came up with 13 inches for the Fox, 15 inches for the Model 3200 and 22 inches for the Model 11-87. Switching to my homebrewed spreader load, I found that respective pattern diameters from those guns increased to 21, 23 and 30 inches. In other words, patterns delivered by the spreader load from the two barrels with Extra-Full chokes were as large in diameter as those delivered by ammo loaded with round

Safety glasses and hearing protection should be worn at all times while shooting. A detachable sling is nice to have on a waterfowl or turkey gun. The Bushnell laser rangefinder is used to determine the distances to various natural landmarks before the ducks or geese arrive.

shot and fired from the barrel with a Skeet choke. Just as interesting, the spreader load increased pattern diameter of the skeet choke from 22 to 30 inches for an increase of over 35 percent.

So which of the three spreader combinations worked best? The load containing a half-charge of flattened pellets positioned beneath a half-charge of round shot delivered patterns of considerably smaller diameter than the other two loads. The load with all flattened pellets produced patterns of about the same size as the load with its flat pellets riding up front but its patterns were not as uniform. Either of those two loads would work but the one with the flattened pellets loaded atop the round pellets delivered patterns of greater uniformity.

The Laser Rangefinder

A laser rangefinder is one of the handiest modern marvels this shotgunner has discovered, because it enables me to mentally draw what I have been known to describe as a circle of certain death around my position. If, for example, I have decided that a particular gun/load combination I happen to be using while hunting waterfowl should be restricted to a maximum range of, say, 30 yards, I use the rangefinder to determine what natural landmarks or other objects located around the spot I am sitting on are at or close to that range. Regardless of what I come up with – a particular decoy out front, a rotting

tree stump to my right, a clump of cattails to my left, a patch of snow behind me or whatever – I know that a duck or goose that flies between me and one of those markers is in grave danger of either dying or embarrassing me in front of friends. I use the rangefinder in the same way when setting up to call in a turkey gobbler.

For the benefit of those who are not familiar with the laser rangefinder, I will mention that it measures distance with incredible accuracy by electronically timing an eye-safe laser beam as it travels out to the target and is then reflected back to the receiving lens of the rangefinder. When first introduced several years ago, they were about the size of a portable television and cost as much as a dozen Remington 870s. This no longer is true. The Bushnell Yardage Pro Scout I take on all my waterfowl hunts weighs only 6-1/2 ounces, takes up no more room in my pocket than three 10-gauge shells and it is affordable to anyone who can afford to hunt. Depending on the reflectivity of the target being ranged, its maximum capability will vary from 300 to 700 yards, making it also quite suitable for big-game hunting. It is as easy as pie to use; simply look into its eyepiece, place the X on whatever you'd like to range, push the button and you've got the exact distance.

Notes on Shooting Glasses

Considering the fact that we are issued only one

pair of eyes per lifetime, I never cease to be puzzled by the number of hunters I see shooting with no eye protection whatsoever. How downright foolish they are! Those who wear regular corrective eyeglasses from a local optometrist are not much better off since as a rule, the glasses they prescribe for everyday wear are not designed to protect the eyes from heavy impact. One steel or lead pellet fired from a shotgun is all it takes to put out the lights, so what you will pay for top-quality safety glasses is dirt cheap compared to the cost of suddenly being blind in one or both eyes. In addition to having lenses tough enough to resist penetration by shotgun pellets, really good shooting glasses share other favorable characteristics. They are light, they are comfortable to wear, they are durable and they come with a no-hassle guarantee. I also like glasses with interchangeable lenses so I can switch colors as ambient light conditions change.

I have worn Randolph Ranger and Zeiss shooting glasses for several years now and have yet to find anything better. Of mild wraparound style, they weigh but a few ounces and yet are quite durable. They are also comfortable enough to wear all day long, day after day, without causing your nose or ears to fall off. Their makers do a good job of standing behind them too. After a couple of years of steady wear, I accidentally broke the frame of the first pair of Rangers I owned, and even though the fault was mine, the frame was quickly replaced with no questions asked and at no charge. Lenses come in a dozen colors and are quickly and easily switched. I most often use the clear, yellow and bronze lenses when hunting, the latter just the ticket for pass shooting on extremely bright sunlit days. When shooting clay targets on hazy days, I prefer an orange lens.

The Electronic Ear Muff

Hearing loss is a permanent thing, and once it is gone there is no way you'll recover it naturally. Back when I was growing up, nobody told us to protect our ears when shooting, and I am now paying for it with some loss in my right ear and even more in my left ear (which is common for a right-handed shooter). Without doubt, the electronic ear muff is one of the best inventions to come down the pike, not only for those of us who desperately want to keep what hearing we have left, but for those who desire to keep their hearing as pristine as possible. It works by blocking out gunfire and other extremely loud sounds while at the same time allowing the wearer to carry on a normal conversation. The Remington R2000 muffs I wear while shooting trap, skeet and sporting clays enables me to communicate with the trapper when necessary, and it even allows me to hear the target leave the trap. And yet, my hearing is protected from the muzzle blast of my shotgun as well as those of other shooters in my squad.

I have also worn the R2000 when wingshooting and find that its ability to actually amplify low-decibel sounds offers advantages there as well. It has a separate volume control for each ear, and its stereophonic qualities allow me to determine from what direction a sound is coming, something not possible with all devices of this type. During a duck hunt in Old Mexico, several other shooters and I were positioned about 100 yards apart along the edge of a thick forest. Ducks that rocketed in from over the tall trees were here, there and long gone forever before my hunting companions could get off a single passing shot. But since my battery-powered muffs allowed me to actually hear the birds winging our way before they blasted into view over the treetops, I was ready and waiting with a 12-gauge welcome. Thanks also to the R2000, I can once again hear a turkey gobble a long way off and the sound of a quail flushing from the broom sedge is even louder to me now than it was 40 years ago. I can also hear a mourning dove's wings as it whistles in for a rear attack. Like many good things in life, the e-muff is not perfect as it can be a bit uncomfortable to wear for any great length of time during hot weather, but I consider that a small price to pay for its benefits.

The Carrying Sling

Having a carrying sling on your shotgun leaves both hands free for toting other gear when heading to a duck blind, when carrying a dead turkey gobbler from the woods or for climbing steep cliffs in chukar country. I also like to have a sling on any shotgun I use for hunting deer. I prefer quick-detachable swivels so I can remove the sling anytime I want to. One of the best slings I have used on waterfowl guns is called The Claw. It is available from Quake Industries. In addition to being quite comfortable, it should last about as long as its owner. All component parts, including its quick-detach (and no-squeak) swivels, are made of synthetic materials, so nothing about the sling will rot or rust regardless of how long it stays wet. Permanently molded directly onto a length-adjustable nylon strap, the 2-inch-wide, non-slip rubber shoulder pad is rated chemical-resistant, isn't supposed to fade or crack when exposed to sunlight, won't soak up water and is guaranteed to stay soft and flexible at temperatures as low as 40 degrees below zero. The standard version I am using works on any rifle or shotgun equipped with quick-detachable swivel posts. Another type is designed to work on shotguns that have no swivel posts; a loop on each end slips over the barrel and butt of the gun.

Company Contacts

Allen (Bob) Sportswear
220 South Main St.
Osceola, IA 50213
800-550-2698

Alliant Powder
Route 14, Box 6, Bldg 229
Radford, VA 24141
540-639-8503

Amateur Trap Shooting Association
601 West National Rd.
Vandalia, OH 45377
937-898-4638

Americase
P.O. Box 271
Waxahachie, TX 75165
800-972-2737

Baker Engineering
(Targomatic)
P.O. Box 857
Fort Jones, CA 96032
800-516-8708

Benelli USA
17603 Indian Head Hwy
Accokeek, MD 20607
301-283-6981

Beretta USA
17601 Beretta Dr.
Accokeek, MD 20607
301-283-2191

Bienville Plantation
P.O. Box 241
White Springs, FL 32096
800-655-6661

Birchwood Casey
7900 Fuller Rd.
Eden Prairie, MN 55344
800-328-6156

Black's Wing & Clay
P.O. Box 2029
Red Bank, NJ 07701
732-224-8700

Boyt Harness Co.
220 South Main St.
Osceola, IA 50213
800-550-2698

Briley Manufacturing
1230 Lumpkin,
Houston, TX 77043
800-331-5718

Brownells
200 South Street
Montezuma, IA 50171
800-741-0015
FAX: 800-264-3068

Burris Optics
331 East 8th St.
Greeley, CO 80631
970-356-1670

Cabela's
400 E Avenue A
Oshkosh, NE 69190
800-237-4444

Dillon Precision Products
8009 East Dillon's Way
Scottsdale, AZ 85260
800-762-3845

Ducks Unlimited, Inc.
One Waterfowl Way
Memphis, TN 38120
901-758-3937

Estate Cartridge, Inc.
12161 FM 830
Willis, TX 77378
409-856-7277

Federal Cartridge Co.
900 Ehlen Dr.
Anoka, MN 55303
612-323-2300

Fiocchi USA
6930 Fremond Rd.
Ozark, MO 65721
417-725-4118

Flying B Ranch
Route 2, Box 12C
Kamiah, ID 83536
208-935-0755

Franchi USA
17603 Indian Head Hwy
Accokeek, MD 20607
301-283-6988

Harris Springs Shooting Preserve
P.O. Box 278
Cross Hill, SC 29332
854-677-3448

High Desert Hunt Club
P.O. Box 89
Gorman, CA 93243
888-425-4868

Highland Hills Ranch
Condon, OR
866-478-4868
www.highlandhillsranch.com
info@huntingseminar.com

Hodgdon Powder Co.
P.O. Box 2932
Shawnee Mission, KS
66201
913-362-9455

IMR Powder
1080 Military Turnpike
Suite 2
Plattsburg, NY 12901
518-563-2253

Irish Setter Boots
314 Main St.
Red Wing, MN 55066
888-738-8370

Ithaca Classic Doubles
The Old Station
No. 5 Railroad St.
Victor, NY 14564
585-924-2710

Kent Cartridge
P.O. Box 42
Kearneysville, WV 25430
304-725-0452

Knight & Hale Game Calls
Box 468, Industrial Park
Cadiz, KY 42211
502-924-1755

Knight Muzzleloaders
Modern Muzzleloading,
Inc.
P.O. Box 130
Centerville, IA 52544
515-856-2626

Little River Plantation
P.O. Box 1129
Abbeville, SC 29620
864-391-2300

Magnum Performance Ballistics
P.O. Box 7916
Macon, GA 31209
800-998-0669

Marlin Firearms Co.
100 Kenna Drive
North Haven, CT 06473
203-239-5621

Michaels of Oregon Co.
P.O. Box 1690
Oregon City, OR 97045
503-655-7964

Midway USA
5875 W. Van Horn Tavern
Rd.
Columbia, MO 65203
800-243-3220

National Rifle Association of America
11250 Waples Mill Rd.
Fairfax, VA 22032
703-267-1000

National Skeet Shooting Association
5931 Roft Rd.
San Antonio, TX 78253
800-877-5338

Navy Arms Co.
815 22nd Street
Union City, NJ 07087
201-863-7100

Noggin Tops
P.O. Box 160
Congerville, IL 61729
877-943-4287

Pintail Point
511 Pintail Point Lane
Queenstown, MD 21658
410-827-7065

Ponsness-Warren
P.O. Box 8
Rathdrum, ID 82858
208-687-2231

Primland Resort
4621 Busted Rock Road
Meadows of Dan, VA
24120
540-251-8012

Quake Industries, Inc.
732 Cruiser Lane
Belgrade, MT 59714
406-388-3411

Remington Arms Co.
870 Remington Dr.
P.O. Box 700
Madison, NC 27025
800-243-9700

RCBS
605 Oro Dam Blvd
Oroville, CA95965
800-533-5000

River Bend Sportsman's Resort
P.O. Box 279
Fingerville, SC 29338
864-592-1348

Rock Springs Lodge
11000 Old Hernandez Rd.
Paicines, CA 95043
800-209-5175

Schnee's Boots
6597 Falcon Ln.
Bozeman, MT 59718
800-922-1562

Shotgun Sports Magazine
Shooting Accessories, Ltd.
P.O. Box 6810
Auburn, CA 95604
800-676-8920

SIGARMS
18 Industrial Drive
Exeter, NH 03833
603-772-2302

Sporting Clays of America
9257 Buckeye Rd.
Sugar Grove, OH 43155
614-746-8334

Stoeger Industries
17603 Indian Head Hwy.
Accokeek, MD 20607
301-283-6300

Thompson/Center Arms
P.O. Box 5002
Rochester, NH 03867
603-332-2394

Tobacco Stick Hunting Preserve
P.O. Box 310
Candor, NC 27229
910-974-7100

Trek International Safaris
P.O. Box 1305
Ponte Vedra Beach, FL
32004
800-654-9915

Turnbull Restorations
P.O. Box 471
Bloomfield, NY 14469
716-657-6338

Weatherby, Inc.
3100 El Camino Real
Atascadero, CA 93422
805-466-1767

Willows Sporting Clays
13615 Old Highway 61 N
Robinsonville, MS 38664
662-357-3111

Yale, David & Kathy
P.O. Box 277
Yellow Jacket, CO 81335
970-562-4225

Zeiss Sports Optics
13005 North Kingston Ave.
Chester, VA 23836
800-441-3005

Index